GOD DOES EXIST!

Examining the Major Formal Arguments for and against the Existence of God

By Daniel H. King, Sr.

© **Truth Publications, Inc. 2020.** All rights reserved. No part of this book may be reproduced in any form without prior written permission from the publisher. Printed in the United States of America.

ISBN 10: 1-58427-231-7

ISBN 13: 978-1-58427-231-1

Cover graphics: istockphoto.com

Truth Publications, Inc.
CEI Bookstore
220 S. Marion St., Athens, AL 35611
855-492-6657
sales@truthpublications.com
www.truthbooks.com

Dedication

This book is dedicated to my wife Donna. She is responsible for this book being written. After she heard me deliver a series of lectures on this topic, she said I should write a book about it. And so I did. "Her children rise up and call her blessed; her husband also, and he praises her" (Prov. 31:28).

Table of Contents

Preface 9

Chapter 1: What This Study Is about: An Ancient Question 17
    Answering the Question at the Most Basic Level
    Philosophical and Logical Argumentation
    In Pursuit of the Solution to the Puzzle of God's Existence
    Preliminary Summation of the Arguments for the Reality of God
    Conclusion

Chapter 2: The Contingency Argument 32
    Nothing Comes from Nothing
    The Argument Stated
    Examining the Argument More Closely
    The Science of Beginning
    Conclusion

Table of Contents

Chapter 3: The Five Cosmological Arguments 44
    The Argument from Motion
    The Argument from Causation
    The Argument from Contingency
    The Argument from Degrees
    The Argument from Teleology or Intelligent Design
    Conclusion

Chapter 4: The Ontological Argument 63
    The Argument as Described by Anselm of Canterbury
    René Descartes and the Argument
    Kurt Gödel's Form of the Ontological Proof
    Think of Something That Does Not Exist
    Logically Incoherent Ideas
    God as the Maximally Great Being
    The Plantinga Version of the Argument
    Atheistic Response to the Argument
    Conclusion

Chapter 5: The Teleological Argument 75
    The Argument Stated
    William Paley's Analogy
    Necessity, Chance or Design?
    Alternative Theories of the Origin of Complexity
    How Do We Determine Whether Design Is Present or Not?
    A Few Examples of Astonishing Design Features in Nature
    Conclusion

Chapter 6: The Fine Tuning Argument 119
    A Statement of the Formal Proof
    The Anthropic Principle
    Our Extraordinary Good Fortune
    The Explanatory Filter: The Specified Complexity Test
    Examples of Anthropic Coincidences
    Conclusion

Chapter 7: The Probability Argument 143
    Stating the Formal Argument
    Random Universe or Universe on Purpose?

GOD DOES EXIST!

What Are the Chances of Life Appearing by Accident Rather Than by Design?
What Are the Obstacles to a Single Functional Protein Randomly Appearing in Nature?
Chance of a Single Functional Protein Appearing in Nature: A Test Case?
Attempting to Prove the Impossible
Conclusion

Chapter 8: The Moral Argument 174
Early Forms of the Argument
Immanuel Kant
The Kantian Version of the Argument
The Moral Law Within
The Contemporary Iteration of the Argument
Conclusion

Chapter 9: The Intelligence Argument 207
Elusive Definitions
Intelligent Machines and Their Makers
What is the Origin of Mind, Thought, and Intellect?
The Argument for God from Intellect
The Evolutionary View of Brain Development
Problems with the Evolutionary Picture of Human Brain Development
The Brain and the Mind
Descartes: Can An Atheist Know That He Exists?
Exploring Cartesian Dualism
Conclusion

Chapter 10: The Consciousness Argument 241
Easy but Hard
Theories of How Consciousness Came to Be
Evolution and Consciousness
Miscellaneous Materialist Arguments
The Argument from Consciousness for God's Existence
Conclusion

Table of Contents

Chapter 11: The Science Argument 267
    Science and Atheism
    Science Employed as a Weapon against Theism
    A Hypothetical Syllogism
    "Dangerous Sexual Repression"?
    Frontal Assault on Religion
    What is Science Anyway?
    Naturalism, Empiricism and Good Science
    Evidence for God from Science
    Conclusion

Chapter 12: The Argument from the Existence of Evil 338
    The Problem Stated
    How Can There Be "Moral Evil" without God?
    Epicurean Denial of God
    Hidden Assumptions
    Physical Existence and Its Inherent Dangers
    "If I Were Running Things, It Would Be Different"
    Job and Suffering
    Types of Suffering
    Intellect and Emotion
    Suffering as Discipline
    What about the Good?
    Free Choice
    How Did Man Go So Wrong?
    Is There a Solution?
    Why So Much Evil?
    Conclusion

Chapter 13: The "Hiddenness of God" Argument 359
    The Problem Stated
    Coming to Know God on His Terms
    Selfish Demands
    How "Hidden" Is He?
    Seeing is Believing?
    "God with Us"
    Conclusion

Bibliography 376

Preface

Author's Biography........386

It is a lonely feeling to be a young Christian in a University classroom listening to lectures daily that question or else directly challenge all that you believe and hold dear. That is often the case these days for young Christian men and women. Unfortunately, in the post-Christian West this has been so for many years. Obviously even the best academically trained student who is fresh out of High School is unprepared to deal with this experience.

From my own High School class I recall a young man who graduated with me and took many of the identical science classes that I took both in High School and then at the University. He became a Christian be-

GOD DOES EXIST!

fore I made that same commitment. We were close friends and waited on the Lord's Table together as young men. Both of us led prayers over the bread and the cup representing the body and the blood of Christ at the Communion table. I had no reason ever to believe that he was anything except sincere in his convictions about what he was doing. By his third year of University course work he had become an avowed atheist. He said many unkind and hurtful things to his humble Christian parents after his change, attempting to humiliate them for their beliefs. He sounded exactly like the professors we were listening to daily at the University.

There is little doubt that this was precisely the aim of the professors he studied under, because I studied under the same ones, and it became clear to me early on that this was their principal intention: to divest young believers of their faith and make atheists out of them, or at least destroy their belief in the Bible. Frankly, it was like going through an attempted brainwashing. Now, of course, they intended to teach a little real science along with their atheism, and they did. Our High School science teachers had not sounded nearly so radical. They were unbelievers, many of them, but apparently the issue of job security was more important for them. The University professors were tenured and had nothing at all to worry about. They were guaranteed their jobs whatever crazy things they said, so they at times espoused some pretty weird stuff. For the first two years of my education I was a science major, as was he, and so I studied Biology, Zoology, Chemistry, Anatomy, Anthropology, etc. It was a very challenging experience, but I did not lose my faith over it. I did spend, though, many lonely hours puzzling over the questions they posed and poring over books in the library, at the time and for many years afterward. Their intellectual assaults on our faith only served to make some of us stronger.

Do not misunderstand. I did not have all the answers to the questions the professors were raising then, and I am sure that I do not have all the answers to them now. But many of the questions they asked had no real answers. That is true because some things are beyond any of us knowing. Fact of the matter is, they had a lot fewer real, substantive answers then than they pretended to have when they appeared so cocksure of themselves at the time. This book underscores a great num-

Preface

ber of them. But looking back at that experience after fifty years or so, I am absolutely certain that many of the deepest and most important questions about life had already been answered for me satisfactorily. I did not learn those at the University. I learned them as I listened to simple men preach the Word of God from the pulpit at church services. I learned them in Bible Study classes. And I came to know them as I beheld the lives of godly men and women who loved the Lord and revered all that is holy and good. Among such people were my own blessed parents. God blessed me to know Christ through the examples of these simple people of faith.

As previously noted, I did not lose my faith during that experience. I changed my major field of study and transferred to a different school afterwards. But it has haunted me throughout the years that my friend was so easily swept off his spiritual moorings by the incessant barrage of abstruse and new information being thrown at him. Sadly, he did not share with me his struggles. I moved away just as he was leaving the church. But I always wished that I had been able to procure a book of the sort that I have written here to fortify my own faith and perhaps even be of some help to someone like him throughout the experience he was going through. Personally, I certainly needed a "ready reference" to help me get through that period of challenges.

And so, knowing there are others today who are facing the identical challenges I went through so many years ago, I have written this material to provide the reader with a general introduction to the philosophical and logical arguments, and some of the fallacies, that are so nonchalantly (and often uncritically) presented by many both in and out of academia. From generation to generation the arguments are pretty much the same. Academic opinion has been monolithic on matters associated with cosmology and the origin of life over the past seventy-five years or so.

Presently, as new information has continued to pour in from the different fields of scientific research, of course, the nature of the argumentation has changed subtly as the years have passed by, and as new theories have been propounded by a newer generation of scientists, and thus we are confronted with an altered perspective along with some different challenges. But basically there is little that is "new under the sun", to quote the book of Ecclesiastes. Wording of some of the argu-

GOD DOES EXIST!

ments may change ever so slightly, but they boil down to a colostrum of essential neo-Darwinian doctrines, part and parcel of the "Nicene Creed of the Church of neo-Darwinism."

One thing has changed markedly, though, and for the better. The present day is so much improved for the young Christian now than it was when I was a student. There are many great books available for study and research and a great host of marvelously capable people who have written and lectured widely on the subject of Christian apologetics. Some Christian scientists have also "broken ranks" and have even occasionally "broken the mold," providing books of amazing brilliance, from within the scientific community, courageously swimming against the tide of the times.

Some of the real standouts of our day are people like: Michael Behe, William A. Dembski, Stephen C. Meyer, and William Lane Craig. They are my own personal favorites. These are men of incomparable skill and intellectual stature. Almost anything that is written by one of these scholars is worth reading, not to say that we agree with one hundred percent of what they write (that is seldom the case, even with the best of my friends), but that their writings are always worthy of the time spent on them. These men are giants, make no mistake about it! And in the area of Christian apologetics they have few peers. Dembski's *Intelligent Design* and *The Design Inference*, Meyer's *Signature in the Cell* and *Darwin's Doubt*, Behe's book *Darwin's Black Box* and *The Edge of Evolution*, and Craig's *Reasonable Faith* along with his books *The Kalam Cosmological Argument* and with Quentin Smith, *Theism, Atheism, and Big Bang Cosmology*, in my opinion are already classics of our time.

In each of their own special niches, these works are worth their weight in gold. They belong in the library of anyone who hopes to respond to the high-sounding claims of modern academics and give encouragement to students of faith at College and University. We are glad to report that there are very many others who are like these notables that have produced helpful works like the ones named above, which are cited throughout this book and are included in the list of written works at the end.

As an explanatory prefatory note to the reader, I would like to mention in advance that one of the unique features of the present book is ved that I have selected and used a considerable number of recent studies and research projects in several of the sciences, especially physics, biology, and genetics. This was done specifically in order to make a point. This book was written in 2020, and many of these studies and projects are probably not of great or enduring importance, other than for purposes of making that point. They are not employed in order to "date" the book to a particular era of scientific investigation, but simply for illustrative purposes. Most of them were carried out in the last ten to twenty years, and they demonstrate that in spite of the fact that multiple voices both inside and outside of these disciplines are calling for some response to the larger question of probability, these voices are going unheard and research continues apace with the identical unsupportable presuppositions in place, even though they are utterly implausible. This issue of likelihood cannot be treated as an aside.

When legitimate questions are directed to researchers about how statistics being applied to any given situation, in science or elsewhere, eliminates chance as the cause for anything, these appeals for logical justification are generally ignored. This is so even though the appeals are sincere and the statistical and other information are admitted to be legitimate by all concerned. The scientists do not deny the numbers. They try to explain them away, but they do not deny them. In this vein, William Dembski speaks of the regulative principle of probability called the Law of Small Probability, which asserts that specified events of small probability do not occur by chance. In every other area of human understanding, this principle is as solid as the Rock of Gibraltar.

But in the sciences, largely controlled by atheists, it is ignored. Dembski makes the point as follows: "This principle engenders a form of inference called the design inference, and a mode of explanation called design. To infer design in explaining an event is to eliminate decisively explanations of that event which appeal to law-like regularities or chance." The leading lights in the sciences will persist in ignoring these observations and the questions that are raised by them until the general public "holds their feet to the fire" by asking them often enough that it forces them to respond. In our view the reason for their code of silence on this subject is that they know that this road leads one way: straight to God. God must be the one responsible for these undeniable

GOD DOES EXIST!

design features of the universe and of the living systems on earth. Law and chance will not explain them.

So, God must exist. No one knows this better than the scientists themselves, so avoidance is the chosen method. Therefore, they plan to act as if there are no logical alternatives to atheism and evade the question as long as it is possible for them to do so. But avoidance and evasion are not an answer. All of us must keep these questions and issues in the foreground and not permit them to be ignored. The evidence is solidly on the side of the believer.

One other note is deemed important as a prevenient explanation to readers: Throughout this work there are repeated references to the age of the earth and of the universe as they are understood by many in the scientific community. It is not our intent to argue this issue in the present context of this book. We have resisted that temptation at every turn. Our subject is the existence of God. This author's view of the topic is well understood by those who have read after him in the past. These explanatory paragraphs are for the sake of those who have not done so or may misunderstand our approach to the subject. We believe the Bible gives a description of the origin of the earth and of the universe from the perspective of the only One who was present at the time of its creation, so we have complete faith in the accuracy of that narrative. Seven twenty-four-hour days were ample time for God to create the universe. In fact, if he had been so minded, a microsecond would have been enough. But he chose what is described in Genesis one for his own reasons. We have no reason to second guess his choice or attempt to reinterpret it to bring it into line with modern thinking on the question.

Moreover, anyone who is aware of the background of the controversy which has swirled about the topic historically speaking, even in a cursory way, will know that the general perspective on that issue as embraced by the majority of elite scientists, is only as old as 1830. This is when the doctrine of Uniformitarianism (the Doctrine of Uniformity or the Uniformitarian Principle) was initiated by Charles Lyell and James Hutton. That theorem states that, essentially, "the present is the key to the past". It is this assumption which lies at the bottom of the modern theories about the age of the earth and of the larger universe. It posits that the identical processes which we now observe as causing the vari-

Preface

ous phenomena on earth, such as volcanic eruptions, earthquakes, localized flooding, soil erosion, gradual deposition of layers of sediment, etc., have always been the formative influences in the earth's crust over vast eons of time. It deposed the long-held view that catastrophic events, such as the biblical flood (Catastrophism), were responsible for observable layering in the crust of the earth. Lyell's book *Principles of Geology* altered the landscape of geological research and set the stage for broad acceptance of Darwin's theory of evolution over vast ages of time. Darwin's hypothetical postulate required immense periods of time to make it in the least plausible, and Lyell's book provided the time element to make it acceptable for those who embraced it.

Frankly, in our view, the entire ideological framework is hypothetical in the extreme. All input into this widely-held theoretical regime is based on one huge and unprovable assumption: that the various observable and measurable phenomena witnessed by the modern scientific researcher have been the same into the almost infinite past, clear back to the origin of space, time and matter. Every one of us knows that a supposition of this magnitude is not provable. It cannot now be established, and it will never be demonstrable. Past events, especially those in the ancient, prehistoric era, cannot be measured. They can only be guessed at. And that is what is happening in this regard. Those who make pronouncements about such things are always doing so from the perspective of the Doctrine of Uniformity. They have embraced the doctrine, and so it has become their operational presupposition. It is always at the back of their minds. They cannot divorce themselves from it. It is an essential element of their thinking.

And, in our estimation, that is no less doctrinaire than an ecclesiastical proclamation from the Pope in Rome informing Catholics what they must believe. To view the matter differently is to ignore altogether the facts of the case, logically speaking. So, we have no precise data as to how old the world is, or the universe. No one does. But we reject the commonly accepted theoretical timeline regarding them both. They are based on unprovable assumptions. We appreciate how difficult this is for some readers to accept. Every age of man is burdened with its own set of unproven and unprovable presuppositions. Our age has many of its own, and this is one of them. This should be kept in mind by the reader as he makes his way through this book. It is our plan to mention this but once and trust the reader to understand this as the discussion moves forward. Just because we quote various research reports or allude to these presumptive timelines without comment, that does not mean that we have embraced them. They are the personal preferences of the authors being cited, not the view of this writer.

Thanks are due to the Board of Directors and the Editorial Committee of Truth Publications, publisher of all of my books. Special notice should be given to Mark Mayberry, Kyle Pope, and Mike Willis, my dear friends and fellow editors, with whom I have worked pleasantly for a number of years. They were enormously helpful in bringing this book to its final form.

Chapter 1
What This Study Is about: A Very Ancient Question

The Bible begins with a statement about God. It does not start with any sort of argument about whether He exists or not. That is left to others. It simply assumes that He is the decisive factor in the origin of the physical universe. Genesis 1:1 says without any fanfare at all: "In the beginning God...." Then it proceeds to outline the general sweep of the material and living world as it was "created" and "made" by the Creator, God. Genesis is not a book of science and it is not intended as a primer of logic. It is not well-suited to either purpose and those who have attempted to make it either one have been frustrated in their efforts.

It is commonplace in our time for writers to enter into some method of dialectic when they discuss issues or topics that are debatable or highly controversial. But the biblical authors are never given over to

GOD DOES EXIST!

such discussion and reasoning as a technique to ascertain whether deity is real or not. That is what philosophers do.

And these writers were not philosophers, nor were they bent in the direction of philosophy or of the philosophical method. Their special province was *revelation*. They were, in point of fact, apostles and prophets (Eph. 2:20; 3:5; 4:11; 2 Pet. 3:2; Rev. 18:20). The unique thing about them was that they enjoyed an *experience of God*. God prepared them, *sent* them and *spoke through* them. They knew God and knew about God in a special way that others did not. They were not speculating about God. Neither were they engaged in a formal or even informal investigatory exploration of the realm of the divine. Essentially, they reported what they saw and heard.

Therefore, the importance of their work in making known the will of God to the human family represents a whole different category of literature from the ancient sophists, rhetoricians and philosophers of the Greek world who have so profoundly affected the Western intellectual tradition. They wrote about what they had come to know by direct communication with God. As the prophet Jeremiah said, "Now the word of the Lord came unto me, saying. . ." (Jer. 1:4), and Isaiah explained, "The vision of Isaiah, the son of Amoz, which he saw. . ." (Isa. 1:1), and Ezekiel noted, ". . . the heavens were opened, and I saw visions of God. . . " (Ezek. 1:1). All of the Hebrew prophets spoke similarly. Clearly, our own research in this modern era is of a different type and thus must employ a different methodology!

For now, and for our purposes here, it is important to observe that the dialectical method would have been of no use at all to them in dealing with the question of God's existence, even though it may be critical for us as it was for the ancient Greeks and every Western civilization that has risen since the writings of Plato and Aristotle. The Hebrew prophets lived in an age of the disclosure of religion. We live in a time altogether different from theirs, wherein we are completely dependent upon the disclosures made to and through them. The further significance of this we shall take up in the chapters that are to follow.

Suffice it to say, then, that when this particular author of this part of Holy Scripture makes this introductory assumption about the being

What This Study Is about: A Very Ancient Question

of God and sets forth this definitive declaratory statement about God's creation of the heavens and the earth, he is going "a bridge too far" for some modern readers. How can he say these things without attempting to prove them? Why does he not provide support for his contentions? Hence, it might be asked whether he may be being more than a little too presumptuous? Or, on the other hand, could he merely be stating the obvious?

Of course, there are those who consider the writer to be overstepping due bounds of logical propriety and courtesy when he unhesitatingly moves forward from this point without making the intellectual case for deity. Admittedly, this is a curious thing. In point of fact Scripture never deals with this matter in any great detail in the 66 books of the Bible, as though the nonbeliever's point of view was somehow moot, relatively speaking, and thus deprived of any real practical or intellectual significance. Why this particular approach? Was it because the world was full of pagan idolaters and there were no infidels at all? Few of us would accept this as the explanation. The world has always had its unbelievers. It was not different then. Why then did he and all of the others who followed him dare to ignore the case for skepticism? How could he treat the skeptic with such indifference? How could he leave the atheist and the agnostic in the lurch without even a word, as though they did not exist at all? In our view he was simply stating the obvious. Some things are so blatantly apparent that they do not require to be proven.

There are a good number of things in life that fit into this category. We feel no need to make a logical case for them or prove them. For example, the fact of one's own existence does not require to be established for most of us. "Je pense, donc je suis", or in English, "I think, therefore I am," as the French philosopher René Descartes put it in his work *Discourse on the Method*. We understand that there are intellectuals who question even this basic premise, but for most of us this is a quibble not worth our time to rebut.

Likewise, for those of us who believe in God the evidence is everywhere about us on so grandiose a scale that in general we feel no strong compulsion to be continually making the case that God exists and cares for us. In our estimation, His fingerprints are on every aspect of the

GOD DOES EXIST!

material and living world. When we see the sun rise, we see His hand there. When the thunder rolls during a rainstorm, we hear His mighty voice in it. In the sweet music of the songbirds in springtime, we hear Him also. The flowers that cover the hillsides and the butterflies that flit among them remind us that He is never far from any of us. An amazing mountain vista is His handiwork. The brilliant fall colors of an Eastern woodland are a canvas painted through His genius. No human painter can compare with the masterpieces He has left us. No camera can produce a photograph that does it justice. Too, the more we learn about the universe and our world within it, scientifically and otherwise, the more evident to us is His wisdom and creative power. We cannot see anything beautiful without seeing Him in it. We cannot hear anything lovely without hearing His voice in it.

God is, of course, invisible to the naked eye and so unprovable in the physical world by its various modes of proof. But "the things that are made" give ever present and undeniable evidence of His spiritual and metaphysical reality. The result of this is that unbelievers are "without excuse." What does this imply? It says that they have no genuine basis upon which to sustain their negative case against God's existence. Those who consider themselves to be astute tormentors of believers poke questions at us like these, "Where is God? Show Him to us and we will believe in Him." Or, "Who made God?" But such questions and challenges do not discourage us. What they cannot see at all, we see plainly. What is invisible to them is undeniable to us.

This is like the woman who called the 911 operator because she heard a sound in her house one dark night when she was alone. The voice on the other end of the phone inquired as to whether or not she had checked the house thoroughly to see whether there might be someone in the home. She replied that she had gone through the place quite thoroughly and found no one there, but afterward heard the noise again. "Did you check under all of the beds?" she was asked. "Of course," she replied. "Could you have missed one?" came the follow-up. "I suppose I could have," she said. "Did you check in every closet and cupboard?" was the next question. "I thought that I did," she answered. "Could you have missed one?" the 911 operator said. "Well, I guess I might have," was again her response. The operator was trying to get her

What This Study Is about: A Very Ancient Question

to see that in that one place she had missed, that is precisely where the intruder could be.

It is always impossible in real terms to prove a negative. The atheist places himself in an unenviable position. He asserts that God is nowhere to be found in his modes and methods of analysis and yet never acknowledges that where he has not looked, or even where he has looked without seeing, that is exactly where God is to be found! At the same time, the believer casts his eyes about and sees evidence of Him everywhere he looks! His fingerprints are on everything! As Paul explained:

> For what can be known about God is plain to them, because God has shown it to them. For his invisible attributes, namely, his eternal power and divine nature, have been clearly perceived, ever since the creation of the world, in the things that have been made. So, they are without excuse (Rom. 1:19-20 ESV).

It is for this reason that it is altogether appropriate to label one who takes the alternative viewpoint a "fool." If the evidence is indeed all around him, and still he denies it at every turn, is this not an appropriate designation to apply to him? That is exactly how the Psalmist saw it, with just one additional caveat which he has to offer: he says that this fellow is not really being perfectly honest in framing this matter as an intellectual adventure but instead is motivated by impure and corrupt motives. He explains:

> The fool says in his heart, "There is no God." They are corrupt, they do abominable deeds, there is none who does good. The Lord looks down from heaven on the children of man, to see if there are any who understand, who seek after God. They have all turned aside; together they have become corrupt; there is none who does good, not even one (Ps. 14:1-3).

Even in ancient times the evidence was powerful and difficult to explain away. But evidence is not all that moves the mind to make a judgment about a matter. It should be noted that the Psalmist ascribes to the "fool" of this text an underlying sentiment that moves him toward this skeptical perspective which he is said to take on the issue of the existence of God.

Why is this true? The answer is transparent. People are motivated by self-interest. All will admit that human beings believe many of the

GOD DOES EXIST!

things they do because this is what they want to believe. They will even lie to themselves when there is some perceived benefit for doing so. We could wish that everyone made decisions about weighty matters on the basis of logic and reason. The world would be a better place if this were so. But, alas, that is not reality in all cases.

In our time most of those who claim to be atheists and agnostics do so on the ground that they have one or more legitimate intellectual objections to the notion that there is a God. This Psalmist denies the credibility of their claims. He alleges that they believe what they want to believe in order to live as they want to live. That is the benefit they enjoy from this lie that they tell themselves. They refuse "to have God in their knowledge" because they refuse to be in any way inconvenienced by His laws. "They have become corrupt" he asserts, and "there is none who does good, not even one."

Answering the Question at the Most Basic Level

Having noted what the Psalmist says in one instance already, it is appropriate to observe that in another place the Psalmist points out that in the starry night sky there is ample proof of God's creative genius. In addition, he asserts that it is easily and readily accessible to any open mind. "Just look up!" He says to those who are inclined to listen. One does not have to know any science at all to take in the information this author describes. He does not need a telescope either. His powers of observation alone will suffice.

Since time began, men have peered into the night sky after the clouds have rolled away and wondered at the thousands of points of light which populate the blackness above them. What we today know about those bright spots above us, since the first giant observatories and their gigantic telescopes, not to mention the Hubble telescope that hangs in orbit above earth's atmosphere, is amazing beyond description. Often a single speck in the sky represents thousands of stars, and even galaxies of stars akin to our own Milky Way. How did all of this majestic cosmos come to be? What is its explanation? Who or what brought it about? These are all questions that inevitably come to mind as one surveys the heavens above.

What This Study Is about: A Very Ancient Question

And so, what this writer observes is really simple and basic, but at the same time it is quite profound. He plays upon the inner curiosity of every human being who stares at the night sky in wonder and awe at what he sees.

But he goes beyond simple wonder. He delves into the realm of metaphysics as he makes an assertive statement about it. In his reverie he observes that even though the heavenly bodies have no voice with which to communicate, they scream aloud to any open ear that is willing to give heed to their proclamation. They have something to say that must not be ignored. They tell us a great deal about that One who made them, their Creator:

> The heavens declare the glory of God, and the sky above proclaims his handiwork. Day to day pours out speech, and night to night reveals knowledge. There is no speech, nor are there words, whose voice is not heard. Their voice goes out through all the earth, and their words to the end of the world (Ps. 19:1-4).

Philosophical and Logical Argumentation

The people who are best trained and most qualified to deal with these issues at the technical level are philosophers and logicians. That said, what is a philosopher anyway? The Athenian Plato, disciple of Socrates, said a true philosopher is "a spectator of all time and existence ... a gentle and noble nature" who "desires all truth," and who "seeks to be like God as far as that is possible for man."

Now in these few brief phrases the inimitable Plato may have been drawing unconsciously a perfect representation of his own nature and personality. At the same time though, quite apart from the personal depiction, he intended to give a characterization of what the ideal philosopher was to be. And while most of those who pursue the vocation today (as in the days of the apostle Paul; cf. Col. 2:8), do not live up to this high standard, certainly the ideal itself is a worthy goal.

The professor of logic pursues the science that deals with the principles and criteria of inference and demonstration, i.e. "the science of the formal principles of reasoning." Debate is the logician's mode of testing the various data points in order to see which ones are valid and which are not. Again, in Paul's day the professional scribe, the philosopher and

GOD DOES EXIST!

the debater all failed to know God, and so "the foolishness of preaching" was the vehicle that God chose for revealing Himself (1 Cor. 1:20-21). The primary means at the philosopher's disposal was not, all by itself, capable of rendering a full understanding of deity and His nature. Some things it could figure out. Other things were quite beyond the scope of its methodology.

Like the reader, this writer is not a philosopher. And, like the reader, this writer is not a logician. Although trained at the university level in the various sciences, I am not a scientist either. My special area of expertise is biblical and religious studies. So on a personal or professional basis, we do not feel fully qualified to frame these arguments on our own prerogative or in our own words, except at the most rudimentary level. Some of the topics treated in this book breath the rarefied air of some of the specialty sciences, and for the most part, ordinary readers do not even "speak the language" of those specialized disciplines. For this we sincerely apologize at the outset. If it were possible for this to be avoided, we would have done so. But, frankly, some of the most powerful and incontrovertible evidence that exists comes from these areas of expertise. Microbiology, biochemistry, physics, genetics, statistics, mathematics, logic, philosophy and even artificial intelligence are critical areas of concern for this subject. This is indeed a diverse medley of distinctively different and seemingly unrelated fields. All of them are essential to the purpose of this book. For this reason we cannot ignore what they have to contribute, even though they are highly technical and some of what they offer is difficult to comprehend.

On this account we shall not attempt to tackle these topics except in general outline form in as rudimentary a way as is possible. Also, we will put them before the reader just as we have gleaned them from the writings of those highly qualified, intellectually gifted, and educationally suited individuals who are cited as sources throughout this book and particularly under the rubric of the specialized bibliography at the end of this work. If the reader should desire to investigate any particular aspect of any of these topics further, that is the place to begin. Because of the unique nature of this particular topic, this is the most heterogeneous bibliography this writer has ever produced and it is rich with source materials that any interested party could spend a lifetime researching.

What This Study Is about: A Very Ancient Question

The arguments that we plan to cover in this material represent the sum and substance of Christian Evidences or Apologetics on the general topic of the existence of God. Of course, "Evidences" is a much broader subject than whether or not God exists, but all will surely agree that this is the starting point for the sincere investigator as well as the one special piece of ground that must be won at all costs by the earnest student or, quite simply, all else is lost as regards that area of study. Here is why:

If God does not exist, or it cannot be established by sound reasoning and logical argument that He does, then what does it matter that we hold to notions such as the inspiration and authority of the Bible, or the fact of Jesus's qualification to be the Jewish Messiah, or that He rose from the dead on the third day, any of the other considerations that are treated in that noble discipline? That is the quintessential problem, and so it is the first order of business to which we must attend. The existence of God has to be explored with some amount of depth and seriousness in order for it to be possible to move with confidence beyond this most elemental concern.

Why should we bother with this heady and complicated subject? Why not let others worry with such things? After all, delving into these areas of thought are, admittedly, challenging at every level. For the person whose faith is constructed on shaky ground, a study of this sort could prove to be encouraging in the most absolute sense of the word. For the sincere truth seeker who has had no previous opportunity to look into this topic, it could be life-altering. But for some, even believers, it may seem daunting and perhaps even frightening. Plainly, it introduces us to a world of thought and methods that we are not accustomed to, have little or no experience with, and in some instances we do not even "speak the language" of the discipline.

Unfortunately for those who tend to be spiritually lazy, these topics are unavoidable. They have to be considered, at least at some level, by all who have been enrolled in the family of God. There will be times when teachers, preachers, and other religious leaders will not be present to respond when error on this subject is being presented as truth. You may not be able to depend on someone else to make the case for God's existence. Peter said that Christians have an obligation always to be prepared to make a defense of their faith:

GOD DOES EXIST!

> Always be prepared to make a defense to anyone who calls you to account for the hope that is in you, yet do it with gentleness and reverence... (1 Pet. 3:15).

Our faith in God must be defended. All of us need a basic understanding of these matters and an ability to deal with them on a rudimentary level, at the very least. That does not necessarily mean that you may be forced to meet an accomplished and well educated atheist or agnostic professor in a public debate. This is not what you need to be worried about. There will always be someone who is just as accomplished and as well educated and who will be anxious to handle that situation. In the majority of instances of that sort, you will only hear "bluff and bluster" anyway, and the boastful skeptic will usually cower and make excuses when publicly challenged to defend his position.

Usually it is far less daunting than this and far more ordinary. In most cases where someone calls into question whether God exists or not, he or she will only be an individual who is generally uninformed and who expresses a lack of knowledge of the subject. At the same time, you may be the only person available on that occasion to answer the challenge. There may be no one else present to respond to the question or else no one who has the courage or training to speak out. Hence, it is critical that you prepare for that moment when a defense of truth may fall to you, and yours will be the lone voice to speak out in defense of what is right. Knowledge is power. Information is critical to understanding. Confidence grows out of being well informed. And being well informed is inextricably associated with the reading and study of books. Books like this one.

Concerning the question of God's existence, this series of studies is written in order to give the student a basic understanding of the major arguments, both for and against, so that you will be well prepared to wrestle with the issues involved and respond appropriately when challenged. The student should not be fearful when that time comes. The evidence is plentiful and powerful, and clearly on the side of the conscientious believer, as we shall demonstrate on the pages that follow.

In Pursuit of the Solution to the Puzzle of God's Existence

Is the physical world all there is? Did it somehow explode into existence from pre-existing matter? Did it just appear from nothingness without any cause or reason behind this mysterious process? Or, did the

What This Study Is about: A Very Ancient Question

physical universe come about because of a Creator who shaped and formed and thus "created" everything? Are questions like these a matter of one's faith-stance or philosophical leaning, or are they answerable from the standpoint of logic and reason?

These are all profound questions that beg for some response. But, are they subject to an approach which might yield a logical and reasonable answer? Surely if God was behind all of this "stuff" that surrounds us, He left some appreciable evidence to show His part in all of it?

Throughout the centuries wise and thoughtful men have wrestled with such questions and over the course of the years have distilled and formalized their arguments into practical and understandable statements which are useful vehicles that communicate these ideas so that later generations of men and women could appraise and perhaps also imbibe their speculations and ruminations. The product of their research has been a formidable collection of formal arguments. It is our plan in this series of studies to explore these questions by looking at these formal arguments set forth by philosophers, logicians and theologians in order to explore the answers to these eternal questions.

Our approach to these rather heady and complex issues in the chapters ahead aims at simplicity. But that does not mean that this study will be easy. We intend it to be very basic, and will try to keep it from being too complicated. We will try with all our might to make it understandable and as comprehensible as is realistically possible, while at the same time honoring the true nature of the topic under discussion.

However, due to the essential nature of this discussion, being that it is a dialogue in the context of philosophical thought and formal logic, we must therefore utilize the somewhat sophisticated language of philosophy and of formal logic. Philosophy is a discipline that utilizes a certain methodology and a specific vocabulary that is uniquely suited to its various conceptual pursuits. As well, formal logic is a special discipline with a long history and a well-worn *modus operandi*.

This is true and must be recognized and appropriated on a rudimentary level at least in order to deal with the present subject in spite of the fact that it may be quite foreign to most students today. Years ago it was considered a practical and useful part of a basic education in the

GOD DOES EXIST!

Western world. It should still be so today, because it is tantamount to teaching people how to think and reason. This is so because it teaches people how to think and reason to a logical conclusion about any matter. This is a critical aspect of education.

Unfortunately the great majority of what is done in the name of teaching today is about one thing: propaganda, i.e., selling the agenda of the political left, and thus, telling young people *what* to think, rather than *how* to think. It is about feeding them liberal ideology rather than instructing them in the basics and allowing them to think for themselves. Clearly some who are in control of the educational system are fearful that they might think for themselves and come to the wrong conclusions. Hence, like so many other aspects of Western education in the twenty-first century, instruction in reason and logic has been dropped from the curriculum of public education in favor of less worthwhile but more politically sensitive subject matter. But I digress.

As a result, some of what we will pursue along these lines may seem foreign and may utilize terms that are not at first familiar to the student. We shall attempt in every instance to explain the special terms as we employ them, and take the additional space necessary to provide enough background information so that the reader is not lost in the course of the study.

At the same time, we would suggest that the reader keep a good English dictionary close at hand and use it immediately when a strange term or idea is presented that needs further explanation or more specific definition. The language of logic and philosophy is a highly specialized vocabulary that may sound unfamiliar at first, but is entirely within the grasp of any person who is willing to put forth the effort to understand it. Take the time necessary to comprehend both the terms and the concepts being utilized. It will pay rich dividends later on.

Preliminary Summation of the Arguments for the Reality of God

An argument is a series of statements or premises which logically lead to a conclusion. Sometimes, especially in a formal presentation of the case, such an argument may be stated as a syllogism, with supportive major and minor premise(s) and then a conclusion. Sometimes there are several conclusions.

What This Study Is about: A Very Ancient Question

A valid argument must obey the rules of logic: its conclusion must follow from the premises. The premises need to be true, supported by the evidence available (more plausible than their opposite). An argument of this sort is sufficient to establish the truthfulness of the conclusion it is set forth to prove.

It will be noted in the pages that follow that there are a great many arguments of this kind and even if the reader should see one or two of them as unconvincing, the fact that there are so many of them is a powerful argument itself! Too, even those arguments that have been propounded by atheists to make their case against the existence of God, when looked at from another and more objective angle, in truth offer compelling and very persuasive evidence in favor of deity. Thus, a student must be willing to examine the arguments from different angles or perspectives.

The following is a helpful summary of the arguments for and against God's existence:

- Contingency Argument
- Cosmological Arguments
- Ontological Argument
- Teleological Argument
- Fine Tuning Argument
- Probability Argument
- Moral Argument
- Intelligence Argument
- Consciousness Argument
- Science Argument
- Existence of Evil
- Hiddenness of God

Conclusion

It is our plan to take up each of these points in its own turn in the chapters that follow. A close look at this list will suggest immediately to the mind of the observer that these propositions are not remotely either biblical or theological. As we have suggested above, they are of the nature of a coherent and reasonable series of philosophical and logical reasons or statements of facts that are intended to make the case for a certain point of view. All of these arguments, even the ones proposed

GOD DOES EXIST!

by skeptics, take us to the identical place. That is intentional. The point of view they set forward is that God does, in fact, exist.

Questions for Discussion

1. Why does the biblical writer of Genesis 1:1 not enter into a logical or carefully reasoned argument for the existence of God?

2. What is the major difference between the biblical writers in general and a philosopher?

3. Dialectic is the term popularized by Plato in his description of the Socratic dialogues. It represents a discourse between two or more people holding different points of view about any subject, in an effort to establish the truth through reasoned arguments. Does this philosophic method have cogency in a discussion about the existence of God? Should we expect to see this sort of discussion on the pages of the Bible in regard to God's existence, or any other subject for that matter?

4. What is the difference in perspective between the believer and the unbeliever? Is it important that the nonbeliever has put himself in the position of affirming a negative, i.e. affirming that God does *not* exist?

5. Read Romans 1:19-20. *Eternal power* and *divine nature* are the two emphases of this important text. How is each of these aspects of deity demonstrable in the material world?

6. Is it fair to call the skeptic a "fool," as the Psalmist does in Psalm 14:1? Is there no such thing as an intelligent skeptic who honestly and sincerely examines the issues involved and concludes that there is no God?

7. The statement found in Psalm 14:1 is attributed to David in the tenth century BC. Is there much more evidence of a scientific nature known to those of us who live three thousand years later?

8. Does self-interest enter into the question of whether or not one believes in God? Is it possible that one is protecting some desire to leave God out of the picture and ignore His moral laws, while claiming to believe that the evidence is against His existence?

What This Study Is about: A Very Ancient Question

9. Basically the Psalmist says, "Just look up at the heavens," as his argument for God's existence and power. Of course, modern observatories and telescopes in orbit around the earth give us much more than the naked eye could see in ancient times. Is this an argument that you deem to be valid?

10. How do the logical and philosophical pursuits influence our study of the existence of God? Is it fair to use their methods to explore such intrinsically biblical questions and their resolutions? Or, ought they to be left aside entirely for another method of exploration? What would that method be?

Chapter 2
The Contingency Argument

The esteemed German mathematician and philosopher Gottfried Wilhelm Leibnitz puzzled over the eternal question: "Why is there *something* rather than *nothing*?" This is a question that is well worth asking. Of course, we all agree to the proposition that there is something because we are here. That is not a question that most of us consider arguable, although we must admit that there are those who wish to argue even this issue.

For now, though, let us assume that this matter is settled, in spite of the fact that there are occasional detractors. We are here and we exist. The universe is here and it exists. Being that we are here, then there is something instead of nothing. *But why is this so?* Why is there something? Why is there not simply nothing at all?

The Contingency Argument

Aristotle called this "the most basic question of all," and said that it was at the very root of philosophy. More than that, though, it is the one question that is at the root of existence itself. All thoughtful people should give some careful consideration to this issue, therefore. Admittedly there are a whole host of people who live their lives through and never pause long enough from their activities to contemplate the quintessential issues involved with this or any other critical query.

But such is not the case with everyone. Philosophers are an exception to this general rule. In point of fact, no philosopher who ever was serious about his life's work would go for very long without spending serious time entertaining the notion of which we speak and deliberating over its exciting potentialities and interesting possibilities. At its heart, then, this is most assuredly a philosophical question. It is the sort of thing philosophers ponder regularly. Even though we are not professional philosophers, we need to think about it also. And so we shall.

Nothing Comes from Nothing

Attendant to this question is the realization that nothing produces nothing. Put another way: From nothing, nothing comes. Let us illustrate this point in a practical way. A vacuum tube may be manufactured that has within it a perfect vacuum. Let us postulate that it is tested and shown to contain zero molecules of any form of gas. This, of course, might be practically unachievable but it is theoretically conceivable, and that is all that is necessary for our purposes in this simple experiment.

Now, let us wait for fifty years to observe what happens within the inner space of the tube. All will agree that even after fifty years, as long as the tube remains intact and does not leak any gas molecules into the inner space from the outside of the tube, no molecules will be found inside. Now wait one hundred years. Once again, so long as there is no leakage, zero molecules will be found within. Extend the duration of the test as long as you wish: one thousand years or even one million (if such were even possible), and the result is perfectly predictable.

If molecules do appear in the tube at some point, it will be suspected that leakage has occurred. It will never be supposed that molecules have appeared inside on account of some type of "spontaneous generation." That is a theoretical postulate that was once thought possible but

GOD DOES EXIST!

is now considered ridiculous. Molecules have not suddenly and inexplicably appeared in the tube. Why not? Because we all understand the fact that from nothing, nothing comes.

To argue otherwise is not only utterly preposterous but counter intuitive and obviously against all of human experience, as well as absolutely unscientific! Things simply *do not* pop into existence. As we have heard Dr. William Lane Craig say repeatedly, "At least in the case of the magician who pulls a rabbit out of a hat, you start out with a magician and a hat!"

Here we start with nothing and, quite suddenly, and totally without an adequate explanation, we have everything! For, you see, we are not really discussing a simple experiment involving an empty vacuum tube over an indeterminate span of time. Rather, we are talking about the origin of the material universe. And so, by some very intelligent theoreticians we are being told with all seriousness that *from nothing everything comes*. A proposition of this sort makes no sense at all in any other context, but in this case it is set forward in all seriousness as the only truly logical approach to the origination of all that exists.

Thus, atheistic scientists argue, not on the basis of hard science or solid logic but of *a priori* theoretical constructs, that the universe at the time of the Big Bang exploded into existence out of absolute nothingness. And with that, absolutely everything began. In other words, they make the deadly serious claim that out of nothing not only something but everything that now exists came to be, i.e., the physical cosmos and all that is contained within it.

Believe it or not, this is in fact what they are alleging. Make no mistake about it, as crazy as it sounds, it is their position on the matter. They attempt with all of their might to make the case sound logically possible, philosophically credible, and scientifically feasible. And they make this effort in spite of the fact that all of our five senses, all of human experience, along with the concerted voice of all of the available evidence on the subject, tell us that it is logically impossible, philosophically incredible, and scientifically infeasible.

The Argument Stated

This brings us to the Contingency Argument itself. Below the reader will find the argument from contingency as stated in a brief syllogism.

The Contingency Argument

But first let us define and explain this important term. Syllogisms were first utilized in formal logic by Aristotle in his studies on the art and method of correct thinking. Known collectively as the *Organon*, Aristotle single-handedly in this series of works set forth the most efficient method in the proper analysis of any argument. In his treatise *Prior Analytics* he distinguished between inductive and deductive reasoning, and more importantly, introduced the concept of the syllogism. Will Durant called it "the most characteristic and original of Aristotle's contributions to philosophy." Moreover, it has become one of the most essential aspects of formal logic down to our own time.

Hence, a syllogism is defined as a deductive scheme of a formal argument consisting at the minimum of a major and minor premise and a conclusion. Such a scheme is useful in the analysis of any point of view in order to ascertain the truth or falsity of the proposition in question. So, it is assuredly a key tool for the investigation of the query into whether or not God exists.

The contingency argument is as follows:

Premise 1: The universe exists (space, time, matter).
Premise 2: Everything that exists has an explanation of its existence, either in the necessity of its own nature or in an external cause.
Premise 3: If the universe has an explanation of its existence, that explanation is an external, transcendent, personal cause.
Conclusion: Therefore, the explanation of the existence of the universe is an external, transcendent, personal cause (an unembodied mind, i.e. God).

Examining the Argument More Closely

If one believes in God, then there is one thing that is self-evident at the outset. By very definition, God exists by the necessity of His own nature. Therefore, the one whom we describe as "God" cannot have an external cause. This is so because whatever caused God, if God were to have a cause, would logically have to be God. The origination and explanation of this proposition takes us back once more to the question of infinite regress. We all have heard the silly question that is quite often asked by shallow minded atheists, namely, "Who made God?" The ques-

GOD DOES EXIST!

tion itself is nothing more than a ridiculous distraction. Infinite regress is impossible.

It would be absurd to permit any moderately reasonable person to begin a discussion of this sort with a definition of God that makes Him a dependent being. Such a definition is self-contradictory. It would be like saying that the divine being we are talking about is not divine! What would God be dependent upon for His being? Again, what caused God would have to be God, by definition! So, no matter how many steps we take backward in our reasoning process, we will always wind up at the same point. If God exists at all, then God exists by the necessity of His own nature. He depends upon nothing outside of Himself for His being. He is the one non-contingent being.

Akin to this point, there is another issue that deserves to be dealt with at this juncture in the present discussion. It also presents a logical challenge for us. And it is this: whatever caused the universe to come into existence must, of necessity, be greater than the universe itself. That is inevitably so because any effect must necessarily be inferior to its cause.

This principle is easily demonstrable by virtually everything in our common experience. If I move a glass across the table, that is only a small illustration of what I am capable of moving. I am capable of moving much more. In fact, I probably could move 100 glasses across the table without too much effort. That is not because I am particularly strong or especially powerful. It is because I am an adult male human being with quite ordinary strength. And on account of the fact that almost any adult male human being can perform such a task, I can also do it.

But there is another consideration which must be given some thought to in a more general sense. It simply turns the argument around in the opposite direction. The reason this is evidently true is that the effect is much inferior to the cause, whatever the effect is and whatever the cause may be. The same wind that causes the trees to sway is perfectly able, in just the right circumstances, to rip those trees from out of the ground. Tornadic winds have frequently performed that frightening feat. This illustrates our point perfectly. The effect is much inferior to the cause, at least in terms of potential.

The Contingency Argument

If a horse transports a small child from one place to another without great effort, it probably would not surprise you to know that the same massive animal could take three full-grown adults the identical distance without much strain. None of us is very surprised to know any of this. A horse can weigh from 700 to 2200 pounds. An animal of that size and weight is enormously powerful. The concept of "horsepower," which is a common measurement of power in a steam-driven, gasoline powered, or any other type of mechanical engine, is based on the original testing by the 18th century Scottish engineer James Watt. He noted that draft horses on average were capable of lifting 550 pounds one foot in one second. That became the standard by which "horsepower" was measured from his time on, though the history of this measurement has been rather complex over time, since engines also have become extraordinarily complex over the years.

Given these facts, however, a modern engine is powerful at a level that was hard to imagine back in the time of Watt! The human brain and its unique ingenuity is responsible for that. This is even true when the effect seems in its magnitude to overshadow the cause. In the case of an explosive device which is built and detonated by a human being, the effect is of course more powerful than sheer human power unaided to cause harm. But, on the other hand, that same human brain may be capable of building another explosive device that is many times more devastating than the one before. It is the human mind that is in this instance the most powerful cause that is responsible for the devastation. It is the human brain that produced the atomic bomb, the hydrogen bomb, and then the neutron bomb! And so, even here the cause dwarfs the effect that results from it. We understand the principle behind all of these happenings and do not even give any of it much thought in our day.

Volcanoes also illustrate this point well. According to the U.S. Geological Survey, when Mt. St. Helens erupted in 1980 it was estimated that the mountain released 24 megatons of thermal energy. This is equivalent to 1600 times the size of the atomic bomb dropped on Hiroshima. But Mt. St. Helens was not even at the top of the scale of the Volcanic Explosivity Index. According to the Index it was a class 5, whereas the scale reaches up to 8. Class 8 super-volcanoes result in "super-colossal" eruptions which are known to spew forth more than 1000 cubic kilome-

GOD DOES EXIST!

ters of rock and ash, altering the climate of the entire planet for a time. All of the nuclear arsenals of all of the great powers on earth, if each and every one of them were detonated at once, could not match such super-explosions! Even with all of that, the pent up energy within the earth's crust would only be partially released in such a single cataclysmic event! Why is this so? The effect, as great as it may seem, is always ultimately much inferior to its cause. And, as we have seen, the converse is also true: the cause always eclipses the effect.

And so, whatever effect we depict, the causation is superior, sometimes in indescribable degrees of superiority. *Clearly this is the case with God.* The known universe, as grandiose as it may appear, is vastly inferior to its Maker. How do we know this? Because every effect is inferior to its cause, and every cause is superior to its effect.

In other words, we know this in principle and appreciate the universal validity of the principle. The scale of the universe is beside the point. Without question the universe is an impressive effect, but this quite simply suggests that the Cause of this effect is even more impressive, no doubt even by unimaginable orders of magnitude. Simply stated, then, God is greater and vastly more powerful than the universe He created. Therefore, the more amazing and expansive we perceive the cosmos to be, the more impressed we should be with the nature of the One who is responsible for it, the ultimate Cause of it.

This brings us to yet another important and related consideration. Some atheists argue that matter exists by the necessity of its own nature. This answer is often given as a response to the argument which we have set forth above. Of course, this is the only real alternative to the notion that God created matter when He initiated the universe and its other constituents, space, time, and energy. This view, to their way of thinking, offers them an alternative to the necessity of God. For this reason it is a very convenient theory. There is just one problem. And it is an especially thorny one given their boast that they are always on the side of science and that science is always on their side.

Simply stated, the science is now allied on several fronts squarely and powerfully against this view. *Matter is not eternal; it had a beginning.* That we now know beyond any doubt. We may have postulated it at

The Contingency Argument

a previous time in the history of thought on this subject, but now we know it as fact. The science is clear. And the science is indubitable. The cosmos had a beginning-point, a point before which it did not exist. And, if it had a beginning, then it does not exist by the necessity of its own nature. Something or Someone had to cause it.

Moreover, it cannot be deemed as sufficient as its own causation, or its own explanation. Matter did not cause itself. Matter does not explain itself. Something or some Person outside of itself caused it. Something or some Entity outside of itself, therefore, is its explanation. This is an essential inference from the facts of the case. Logic requires it. There is no avoiding this conclusion, at least, if we are willing to allow the science to speak for itself. So, let us have a look at the facts and the science involved.

The Science of Beginning

There are several particulars in the ongoing research that are now beyond challenge in this regard. They establish without question that matter had a beginning. The first piece of evidence is found in the long-understood nature of the second law of thermodynamics. Even though this aspect of the subject has for many years been appreciated, many thought that some sort of "work-around" could be managed for this problem as further study was done.

Eventually, exactly the opposite has occurred. Additional study has provided supportive information for what is inferentially concluded from the law. Basically, the law states that in any isolated system, as energy is being transferred or transformed, there is an increase in entropy or disorder. In short, energy is in a sense degraded over time so that it becomes less useful.

Thus, even though the first law of thermodynamics states that there is a constant *quantity* of energy present in the universe (or in any other closed system, for that matter) and none can ever be gained or lost, the *quality* of that energy is persistently and predictably declining on account of the second law. Hence, the *usefulness* of the energy in the system becomes the critical factor. The amount of energy that is left over after every reaction is less useful than what was available at the beginning of the process. So, the amount of usable energy is constantly being degraded.

GOD DOES EXIST!

This simple observation has enormous implications for our understanding of the physical universe. As a result of our understanding of this principle, it is universally recognized that, left to itself, at some far-distant time in the future the cosmos will run out of usable energy. Total entropy. That will be the end. No more light. No more fiery stars. Nothing. The universe will have "run out of gas" so to speak.

Now, on the other side of this equation, there is the universe's beginning-point. It must also be considered in the light of this physical law as well. At that juncture, when the cosmos first began, the maximum level of usable energy existed in the universe. At that very moment the decline in usable energy began. It has been "downhill" ever afterward.

These facts are not only imminently logical but scientifically demonstrable. Their implications are also considerable. Logically they force us to the conclusion that the universe could not be infinitely old. If, on the other hand, the universe were infinitely old, that is to say, matter were eternal, then it would already have run out of usable energy. If matter existed into the infinite past, it would have "run out of gas" long ago. And so, in no possible reconstruction of events is it plausible to argue that the material universe is infinitely old. It could not be because it is still fully functional and there is lots of energy left in the system. Therefore, the universe has a finite history; it began a finite number of years ago, whatever that number might be. It is that simple.

As already mentioned, this argument from the persistent inclination toward entropy, as important as it is, has been around for many years as an observable scientific phenomenon. Many researchers failed to consider its implications with sufficient gravity, perhaps thinking that eventually these phenomena would be explained in terms of later discovery. Little did many of them understand that eventually solid confirmation of these observations and what they implied would come in the form of other equally undeniable factors with far-reaching implications of their own.

More recently other discoveries have come to light that are even more impressive than the second law and its ramifications. For example, Alexander Friedmann and Georges Lemaitre, working with Einstein's theory of General Relativity, predicted that the universe was expanding.

The Contingency Argument

Their theory was empirically confirmed in 1929 by American astronomer Edwin Hubble in his research in the field of extragalactic astronomy. In the course of his investigations, he was the first to observe the existence of galaxies of stars beyond the Milky Way and of the cosmological "redshift" phenomenon. His observations tied this latter reality to an expanding universe. When an object moves away from us, the light is shifted to the red end of the spectrum, as its wavelengths get longer. If on the other hand, an object moves closer, the light shifts to the blue end of the spectrum, as its wavelengths get shorter.

Hubble noted that nearly all of the galaxies he observed are moving away, and so moving to the red end of the spectrum. The implications of this observation were earth-shattering for scientists in their speculations about the origin of the universe. At the same time it was entirely consistent with what they already knew from the second law of thermodynamics. An expanding universe, they concluded, must have sprung into existence at some point in the finite past. It could not be eternal. It had to have had a beginning, and that beginning was at the point from which it was moving over time.

The final piece of this larger puzzle regarding origins was revealed in 1965 with the discovery of cosmic microwave background radiation. Arno A. Penzias and Robert W. Wilson of Bell Laboratories were testing a sensitive horn antenna designed for detecting low levels of microwave radiation when they detected a low level of microwave background "noise" hindering their studies. It was aggravating and persistent. Upon further investigation, it turned out that this "noise" was coming from interplanetary space.

After considerable additional investigation of the phenomenon, they noted that this microwave "noise" came from every direction in space. It was a distribution of microwave radiation which matched a blackbody curve for a radiator at about 2.7 Kelvins. A group at Princeton had earlier predicted that there would be a residual microwave background radiation left over from the Big Bang and had planned an experiment to attempt to detect it. Penzias and Wilson finished their studies first and so were awarded the Nobel Prize in 1978 for their work on the phenomenon.

GOD DOES EXIST!

This evidence confirmed, in a quite accidental but most extraordinary way, the existence of a finite universe. The material universe had a beginning and so, given the implications of the second law of thermodynamics, would eventually have an end. Certainly the beginning was now confirmed to have taken place. All "eternal universe" models that have been theorized by various scientists after these important discoveries have failed miserably. They simply cannot account for or explain these phenomena, nor can they be viewed as convincing in the light of these three phenomena.

Hence, the Borde-Guth-Vilenkin Theorem became predominant, demonstrating that any expanding universe cannot be eternal in the past. And, as Alexander Vilenkin wrote, "It is said that an argument is what convinces reasonable men and a proof is what it takes to convince even an unreasonable man. With the proof now in place, cosmologists can no longer hide behind the possibility of a past-eternal universe. There is no escape, they have to face the problem of a cosmic beginning" (*Many Worlds in One*, 176).

Conclusion

Of course, there are those who will not be satisfied and cannot give up their only hope for their opposition to the God hypothesis. "The universe has no explanation." Some atheists say this because that is the necessary inference that is to be drawn from their persistent assumption that God does not exist. A universe that had a beginning, must also have an explanation, whereas a universe without a beginning can be said to have no explanation. Whatever caused it to be is the explanation of it. If it has always been, then in their way of thinking it needs no explanation.

That is their way of working around the philosophical and logical necessity of cause and effect. To their minds, either the essential matter which constitutes the physical universe is itself eternal in the past, which some still stubbornly allege in spite of these rather impactful recent discoveries that seem to make it an impossibility, or else it exists by the necessity of its own nature. Either way, they are not obligated to explain it. However, neither of these alternatives is particularly enticing because of the mounting and overwhelming scientific evidence against them. Their hope for some future alternative theory or antithetical discovery that will blow all of this data out of the water appears to be a mere "will-of-the-wisp," an *ignis fatuus*, without substance.

The Contingency Argument

Consequently, if the cosmos has an explanation, and everything within it certainly does, then God exists. God is the cause of it, and God is the explanation of it.

Questions for Discussion

1. Is the following question worthy of our consideration: "Why is there something rather than nothing?"
2. "From nothing, nothing comes." What are your thoughts on this statement?
3. Is it true to say that it is the position of many skeptics that, "From nothing, everything has come"?
4. Summarize the Contingency Argument for God.
5. Why is it important to understand that by definition God exists by the necessity of His own nature?
6. Is it logical to state that whatever caused the universe must be greater than the universe?
7. Is it correct to argue that whatever causes anything is necessarily greater than the effect that was caused?
8. Is it correct to argue that whatever is caused by something else is necessarily inferior to that which caused it?
9. What three scientific factors make it incredible to believe that the universe had no beginning in finite time?
10. How do atheists yet make the case that the "God hypothesis" is not trustworthy?
11. In your view, what is the explanation of the material universe?

Chapter 3

The Five Cosmological Arguments

In Book 12 of his *Metaphysics*, Aristotle in his examination of the notion of movement, spoke of the primary cause or "mover" of all of the motion in the universe. Also, in Book 8 of his *Physics*, he noted that "there must be an immortal, unchanging being, ultimately responsible for all wholeness and orderliness in the sensible world." He spoke of this prime mover as *prōton kinoun ariskēton*, which he further characterized as "an independent divine eternal unchanging material substance" (Sir David Ross, and John Lloyd, *Aristotle*, 6th rev. Edition, 2006; pp. 188, 190). In his way of thinking, the very existence of change requires a first unmoved mover in order to begin the entire process.

It is suggested by some scholars that Aristotle probably derived this theory from earlier speculations by Greek philosophers who came before him. He is certainly dependent on the thinking of others who

The Five Cosmological Arguments

preceded him in other areas of his thought (e.g., he adopted the geometrical model of Eudoxus of Cnidus in terms of the motions of the celestial spheres, etc.), so this view, even though it is not proven beyond question, is quite possible. Even so, it's attribution to him is entirely appropriate on account of his first literary mention of the notion.

Because of his wide popularity and considerable influence in every sector of learning and education after his time, Aristotle's concept of the prime mover entered early Christian thought along with Neoplatonist philosophy. Later still, the idea was borrowed by medieval Islamic thinkers, especially in the Sunni tradition. One of the earliest proponents of the concept among the Islamists was Al-Kindi (801-873) in the 9th century. He argued that, "Every being which begins has a cause for its beginning; now the world is a being which begins; therefore, it possesses a cause for its beginning" (*On First Philosophy*; quoted in Seyyed Hossein, *An Introduction to Islamic Cosmological Doctrines*, 168).

The argument was further refined by Al-Ghazali (Algazel; 1058-1111) in the 11th century in his work *The Incoherence of the Philosophers*, and by Ibn Rushd (Averroes; 1126-1198) in his book *The Incoherence of the Incoherence*. Al-Ghazali and Ibn Rushd follow the typical Asharite (Asharite School of Sunni Islam, founded by Arab theologian Abu al-Hasan al-Ash'ari) *kalam* cosmological argument in that they argue the scientific evidence for the temporal origin of the world, and then reason from that to the existence of a Creator. The word *kalam* is the Arabic term for medieval theology. The two writers had differences in regard to various specific points, but agreed on this matter. In his work *Decisive Treatise*, Ibn Rushd summarily reduced the argument between Asharite theologians and the ancient Greek philosophers to one of simple semantics. Regarding the question of the Prime Mover, both men were clearly Aristotelian in their approach. William Lane Craig popularized the term "*kalam* cosmological argument" in current philosophical thought, because of its historic roots in medieval Islamic theology. In 1979 he titled a rather extensive book on the argument by this name.

On the other hand, it is generally recognized that the brilliant Dominican priest, theologian, and philosopher Thomas Aquinas (1225-1244) gave the Christian world and its Western societies the classical statement of the Cosmological Argument for God. In the *Summa Theologiae*,

GOD DOES EXIST!

he set forward five proofs for the existence of God. Aquinas thought in terms of an "Unmoved Mover," or "Prime Mover," an "Uncaused First Cause," and of a "Necessary Being," as opposed to other beings that he described simply as "contingent beings." Aquinas, considered one of the greatest Christian philosophers in human history, started his thought process about this subject from an *a posteriori* position. The human experience of the material universe is key. To his mind, motion would include any sort of change, such as growth, for instance. The natural condition is for things to remain at rest. Something which is moving is therefore in an unnatural state, and so must have been put into that state by some extra-ordinary being, an external supernatural power.

No less a scientist and theoretical genius than Albert Einstein is quoted in agreement with this set of proposals: "I see at the beginning of the cosmic road—not eternal energy or matter, not 'inscrutable fate,' not a 'fortuitous conflux of primordial elements,' not 'the Great Unknown'—but the Lord God Almighty" (quoted in "Identifying Einstein's 'Creative Force,'" *The Evidence for God in an Expanding Universe,* ed. John C. Monsma, 68).

The following cluster of arguments are all related to one another in that they are grouped within the larger category of "cosmological" arguments, that is to say, arguments that are based on the essential nature of the observable cosmos. They attempt to explain its complexity and obvious design features in terms of such an "Uncaused First Cause" or an original "Prime Mover." The influence of the inimitable Aquinas is evident throughout this presentation of the arguments.

1. The Argument from Motion

We currently live in a world in which things are in motion. The wind is moving. The trees and the grasses are in motion on account of the wind. Water is flowing. Cars are moving. Trains are moving. Planes are moving. People and animals are in motion. Even when their bodies are at rest, their hearts are beating and their lungs are moving as they inhale and exhale. Motion is a constant in our material world.

Movement is caused by movers (things that cause motion). When the wind blows it sets the ocean waves in motion. In the case of a sailing ship, the sails propel the ship forward on account of the movement

The Five Cosmological Arguments

of the wind. Too, the movement of the waves causes the ship to move back and forth on the surface of the ocean. If the waves move violently enough, things like chairs and tables will shift inside the ship. This motion may cause the inner ear mechanism of the passengers on board to experience "motion sickness" or to become "seasick." In this scenario the wind is the prime mover that sets all of the other objects in motion. But the identical principle is at work whenever and wherever there is motion in our physical world.

Behind all of this there is a universal principle at work. Everything that is moving must have been set in motion by something else that was moving. A still object does not move another object. Only a moving object can set another object in motion. If you have seen dominoes set beside one another in a long chain you will be well aware that this is true. As long as the first domino is unmoved, or left alone, the entire chain remains motionless. But once the first domino falls, it sets in motion an absolutely inevitable chain of events.

However many there are, whether a dozen or a thousand, that are set near enough to one another to create a particular chain of events, they will all fall one by one, until they have all fallen in a heap. That first gentle touch by a single human hand will set the dozen or the thousand into motion. That is the way our physical world works. Wherever and whenever there is motion there is causation. In every instance, something or someone started the process. That is for certain!

That is on the micro level, of course. But what about at the macro level? Who or what started all motion? Are we to believe that this principle which is so clearly and forthrightly taught to us by virtually everything around us is also not true at the macro level? And so, our point is this: Something or someone must have started the movement in the first place. We call that something or someone God.

Infinite regress, on the other hand, is impossible. Despite claims to the contrary, no proof is ever forthcoming to establish a different hypothesis. At the same time, an infinite regress of movement is the only other alternative to a "Prime Mover" (or Unmoved Mover).

Stated succinctly, then, the syllogism which lays out the argument is as follows:

GOD DOES EXIST!

Premise 1: Objects are in motion.
Premise 2: Everything in motion was put in motion by something else.
Premise 3: There cannot be an infinite regress of movers. Movement must begin somewhere with something or someone.
Conclusion 1: Therefore, there must be a First Mover, itself unmoved, and that is God.
Conclusion 2: Therefore, God exists.

2. The Argument from Causation

This argument may be stated in very few words and without much elaboration. It is based on the observation that all we know and experience in the cosmos, somehow or other, has a cause. But what sort of thing could be responsible for causing an entire universe to come into being? That is a most natural question, and one that cannot be avoided, if cosmology is permitted to ask all of the appropriate questions. So, here is the argument itself.

Premise 1: Whatever begins to exist has a cause.
Premise 2: The universe began to exist.
Conclusion: Therefore, the universe has a cause.

What follows now is the reasoning that grows out of the pursuit of the question to its logical end. The answer to the question of who or what might be responsible for causing a universe to exist is an interesting one. Frankly, *it can only lead back to the concept of God*. Think of it this way: whatever caused the universe to exist must itself be uncaused since it is impossible to have an infinite regress of causes. Mathematician David Hilbert rightly said, "Infinity is merely an idea; the infinite is nowhere to be found in reality." Hilbert's research on the notion of mathematical "infinity" is legendary. Hence, an infinite regress of causes is not credible. Too, the cause of the universe must be immaterial, or non-material, since it existed prior to the beginning of the material universe. It must be eternal, or timeless, since it existed before time and ultimately created time. It must be omniscient, being that it possessed sufficient genius to design and manufacture a universe. It must be omnipotent, since it had the virtually unlimited power essential to create a universe. It must have a personal will, since it decided to bring the universe into

The Five Cosmological Arguments

being. And the principle of Occam's Razor (the law of simplicity: "entities should not be multiplied unnecessarily") says that there is likely to be just one cause and not many. So, at the end of the process of reasoning about the cause of the universe, we have described God in every particular. *Therefore, it should be concluded that God is the cause of the universe.*

But, having said all this, let us return for a moment and explore the original question itself, which lies at the root of the first and second premises of the argument. Once more, we may draw hundreds of illustrations from what we see about us in the material world, but a few very obvious ones will suffice. If we happen upon a field of old magma, such as is frequently found in nature, we may conclude that at some time in the past, whether in the ancient past or more recently, a nearby volcanic source produced that field of hardened stone. A specific volcanic event caused the deposition of that field of igneous rock. All observers would reach the identical conclusion in this regard. Some might debate the precise point in time when it was laid down, whether two-hundred years ago, or five-hundred years ago. However, not one person would ever argue that it appears there uncaused. We always and inevitably look for the cause or causes of any particular phenomenon. It is then *explained* in terms of its causation. In this case the cause was a volcano.

Likewise, if we were to find a deep bog, filled with sedimentary layers, we might speculate about its origin. This wet, spongy ground seems to represent the accumulation of organic debris from many years of growth of some particular type of flora that is still living in the topmost layer of the bog. Different views might be expressed by various observers of the phenomenon, in their exploration of the layers that comprise it, as to how or why it has come to be as it has. But it would be deemed unscientific and illogical to argue that it appears as it does without some explanation, some cause. All might not agree as to the precise nature of the cause of it, but all would say that there was a cause for it and that through careful analysis of the layerings the cause or causes, in all probability, could be determined with some relative degree of certainty.

Fossils found in sedimentary rock are immediately recognized as representing the bony structures or even in some cases the soft tissue of ancient life forms which were alive at the time of the deposition. Their skeletons appear in the rock layers because they were somehow caught

GOD DOES EXIST!

up in a series of cataclysmic events that led to their death and deposition. When the rock hardened over time, their skeletal remains were left as imprints in the stone, evidence of the fact that they once lived, and of what they were like when they were alive. Some such explanation of their presence in the rock layering would be agreed to by one and all. There might be different opinions and variants as to the exact mode of their deposition in the sediment, but it would be universally recognized that this is what caused the phenomenon.

Science always looks for an explanation for what the cause of some phenomenon might be. This is true with logic as well. What caused a thing, and how may it be explained? There are no exceptions to this general rule. Things do not happen in nature without causes. Yet many scientists break this rule in regard to their analysis of the sum of all of nature's parts. The logic requires that if it is true with respect to each and every part of the natural world, then it is true also of the sum of its parts. Even the dedicated atheist, David Hume, admitted, "I never asserted so absurd a proposition as to say that anything might arise without a cause."

So, let us state this fact in the form of a set of propositions. This set will be more complete than the earlier one given above. They will also include some of the elements which we have introduced since we looked at the other more elemental set. The syllogism would appear as follows:

Premise 1: Some things are caused.
Premise 2: Anything caused has to be caused by something else (since nothing causes itself).
Premise 3: There cannot be an infinite regress of causes.
Conclusion 1: Therefore, there must have been a First Cause, itself uncaused, and that is God.
Conclusion 2: Therefore, God exists.

3. The Argument from Contingency

Philosophy rightly distinguishes between what it describes as "contingent beings" and "essential beings." In this respect, how would we mark the difference between human beings and a divine being?

Every human being who exists is a contingent being; he/she might not have existed. The fact that he or she exists is never by necessity. No human is a necessary being. In every instance a whole host of circum-

The Five Cosmological Arguments

stances and events fortuitously came together to make that person's existence in the world a possibility. We could, of course, explore the concept of divine providence in regard to this subject, and that would make the idea more interesting, but that would only complicate our inquiry. In simplest terms, every human person is contingent. What if his father and mother had not met? What if one of them was killed or died from disease during childhood? He would not be and would never have been.

Among the Western societies after the course of the second great World War, almost an entire generation of young marriageable-age men was wiped off the face of the earth. Those whose bodies were recovered are buried in military cemeteries all around the world. Others are listed as MIA (missing in action) to this day. Most of them never procreated. Therefore, a huge number of children who would have been their legacy to the world were never born. They are the best illustration of how truly contingent every one of us is! We are here, but we might never have been. We are all contingent beings. And, every person who has ever lived was in this sense a contingent being.

However, an infinite regress of contingency is impossible. We cannot have a world where everything and everyone is contingent, because then, by definition, it all could easily have never existed. In fact, nothing would ever have existed if absolutely everything was and is contingent. Logically, it must stop somewhere. Contingency can only go so far. Beyond that it begins to strain credulity.

Therefore, there must be at least one Necessary Being who has always existed, who always will exist, and who can't not exist. He is essential to the entire process. In fact, without Him in the picture at some point, there is no process. All existence begins with Him. All existence is dependent upon Him. He is responsible for the fact that all contingent beings exist.

Stated succinctly, then, the argument would be as follows:

Premise 1: There are contingent things; the world is full of them.
Premise 2: Contingent things can cause other contingent things, but there cannot be only contingent things.
Premise 3: This is true because that would mean that there is an infinite regress of contingency, and a possibility that nothing might ever have existed.

GOD DOES EXIST!

Premise 4: An infinite regress of contingency is impossible.
Conclusion 1: Therefore, there must be at least one Necessary Thing, and that is God.
Conclusion 2: So, God exists.

The key to appreciating the force of this argument is to understand the nature of contingency itself and how truly fragile life is. As much as the odds were against our having ever come to be, to have lived at all, nevertheless, we are here. We have beaten the odds. Here we are.

And so we have arrived at this particular moment in time in order to go beyond merely existing and contemplate the mystery of our being. In so saying, we cannot but admit how genuinely contingent we are. Every generation before us was also. Every person who has ever seen the light of day, whether famous or infamous or merely forgettable, was the same. Not one of us or one of them ever had to be! They were all likewise contingent.

But such a long line of contingency cannot stretch on into the infinite past. Logic will not allow it. The facts of the case would militate against that implausible abstraction. An eternal string of unlikely contingencies is impossible. Our very existence argues vehemently against it. At some point in the finite past a Necessary Being was responsible for this long line of contingencies. It cannot have been otherwise.

4. The Argument from Degrees

In human experience the concept of degrees is fundamental. We take the idea for granted as we go about our daily activities, without much thought of what its implications might ultimately be. All about us there are things that illustrate this point. We characterize them in terms of what is good, better, and best, for example. Or, in terms of what is bad, worse, and worst of all. We think about things that are hot, warm, tepid, cool, and cold. Things are light or dark, lighter and darker, as well as, lightest and darkest. We could go on and on with illustrative comparatives of this kind, all of them describing various degrees of comparison. They would potentially number in the thousands.

Such states of being, along with their comparatives and attendant superlatives, are at the heart of our experience in the material universe.

The Five Cosmological Arguments

That cannot be denied. These simple and pregnant observations form the basis for an argument for the existence of a Supreme Being.

Some have called this the "Henological" Argument. This term derives from the Greek word *hen* which means "one." The concept of "The One" was fleshed out by the late Greek philosopher Plotinus (ca. AD 205-270), who started the trend toward what was later called Neo-Platonism. In our view this is an inappropriate title for the view, since Plotinus in his philosophy of "The One" was describing his theory of the metaphysics of emanation rather than of creation *ex nihilo*, which has always been the Christian perspective. So, to utilize this term to describe Christian theology in regard to God and creation is not consistent with either the philosophy of Plotinus or the philosophy of Thomas Aquinas, who is responsible for the major statement of the argument from the Christian standpoint.

Aquinas iterates the argument as he sees it thus:

> The fourth way is based on the gradation observed in things. Some things are found to be more good, more true, more noble, and so on, and other things less. But comparative terms describe varying degrees of approximation to a superlative: for example, things are hotter and hotter the nearer they approach what is hottest.
>
> Something therefore is the truest and best and most noble of things, and hence the most fully in being. For Aristotle says that the truest things are the things most fully in being. Now when many things possess some property in common, the one most fully possessing it causes it in the others; fire, to use Aristotle's example, the hottest of all things, causes all other things to be hot. There is something therefore which causes in all other things their being, their goodness, and whatever other perfection they have. And this we call God (*Summa Theologiae* 1a, 2, 3).

Intelligent beings arrange things in our experience in terms of more and less, and when we do, we tend to arrange them on a sort of relative scale employing words that characterize them as either more or less (in modern terms from 1 to 5, or even 1 to 10, etc.), and then finally in terms of most and least. Comparatives lead us eventually in the direction of superlatives: good, better, and best.

GOD DOES EXIST!

Light is a perfect example of this. We depict it in terms of lightness as it approaches perfect whiteness. Dark is described in precisely the opposite language. It is considered darker as it approaches total opaqueness. A complete lack of light would therefore constitute "perfect darkness." There would be degrees of dimness and brightness all along the way. The extreme at each end of the spectrum represents the full measure or perfection of that state of being, whether of lightness or darkness. This method of measurement between opposites applies in a whole host of different areas of comparison.

Another logical concomitant follows in the wake of this observation. Sometimes it may be the literal distance between an object and a source of heat or light that determines *how* hot or cold something may be. Now, we understand that things are to be considered more or less warm as they are more or less proximate to the source of the heat or light. A metal object that is left sitting in the fire on the fireplace may glow red from the heat and will certainly be too hot for one to touch it with his bare hands. If it is a few inches away, and left there for a considerable time, it may still be too warm to handle, but not as hot as one left sitting directly in the fire. If it is a few feet from the fireplace, out in the middle of the room, it may be a bit warm, but may easily and without discomfort be handled. We should also note that the heat that reflects from the metal object does not originate in the object itself, but rather from the fire. The object is so close to the fire that it absorbs the heat from it. The closer it is to the fire, the more heat it will absorb. Remember this principle, for we shall return to it momentarily.

In a similar fashion, truth and good and the whole host of the finest qualities of character, represent the most desirable traits for a human being to emulate and perpetuate in his own personal life. Some virtues may have detractors, but most of them do not. We all recognize that it is better, for example, for someone to be brave than to be cowardly. It is preferable for them to be honest rather than deceptive. It is better for them to be courteous rather than rude. Likewise, we appreciate that it is better to be loving rather than hateful, generous rather than selfish, kind rather than spiteful, etc.

We may excuse some of these uglier and less desirable traits in ourselves at times in order to justify our own shortcomings, but we would

The Five Cosmological Arguments

never excuse them in others. We know that they are unpleasant and undesirable. And if we are honest with ourselves, we will recognize that they are areas of our own character at certain times that sorely need correction, and understand that we need to work on the attitudes that underlie them and replace these unsavory vices with virtues.

The concept of truth will illustrate the point. A statement that is made by someone has the potential to be either true or false. In fact, it may be mostly true or mostly false. Or, it may even be half true and half false. If I say that, "John just went out of the room to go home," when it was Michael who just went out of the room to go home, then the statement was half true and half false. If, on the other hand, Michael went out of the room but it was his stated purpose to go to work rather than home, then the statement was wholly false, that is, false in every respect. Statements in general may be said to be more or less true as they approach the perfect standard of accuracy.

States of being in the material universe are also supportive of this notion. When we compare a rock, a plant, an animal, a sloth for example, and a human being, we understand that all of these objects or creatures have a state of being. The rock exists, just as the plant does. So does the sloth and the human being. But we appreciate that the being of the rock is inferior in a very important way to that of the plant, because the plant is a living thing while the rock is merely an inanimate object.

Likewise, the sloth is a living creature which in some sense may be said to be superior to a plant, but at the same time we know that it is inferior to a human being. Its "being" represents a higher form of life than a mere plant, but it does not possess high intelligence and cannot reason or communicate. These are qualities possessed only by human beings.

The living world of plants and animals illustrate this lesson at every conceivable level. And, as human beings, the highest and most advanced of all living things in terms of intelligence and potential, we commonly and rightly make such comparisons. They are a natural element of our communication process at every level. But, are we willing to take the next step and accept the implication of this? Are we prepared to draw a logical conclusion from the universal lesson we learn from the whole of the natural realm, when it is taken together as a full range of

GOD DOES EXIST!

comparatives and superlatives? Clearly, all of this has the potential to carry us to a conclusion that for some of us is viewed as undeniable.

As we have done previously, let us state the consequent proposition plainly: if there are degrees of truth, and good, and of being itself, then there exists some One who is the superlative of all truth and good and of being itself. Moreover, the closer we are to the ultimate source of all virtue, the more virtuous we ourselves will become. God is, in fact, that ultimate source and standard of what is true and good, and even of being. The nearer we draw to Him, the more we come to know of Him, the greater our love and respect for Him, the more we will be like Him and share His nature.

Once more, this point may be stated philosophically and propositionally in the form of a logical syllogism. The argument may be set forth as follows:

Premise 1: Properties come in degrees.
Premise 2: In order for there to be degrees of perfection, there must be something perfect against which everything else is measured.
Premise 3: God is the pinnacle of perfection.
Conclusion: Therefore, God *must* exist.

In order for there to be degrees of perfection, there must be something perfect against which everything else is measured. God is that pinnacle, that superlative of perfection. Thomas Aquinas was keen in his perception of the world in making the inferences that he did with regard to degrees. Shallower minds would never have thought through what is commonplace to all but has such profound implications when analyzed. He paused long enough to think about and attempt to understand the ramifications of what was to be observed in the natural realm and in the human condition. It was everywhere about him, just as it is everywhere about every one of us. But the scholarly Aquinas took careful notice of it and contemplated what it all might imply. He perceptively observed that the range of possibilities must stop somewhere. The scale of comparatives must have an ultimate goal, logically and philosophically. From this he necessarily inferred the existence of God.

Many other great philosophers have tended to draw the same conclusion that he did. God is the realization of all comparisons that have

The Five Cosmological Arguments

to do with truth, and virtue, good, and even of the notion of being itself. He is the superlative of all that is true and virtuous.

God is perfect truth, devoid of all falsehood. God is incomparable virtue, bereft of any negative quality or inclination toward evil. Finally, God is the perfect and ultimate being, at the very top of the scale of being. We exist as human beings only because He willed for us to exist. Those who live their lives in isolation away from Him cannot appreciate how deeply changed and altered they might have been if they had sought out His fellowship.

Some of us will remember the film, "The Life and Times of Grizzly Adams" a 1977 story about a mountain man and a grizzly bear cub that he raised to become his companion. This giant creature, if we were to encounter it in the wild, would be terrifying. Humans are killed and sometimes even eaten by grizzlies almost every year. And yet, its friendship with a particular human being had made of it a gentle giant, a downright friendly monster. We watched in stark amazement as Dan Haggerty, the show's lead actor, interacted with gentle Ben, a predatory carnivore of massive size and phenomenal strength, and surprisingly demonstrated the demeanor of a collie puppy.

Friendship with God can do the same for the most uncivilized and uncouth among us. His friendship can make us what we ought to be and what we were originally intended to be. Those of us who work constantly in the province of connecting people with their God through Jesus Christ have seen this outcome hundreds of times. While some may doubt the seriousness of what we do, the results of such labors have to be conceded by one and all. Changed men change the world for the better one person at a time. And it is clearly their newfound nearness to deity that has made all of the difference. So, as Thomas Aquinas prayed, so should we:

> Grant me, O Lord my God,
> A mind to know you,
> A heart to seek you,
> Wisdom to find you,
> Conduct pleasing to you,
> Faithful perseverance in waiting for you,
> And a hope of finally embracing you. Amen.

GOD DOES EXIST!

5. The Argument from Teleology or Intelligent Design

Teleology is the study of design in nature. The word itself derives from the Greek terms *telos* and *logia*. The former term means "end" or "purpose." The concept behind our use of this term to describe the material world is the very common observation of patterns and complexity which seems to indicate planning and purpose and militates against the idea that the natural world has come about through blind chance.

Thomas Aquinas framed the argument thus:

> The fifth way is taken from the governance of the world. We see that things that lack intelligence, such as natural bodies, act for an end, and this is evident from their acting always, or nearly always, in the same way, so as to obtain the best result. Hence it is plain that not fortuitously, but designedly, do they achieve their end. Now whatever lacks intelligence cannot move towards an end, unless it be directed by some being endowed with knowledge and intelligence; as the arrow is shot to its mark by the archer. Therefore, some intelligent being exists by whom all natural things are directed to their end; and this being we call God.

Aquinas based his argument on Aristotle's understanding of the various biological processes in nature which clearly show design features. Hence, by observing certain aspects of the cosmos, it may be concluded that it gives the appearance that a great many things both in the natural world and in the biological realm are perfectly adapted to fulfill their role and function. At the most rudimentary level the human body illustrates this important observation. A single human body is organized from the ground up into a final product, from the most basic to the most complex in the following orderly and systematic way: atoms, molecules, cells, tissues, organs, organ systems, and finally a fully functioning organism.

Such complex organs and their systems in nature, such as the eye, the ear, the brain, the circulatory system, the nervous system, the digestive and excretory systems, the skeletal system, the muscular system, the endocrine system, the lymphatic system, the reproductive system, and the integumentary system which encloses it all, provide the keen observer with the firm indication that they were deliberately designed for these special purposes. The fact that no part of these can stand alone

The Five Cosmological Arguments

without all of the others working smoothly together suggests the relative impossibility that they developed gradually over time through a process of chance happenings. How would the creature survive prior to the full development and functionality of these exceedingly complicated systems? That is the question that those who postulate a gradual development scenario cannot answer.

Further, as research has advanced our knowledge of the conditions that are essential for life to exist, we have come to understand that the universe as a whole is somehow "fine-tuned" for the existence of life. This fact is well established by a whole host of scientific observations. We shall put off until the fifth chapter of this book a closer look at some of these rather complicated issues and their weighty implications. Suffice it to say for now that many of them are so precisely configured that they give the outward impression of "fine-tuning" and not of accidental or fortuitous causation and sequencing.

What is the explanation for this? There are only three possible ways of solving this puzzle. The fine-tuning of the universe is due to either *physical necessity, chance, or design*. What would be the basis of this physical necessity if it existed? Those who make the case for chance as the ultimate explanation tell us that given enough possible worlds, even the most unlikely scenario that one could imagine would eventually, and even inevitably, occur. But this is a theory that is the last bastion of a desperate mind.

To their way of thinking this talk of "possible worlds" seems to offer them a sophisticated way of avoiding what appears to theists to be the only possible explanation. But they have to admit that they cannot prove the existence of even one other possible world than that one which is observable to us. The existence of other possible worlds represents only an intellectual exercise, not a genuine logical alternative. By grasping at straws called "the multiverse" then, they admit not only the unlikelihood of their hypothesis but it's sheer impossibility. "Other possible worlds," and multiple universes, are the last refuge of desperate men! Raw chance cannot explain what our eyes behold and what our other senses detect in the natural world! Anyone with normal intelligence, and who is not trying to give atheism a way out of this logical conundrum, would have to admit that.

GOD DOES EXIST!

So, it is not due to physical necessity or chance; both options are implausible. Therefore, it is due to design. This is the only other logical possibility. And the presence of so many thousands of design elements at every level in both the physical cosmos and the biological diversity in the sphere of living things, necessitates the existence of a Designer. Not only so, but a Designer whose intelligence and sophistication is beyond our capacity fully to comprehend and appreciate. Some of these organic systems have required the coordinated efforts of thousands of scientists over hundreds of years even to begin to comprehend their processes and procedures. God, therefore, is the only reasonable explanation for the facts thus described.

So, again, to state the argument succinctly in propositional form:

Premise 1: The universe is fine-tuned to accommodate life.
Premise 2: The fine-tuning of the universe is due to either physical necessity, chance, or design.
Premise 3: Its fine-tuning cannot be due to physical necessity or chance.
Premise 4: Therefore, it is by design.
Conclusion 1: The existence of design necessitates a designer.
Conclusion 2: Therefore God, the Designer, exists.

The effectiveness of these arguments set forth by Aristotle and Aquinas may not be in the persuasiveness of any one of them by itself but rather in the cumulative force of the five of them together. Each of them is persuasive in its own right. But all of them put together magnify the evidence and produce a bedrock foundation for belief in God.

Conclusion

These arguments have frequently been made by believers since the time of Aquinas. Each one is fairly simple and straightforward. But that does not mean that they have been generally accepted or that skeptics have all been convinced by them. The response which has often been heard from unbelievers after hearing them presented, and even if they recognize the force and cogency of one or more, or acknowledge the reasonableness of all of these cosmological arguments put together, is at times disappointing. It may sound something like this: "Well, all you seem to have established is the strong probability of the existence of

The Five Cosmological Arguments

an "Unmoved Mover" and an "Uncaused First Cause," etc. You have not proven the existence of the Hebrew God or the Christian Christ, or anything of that sort. You have not even established whether God is plural or singular in number?"

That point has some legitimacy. It should be stressed that this is not the purpose of these proofs. These arguments are simply introductory to the larger set of questions that need to be addressed. The aim of such reasoning as this is to set the stage for further exploration of those other issues. But first things first. How do any of these other things matter to us if we cannot be convinced initially to believe in the notion that God, or any deity at all, is possible conceptually? This is the most basic requirement, and it is precisely what these arguments are intended to authenticate.

What Aquinas was trying to prove, and what we are trying to certify, first and foremost, is that God exists. That is the sum and substance of what we are interested in pursuing. After we have established this proposition as more plausible than not, then we may proceed with some considerable confidence toward examining the evidence as to which of the possible options would be most reasonable in those other and equally important areas of contention. But establishing that it is reasonable to believe in God is step one. And, this is the stated objective of these arguments.

For our purposes the issue of what the nature of God is and whether or not he is the God of Abraham, Moses, Elijah, and Jesus is a discussion that we shall leave for another day. Suffice it to say for now that the five formative arguments posed by Aquinas have been powerful and convincing for a great number of people in their own right, and they have never been adequately answered, and they certainly have not been debunked.

This is so in spite of the fact that there have been a good many negative responses to them throughout the years since they were first formulated and recorded for the benefit of posterity. White noise, however, will not suffice to convince thoughtful believers that they are invalid, and up to now that is all that has been forthcoming to answer these five convincing proofs.

GOD DOES EXIST!

Questions for Discussion

1. What part did the ancient philosopher Aristotle play in framing the cosmological argument for the existence of God?
2. Describe the perspective of Thomas Aquinas in his presentation of the cosmological argument.
3. Aquinas spoke of five separate and distinctive angles in his look at the argument for God from cosmology. Can you name them all?
4. Summarize the argument from motion in the universe for God's existence. Do you consider it to be valid?
5. Summarize the argument from causation for the existence of God. Do you consider it to be plausible?
6. Summarize the argument from contingency for the God hypothesis. Is it persuasive?
7. Summarize the argument from degrees for the existence of a Higher Power. What do you think of this approach?
8. Summarize the argument from teleology or "intelligent design" for God as the Designer of the cosmos.
9. What is the cumulative effect of these five arguments taken together? Are they more forceful given the fact that there are five of them rather than just one representing a single line of approach to the question?
10. What is your view of the argument made against the cosmological perspective which says that these points are weak because they do not establish which God is the true one or even whether there is one God or many?

Chapter 4
The Ontological Argument

The Argument As Described by Anselm of Canterbury (1033-1109)

Ontology is a word that is not regularly in our vocabulary. So, it would be entirely appropriate to provide a working definition of the idea for the sake of the uninitiated reader. The term refers to "the study of the nature of being and existence." Speaking formally, it is a branch of metaphysics and philosophy that deals with the nature of existence, becoming, and reality. It deals with questions that concern what entities exist or may be said to exist. And so it is a term that is useful in relation to the question of whether or not God exists.

In chapters 2 and 3 of Anselm of Canterbury's book *Proslogium* (1078), he fleshed out the argument that has been described as the Ontological Proof for God. In speaking of the fool who claims that there is no God, he remarked in regard to the Creator, "we believe that thou art

GOD DOES EXIST!

a being than which nothing greater can be conceived." He went on to say that, "By 'God' we mean an absolutely unsurpassable being, a being that cannot be conceivably improved upon." Anselm proposed that we ought to treat the understanding or the mind as if it were a place, and thus to speak of things existing "in the understanding." From this he went on to argue:

> And assuredly, that than which nothing greater can be conceived cannot exist in the understanding alone: then it can be conceived to exist in reality, which is greater.
>
> Therefore, if that than which nothing greater can be conceived exists in the understanding alone, the very thing than which nothing greater can be conceived is one than which a greater can be conceived. But obviously this is impossible. Hence there is no doubt that there exists a being than which nothing greater can be conceived, and it exists both in the understanding and in reality.

Thus, Anselm made the observation that the fool had conceded that God exists in the understanding (he admits this by his denial of his existence), but he concludes that it is impossible for him to exist in the understanding alone. Being that He is such as He is, he cannot exist only in the mind. Here is a basic outline of the argument:

1. Suppose (with the fool) that God exists in the understanding alone.
2. Given our definition, this means that a being than which none greater can be, exists in the understanding alone.
3. But this being can be conceived to exist in reality. That is, we conceive of a circumstance in which theism is true, even if we do not believe that it actually obtains.
4. But it is greater for a thing to exist in reality than for it to exist in the understanding alone.
5. Therefore, we seem forced to conclude that a being than which none greater can be conceived can be conceived to be greater than it is.
6. But this is self-contradictory, and thus impossible.
7. So, point 1 must be false. God must exist in reality as well as in the understanding.

The Ontological Argument

René Descartes and the Argument

René Descartes (1629-1649) also wrestled with this concept in his philosophical writings, but from a slightly different angle. Descartes approached the argument differently but ended up with practically the same conclusion. His special line of reasoning was drawn from two central tenets of his personal approach to philosophy: the theory of innate ideas and the doctrine of clear and distinct perception. He saw the ontological proof not as a formal argument as such, but as a self-evident axiom grasped intuitively by a mind free of philosophical prejudice. He often compared it to a geometric demonstration. He argued that necessary existence cannot be excluded from the idea of God anymore than the fact that its angles are equal to two right angles can be excluded from the concept of a triangle.

God's existence is thus purported to be as obvious and self-evident as the most basic mathematical truth. He also considered this as a proof from the "essence" or "nature" of God. He maintained that necessary existence cannot be separated from the essence of a supremely perfect being without contradiction. He made a distinction between a thing's essence and its existence. Descartes iterated the argument in this way, and please note the extreme simplicity of his wording, for it is obvious that this is precisely what he was striving for. Hence, it is the essence of simplicity:

Premise 1: I have an idea of a supremely perfect being, i.e. a being having all perfections.
Premise 2: Necessary existence is a perfection.
Conclusion: Therefore, a supremely perfect being (God) exists.

Kurt Gödel's Form of the Ontological Proof

Kurt Friedrich Gödel (1906-1978) was one of the greatest mathematicians and logicians of the twentieth century. In fact, he is classed with Aristotle and Gottlob Frege as one of the most important logicians in human history. His brilliance is attested by the fact that his good friend Albert Einstein, who worked with him at the Institute for Advanced Study at Princeton University said that he came to the Institute "to have the privilege of walking home with Gödel." His conversations with Gödel were among his favorite things in life. For his seventieth birthday in 1949, he gave Einstein a strange birthday gift: a rotating universe. In

GOD DOES EXIST!

studying Einstein's relativity equations, he found a solution for a rotating universe. Not that our universe rotates, or that it contains the mass distribution his universe required, but it did demonstrate that such a universe is consistent with the theory that describes most precisely the events witnessed in space and time. One of the most stunning aspects of his discovery was that his universe contained closed-loop time-like paths. It therefore suggested the possibility of time travel. His demonstration of the existence of solutions to Einstein's field equations in general relativity, involved closed timelike curves. Modal logic is a branch of logic that is useful in proof theory, the study of that which can and cannot be proven in mathematical systems. Interestingly, the most common setting for the discussion of ontological arguments for the existence of God is the framework of modal logic. For the ordinary person, Gödel's ontological proof for God is utterly incomprehensible, since it is written in modal logic symbols.

However, it is composed of four theorems and the following is a simplification into ordinary language of the proofs:

Proof of Theorem 1:
>We call a thing godlike when it has every good property.
>Being godlike is good.
>(No Atheism): It is therefore possible that something godlike exists.

Proof of Theorem 2:
>If a thing is godlike, then being godlike is its essence (if it has an essence).

Proof of Theorem 3:
>We call a thing godlike if it has all of the good properties (by definition) and no bad properties. So any property that a godlike thing has is good, and is therefore necessarily good, and is therefore possessed by anything godlike.
>We call a thing indispensable when something with its essence (if it has an essence) must exist.
>Being indispensable is good.
>Something godlike necessarily exists.

The Ontological Argument

Proof of Theorem 4:
>If something is godlike, it has every good property by definition.
>
>In particular, it is indispensable, since that is a good property; so by definition something with its essence, which is just "being godlike" (by Theorem 3), must exist.
>
>In other words, if something godlike exists, then it is necessary for something godlike to exist.
>
>But by Theorem 2, it is possible that something godlike exists; so it is possible that it is necessary for something godlike to exist; and so it is, in fact, necessary for something godlike to exist.

It should be noted that in its essence it is the same basic proof as was set forth by those who framed the argument before him, even though he added the dimension of making the argument in the form and symbols of modal logic. What motivated him to pursue this question as a logician was the question whether it is possible to deduce the existence of God from a small number of foundational (but debatable) axioms and definitions, with a precise, formal argumentation chain in a well defined logic. In theoretical philosophy, formal logical confrontations with such ontological arguments had been thus far (mainly) limited to paper and pen. Up to that time, the use of computers was prevented, because the logics of the available theorem proving systems were not expressive enough to formalize the abstract concepts adequately. His proof changed all that. He employed "higher-order modal logic" (HOML) to handle concepts such as *possibility* and *necessity* and to support quantification over individuals and properties. Thus, he defined God as possessing all *positive* properties (cf. Benzmuller and Paleo, 93).

His work on these four theorems was not disclosed until near the time of his death. Given his brilliance and his unique approach to the subject, considerable discussion has followed in the wake of his reasonings. Dana Scott later elaborated this approach to the question, but then J. Howard Sobel critiqued it arguing that the reasoning behind it was defective. C. Anthony Anderson, set forth a new version of the language of the argument, which he alleges "does not engender modal collapse" as the earlier version did. If the reader wishes to pursue the deeper implications of this particular form of the ontological proof for God, then Anderson's essay is recommended reading (cf. C. Anthony Anderson, "Some Emendations of Gödel's Ontological Proof," *Faith and Philosophy* 7 (July 1990): 291-303).

Think of Something That Does Not Exist

Critical to all of the arguments of this sort is the question of whether it is at all possible to conceive of something that is nonexistent. An important notion to consider, then, is whether this argument is valid. Is it really possible to think of something that does not exist? Any reader is likely to think at first that it is really possible to do so, to think of something that does not actually exist. But is that *really* possible? You see, what we generally think about when asked this question, is not what the question in truth entails. What is being asked must be defined in order for us to grasp the full implications of the question. What is being asked is this: "Can you think of something that has never been thought of previously, not merely some new combination of elements with which you are already familiar, but something that is absolutely and completely new?" That is where this question becomes particularly interesting. And it requires a little explaining on our part.

The jet plane is a good illustration of this point. When these new flying machines were first introduced they would have had to be described in terms with which everyone was already familiar. Previously existing airplanes would have suggested almost everything about the new airframes, except the new means of propulsion. And even there, there were parallels. One might have said, "It is much like a DC-6, except that it is much larger, having a wider wingspan, and more powerful engines, and is therefore capable of greater payloads. It is unusual in that unlike previous planes, it has motors that have no propellers. Rather than being pulled along through the air by the props, they are pushed forward by the exhaust from the jet engines" (Cf. Baxter, *I Believe Because,* 42-43).

Notice that in every comparison of the two types of airplane, what is known becomes the introduction to what is unknown. What we know about already explains what we do not know about. This is true because the jet plane was very much like earlier planes except in a few newer and better features. Most of what we learn about almost anything is

The Ontological Argument

taught to us this way. We learn from what we already know about. It is this critical principle upon which the ontological argument is based. It concludes that man cannot think, in an absolute sense, of something that does not exist. If he can think about it, then it exists. Therefore, the argument goes, when a man thinks of God, when he contemplates his perfection of being, the very thought itself is an argument that God must necessarily exist. If He did not exist, we could not have Him in our thoughts. The very thought that we can contemplate Him is itself a powerful proof that He exists. And so, as Anselm argued, the fool proves the existence of God by his fierce denial of Him! By contemplating His being, even to deny it, he establishes the fact of it.

Logically Incoherent Ideas

Let us stretch our minds a little further. Having embraced the notion of God in terms of the ontological proof, we need to consider other possibilities along this same line. All sorts of ideas run through the human mind. A few have validity, while others may stretch the bounds of imagination. Some ideas, however, are logically incoherent and so could not exist in any possible world. This would be the case with a married bachelor, for example. It would also be the case with a round square. Neither of these ideas are coherent. What is conceptually irrational is not conceivable in any possible world. So even though our minds might entertain such notions, the incoherence of them would cause us to reject them and forget them.

Other ideas do not exist in the actual world (unicorns), but might exist in some possible world. In other words, they might exist in some fantasy world in the imagination of a storyteller. There is nothing about them that is utterly unique or entirely new. They resemble a horse in most ways, except for their single horn on their head. And we know all about both horses and horns, even though we have not seen actual horses with horns. It could be argued that such creatures could potentially develop over time in the horse family if just the right genetic development occurred over many years of special selective breeding. In that case, a unicorn might be said to exist in the world of genetic potential. Neither of these are the real world, of course, but they would qualify as "possible" worlds.

GOD DOES EXIST!

Where does the idea of God fit in? The ontological argument answers this question. It states that "if God possibly exists, then God actually exists." At first this method of reasoning through the question may not sound convincing to us. But the logic of the issue must be followed to its conclusion in order to appreciate the force of it. For ordinary things the logic will not work and could not work. That of course is the problem that must be reasoned through by the philosopher. When we are dealing with the notion of God, we are no longer talking about ordinary things. We are now addressing extraordinary things.

For example, we may speak of any ordinary thing, let us say, a grasshopper which can ice-skate, or a frog with wings that flies, or a flea as large as a horse. Each of these is something with which we are familiar on the one hand and yet possessing some trait that would not ordinarily be found in nature associated with that particular creature. To imagine any of these things is not to say that it does exist, of course. That goes without saying. But, once more, we could conceive of them in some possible world because in each instance we are describing something that we know and understand, only having some aberration from the norm. So it could exist in some possible world. However, God is clearly different from any of these ordinary things in the material world in a whole host of ways. But this is so in one way especially.

God as the Maximally Great Being

To begin with, it is critical that we understand what we mean by "God." God is the idea of a maximally great being (all powerful, all knowing, and morally perfect). Throughout the history of the human family there have been all sorts of concepts of deity or "godhood." All of them do not necessarily encompass these essential ideas of God. Pantheism, panentheism, henotheism, polytheism, monism, monotheism, etc., each has captivated the imagination of some group during a particular era and some of them are prevalent even today in the thinking of multitudes of people. However, under these various ideas of God and religion, each aspect of what we have described as "God" above has been challenged or denied by many. So, it is clear that we ought to explore this notion to some extent, especially in the context of being and existence.

The Ontological Argument

Only the three great monotheistic religions have viewed God in the way that we have described, namely as all powerful, all knowing, and morally perfect. Paganism, which has viewed God in terms of polytheism, sees many divine persons inhabiting the heavens, all of them being morally imperfect (sometimes depraved). They are rather like grander versions of ourselves. The myths that tell their stories are all filled with tales of their lying, fornication, adultery, cheating, and stealing. Moral perfection is not a prevalent concept in polytheism, if it is a concern at all. Moreover, the various gods are more or less powerful in terms of the chief god of the pantheon.

Zeus, for example, was the king of the gods in Greek mythology. He was seen as being a god of the sky, lightning, and thunder. This was his special province and power. The favored title for him is "cloud-gatherer" (*nephelēgereta*). He was not omnipotent. Nor was he self-existent. Zeus was born in the natural way. He was conceived by Cronus and Rhea. Paganism was not at all troubled about the seeming inconsistency of this. And in this regard he is not alone. He has often been compared with Indo-European gods like Jupiter of the Romans or the Norse god Thor. In most of the myths he is seen as the husband of Hera and the father of Ares, Hebe, and Hephaestus. In other words, he is more human in nature than god-like. In general, this is what polytheism is like. The gods are more like men than they are gods. They are also morally flawed like ordinary humans.

Monotheism, on the other hand, sees God as all powerful, all knowing, and morally perfect. So, only in the case of monotheism are we able to speak of God in these terms, and so view him as a "Maximally Great Being." Consequently, if it is possible that a Maximally Great Being exists; then we can say that He exists in some possible world. But a Maximally Great Being would not be maximally great if He existed in only *some* possible worlds. To be maximally great He must be so in *every* possible world, or He is not maximally great, and that includes the real world, the world of true being. The conclusion which must be drawn from this set of observations is that God exists in the actual world, and so, quite simply, it may be stated with assurance that God exists.

GOD DOES EXIST!

The Plantinga Version of the Argument

This argument is still very popular today. Below we have listed a version of the argument in syllogistic form, after the fashion of Dr. Alvin C. Plantinga, noted philosopher and professor at Calvin College. His is no doubt the most creative version of this proof for God and is employed by many philosophers today:

Premise 1: It is possible that a Maximally Great Being exists.
Premise 2: A Maximally Great Being exists in some possible world.
Premise 3: If a Maximally Great Being exists in some possible world, then it exists in every possible world.
Premise 4: If a Maximally Great Being exists in every possible world, then it exists in the actual world.
Conclusion 1: A Maximally Great Being exists in the actual world.
Conclusion 2: Therefore, a Maximally Great Being exists.

Dr. Plantinga's propositions are relatively uncontroversial, much like their prior exemplars, except for his first premise. The other premises are incontrovertible; they follow naturally and logically from the first premise. It is the first premise where the debate concentrates its energies. You see, in order for an atheist to falsify this argument, he is forced to object to the first premise. In fact, he must prove, not that God does not exist, but that it is impossible that God exists. God could not exist, even in the realm of ideological possibility, or else this argument must be surrendered to as altogether plausible. If God is possible or even conceivable as the Maximally Great Being, then logically it cannot be denied that He exists.

Atheistic Response to the Argument

The response to the argument that has typically come from atheists is for them to try to create a parallel to it which, to their way of thinking, demonstrates the absurdity of the concept. For example, they speak of a "maximally great island" as a case in point. But in fact this proves nothing; such a thing as they describe is incoherent. Too, it is entirely subjective. It would be different for almost everyone. What type of island would be your preference? Would you prefer a dry and sandy island or one that is covered with jungle? Would you prefer it to be empty of inhabitants in order to enjoy the isolation, or covered with people, hotels,

The Ontological Argument

and resorts? Each person would have a favorite type, with variations of all kinds, so it might be great for one person but not so great for someone else, and thus it could never be "maximally" great. A "maximally great island" is, therefore, an impossibility. It might be great to some people, but it could never be "maximally great" for everyone.

Again, that faulty concept is incoherent and too individually subjective to provide a true comparison. The same would be true of a "maximally great dog" or "car" or "pizza" or anything else. This approach to the argument will not work. It certainly does not refute the proposition. It provides only a poorly contrived parallel, which is in fact imperfect at its most critical juncture.

Conclusion

So, we are left with the force of the argument intact. Whether it is considered to be compelling or not is a matter of personal reflection. Many believers hold that it is too subjective for them to be convinced by it. At the same time, some of the most capable and insightful of modern philosophers still esteem it to be definitive, decisive, and even unanswerable. The individual reader must assess its cogency and persuasiveness for himself. Assuredly, on account of its historic place in the thinking of Christian scholarship and the language of natural philosophy, it deserves serious deliberation by those who wish to consider all of the arguments for the existence of God. Men of the stature of Anselm, René Descartes, Kurt Friedrich Gödel, and Alvin C. Plantinga should not be brushed aside too readily. It could be that if you think it is unconvincing, perhaps you have not yet thought deeply enough about it.

Questions for Discussion

1. What did Anselm have in mind when he spoke of "that than which nothing greater can be conceived"?
2. How did the unbeliever or "fool" play a part in the construction of the ontological argument?
3. Summarize Anselm's reasoning on this question.
4. Summarize Descartes's statement of the argument.
5. How does the idea of conceiving of something altogether new play a part in this argument? Try to think of something completely and entirely new. Why is it such a challenge?

GOD DOES EXIST!

6. Certain ideas are logically incoherent and could not exist in any possible world. Give an example of this.

7. Other ideas are possible in some conceivable worlds, but may not exist in the actual world. Can you provide an example of something like this?

8. What do we mean by "God"? How has this concept changed over time? How does monotheism solve many of the issues that are raised by polytheistic belief?

9. Summarize Dr. Alvin Plantinga's version of the ontological argument.

10. What is the usual reply that is given to the ontological argument by modern atheism, and why is it inadequate to refute the argument?

Chapter 5
The Teleological Argument

Since ancient times observant men have noted evidence of design features at almost every level in the physical universe. It will be recalled that Thomas Aquinas listed this as his fifth proof for the existence of God. Too, Aristotle spoke of "four causes" as being fundamental to an understanding of the "why" of anything, that is to say, its cause for being (Greek, *aitia*), or as his choice of words implies, its causal explanation.

These factors included: (1) the material cause (*hule*), the nature of the raw material employed ; (2) the efficient cause (*kinoun*), or agent which brings about the end result; (3) the formal cause (*eidos*), the form or idea that provides a pattern of the thing; and, (4) the end, or final cause (*telos*), or the purpose of a particular thing, its *raison d'être*.

The standard example which a good number of philosophers employ in order to illustrate these four causes would be Michelangelo's statue of David. The material cause is what it is made of, in this case, marble. The efficient cause is the immediate activity that produced the statue, Michelangelo chipping away at the stone to shape it with hammer and chisel. The formal cause is its structure; it is a representation of the figure of David as it is imagined in the mind of the artist, and not a random, formless, chunk of marble. And the final cause is its purpose; presumably it was created to beautify some Florentine palace (Cf. W. Dembski, *Intelligent Design*, 123).

It is noteworthy that Aristotle gave equal weight to all four causes. In particular the great philosopher would have regarded any inquiry that omitted one or more of his causes as fundamentally flawed and woefully deficient. In other words, he would have objected strenuously to the modern tendency to exclude design from the discussion of the origin of the universe and of the life-forms which exist within it. For the believer, the formal cause involves design and the efficient cause is the activity of the Designer to bring it into existence. The final cause is the purpose for which it was created.

All three of these aspects seem to suggest the necessity of design, and design suggests a Designer. In all the rest of our experience in the present realm, we utilize all four of these features of analysis in regard to any object or thing. It would appear logical therefore to employ these four means, just as Aristotle did, to the totality of the universe and all that is within it. And yet, such considerations are excluded from the process by those who *a priori* reject the notion of design in nature. But, in spite of their protestations the evidence for design is difficult for many of us to ignore, in spite of the determined tendency to do so by materialistic skeptics.

The conclusion that has been drawn from this by open-minded scientists as well as serious and thoughtful onlookers is that the universe and its multitudinous non-living and living illustrations of complexity provide evidence of a preconceived and well executed plan. They constitute proof that an intelligent mind was behind the whole of it. Could these intriguing phenomena have just happened, as skeptics and atheists have alleged? Not hardly. Many of these "design elements" are far too complex and rendered utterly useless without even a single element wrapped up in the package to be attributed to mere chance alone.

The Teleological Argument

From these observations has developed a formal argument which has come to be described as the Teleological Argument for God. This is essentially an argument from *cause and effect*. The idea that lies behind the logic of it is that if an effect is observable, then an adequate and sufficient cause is necessary in order to explain it. Natural law and blind chance are not adequate to explain these effects that we encounter in nature. In this case it is the sheer immensity and scale of what is observable in the material universe that forces so many observers to conclude that a being of inexplicable power and wisdom is responsible for it. God is the only cause that is adequate to explain them.

The Argument Stated

The classical design argument begins by noting certain highly ordered or complex features within nature such as the configuration of the planets in our solar system or the architecture of the vertebrate eye. It then proceeds to argue that such noteworthy features could not have arisen by chance or natural selection, and so without the activity of a pre-existent intelligence (typically equated with God). God is the only plausible explanation for these features of the material creation. Throughout history in the West, many philosophers and scientists have formulated such empirically-based theistic arguments, stated in various but obviously kindred ways.

Typically the argument itself has been stated in terms that are very basic and understandable by most everyone. The following syllogism sets forth the argument in three rudimentary statements:

Premise 1: Evidence of design exists in great profusion in nature and in the universe generally. In that sense, then, an *effect* is observed.

Premise 2: Design provides evidence of a Designer; from this *effect* we infer an essential *cause*.

Conclusion: Therefore God, the Designer of the universe, and its essential cause, must exist.

How do we go about assessing the value of this simple set of propositions? Just as simply as it is stated. In point of fact, in all other aspects of our lives we infer an adequate cause to explain every effect that we observe. The cause must be sufficient to explain the effect in

GOD DOES EXIST!

every instance. If we descend the stairs in our home, and a toy is lying at the bottom of the flight, in perfect position to cause a fall, we assume that one of our children quit playing with it and left it there. Problem solved. Unless some other family member is planning to kill us, some such answer as this is the "short and sweet" route to solving the puzzle. Is the cause sufficient to explain the effect? Yes, it is. Daily we assess just such situations without excessive thought and without much strenuous brain activity.

But, suppose that we take this matter of adequate causes a step further in ordinary life. If a car is parked in front of someone's house, we would never surmise that a cow or a goat may have put it there. Worse still, would be the theory that it just appeared there without any explanation at all. Intelligent people would never speculate along those lines. Perhaps the husband parked it there? Someone might suppose that to be so. Maybe the wife drove it there? Someone else might think that this is the right solution. One of the children could have left it out front? That could be the answer. Any of these would be realistic explanations that provide an adequate cause which might explain the observable effect. Something else might explain it adequately as well. A neighbor could have left it there? But the cow explanation will not work. The goat theory is lacking also. Interestingly enough, the idea that "it just appeared there" is the least convincing of all of the options. Why is this so? Things do not just appear without any adequate explanation!

The magnificent material universe with all of its beauty and complexity is an effect which deserves an explanation that is worthy of the observable intricacy and majesty of it. But this creates an immediate problem for any of us. It takes the observer outside the realm of his ordinary experience, for in this particular instance, the cause cannot be ordinary, for it must be sufficient to explain such an astonishing and awe-inspiring effect. The prevailing atheistic view which says that it just appeared without any adequate explanation is, unsurprisingly, the most unconvincing of all answers to the question of origins for the vast majority of the human population. A long series of wonderful accidents to bring it to its current form, as an explanation, may indeed be enough to satisfy the curiosity of some researchers, but for most people God is the only satisfactory answer. The reason this is so is on account of the

The Teleological Argument

practical, everyday, *teleology* that they encounter constantly as they make their way in the world. They explain what they experience based on this cause and effect relationship. And they conclude that this case should not be treated any differently.

On every hand believers see the evidence of it and they cannot explain it otherwise than as the intelligent action of an infinite mind, a "Maximally Great Being." Skeptics instinctively fire back with the charge that "this is the god of the gaps mentality"! In other words, whenever we cannot figure out the science of a thing, that is, either how some inorganic or organic evolutionary process may have produced the particular result in question, that is where (a gap) we tend to insert God into the process and have Him intelligently manufacture the particular result in question. That is the allegation that is levied against believers, at any rate. It satisfies the minds of skeptics generally, but does it really offer a cause adequate to explain the effect? No, it does not. It only takes what we consider to be a "cheap shot" at theists. It does not resolve the issue raised in any satisfactory manner.

As science has revealed complicated biological mechanisms and uncovered extensive biochemical processes at the cellular level over time, though, and discovered the profoundly complex prerequisites for life to exist in the universe, this argument has begun to sound more and more hollow as the evidence has piled up. It has become increasingly impossible to put anything else except an omnipotent God into these "gaps", which are in fact not small "gaps" in any sense of the word, but massive chasms of information technology and biological systems lacking any sort of logical explanation in regard to the "how" of their origin. Whereas in the past atheists have spoken of "the god of the gaps," we now are in a position historically to speak of Darwinian gradualism as a theory without any serious hypothetical reconstruction of how these extremely complicated biological information systems and biochemical pathways could have developed over any conceivable amount of time through any series of fortuitous accidents and propitious genetic mutations. Let us say again, these "gaps" are not merely small patches that may eventually come to be explained in terms of how they mysteriously developed on their own under the unintelligent oversight of natural law and the mindless agency of blind chance.

GOD DOES EXIST!

Thus, Darwinism with its methodology has become a sort of idol that must be salvaged at all costs, even if the full weight of science is against it. It is reasonable to conclude therefore, that Darwinism has become in point of fact "the god of the gaps" that atheistic scientists have alleged intelligent design to be. Darwinism is a religion, pure and simple. Darwinian expectations of beneficial outcomes answer all of the unanswerable questions of the present day and solve all of the riddles and mysteries uncovered by future investigation. They are always the presumptive answer to every potential question or mystery, even though other explanations appear to be the only sensible possibilities. Many scientists today, especially in the biological disciplines, cannot think beyond Darwinism because this mode of resolving complicated problems has become a virtual religious zealotry. According to David Berlinski:

> The effort by Darwinian biologists to promote Darwin is simply explained. Within the English-speaking world, Darwin's theory of evolution remains the only scientific theory to be widely championed by the scientific community and widely disbelieved by everyone else. No matter the effort made by biologists, the thing continues to elicit the same reaction it has always elicited: You've got to be kidding, right? There is wide appreciation of the fact that if biologists are wrong about Darwin, they are wrong about life, and if they are wrong about life, they are wrong about everything....
>
> Suspicions about Darwin's theory arise for two reasons. The first: the theory makes little sense. The second: it is supported by little evidence... (*The Devil's Delusion,* 186-187).

The situation is changing, however. A groundswell reawakening is taking place in the scientific disciplines, in spite of the powerful forces allied against the notion of an Intelligent Designer being behind all of these sophisticated, elaborate, and sometimes labyrinthine biological and chemical systems. It has become more and more difficult, as we have come to understand their baffling obscurities in greater detail, to convince ourselves that these systems could ever have come to be as a result of a series of amazingly fortuitous accidents. Steadily the number of research scientists has grown who recognize that many of the theoretical reconstructions of events postulated at an earlier stage in the research are not only highly unlikely but are in fact implausible in the

The Teleological Argument

extreme. These things could not have happened in any possible world without intelligent assistance!

William Paley's Analogy

Let us return momentarily to a simpler time, when a very rudimentary illustration held great weight in the thinking of most people, both intellectual and uneducated alike. William Paley's nineteenth-century watch analogy (*Natural Theology*, 1852) has come to be identified very specifically with this argument concerning teleology. In spite of the fact that it was penned many years ago, it has never lost its lustre. The idea behind it is that things which are complex do not occur by chance, or appear randomly in nature. In our experience as human beings we see them all the time. All sorts of marvelous inventions surround us in our work and even at play. Occasionally we see a new one for the first time. That makes no difference to us, though. Even upon seeing a new machine or device for the first time, we still instantly identify it as a product of human ingenuity, that is, of intelligent design.

In fact, all of these ingenious playthings, devices, and tools that we utilize in our day have the definitive marks of being "created things." They are all the result of an engineering and manufacturing process. We may not have seen them being made, or even have any idea of how they might have been made, but we know that they were made. Intelligent human beings conceived of them and then made them. We readily distinguish them from what we find ordinarily in a natural environment. And we always attribute them to intelligent design. That is the whole point. We would never think of attributing their occurrence to chance or random appearance.

Here is Paley's illustration: If a beautiful watch were to be found in a meadow, no thinking person would ever posit that it just happened to be there accidentally or appeared there out of nothing and for no apparent reason. A suggestion of that sort would not be taken seriously. It's complexity and obvious design features would cause a rational person to assume it was a product of intelligent engineering as well as a sophisticated manufacturing process. It's presence in the meadow might lead one to conclude that at some time prior another human being had passed that way and had either lost his timepiece or perhaps had dropped it to the ground and left it there intentionally.

GOD DOES EXIST!

Why would we resolve the question so easily and in this particular way? Because, such things do not just "pop into existence." Complicated Swiss timepieces do not appear in meadows without being manufactured by intelligent watchmakers and brought there and left by some person or thing. That kind of phenomenon does not happen in our experience. We have never seen or heard of any such thing happening in our personal experience or anyone else's. And yet, atheists and other skeptics tell us that a complex universe just popped into existence. Then, from that original explosion of random matter came the present diversity and complexity of life that surrounds us on all sides in all of its wonderful profusion. Millions of different types of creatures, plants, insects, animals, single-celled, and multicellular living things, bacteria, viruses, molds, mildews, etc. Of course, they utilize much more sophisticated language to describe the whole process, but in the final analysis this is precisely what they are saying.

Is it not then justified for us to ask the following? Why do not horses just appear, or cars, or trucks, or watches, or computers? Why do only universes appear randomly; and will another one randomly appear today? If not, why not? Naturally, all of this sounds rather absurd. But this absurdity of which we speak is in fact the heart of modern cosmology. It is believed by the majority of atheistic scientists that the universe of which we are all a part simply appeared at some point in the distant past. And why do we not observe the spectacular changes taking place around us even as we are told they have been taking place over the millennia, which has led to the tremendous variety of life-forms? We are told that it is so gradual that we are not able to see it happen. But, does that really answer the question? Surely we can observe it as it happens *somewhere* in the present time! If literally millions of such transformations have taken place since the beginning, why are some of them not observable presently?

These questions, even though they may sound ridiculous, are quite relevant and in fact get to the heart of this inquiry. Never mind the high-sounding rhetoric intended to distract us from pressing questions of this sort. Such queries are entirely legitimate and they deserve good answers and not just bloviating and deflecting in response.

The Teleological Argument

Necessity, Chance, or Design?

Modern science has struggled with the problem of how to deal with three realities: necessity, chance, and design. The material universe came about by one of these means or another of them, and life began by one of these means or another of them. During the Middle Ages, the great Jewish rabbi Moses Maimonides (1138-1204) in his 14-volume compendium of Jewish law, *Guide of the Perplexed,* contended in opposition to the Islamic interpreters of Aristotle who viewed the heavens as "the necessary result of natural laws," that they were actually the result of design. For him the irregularity of the distribution of the stars in the heavens demonstrated contingency rather than necessity. Random chance was also at the bottom of his list. He explained it thus:

> But if we assume that all this is the result of design, there is nothing strange or improbable; the only question to be asked is this: What is the cause of the design? The answer to this question is that all this has been made for a certain purpose, though we do not know it; there is nothing that is done in vain, or by chance... (188).

Newtonian mechanics, construed as a set of deterministic physical laws, seemed only to permit necessity. Yet, even Newton left room for design. He argued that the stability of the planetary system depended not only on the regular action of the universal law of gravitation but also on the initial positioning of the planets and comets in relation to the sun. This aspect, he said, "could only proceed from the counsel and dominion of an intelligent and powerful being" (*Mathematical Principles of Natural Philosophy,* 543-44; quoted in Dembski, "The Third Mode of Explanation," 46, n. 30). So, in the end, Newton saw both necessity and design as participants in the process. But he placed little faith in the viability of blind chance as an explanation for anything.

Since the time of Laplace, however, this situation has reversed itself. Science as a formal discipline has largely dispensed with design as an explanation for anything. The reasoning of Charles Darwin was that many things work as though they were designed to function as they do, but there is another explanation for that generality. What appears on the surface to be so is not what it appears to be. In the case of biology, for example, natural selection seems over time to resemble selective breeding in its result. It is as if an intelligent agent were at work in the process, but in fact it is only a case of blind chance working through natural laws over long periods of time. Beneficial traits which appear randomly are selected by environmental and other factors, and become dominant in any population of plants or animals.

Nature's Laws

At this juncture it would be helpful to make a simple observation regarding nature's laws that is not commonly observed or recognized. As C. S. Lewis rightly pointed out: "In the whole history of the universe the laws of Nature have never produced a single event" (*God in the Dock*, "The Laws of Nature," 77). In reading the literature of modern atheists, one would think that almost everything that is observable happened as a result of either one of the laws of Nature or else from a confluence of several of them. The importance of Nature's laws in what we see around us should not be minimized. As Lewis went on to say, "They are the pattern to which every event must conform, provided only that it can be induced to happen."

However, here lies the rub. The laws of Nature do not cause things to happen. All events do indeed obey them. But it is the events themselves that we are puzzled about. What makes them happen? What is it that caused them in the first place? We know from physics about the laws of motion. But what started things in motion? The laws of physics do not answer that question. They provide us with no help at all on the matter. This is where the atheist runs into a brick wall, an immovable obstacle. Just as the laws of arithmetic are employed in the world of finance and the handling of money, all operations must abide by and be explained in terms of those arithmetic laws, so it is in the natural world with Nature's laws.

As a matter of fact, not one thin dime is produced as a result of the laws of arithmetic. Mathematics alone will not put a dollar into your pocket or mine. The laws regulate it once it is there. If you have it in your pocket already, and then you spend a dollar, then simple arithmetic says that you now have zero dollars in your pocket. We cannot increase our income by performing arithmetic formulas. If our pocket is empty we must somehow put some money in there in order for the laws of arithmetic to be able to regulate it. This is precisely how the laws of Nature work. They do not produce anything, but they do regulate everything. They provide the pattern to which events conform, but the source of all events must be sought elsewhere.

The Teleological Argument

This is an uncomfortable fact that is generally ignored by atheistic thinkers. They go about their task of explaining this magnificent, multifaceted universe as if the laws of Nature cause everything to happen. The reality is that *they cause nothing to happen*. They merely regulate what does happen, when it happens.

As Lewis further noted:

Where, then, do actual events come from? In one sense the answer is easy. Each event comes from a previous event. But what happens if you trace this process backwards? To ask this is not exactly the same as to ask where *things* come from—how there came to be space and time and matter at all. Our present problem is not about things but about events; not, for example, about particles of matter but about this particle colliding with that. The mind can perhaps acquiesce in the idea that the "properties" of the universal drama somehow "just happen to be there": but whence comes the play, the story?

Either the stream of events had a beginning or it had not. If it had, then we are faced with something like creation. If it had not (a supposition, by the way, which some physicists find difficult), then we are faced with an everlasting impulse which, by its very nature, is opaque to scientific thought. Science, when it becomes perfect, will have explained the connection between each link in the chain and the link before it. But the actual existence of the chain will remain wholly unaccountable. We learn more and more about the pattern. We learn nothing about that which "feeds" real events into the pattern. . . .

The smallest event, then, if we face the fact that occurs (instead of concentrating on the pattern into which, if it can be persuaded to occur, it must fit), leads us back to a mystery which lies outside natural science. It is certainly a possible supposition that behind this mystery some mighty Will and Life is at work. If so, any contrast between His acts and the laws of Nature is out of the question. It is His act alone that gives the laws any events to apply to. The laws are an empty frame; it is He that fills the frame—not now and then on specially "providential" occasions, but at every moment (ibid., 78-79).

All of this has been consistently ignored by the majority in the scientific community. Natural law has been treated as a creative reality, not as a regulatory reality alone. And this is true in spite of the lack of any scientific demonstration of its creative power to initiate anything. Consequently, the search for the laws, phenomena, and conditions which are supposed to have led to various realities, as they are observable in the universe and among living things, has become the norm. And so, blind chance over long epochs of time has become the universal explanation for those realities in the minds of a great many scientists. There have been exceptions to this generality, of course, but atheism has become the motivating ideological influence for the majority of scientists. Design and purpose are no longer topics worthy of discussion in the arena of science as far as the leaders in most fields are concerned. Even some scientists who have a personal commitment to religion in some form have given up considering design and purpose in pursuit of the scientific endeavor.

Moreover, with the rise of statistical mechanics and then of quantum mechanics, the role of chance in physics came to be regarded as ineliminable. Especially convincing in this regard was the failure of the Bell inequality (cf. J. S. Bell, *Speakable and Unspeakable in Quantum Mechanics*, 1987). As a result, a deterministic, necessitarian universe has given way to a stochastic universe in which chance and necessity are both regarded as fundamental modes of scientific explanation, neither being reducible to the other. The result of this line of reasoning in scientific endeavor was to permit a principled distinction between necessity and chance while repudiating design, "the third mode of explanation," altogether as a possible explanation for natural phenomena (Dembski, "The Third Mode," 19-20). Design was out of favor. But was science right to repudiate design? In *The Design Inference* (1998) William Dembski made the case, successfully in our view, that design *is* a legitimate and fundamental mode of scientific explanation. His aim was not to establish creationism but rather to rehabilitate design as a mode of explaining certain realities in science.

How complexity in the natural world is to be viewed changed gradually and rather radically during the twentieth century. Scientific evidence flowed in from numerous sources to alter the direction of both scientific thinking and philosophical theorizing. The theory of general relativity as suggested by Albert Einstein (1915-16), started the revolution. At the time, few would have expected it to turn out as it did. Newton's view of a static universe quickly fell to the new way of thinking, which postulated that the universe was simultaneously expanding and

The Teleological Argument

decelerating. According to the relativity theory, massive bodies alter the curvature of space so as to draw nearby objects to them. He further theorized that all material bodies would congeal unless the effects of gravitation were continually counteracted by the expansion of space itself. So the theory implied an expanding, not a static, universe.

Ultimately, of course, the legitimacy of Einstein's points was confirmed by Edwin Hubble's astronomical discoveries and the Bell Labs researchers Penzias and Wilson. This was demonstrated when they detected cosmic background radiation left over from the origin of the universe. This discovery proved that the universe had a beginning, disposing of all of the cosmological models that opted for a "steady state" view of the universe, namely that it was infinite in nature. The particulars of these epoch-making developments are treated elsewhere in the present book in greater detail.

At any rate, when it became obvious, perhaps even undeniable, that the universe had a beginning, in spite of the fact that over a long period of time it had previously been speculated that it did not, a good number of philosophers of science started to suggest that it might also have a purpose. After all, what do design features tell us? When we discover them, how do we gather information from them? Design has always been associated with purpose, as indeed it ought to be, since in all other areas of our experience the two are integrally associated with one another. Things are designed by an intelligent agent, like man, with a purpose in mind. A tool like a hammer, for example, might have a flat and rounded head for hammering, a claw for extracting nails, and a handle that fits the hand of a human carpenter. The design features of the object are suggestive of its purpose. To conclude that the object has these characteristics of design but these are not permitted to imply anything at all to us about how it came to be or why it is found in exactly the form that it has, does not seem quite fair, does it? Yet this is precisely what we are told by a great many leading lights in science about the design features of the universe and of the living systems within it.

Alternative Theories of the Origin of Complexity

Modern science has worried that something might be falsely attributed to design and then later have it overturned and categorized as attributable to some other criterion. This concern, though perhaps justified in the past, is no longer tenable. There does in fact exist a rigorous criterion for distinguishing intelligently caused objects from unintelligently caused ones. Many special sciences already employ this criterion in their methodology. Though most of them use this criterion in a pretheoretic form, it is already at work in several of these disciplines.

For example, intelligently produced items are readily distinguished in forensic science, artificial intelligence, cryptology, archaeology, and in the Search for Extraterrestrial Intelligence (SETI). The great breakthrough of the intelligent design movement in science has been to isolate and make more precise the criterion itself. Michael Behe's criterion of irreducible complexity for establishing the design of biochemical systems is a special case of this general standard for detecting design (Cf. Behe, *Darwin's Black Box*; Dembski, *The Design Inference*; and *Intelligent Design*, 127). For a good number of theoreticians his work has changed the landscape. Intelligent design has begun to make sense in a circumstance where researchers seem to be out of workable alternative hypothetical reconstructions. And make no mistake about it, most of them are out of ideas! They seem to have exhausted all of the viable options and have nowhere else to go to look for explanations.

By the phrase "irreducibly complex," Behe means a single system composed of several well-matched, interacting parts that contribute to the basic function, wherein the removal of any one of the parts causes the system, effectively, to cease functioning. He explains that:

> ... An irreducibly complex system cannot be produced directly (that is, by continuously improving the initial function, which continues to work by the same mechanism) by slight, successive modifications of a precursor system, because any precursor to an irreducibly complex system that is missing a part is by definition nonfunctional ... it would have to arise as an integrated unit, in one fell swoop, for natural selection to have anything to act on (39).

Darwin's gradualism simply will not work as a means to the end of producing a single fully functional irreducibly complex system, of any kind, and there are literally thousands of them in the natural world.

Hence, Behe rejected gradualism as well as the two prevailing theories for the rapid assembling of complex systems proposed by scientists. The first of these is the symbiosis theory. This view has some encour-

The Teleological Argument

agement in the form of observable symbiotic relationships which exist commonly in nature. Lynn Margulis, while still a graduate student, theorized that in the place of the Darwinian view of progress by competition and strife, cells developed these systems by cooperation and symbiosis. As a case in point, Margulis believed that at one time on the ancient earth a larger cell "swallowed" a bacterial cell, but did not digest it.

Hypothetically, the two cells then adapted to the situation. According to this reconstruction of events, the smaller cell then received nutrients from the larger one, and, in return it passed on some of the stored chemical energy it made to the larger cell. When the larger cell reproduced, the smaller one did too, and its descendants continued to reside inside its host. Over time the symbiotic cell lost many of the systems that free-living and independent cells need, and specialized more and more in providing energy for its host. The host cell became increasingly dependent on the bacteria living inside of it for energy. Eventually this once independent bacterial cell became what we identify as a mitochondrion.

Today an ordinary cell contains about 2000 of these mitochondria, occupying about twenty percent of the cell's volume. These organelles, as they are called, constitute the "energy factories" of the eukaryotic cell. They oxidize sugars and fats to produce energy in the process we describe as respiration. The natural question to ask, however, is this: What did these cells do for energy prior to their symbiosis with their new "mitochondrial bacterium" friend? How did they function without them? They certainly could not function without them now!

At first the Margulis theory was scoffed at, but over the years it has gained a considerable following in the scientific community. The most important question for biochemists, however, is whether or not symbiosis can explain the origin of complex biochemical systems themselves. And the answer to that is, clearly they cannot. The essence of symbiosis is the joining of two separate cells, or two separate systems, *both of which are already functioning*. In the mitochondrion scenario, one preexisting viable cell entered a symbiotic relationship with another such cell. But neither Margulis nor any of her supporters have offered a detailed explanation of how the preexisting cells originated. So, in the end, the symbiosis theory fails to explain the very thing that it was hoped it would definitively elucidate.

GOD DOES EXIST!

"Complexity Theory" is the other view that has developed over the years to displace the Darwinian model of gradualism. Stuart Kauffman championed this hypothesis. He theorized that systems with a large number of interacting components spontaneously organize themselves into ordered patterns. He could not point to any cases of this happening in nature. Essentially this view grew out of Kauffman's observation of computer systems and of the software systems that run them. Proponents of the view point to the behavior of computer programs and assert that the functioning of a computer program resembles the behavior of biological systems. Kauffman postulated that small changes in DNA have the potential to produce large, coordinated biological changes, being that this is the way software sometimes acts in producing data output on a computer system. At this juncture, however, "complexity theory" represents little more than an idea. There have been no biological case studies to advance the view, and so over time its popularity has also waned. Not many strong advocates of the view are found in the sciences today.

But let us be clear on this matter. Neither of these views has the potential to explain the appearance of complex systems in nature. They may be capable of explaining minor changes within a system that is already fully functional, but they cannot explain its appearance. The theory of Margulis is not a workable explanation because symbiosis starts with complex, already-functioning systems. It cannot account for the fundamental biochemical systems that appear in such profusion in the natural world. This was Behe's strongest point, and Margulis's weakest. He observed that this view might be capable of explaining some aspects of development of life on earth, but it cannot explain the ultimate origins of complex systems (*Darwin's Black Box*, 189). He is right in his assessment.

Likewise, complexity theory envisions a complex, interacting mixture of chemicals which might have occurred on earth before life developed (although there is virtually no evidence to support this idea), but it would not have mattered once cellular life began. The essence of cellular life is regulation. The cell controls how much and what kinds of chemicals it makes. This is accomplished through the central processing system of the cell, it's control room, where DNA and messenger RNA

The Teleological Argument

determine the types and precise amounts. When it loses control, it dies. If there is a systemic breakdown, it is deleterious, never beneficial. And yet this is the very thing that alternative theories depend upon entirely: beneficial "mistakes" in the process.

The upshot of this is that a controlled cellular environment does not permit the serendipitous interactions between chemicals (always unspecified) that Kaufman and other theorists require in order to establish that the theory is workable. Because a viable cell keeps its chemicals on a short leash, it would tend to prevent new, complex metabolic pathways from originating by chance (*Darwin's Black Box*, 191-92). Complexity theory, therefore, is best restricted to mathematics and computer science where it originated. Its usefulness in the area of biological and biochemical complexity is purely hypothetical and has not been proven.

In the end, neo-Darwinism is left without viable alternatives. It is bereft of an explanation for the development of complex biological systems and should be rejected as a working hypothesis once and for all. Its proponents have not been able in 160 years of study and speculation to produce a logical presentation that accounts for these monumental systems observable in nature. How did they appear? What is the mechanism by which they developed? Darwinism has no good answer for these all-important questions. As Behe noted:

> "Publish or perish" is a proverb that academicians take seriously. If you do not publish your work for the rest of the community to evaluate, then you have no business in academia (and if you don't already have tenure, you will be banished). But the saying can be applied to theories as well. If a theory claims to be able to explain some phenomenon but does not generate even an attempt at an explanation, then it should be banished. Despite comparing sequences and mathematical modeling, molecular evolution has never addressed the question of how complex structures came to be. In effect, the theory of Darwinian molecular evolution has not published, and so should perish (*Darwin's Black Box*, 186).

How Do We Determine Whether Design Is Present or Not?
What do we mean by the term "design"? In brief, design is *the purposeful arrangement of parts*. In the case of Paley's watch, there is a watch case, a watch face with numbers on it, a minute hand along with a hand to point to the hour, attached to the face with a tiny post. When

GOD DOES EXIST!

you remove the back there are many parts within that all fit together and work in synchrony. Clearly the thing was designed. The purposeful arrangement of its various parts prove this fact beyond any possible alternative view of its origin. Other hypothetical reconstructions of events could be propounded that might attempt to explain the shiny object, but none of them would prove to be very convincing.

How is it possible confidently to detect the presence of design? When is it reasonable to conclude, in the absence of firsthand knowledge or eyewitness accounts, that something has been designed by an intelligent agent or engineer? For discrete physical systems, like Paley's watch or any other physical object manufactured by humans, where there is no possibility of a gradual route to their production, design is evident when a number of separate, interacting components are ordered in such a way as to accomplish a function beyond the capabilities of the individual components if left to themselves. The greater the specificity of the interacting components required to produce the particular function, the greater our confidence should be in concluding that design is indeed present.

In the case of a mechanical object we may not always be able at once to discern the purpose of it or its function in some system of other parts, but its shape and the material out of which it is constructed will likely provide a clue that it is intended to work together with other parts in order to perform some special function.

In addition, it should be noted that intelligently produced objects in many instances bear the imprint of their makers, in some way or another. Sometimes a company logo is present, a set of initials, or even a company name may be imprinted on the object. At other times unique methods and production procedures prove the identity of the manufacturer. Paley's watch may have had "Swiss Made" imprinted on its face along with the name of the company that designed and manufactured it! Too, certain traits that are unique to watch-makers in Switzerland would inevitably be present. These would be distinctive and would clearly indicate their place of origin. This would not be at all unusual. In fact, in modern times we have come to expect such indications to be present on almost all of the products we buy and use.

The Teleological Argument

Of course, it would be difficult to imagine an exact parallel to this in nature. At the same time, it would not be at all far-fetched to find aspects of the creation, if we may assume for the moment that there is a Creator who planned and brought the sum and substance of it all into existence by His creative power, that have the imprint of their manufacturer on them. This is not to say that His name would be emblazoned on the product of His creative efforts, but that He might leave markers of His creative genius at various points in the inner workings of those things He has produced. It is precisely this sort of thing that careful observers ought to be on the lookout for as they study the natural world and especially the living things that inhabit it.

Another important criterion that is a marker for intelligence is communication. Intelligent beings are able to communicate with one another. Patterns of words and sounds make up the grammatical "stuff" of human communication, for example. If we were to happen upon a Scrabble board with the phrase, "Happy days are here again," spelled out perfectly, it would never occur to us that the pieces had been poured out randomly on a table with this sentence being the result. Even though we know that it is possible that a few words might fall into such an unlikely pattern, we also appreciate how extremely remote the chances of that would be. A person might pour out letters on the table every few seconds for one thousand years, if that were even possible, and never accidentally produce an intelligible sentence! This being so, we would readily exclude random chance as a potential explanation for what lies on the table.

We would conclude instead that an intelligent being had placed the pieces in precisely this order intentionally. In fact, if any intelligible sentence or phrase appeared thus, this would be our conclusion. We would never attribute intelligent spelling and word structure to blind chance or randomness. Why is this so? Because intelligent communication is a product of an intelligent source, a thinking being.

Radio astronomers have searched the heavens for signs of extraterrestrial life for many years, starting in the 1980's. To increase their chances of finding some indication of extraterrestrial intelligence, SETI researchers monitor millions of radio signals from outer space. However, the primary challenge is to distinguish intelligent communication of some sort from the natural sounds that occur regularly, since many natural objects in space produce radio waves. Neutron stars or white dwarfs, for example, emit a beam of electromagnetic radiation. Hence, they are sometimes referred to as "pulsars." Looking for signs of design among all of the naturally produced radio signals is like searching for a veritable needle in a haystack.

In order to sift through all of these naturally occurring radio signals and look for the presence of intelligence, SETI researchers run the signals they monitor through computers programmed with pattern-matchers. So long as a signal does not match one of the preset patterns, it will pass through the pattern-matching sieve (and will do so even if it has an intelligent source). On the other hand, if it does match one of these patterns, then depending on the pattern matched, the SETI researchers may have good reason to believe that they are dealing with an intelligent source being responsible for the signals.

What characteristic about a particular signal would seem to indicate design, and therefore suggest the presence of intelligent communication? Generally speaking, whenever we infer design, we must establish three things: contingency, complexity and specification. Contingency ensures that the object in question is not the result of an automatic and therefore unintelligent process that had no choice in its production. By being compatible with but not required by the regularities involved in its production, an object, event or structure becomes irreducible to any underlying physical necessity such as natural laws or algorithms. Complexity ensures that the object is not so simple that it can readily be explained by chance. Complexity, in a sense, is a form of probability. Complexity and probability vary inversely: the greater the complexity, the smaller the probability. Finally, specification ensures that the object exhibits the type of pattern that is characteristic of intelligence.

So, when called upon to explain an event, object, or structure, we have a decision to make. Are we going to attribute it to necessity, chance, or design? According to the complexity-specification criterion, to answer this question is to answer three very simple questions: Is it contingent? Is it complex? Is it specified? (Cf. Dembski, *Intelligent Design*, 128-33). We shall see later that the communication that takes place regularly in the cell through the DNA and RNA molecules is indicative of

The Teleological Argument

both intelligent design and of communication. It fits all of these criteria. It is contingent. It is complex. And it is specified. So it is clearly the product of the design of an intelligent agent.

A Few Examples of Astonishing Design Features in Nature

During the last fifty years or so, developments in physics and cosmology have placed the word "design" back in the scientific vocabulary, after it had experienced a long quietus. Several factors have entered into this change in circumstances. As an example, it has been discovered that life in the universe depends upon a highly improbable but precise balance of physical factors. The constants of physics, the initial conditions of the universe, and many other of its features appear delicately balanced to allow for the possibility of life. Even very slight alterations in the values of many factors, such as the expansion rate of the universe, the strength of gravitational or electromagnetic attraction, or the value of Planck's constant, would render life impossible. All of this has been generally unexpected on the part of researchers, but has proven to be a boon to the concept of design in the universe. What shall we make of these surprising facts? What may we necessarily infer from them? Consider the following illustration:

> Imagine that you are a cosmic explorer who has just stumbled into the control room of the whole universe. There you discover an elaborate universe creating machine, with rows and rows of dials each with many possible settings. As you investigate, you learn that each dial represents some particular parameter that has to be calibrated with a precise value in order to create a universe in which life can survive. One dial represents the possible settings for the strong nuclear force, one for the gravitational constant, one for Planck's constant, one for the speed of light, one for the ratio of the neutron mass to the proton mass, one for the strength of electromagnetic attraction, and so on. As you, the cosmic explorer, examine the dials, you find that they can be easily spun to different settings that they could have been otherwise. Moreover, you determine by careful calculations that even slight alterations in any of the dial settings would cause changes to the architecture of the universe such that life would cease to exist. Yet for some reason each dial sits with just the exact value necessary to keep the universe running like a giant safe with multiple combination-locks each of which has been opened. What do you infer about the origin of these finely-tuned dial settings?

GOD DOES EXIST!

Not surprisingly, physicists have been asking the same question (Stephen Meyer, "Return of the God Hypothesis," 9).

A considerable number of physicists now refer to these factors as "anthropic coincidences" (because they make life possible for man) and to the extremely fortunate convergence of all these coincidences as "the fine tuning of the universe" (K. Gilbertson, "The Anthropic Principle," 150). Given the improbability of the precise ensemble of values represented by these constants, and their specificity relative to the requirements of a life-sustaining universe, many physicists have noted that the fine tuning strongly suggests design by a preexistent intelligence.

As Paul Davies, a well-known British physicist expressed it, "the impression of design is overwhelming" (*The Cosmic Blueprint,* 203; quoted in Meyer, "Evidence for Design in Physics and Biology," 57). Being that we intend to spend an entire chapter on this topic, however, we shall put off for now a discussion of these matters in greater detail until later in this book.

Cases of astonishing complexity in the natural or biological world number in the millions. We would not presume to summarize even a small sampling of them. The consistent forward movement of science has uncovered more and more of these cases. In some sense it could be argued that they are present in almost every living thing on the cellular and biochemical plane. But even in this case, some instances are more amazing in the level of their sophistication, and thus more indicative of special engineering and ingenious design, than others. It will be helpful in the present work to characterize a few cases that illustrate this point. We ask the reader's indulgence through the highly technical jargon necessary to adequately demonstrate the irreducible complexity of these examples.

1. *The Clotting of Blood.* One of the illustrative systems demonstrating incredible complexity in the natural world that is cited by Michael Behe in his book *Darwin's Black Box* (81ff.), is the cascade of events that occur when blood clots. When the human body springs a leak, in the sense that an open wound causes blood to flow out of the system, the blood behaves in a most unusual way. We usually watch the process happen without much thought for what makes it happen. But this is

The Teleological Argument

no "simple" process, biochemically speaking. If a container of milk, or orange juice, or even syrup is punctured, it will empty completely, either quickly or slowly, depending upon the viscosity of the liquid inside of it. But blood does not do this, generally speaking. Ordinarily we bleed for a moment or two and then it slows and stops completely. A clot, or platelet plug, stops the flow of blood and permits the wound to begin the process of healing. All of this takes place automatically in the body.

We take little thought of the process, if we "nick" a finger with a knife, unless of course we are taking certain medications that may hinder clotting, in which case we are very careful about allowing such wounds to happen in the first place. And we are diligent to apply pressure to the area until the clotting happens when we have an accident. Blood clotting occurs in a multi-step process known as the coagulation cascade. The process involves many different proteins as well as many different chemical reactions. The cascade is a chain reaction in which one step leads to the next. In general, each step produces a new protein which acts as an enzyme, or catalyst, for the next step. The chemicals involved in the coagulation cascade are called clotting or coagulation factors. There are twelve clotting factors, which are numbered with Roman numerals and given a common name as well. The factors are numbered according to the order in which they were discovered and not according to the order in which they react. Other chemicals are needed for blood clotting in addition to those numbered in the coagulation cascade. For example, vitamin K is an essential chemical in the blood clotting process. That is why we are told to eat our leafy greens, because they contain this important clotting vitamin.

It would surprise most people to know that this process requires extreme precision and is extraordinarily complex biochemically. When a pressurized blood circulation system is punctured, a clot must form very quickly or the person or animal involved will bleed to death in just a few moments. On the other hand, if blood congeals at the wrong time or place, the clot may block the blood circulation, as it does in heart attacks and strokes, and the person or animal will expire on that account. If we are cut, a clot must form that will stop the bleeding all along the length of the cut, sealing it off completely. At the same time, however, the clotting must be confined to the area of the cut or else the entire blood flow will solidify, also causing death. Hence, this process must be tightly controlled so that clots are only formed when and where they are needed, but nowhere else.

The most important initial chemical ingredient in this process is fibrinogen, a composite molecular structure composed of six protein chains, containing twin pairs of three different proteins. The substance itself is dissolved in blood plasma, floating through the circulatory system until needed. But if and when a cut or injury occurs, and bleeding starts, then another protein, called thrombin, slices off several small pieces from two of the three pairs of protein chains in the fibrinogen. The trimmed protein is now called fibrin, and it has sticky patches exposed on its surface that had been covered previously by the pieces that were shaved off. Because of the unique shape of the fibrin molecule, long threads form, cross over each other, and make a protein meshwork that looks like a fishing net and traps blood cells, keeping them from escaping out of the wound. This is the initial clot. This process continues building up until the blood stops flowing from the laceration altogether. But thrombin is dangerous. If it were to do its work without regulation, it would shortly cause the death of its host. The blood would solidify throughout the system.

To regulate such systems as this, the body commonly stores enzymes, the proteins that catalyse a chemical reaction, in an inactive form for later use. These inactive forms are referred to as proenzymes. When a chemical signal is received that a certain enzyme is needed, the corresponding proenzyme is activated to produce the mature and usable enzyme. As in the case of the conversion of fibrinogen to fibrin, proenzymes are often activated by cutting off a piece of the proenzyme that is blocking a critical area that is needed for the reaction to take place.

Thrombin initially exists in its inactive form, called prothrombin. Another protein called Stuart factor cleaves the prothrombin, turning it into active thrombin which can then cleave fibrinogen into fibrin to form a blood clot. But Stuart factor is also dangerous. Left to itself it would rapidly trigger the clotting cascade, congealing all of the blood of the organism. So Stuart factor also exists in an inactive form that must first be activated in order for it to do its important work. In this case, accelerin is required to activate the Stuart factor, and then cleave

The Teleological Argument

the prothrombin. But accelerin also initially exists in an inactive form, called proaccelerin. What activates it is thrombin. It seems that there is always a trace of thrombin in the bloodstream, just enough of it to allow proaccelerin to be cleaved into accelerin when needed but not enough to cause the clotting cascade to begin by cleaving fibrinogen into fibrin.

This is where the process gets especially complicated. Prothrombin as it is initially produced by the cell cannot be transformed into thrombin, even in the presence of Stuart factor and accelerin. It must first be modified. This process is performed by ten specific amino acid residues, called glutamate (Glu) residues, changed to γ-carboxyglutamate (Gla) residues. This allows the prothrombin Gla residues to "bite" into calcium, and bind with it to permit prothrombin to stick to the surfaces of cells. It is only this fully developed, modified calcium-prothrombin complex bound to a cell membrane, that can be cleaved by activated Stuart factor and accelerin to give thrombin. This modification of prothrombin requires catalysis by a specific enzyme. In addition to this enzyme, however, the conversion of Glu to Gla needs a small molecule called vitamin K.

Another part of this process is a protein called Hageman factor. When a cut occurs this protein sticks to the surface of cells near the wound. Bound Hageman factor is then cleaved by a protein called HMK to yield activated Hageman factor. Immediately the Hageman factor converts another protein, called prekallikrein, to its active form, kallikrein. This protein helps HMK speed up the conversion of more Hageman factor to its active form. Activated Hageman factor and HMK then together transform another protein, called PTA, to its active form. Activated PTA in turn, together with the activated form of another protein called convertin, switch a protein called Christmas factor to its active form. Finally, activated Christmas factor, together with antihemophilic factor (which is itself activated by thrombin in a manner similar to that of proaccelerin) changes Stuart factor to its active form.

What we have just described here is what is called the "intrinsic pathway" where all of the proteins required for clotting are contained in the blood plasma itself. In the "extrinsic pathway" some of the proteins occur on cells rather than in the plasma. This latter pathway is also a cascade of activators and their counterpart proteins. The two pathways intersect at a number of junctures, but they represent two different routes to the same objective: blood clotting and wound healing. Ten different proteins, or coagulation factors, are involved in this chain of reactions.

The point of our summary of this important cascade of events in the process of blood clotting is to show the reader that this series of reactions perfectly illustrate the irreducible complexity of the biochemistry of this extraordinary system. Even a single reaction, if it were removed from the chain of events, would thwart the entirety of the process. Either clotting would not occur, or the missing component would turn the entire blood stream into a solid mass. If either one of these results were to occur, the animal or human being would immediately expire. Moreover, no single part of this cascade would be of any real value alone. Every part is dependent on every other part of the process.

Gradual development of such a system is extremely unlikely, if not impossible. How would one go about the matter of describing a way such a complexity of reactions would develop over time by a process of fortuitous accidents or of fortunate genetic anomalies? Frankly, the whole idea is so ludicrous on the face of it that no one has really ever made a serious effort to that end. But if the neo-Darwinian model crashes and burns in the face of such an amazing illustration of biochemical complexity in the natural world, which it does in spades, then why is intelligent design considered out of the question in this instance? It is only because the idea of God is considered so repugnant to a good number of leading scientists that the notion of divine design of the system is ruled out of bounds at the start of the discussion.

2. *The Krebs Cycle.* Another of the many incredibly complex biochemical processes which has proven to be impossible to explain in terms of its origination is the Krebs Cycle (first identified in 1937 by and named after Sir Hans Adolf Krebs and William Arthur Johnson at the University of Sheffield; Krebs received the Nobel Prize in Physiology or Medicine for its discovery in 1953); it is also referred to as the Tricarboxylic Acid, or Citric Acid Cycle.

This "cycle" or system is a series of chemical reactions used for the generation of energy in the cell whereby glucose is broken down into Carbon Dioxide (CO_2) and water (H_2O). It also oxidizes acetyl CoA which is produced from the breakdown of carbohydrates, lipids, and proteins.

The Teleological Argument

This is an exceedingly sophisticated series of chemical reactions that take place inside all aerobic organisms. Put another way, its end purpose is to release stored energy. It accomplishes this feat through the oxidation of acetyl-CoA derived from carbohydrates, fats, and proteins into carbon dioxide and chemical energy in the form of adenosine triphosphate.

In Eukaryotes (organisms composed of one or more cells containing visibly evident nuclei and organelles), the matrix of mitochondria accomplish this process. The Krebs Cycle releases energy (ATP) required for the various metabolic activities of the cell. Moreover, intermediate compounds formed during the cycle are used for the synthesis of biomolecules like amino acids, nucleotides, chlorophyll, cytochromes and fats, etc. As well, the carbon skeletons which are freed up during the cycle are used in the process of growth and maintenance of the cells. The process involves four dehydrogenation steps and two decarboxylation steps. Nine major steps in all are apparent (along with several minor ones):

1. **Condensation**: Acetyl CoA combines with oxaloacetate in the presence of the condensing enzyme citrate synthase. From this reaction CoA is released.
2. **Isomerisation**: In the presence of the iron containing enzyme aconitase a molecule of water is released and citric acid is changed into cis-aconitate (dehydration); then Cis-aconitate combines with a molecule of water and forms isocitrate (rehydration).
3. **Dehydrogenation**: Isocitrate undergoes dehydrogenation in the presence of the enzyme isocitrate dehydrogenase. Mn_2^+ ion is required for the functioning of this particular enzyme; so it must be present for the reaction to take place. The Hydrogen that is produced by isocitrate is picked up by NAD^+ (Nicotinamide adenine dinucleotide) to form $NADH_2$. After losing its hydrogen, isocitrate is changed into oxalosuccinate (6C).
4. **Decarboxylation**: In this process, oxalosuccinate undergoes decarboxylation. It can only take place in the presence of the oxalosuccinate decarboxylase enzyme, hence oxalosuccinate is changed into α-ketoglutarate.

5. **Oxidative Decarboxylation**: In the presence of enzyme α-ketoglutarate dehydrogenase complex, the 5-carbon compound, α-Ketoglutarate undergoes simultaneous dehydrogenation and decarboxylation. This enzyme complex contains TPP, Lipoic Acid, Mg_2^+ and trans-succinylase. NAD^+ and CoA are required. The products formed from this process are 4-carbon compound succinyl CoA, $NADH_2$ and CO_2.
6. **Substrate level ATP/GTP Synthesis**: In the presence of the enzyme succinyl thiokinase, succinyl CoA is hydrolyzed. As a result, CoA and Succinate are formed. The energy liberated during the process is used in the synthesis of ATP in Plants and GTP (Guanosine triphosphate) or ITP (Inosine triphosphate) in animals. CoA is released as a result of this process.
7. **Dehydrogenation** (Oxidation): During this step, the 4-Carbon compound Succinate is oxidized to form another 4-carbon compound called fumarate with the assistance of the enzyme succinate dehydrogenase and the hydrogen acceptor FAD (Flavin Adenine Dinucleotide). This enzyme is attached to the inner mitochondrial membrane. It contains or non haem iron (Fe-S) protein. This enables the enzyme to link with the electron transport chain.
8. **Hydration**: The eighth step of this process has fumarate reacting with a molecule of water, in the presence of the enzyme fumarase in order to form another 4-carbon dicarboxylic acid called malate.
9. **Dehydrogenation** (Oxidation): The final step of this chemical procedure requires the presence of the enzyme malate dehydrogenase. The malate that is created in the previous process is oxidized to form oxaloacetate. NAD+ is then reduced to form $NADH_2$.

At this point an oxaloacetate formed in this reaction becomes available to combine with acetyl CoA to start a new cycle all over again. It should be observed that the many enzymes required for these different steps in the cycle are located both in the matrix and in the inner membrane of the mitochondrion (cf. www.chemistrylearning.com/krebs-cycle/).

The Teleological Argument

It must be recalled that this complicated series of steps represent only a part of the overall biochemical process with which it has to do more generally. These nine steps (and their intermediates) represent the cyclic process which is used by the cell to oxidize the pyruvate formed during the glycolytic breakdown of glucose into carbon dioxide and water. They are a mere subset of the four phases of complete glucose breakdown. A snapshot of the entire procedure would be helpful at this point.

The overall process in summary is as follows. The initial breakdown of glucose is called glycolysis and it occurs in the cell cytoplasm. In this instance a series of eight individual reactions causes a 6-carbon glucose molecule to be metabolized using two adenosine triphosphate (ATP) molecules to form two 3-carbon pyruvate molecules, two water molecules and four ATP molecules for a net gain of two ATP molecules. ATP is the primary source of energy in human metabolism. In the matrix, or interior, of the mitochondria of cells the two pyruvate molecules yielded by glycolysis are combined with two coenzymeA (CoA) molecules to produce two acetyl-CoA molecules and two carbon dioxide molecules. This initial reaction occurs in a single step and does not require the presence of oxygen.

Next, the Krebs Cycle described above yields two more molecules of ATP, and finally there is the electron transport chain. In this extensive step, which takes place in the inner membranes of the mitochondria, oxygen at last enters the picture. The transporters in this scheme are molecules of NAD and FAD (flavin adenine dinucleotide), the nucleotide intermediaries which participate in the electron transport mechanism in cellular mitochondria. In the presence of six oxygen molecules, protons are passed from NAD and FAD to other NAD and FAD molecules down the chain, allowing ATP to be extracted at various points. The net result of these reactions is a gain of 34 ATP molecules. This last series of procedures thus produces the greatest bulk of ATP for cellular energy (cf. https://sciencing.com/four-stages-cellular-respiration-5241517.html).

Atheistic scientists recognize that they have no clue as to how such a complicated maze of biochemical processes and procedures, with all of their individual constituent parts, could ever have developed by any imaginable process of trial and error, regardless of the strength of the neo-Darwinian concepts of genetic mutation and survival of the fittest, even over vast ages of time! No single stage could stand on its own without the other stages being present, or else there would be no beneficial result that would come of it. Every part requires all of the others. There is little wonder that as these complex features of cellular life have been uncovered in all of their vast complexity, the popularity of Darwinism among non-scientists has begun to wane, and now is considered a pitiful joke to a great many. Outside the collegial brotherhood of scientific academia where the pressure for acceptance of the Darwinian model of origins is not a factor, the average individual is capable of seeing the impossibility of such amazing complexity being the product of a series of fortunate accidents! Only someone who is already convinced that this is how life began could be brought to accept this viewpoint.

Thus, even if one *assumes* the rectitude of the Darwinian model of development, some sort of intelligent oversight and administration is essential to explain the end result. Little wonder that theistic evolution has been growing in its popularity as the biochemical facts have gradually come in. Clearly this extensive series of biochemical reactions with all of their respective reagents presenting themselves at just the right time and place is the product of an intelligent Designer. Frankly, the "faith" of atheists in Darwinian theory, or any other alternative materialistic theory of origins for that matter (i.e., multiverse or inflationary cosmology, etc.), is far beyond what most of us can muster within ourselves, even if we are inclined to believe them. They are just too fantastic to be credible.

3. The Biochemical Cycle of a Light-Sensitive Cell. This process is also very complex, involving twelve very sophisticated biochemical steps. They are as follows:

1. Light strikes the cell, and a photon interacts with a molecule called *11-cis-retinal*.
2. This rearranges within picoseconds (the time it would take light to travel the width of a human hair) to turn into *trans-retinal*.
3. The change in the shape of the retinal molecule forces a change in the shape of the protein *rhodopsin*, to which the retinal is tightly bound.
4. The protein's metamorphosis alters its behavior; it is now called *metarhodopsin II*.

The Teleological Argument

5. The altered protein sticks to another protein called *transducin*.
6. Before bumping into metarhodopsin II, transducin had been tightly bound with a small molecule called *GDP*.
7. When the transducin interacts with metarhodopsin II, the GDP falls off, and a molecule called *GTP* binds to the transducin.
8. *GTP-transducin-metarhodopsin II* now binds to a protein called *phosphodiesterase*, located in the inner membrane of the cell.
9. When attached to the metarhodopsin II group, the phosphodiesterase acquires the chemical ability to "cut" molecules called *cGMP* in the cell. The phosphodiesterase lowers the concentration of cGMP, just as a pulled plug lowers the water level in a bathtub.
10. When the concentration of cGMP is reduced because of cleavage by the phosphodiesterase, the ion channel closes, causing the cellular concentration of positively charged sodium ions to be reduced.
11. This causes a current to be transmitted down the optic nerve to the brain.
12. The result of this cumulative process, when the signal is interpreted by the brain, is vision (cf. Muncaster, *Dismantling Evolution*, 166-67).

Without any thought for this amazing process, the complicated biochemical procedure described above takes place constantly in the light-sensitive cells of the eye and sends their signals down the optic nerve to the brain. The end result is sight. We never are consciously aware of this amazing biochemical process taking place. We just look and see. How could such a sophisticated series of reactions have begun at all unless they happened all at once? No single step in this biochemical process will stand on its own merits. No single step yields any benefit to the organism until the whole complex of steps is put together. When the entirety is assembled into a working "biochemical laboratory," the miracle of vision results. Moreover, the final step mentioned, the processing of the signals that reach the brain so that they are interpreted properly, is as complicated in its own right as are these other operations.

4. *The Information Content of Cellular DNA.* The next area of interest to us represents a relatively recent branch of knowledge that was

GOD DOES EXIST!

not available to the first generations of those who were drawn into the Darwinian attempt at reconstructing the beginnings of life on earth. In our view, it is one of the most powerful areas of study under the rubric of teleological proof for God in the realm of the created order. It is a body of sophisticated and highly technical information that indicates the activity of an intelligent agent's work in the biological realm. It is the presence of genuine information content in the cellular matrix. The information itself is telling. Its existence is a red flag for intelligence. How it is possible for one to work in this field without being convinced that it is proof of the work of an intelligent artificer is difficult for us to comprehend.

The nature of this communication vehicle is impressive indeed. The level of its sophistication is the second marker for intelligence, in fact, not just intelligence, but high intelligence. Perhaps the word "intelligence" is not even itself sufficient to describe it. "Genius" is a much more appropriate choice. The complicated mode of its expression and the extremely sophisticated methodology of its application in real life is the third signal that a genius was at work when this system of information processing was invented. Undoubtedly the information content which lies at the heart of it as well as the system that makes possible its expression and application was the work of a creative genius, a Creator, namely God. Theories that suggest that blind chance over vast stretches of time is capable of producing such exquisite complexity fall flat in the face of the reality of what in this instance has been observed in the natural world. Not only could they *not* happen, they could *never* happen!

A simple illustration will be helpful in our examination of this aspect of the biological basis of life. If we were to encounter a book with hundreds of pages of information, logical and understandable, as well as capable of being translated and understood, our natural impulse would be to ascribe it to the work of an intelligent agent. It would never occur to us that this information-packed object happened in nature by any other means. Information technology of any sort is the product of an intelligent mind. There are no exceptions to this rule.

In addition, information is an entirely different kind of stuff from the physical medium in which it may temporarily be recorded. It would be absurd to try to explain the literary quality or meaning of a book as an emergent property of the physical aspects of its ink and paper. The

The Teleological Argument

message comes from the author. Ink and paper are simply the media by which the communication contained within are recorded. Similarly, the information that is written in DNA is not the product of DNA. DNA may replicate itself, but it is incapable of producing itself. So, it is entirely appropriate to ask another question as a follow-on. Where did the information come from? Who or what is the author of this book that we call the DNA molecule?

Physical laws cannot be the answer to this mystery. Such laws as these may be able to produce some fairly complex structures in nature, such as snowflakes and crystals. But in these instances the laws produce the identical structure over and over again, with only occasional chance variations. However, repetitive order of this sort has a very low information content. The same laws that produce the crystals in the first place, constantly work to prevent any more complex ordering from emerging. Similarly, it is impossible for a coherent book to be produced by randomly combining letters, spaces and punctuation marks. Even a single rational sentence is unlikely to arise from the process. This is so because, just as a book is not merely the physical aspects of its ink and paper, the information content of it is not simply a mix of random letters, spaces and punctuation marks. It is a form of intelligent communication. And we all agree that intelligent communication is the product of an intelligent mind.

Moreover, if we found this book on a machine that interpreted the code behind it and placed it on a viewing screen in the fashion of a computer monitor, we would certainly know that we were dealing with the work of a sentient and wise being. We would not be inclined at first to think that it might have come together fortuitously or accidentally. Information content is indicative of intelligence, never of blind chance. And the machinery that interprets and applies that information to a particular application would be seen in the identical light. A printer, for example, takes information from a computer and prints it on paper. But all of us know that a printer is itself a very complex machine that works in tandem with a computer. It would never be supposed that a printer simply happened somehow by accident. Accidents produce chaos, not order. Accidents cause things to break down. They do not lead to higher sophistication or more efficiency in a system.

GOD DOES EXIST!

This is our common experience in regard to devices and machines that are produced by intelligent beings like humans. If an accident occurs, things do not get better. Systems break down. They get worse. They sometimes fall apart or fail altogether. The same is true of the living world. As a matter of fact, this is precisely what we have in the case of cellular biology. At the heart of the cell, so small it cannot be seen with the naked eye, is an immense body of information technology along with a complicated system for interpreting the data and putting it to work. *It did not happen by accident! And if accidents occur within the system, things do not improve, they degrade or fail altogether. There is no better illustration of this than cancer.*

Dr. Thomas Nagel, an atheist, wrote incisively:

It is prima facie highly implausible that life as we know it is the result of a sequence of physical accidents together with the mechanism of natural selection. We are expected to abandon this naive response, not in favor of a fully worked out physical/chemical explanation but in favor of an alternative that is really a schema for explanation, supported by some examples. What is lacking, to my knowledge, is a credible argument that the story has a non-negligible probability of being true. There are two questions. First, given what is known about the chemical basis of biology and genetics, what is the likelihood that self-reproducing life forms should have come into existence spontaneously on the early earth, solely through the operation of the laws of physics and chemistry? The second question is about the sources of variation in the evolutionary process that was set in motion once life began: In the available geological time since the first life forms appeared on earth, what is the likelihood that, as a result of physical accident, a sequence of viable genetic mutations should have occurred that was sufficient to permit natural selection to produce the organisms that actually exist?

There is much more certainty in the scientific community about the first question than about the second. Many people think it will be very difficult to come up with a reductionist explanation of the origin of life, but most people have no doubt that accidental genetic variation is enough to support the actual history of evolution by natural selection, once reproducing organisms have come into existence. However, the questions concern highly specific events over a long historical period in the distant past, the available evidence is very indirect, and general assumptions have to play an important part. My skepticism

The Teleological Argument

is not based on religious belief, or on a belief in any definite alternative. It is just the belief that the available scientific evidence, in spite of the consensus of scientific opinion, does not in this matter rationally require us to subordinate the incredulity of common sense. That is especially true with regard to the origin of life.

The world is an astonishing place, and the idea that we have in our possession the basic tools needed to understand it is no more credible now than it was in Aristotle's day. That it has produced you, and me, and the rest of us is the most astonishing thing about it. If contemporary research in molecular biology leaves open the possibility of legitimate doubts about a fully mechanistic account of the origin and evolution of life, dependent only on the laws of chemistry and physics, this can combine with the failure of psychophysical reductionism to suggest that principles of a different kind are also at work in the history of nature, principles of the growth of order that are in their logical form teleological rather than mechanistic. I realize that such doubts will strike many people as outrageous, but that is because almost everyone in our secular culture has been browbeaten into regarding the reductive research program as sacrosanct, on the ground that anything else would not be science (*Mind and Cosmos: Why the Materialist Neo-Darwinian Concept of Nature Is Almost Certainly False*, 6-7).

There is a very important reason why men of science like Nagel are willing to go out on a limb and risk their reputations in order to say such, dare I say, "unorthodox" things. The evidence from science is forcing a host of researchers to admit that what they are finding is "teleological rather than mechanistic." It is difficult for them to admit, but the evidence is so powerful and has been so profoundly cumulative over the years of their research that it has become difficult for them to keep quiet about it.

Cellular biology and biochemistry are extremely sophisticated areas of knowledge. The clotting of blood and the Krebs Cycle illustrate this point very well, as we have shown above. In addition to this, getting to the point of understanding the inner workings of the cell, and especially the informational aspect of it has been a long and drawn out affair. Putting all of the pieces of this narrative together is a complicated story all to itself. Hosts of scientists labored over many decades to unravel the mysteries of the various constituent parts of the process. There are too many names involved to begin to mention them all.

GOD DOES EXIST!

This fact alone is a testimonial to the sophisticated nature of the whole process. If it has taken many years and thousands of highly trained and enormously talented intellectuals to uncover the details of these processes, what does that say about the unembodied Mind that is behind what they have unravelled? The wisdom and sophistication of that One cannot be expressed in words or even appreciated fully. But these barely comprehensible truths do move us to wonder and marvel at the ingenuity and sophistication of the works of his hands (Ps. 111:1-10).

By the year 1909 scientists had been able to separate an acidic material from the cell nucleus. At first they described it simply as "nucleic acid" because it came from the nucleus of the cell. Further investigation caused them to label it as "deoxyribose nucleic acid" (DNA) because they were able to identify a deoxygenated sugar molecule called ribose in the molecule. Scientists further determined that the molecule was made of phosphates and four bases called adenine, cytosine, guanine, and thymine. The chemical formulas and structures of these molecular materials had already been known at the time. But the structure and precise form of the entire molecule was not yet determined. Moreover, it was not then known that this molecule had anything to do with the process of passing on hereditary information. That would prove to be the most exciting and fascinating aspect of this series of discoveries.

In the mid-1940s Oswald Avery successfully identified DNA as the key factor in accounting for heritable differences between various bacterial strains. This was an important step, since it centered investigation in a particular molecule among the plethora of potential candidates for special attention. However, it was Watson and Crick's seminal 1953 paper in the journal *Nature* that turned the scientific world on its heels. The article itself was only nine hundred words in length, and it was written by a pair of unknown, comparatively young researchers, J. D. Watson and F. H. C. Crick. It featured the unprepossessing title, "Molecular Structures of Nucleic Acids: A Structure for Deoxyribose Nucleic Acid." It revolutionized biological research into the nature of heritable *information* within the cell.

The Watson-Crick model made it clear that DNA had an impressive chemical and structural complexity. It was a very long molecule composed on the outside of a regular arrangement of sugar and phosphate

The Teleological Argument

groups. But on the inside it could contain many potentially different arrangements of the four base pairs. Thus, it had an impressive potential for variability and complexity of sequence as required by any potential carrier of hereditary information. The precise sequence of the bases formed the code which carried the genetic information.

In Darwin's time few, if any, biologists talked about biological or genetic information, but today they routinely refer to DNA, RNA, and proteins as carriers or repositories of genetic information. Thus, biology has entered its own "information age." *Biological* information, that is. English dictionaries describe this type of information as "the attribute inherent in and communicated by alternative sequences or arrangements of something that produce specific effects" (Webster). It is surprisingly similar to computer code. As it turns out, not only does DNA contain information, but a particular type of information. It stores the "know-how" for building various molecules in the cell. Many different molecular components are required by the cell for it to grow, function, and maintain itself. DNA specifies the construction plans for the manufacture of those components, whether in whole or in part.

Scientists in our time are aware that protein molecules perform most of the critical functions of the cell. Proteins build cellular machines and structures, they carry and deliver cellular materials, and they catalyze chemical reactions that the cell needs in order for it to stay alive. Proteins also perform another critical function. They process genetic information. In order for them to accomplish this important work, a typical cell employs thousands of different kinds of proteins.

Moreover, each protein in the portfolio of possible proteins has a distinctive shape. This is much like the different tools commonly found in a carpenter's toolbox. They all have different shapes related to the type of work that they do. This is true for proteins as well, and for the identical reason. They are shaped differently because they perform different functions. And the particular function determines the shape of the protein. But in the case of a single protein, the shape can be exceedingly complex, not at all simple like a carpenter's tool. In fact, it was its irregularity that especially surprised researchers when they first observed it. It was not at all what they had expected. As John Kendrew, *et al.* noted in regard to the myoglobin molecule:

GOD DOES EXIST!

> Perhaps the most remarkable features of the molecule are its complexity and its lack of symmetry. The arrangement seems to be almost totally lacking in the kind of regularities which one instinctively anticipates, and it is more complicated than has been predicted by any theory of protein structure ("A Three-Dimensional Model of the Myoglobin Molecule," *Nature* [March 8, 1953]: 662-666; quoted in S. C. Meyer, *Signature in the Cell,* 96).

Biochemists soon recognized that proteins exhibit another remarkable property. In addition to their complex shapes and irregular arrangements of amino acids, proteins also exhibit *specificity*. By specificity, biologists mean that a molecule has some features that have to be what they are, within fine tolerances, for the molecule to perform an important function in the cell.

Proteins are specified in two ways. First, proteins display a specificity of *shape*. The strangely irregular shapes of proteins that Kendrew and others discovered turned out to be essential to the functioning of these complex molecules. In particular, the three-dimensional shape of a protein gives it a hand-in-glove fit with other equally specified and complex molecules or with simpler substrates within the cell. And, because of its three-dimensional specificity, one protein cannot usually substitute for another. A topoisomerase cannot perform the job of a polymerase any more than a hatchet can perform the function of a soldering iron or a hammer the job of a wrench. As the expression goes: "Never the twain shall meet." The extraordinary complexity of their differences, even though they are similar in some ways, make this impossible.

To illustrate further, eukaryotic cells have a unique way of storing information in DNA in a highly compact way (eukaryotes are cells that contain a nucleus and other membrane-bound organelles). Strands of DNA are wrapped around spool-like structures called nucleosomes. These nucleosomes are made of proteins called histones. And, once more, it is the specific shape of the histone proteins that enables them to do their job. They fold into a well-defined three-dimensional shape with a precise distribution of positive electrical charges around their exteriors. This precise shape and charge distribution enables DNA strands to coil efficiently around the nucleosome spools and store an immense amount of information in a very small space.

The Teleological Argument

Hence, as a result of this complicated method of nucleosome spooling, the information storage density of DNA is many times that of our most advanced silicon chips (cf. H. Lodish, *et al.*, *Molecular Cell Biology*, 322; Werner Gitt, *In the Beginning Was Information*, 111-12, 127-131; and, S. C. Meyer, *Signature in the Cell*, 97). Silicon chips capable of containing enormous amounts of information and transmitting it for application in what are often very complex usages do not occur naturally in the world without the engineering capabilities of intelligent minds and production facilities and machinery produced by them for this very purpose. Such chips do not appear anywhere advanced civilization and technical expertise are not found. Obviously complex devices are products of both and will never be found where they are absent. This being true, how is it logical to argue that a more powerful and considerably more sophisticated system than this has been produced without the agency of either engineering expertise or high intellect?

But this is not the end of the story. Proteins do not merely display a specificity of shape; they also display a specificity of *arrangement*. Whereas proteins are built from rather simple amino-acid "building-blocks," their various functions depend crucially on the specific arrangement of those building blocks. The specific sequence of amino acids in a chain and the resulting chemical interactions between amino acids largely determine the specific three-dimensional structure that the chain as a whole will adopt. Those structures or shapes determine what function, if any, the amino-acid chain can perform in the cell. They decide whether it will be a structural component or a molecular machine built for the processing of molecular information. It is this specificity of sequence that distinguishes between purposeful proteins which are important for the functioning of the cell and the maintenance of life and ordinary, useless polypeptides.

Gene expression begins as long chains of nucleotide bases are copied during a process known as "transcription." During this process, the genetic assembly instructions stored on a strand of DNA are reproduced on another molecule called "messenger RNA" (or mRNA). The resulting single-stranded copy or "transcript" contains a sequence of RNA bases precisely matching the sequence of bases on the original DNA strand. RNA also uses chemicals called bases to store genetic information, but

GOD DOES EXIST!

it uses a slightly different chemical alphabet from DNA. RNA substitutes a base called uracil for the base thymine used in DNA.

After it is produced, the messenger RNA molecule travels to the ribosome, a molecular machine that helps translate the mRNA assembly instructions. These instructions consist of a series of three-letter genetic "words" called "codons." Each codon consists of three bases and directs the cell to attach a specific amino acid to a growing chain of other amino acids. For example, the mRNA word UUA directs the ribosome to attach the amino acid leucine, whereas AGA specifies the amino acid arginine. Other codons direct the ribosome to start or stop building proteins. This translation process occurs with the aid of specific adapter molecules (called transfer RNAs, or tRNAs) and specific enzymes (called aminoacyl-tRNA synthetases). We say again: How could any of this have evolved separately? What use would any individual part of this system have been without the rest of it? This is obviously an instance of irreducible complexity. No part would have any value at all without the presence of the whole.

So, it is clear from all of this that DNA contains information through its sequential arrangement of the four bases (adenine, guanine, citocene, thymine) that permits the cell to build functional proteins. Moreover, this "living machine language" is extraordinarily complex. Human DNA, for example, contains about 3.2 billion base pairs, which code for approximately 70,000 genes. The count of recognized protein-coding genes has now settled somewhere between 19,000-20,000. In the human cellular matrix genes may vary in size from a few hundred base pairs to more than two million bases. If it were to be unwound and unfolded, it would stretch to about 6 feet in length (approx. 1828.80 mm). Chromosome 1, for example, is composed of about 248,956,422 base pairs, and stretches to a length of about 85 mm. The packaged or folded form of DNA is called a chromosome.

The human genome (the complete set of nucleic acid sequences for human beings, has been intensely studied in recent years, and it is now known that it is encoded within 23 chromosome pairs (22 paired chromosomes, plus the X chromosome; one in males, two of them in females; and in males only, the Y chromosome). These are all large linear DNA molecules contained within the cell nucleus. The genome also includes the mitochondrial DNA, a comparatively small circular molecule

The Teleological Argument

present in each mitochondrion. The Human Genome Project, which intended to "map" the entire human genetic sequence, was completed in 2004. It left only 341 gaps in the sequence. These "gaps" were made up of highly repetitive and other DNA that could not be sequenced with the technology that was available at the beginning of the twenty-first century. Since that time, of course, these data have been used worldwide in biomedical research, anthropology, forensics, as well as many other branches of science.

Though different species may have the same number of chromosomes as humans, the DNA in every case will be distinct and very different. It is the information content encoded in the DNA that separates a human being from a spider or a frog. Too, the DNA strands will be observably different. The ability of strands of DNA (genes) to generate protein products also differs markedly from species to species. All of this, when considered together, raises an important issue currently confronting evolutionists.

If species change from one to another, what is the mechanism that alters the DNA in such a significant way that it encodes for a radically different creature? Even if we assume that it begins merely with a small change which over time and with additional alterations leads to radical changes, the mechanism whereby these changes are made can only be theoretical at this point. There is no evidence to support any theoretical reconstruction of events such as are postulated by those who wish to press the neo-Darwinian theory. Production of an entirely different system, as in the case of the eye for vision or the ear for hearing, would require at least thousands if not millions of additional sets of DNA "instructions" to be encoded for the production of the new system. *Who or what has been writing that code?*

Conclusion

These three areas of intrinsic complexity and sophistication that we have offered from the natural world are not the only ones that exist in nature. But they are clearly illustrative, even though not comprehensive. They establish that it is common in the organic sphere for systems to exist which are not explicable on the basis of blind chance operating over vast expanses of time, *in any possible world.* Alternative "possible worlds" have become the final redoubt, the last haven of desperate but irrational men who argue for irrational possibilities in the face of mounting evidence against the feasibility of their illogical conclusions. No possible world may be conceived wherein such a complicated series of biochemical processes could "develop" or "evolve" into the final forms that are observable in the natural world.

Realization that the "chance explanation" was highly improbable first began to be recognized on a grand scale in a conference of mathematicians and biologists held in Philadelphia in 1966. The conference discussion centered around what it called, "Mathematical Challenges to Neo-Darwinism." The gathering was called at the Wistar Institute to discuss the growing doubts of many mathematicians, physicists, and engineers about the ability of random mutations to generate the information required to produce new forms of life. The skeptics at the conference mainly expressed doubt about the role of random mutations in biological evolution, but the questions they raised had equally important implications for assessing the role of chance in chemical evolutionary theories about how life first arose on the earth.

According to neo-Darwinian theory, new genetic information arises first as random mutations occur in the DNA of existing organisms. When mutations arise that confer a survival advantage on the organisms that possess them, the resulting genetic changes are passed on by natural selection to the next generation. As these changes accumulate, the features of a population begin to change over time. Nevertheless, theoretically, natural selection can "select" only what random mutations first produce. And therein lies the "rub." For the evolutionary process to produce new forms of life, random mutations must first have produced new genetic information for the construction of novel proteins. That is the problem. And a huge problem it is.

The skeptics at Wistar argued that it is extremely difficult to assemble a new gene or protein by chance because of the sheer number of possible base or amino-acid sequences. For every combination of amino acids that produces a functional protein there exists a vast number of other possible combinations that do not. And as the length of the required protein grows, the number of possible amino-acid sequence combinations of that length grows exponentially, so that the odds of building a functional sequence, a working protein, diminish precipi-

The Teleological Argument

tously. Most functional proteins are made of hundreds of amino acids. Therefore, even a relatively short protein of, let us say, 150 amino acids represents one sequence among an astronomically large number of other possible sequence combinations (approximately 10 to the 195th power!). It seems as though successful DNA investigations, with all of their revelations of informational complexity, had effectively "thrown a wrench" into the machinery of neo-Darwinian theory! And it will never be the same again.

Questions for Discussion

1. Discuss the ideas of material cause, formal cause, efficient cause, and final cause in the historic philosophical understanding of how and why things came to be.
2. The final cause of a thing has to do with its purpose. Is it fair to exclude purpose from the discussion of the human family on earth? Atheistic thinkers consider it "out of bounds" to speak of humanity's having a purpose or reason for being. Aristotle thought that it had to be considered. Which is correct?
3. What is your personal view of the notion that the phenomenal variety and complexity of both the non-living and living world provide evidence of a preconceived and well-orchestrated plan? Does the existence of such a plan permit us to infer that there was a Planner behind it all?
4. Is it true to say that in all aspects of our lives we tend to infer an adequate cause sufficient to explain every effect that we encounter in nature? If this is so, then why is the theory that the universe simply "appeared" or "exploded into being", without an adequate cause being behind this stupendous phenomenon, taken seriously as an explanation for it?
5. State the Teleological Argument for God in a simple syllogism.
6. Darwinists and other atheistic theoreticians reject this argument in spite of the fact that it has been viewed as convincing by most of the human population throughout history, even as it is today. Dr. David Berlinski (Ph.D., Princeton University) points out that evolutionary theory is "widely championed by the sci-

entific community and widely disbelieved by everyone else." How is this divergence of opinion to be explained?

7. Simply state William Paley's analogy. Do you consider it to be logical and defensible in the modern era? If not, what arguments can be made to prove it false?

8. What caused the "steady state" view of the origin of the universe to be widely rejected by the scientific community, and why does this rejection lead us back to God as the ultimate explanation for its existence? What factors have convinced scientists that the universe had a beginning?

9. What is "irreducible complexity"? Explain the concept, and give illustrations of it in the natural world.

10. Is it fair to say that in 160 years of study and research by some of the world's most intelligent people Darwinism has been unable to produce a convincing account of the origin of the monumental systems observable in nature? Could this be the reason that Darwinism is believed by most scientists but by almost no one else?

11. Illustrate the notion of "irreducible complexity" in biological systems?

Chapter 6
The Fine Tuning Argument

Exaggerated subservience to the "Copernican principle" has been reacted to quite negatively in recent decades. Nicolaus Copernicus formulated a model of the universe that placed the sun rather than the earth at the center of our planetary system. Copernicus convinced the world that we must not assume gratuitously that we human beings occupy a privileged *central* position in the universe. Unfortunately, there has been a strong, and not always subconscious, tendency to extend this notion beyond its original intent. In fact, it has been converted into a doctrinaire ideology and eventually into a most questionable scientific dogma. It is therefore alleged that our situation as living and intelligent beings on this planet and in this universe cannot be privileged in any sense of the word.

GOD DOES EXIST!

This dogma, which in its most extreme form, came to be identified with the "perfect cosmological principle" on which the steady state theory of the universe was based. This represented an overstatement of the original "Copernican principle" and it was clearly untenable. This was pointed out by Robert H. Dicke ("Dirac's cosmology and Mach's principle," *Nature* 192 [1961]: 440-441), in conjunction with two presentiments: (1) that especially favorable conditions (of temperature, chemical environment, etc.) are prerequisite for our existence, and that, (2) the universe evolves and is by no means spatially homogeneous on a local scale. Research since the time of Dicke's article in *Nature* has tended to confirm his point of view.

A Statement of the Formal Proof

Rather than the raw fact of the existence of life, and in particular intelligent life, being a sort of afterthought in the conditions of the early universe as well as in the universe up to the present time, the special circumstances that have generally prevailed have seemed to be suggestive of a planned series of predominating conditions conducive to their appearance. Planning, of course, seems to imply the existence of a supreme Planner, and so this has been taken by some, in the disciplines of physics, cosmology, and philosophy, to provide formal proof of the existence of God.

It is our contention that it may well prove to be the most compelling one in the arsenal of such arguments. Stated succinctly, it would appear in the form of a syllogism as follows:

Premise 1: Life, and in particular intelligent life, has appeared in the present universe.
Premise 2: Special conditions, requisite to the appearance and maintenance of intelligent life, have made this possible, against all odds.
Premise 3: Fine tuning of the universe, in the physical constants, the biological and chemical constants, etc., is abundantly evident, once more, against all odds.
Premise 4: Such finely tuned constants are indicative of planning, and planning suggests the existence of an intelligent agent.
Conclusion: Therefore, God, the only intelligent agent capable of such planning and fine tuning, exists.

The Fine Tuning Argument

Premises one, two, and three are all simple observations that are not controversial at this point in time. Scientific discovery over the past six decades has made them widely recognized and generally understood. Thus, the only one of the four premises that is subject to formal challenge is number four. And, if the evidence that we are about to examine in some detail in the present chapter is sufficiently compelling, then that premise will also stand up to criticism and will be sustained. With that being the case, the Conclusion is also justified. Thus, the existence of God is established as proven by the fine tuning of the physical constants of the universe.

The Anthropic Principle

Beginning in the 1960s, physicists unveiled a universe apparently fine-tuned for the possibility of human life. They discovered that the existence of life in the universe is dependent upon a highly improbable but precise balance of physical factors. The constants of physics, the initial conditions of the universe, and many other of its features appear delicately balanced to allow for the possibility of life. Even very slight alterations in the values of many factors, such as the expansion rate of the universe, the strength of gravitational or electromagnetic attraction, or the value of Planck's constant, would render life impossible.

Present-day physicists now refer to these facts using the term "anthropic coincidences," because they make life possible for human beings, and to the fortunate convergence of all of these coincidences as the "fine tuning of the universe." Given the improbability of the precise ensemble of values represented by these constants, and their specificity relative to the requirements of a life-sustaining universe, many physicists have noted that the fine tuning strongly suggests design by a preexistent intelligence. As well-known British physicist Paul Davies encapsulated the notion, "the impression of design is overwhelming" (*The Cosmic Blueprint,* 203; quoted in Stephen C. Meyer," Evidence for Design," 56-57).

In 1967, Brandon Carter of the University of Cambridge, had drawn up a long type-written preprint of his thinking on this matter. It was devoted to *the role of fundamental microphysical parameters in cosmogony* which remained unpublished (*The Significance of Numerical Sequences in Nature. Part 1: The Role of Fundamental Physical Parameters in Cosmogo-*

GOD DOES EXIST!

ny). This was conceived as the first part of a projected work (called *the significance of numerical coincidences in nature*) aimed to furnish a "unified treatment" and a "readily accessible and comprehensible" survey of numerical coincidences emerging from physics and astrophysics. In short, the paper represented a stimulating exercise of what Victor Weisskopf would call *qualitative physics*: a genre of physical discussion which had some forerunners (from Galilei's reflections on the size of the animals attributed to Salviati in the second day of his *Discorsi e dimostrazioni matematiche* to Edwin E. Salpeter's speculations of the mid 1960s) and a long list of successors. That, in Carter's words, concerned "the manner in which familiar local phenomena depend qualitatively, and in order of magnitude, quantitatively on the fundamental parameters of microphysics." He also aimed to distinguish those features of large-scale phenomena "which do not depend critically" on the values of fundamental parameters, from "those which depend on numerical coincidences."

In this work the author explored in particular the role and consequences of a series of "relations and coincidences" obtained through the composition of six parameters. Once again, this employs very technical language unfamiliar to some, but Carter explained it in this way:

1. The pseudo-scalar coupling constant of strong interactions g_s, which is approximately 4 in the so-called *Planck units*; i.e. those fundamental units such that $c = G = h/2\pi = 1$. The adoption of these units is customary in this kind of research. Moreover, the corresponding units of temperature are obtained putting Bolzmann's constant $K = 1$.
2. The electron charge e ($\approx 1/12$ in the above-mentioned units). It should be noted that, in Planck units, e^2 is the fine structure constant (being $\alpha \equiv e^2/hc \approx 1/137$).
3. The nucleon mass m_n ($\approx \frac{1}{2} \times 10^{-19}$).
4. The ratio between the pion (π-meson) mass and the nucleon mass, $m_\pi/m_n \approx 1/7$, which suggests the "maximum effective range of the strong interactions."
5. The ratio between the mass of the electron and that of the nucleon: $m_e/m_N \approx 1/1830$.
6. The ratio between the difference between neutron and proton mass and the mass of the nucleon, $\Delta_N/m_N \approx 1/730$.

The Fine Tuning Argument

From the interplay of these parameters it is possible to show not only that the sizes and masses of the planets and the stars must lie in certain typical ranges, but that they have a fundamental role in determining "the character of all important natural phenomena" with the exception of those where high energy physics or cosmological quantities are directly involved. Carter demonstrated how, apart from relatively small adjustment factors, most of the limiting masses of astrophysics arise (in fundamental units) simply as the reciprocal of the gravitational fine structure constant. There was only one notable exception, and it concerns the positioning of the dividing line which distinguishes main sequence stars, i.e. stable hydrogen's burning stars, that transport energy mainly by convection (red dwarfs) from those in which energy is dissipated primarily by radiative transport (blue giants). Carter showed that this line occurs within the range of main sequence stars only as a consequence of the rather exotic coincidence that the ninth power of the electromagnetic fine structure constant (e^2) is roughly equal to the square root of the gravitational fine structure constant. *This coincidence implied indeed a delicate balance.* Had it been the 11th power, all main sequence stars would be convective red dwarfs. This observation prompted crucial developments.

Although this coincidence was a genuine finding, it was intriguing that there was no need to postulate any new physics to explain it. It was entirely predictable in terms of the ordinary theory of stellar evolution, taking into account that the masses of stable stars are necessarily related to the Landau/Chandrasekhar limiting mass. Programatically he then stated that the final task of the 1967 preprint was to furnish the formulae which illustrate the connection between local and cosmological quantities via the timescales of stellar evolution in terms of microphysical parameters. The promised follow-up to this came three years later in a paper for the *Clifford Memorial Meeting* held at Princeton University in 1970. On that occasion he intended to, in his words, "clarify" the "various much publicised [sic] large number coincidences in terms of standard physical theory in conjunction with the orthodox hot big bang model of the universe" (Bettini, ibid., 15-16).

In 1974, Carter, in his study of "Large Number Coincidences and the Anthropic Principle in Cosmology," rejected the thesis that these widely

GOD DOES EXIST!

known "large number coincidences" were to be seen as evidence justifying the introduction of various exotic theories (e.g. involving departures from normally accepted physical conservation laws). He was convinced that these coincidences ought to be taken as confirming "conventional" (General Relativistic Big Bang) physics and cosmology which could, at least in principle, have been utilized to predict them all in advance of their observation.

However, these predictions do require the use of what may be termed the *anthropic principle*, to the effect that what we can expect to observe must be restricted by the conditions necessary for our presence as observers. To this he added, "Although our situation is not necessarily *central*, it is inevitably privileged to some extent" (291). As a footnote to this point, the "anthropic principle" (or "anthropic reasoning," as some preferred to call it) is defined as a cosmological principle that theories of the universe are constrained by the necessity to allow human existence.

We must, at the same time, recognize that this presupposition is in fact a philosophical consideration. It requires that any data we collect about the universe is filtered by the fact that, in order for it to be observable in the first place, it must be compatible with the conscious and sapient life that observes it. Proponents of this perspective reason that it explains why this universe has the age and the fundamental physical constants necessary to accommodate conscious life. As a result, outside the narrow range thought to be compatible with life ("fine tuning"), it would seem impossible that life, and in particular, intelligent life, could develop. It was the "large number" coincidences then evident in physics and cosmology that seemed to suggest to Carter that "our making any scientific observation is necessarily contingent on our existence" as intelligent beings.

Carter went on to observe that Hermann Bondi in his textbook, *Cosmology* (2nd ed., 1960), a formative volume that had enormous influence for decades after its publication, recognized this fact as essential to good science. In his book he speaks of three classes of theoretical predictions in physics: (1) the traditional kind, formulated without the use of the anthropic principle; (2) those which only require the use of a "weak" anthropic principle. Carter further defined this weak principle in these terms: "We must be prepared to take into account the fact that our

The Fine Tuning Argument

location in the universe is necessarily privileged to the extent of being compatible with our existence as observers." Then he spoke of, (3) those which require the invocation of an extended (and hence rather more questionable) "strong" anthropic principle. Carter said of this strong principle that, "The universe (and hence the fundamental parameters on which it depends) must be such as to admit the creation of observers within it at some stage."

Carter himself was an adherent of the "weak anthropic" approach. That was clear in all of his presentations. However, even though several of these predictions had been recognized already as profoundly interesting on many levels, his employment of this special language to describe them caused quite a stir in the intellectual community. "Large number coincidences" are one thing, but to speak of "anthropic centricity" in any context associated with physics and cosmology is another thing altogether. The considerable debate which these references have sparked has engaged the interest of physicists and cosmologists as well as philosophers and theologians since the original publication of his presentations. One of the main reasons for this wide interest surely resides in the teleological overtones of many recent expositions focused on the topic of surprising coincidences deriving from dimensionless combinations of fundamental constants of physics and cosmological parameters, which some have described as being "fine-tuned" for the arrival of living things, and ultimately of intelligent life-forms, such as human beings.

The first 'large number coincidence' on Bondi's list had to do with predictions of the traditional kind. The first consists of the observation that although stars come with widely varying sizes and colors, from red giants to white dwarfs (and more recently neutron stars), they always have a mass equal in order of magnitude (i.e. within one or two powers of ten) to the *inverse* of the gravitational coupling constant. Although Pascuel Jordan in 1947 (*Die Herkunft der Sterne,* 2 Auflage) had postulated that this coincidence required a revolutionary cosmological explanation, it had by that time been widely recognized that it is predicted by the conventional theory of stellar formation by condensation from diffuse gas clouds. The basic idea is that protostars will be unstable to fragmentation or continuous mass loss until they have separated out

GOD DOES EXIST!

into units small enough to be supported at least to a significant extent by non-relativistic gas pressure.

The second "large number coincidence" listed by Carter was a prediction based on the weak anthropic principle. It is the observed fact that the Hubble fractional expansion rate of the universe is equal to within a few powers of ten to the reciprocal of the same large number. Robert H. Dicke (*Nature* 192 [1961]: 440) pointed out that this too could have been predicted, provided we accept that the present age of the universe is *not* determined purely at random but is most likely to have the order of magnitude of a typical main-sequence stellar lifetime. This is plausible, Carter argued, because at times much later than this the Galaxy will contain relatively few (and many very weak) energy producing stars, whereas at times much shorter than this the heavy elements (whose presence seems essential for life) could not have been formed. This second category contemplated "those coincidences whose explanation, although straightforward, requires subjective and probabilistic considerations relating to our own position as observers in the universe."

The third type were "those coincidences which cannot be given a direct physical explanation since they depend more or less critically on the actual values of fundamental or microphysical constants, but which nevertheless could in principle have been predicted in advance of their observational discovery on the ground that they are necessary preconditions for the existence of observers (ourselves) in the universe."

Following the lead of Dicke, Carter discussed the constraints imposed by the existence of observers to the "observed value of the cosmological time," suggesting some further cosmological insights and founding a reason to reject by principle not only Dirac's "revolutionary departure from orthodox physical theory" but also any form of steady-state theory that postulates an independence between the age of the universe and the Hubble constant (cf. Stefano Bettini, "Anthropic Reasoning in Cosmology," 17, n. 107).

Our Extraordinary Good Fortune

What can we conclude from all of this? It seems that we humans are extraordinarily lucky to exist at all, since all universal fundamental constants and life-permitting factors really fall into such a very small

The Fine Tuning Argument

life-allowing region. These phenomena are known as the fine-tuning phenomena. Basically, the definition of fine-tuning can be formulated as follows (cf. Mark Saward, "Fine Tuning," 243-253):

> **Definition of fine-tuning:** A universe Φ is fine-tuned for life if there is some constant σ in a physical law of Φ, such that,
> 1. The range of values of σ compatible with the existence of life (life-permitting range) is much smaller than the range of possible values of σ;
> 2. σ is within the life-permitting range;
> 3. Φ is life-permitting.

Traditionally, the fine-tuning phenomena mainly focus on the fundamental constants and life-permitting range. However, the effects of the fundamental constants also depend on the initial conditions. Therefore it is also very important to consider the fine-tuned conditions for life. Besides, if we further focus on the "intelligence-permitting range," some more fine-tuned parameters and conditions have to be considered. Therefore, we can enlarge the fine-tuning phenomena by including the presence, by whatever means (creation or evolution), of intelligence, especially the eventual presence of human beings. Based on the above reasons, the new definition of fine-tuning can be stated as follows:

> **New definition of fine-tuning:** A universe Φ is fine-tuned for intelligent life if there is some constant σ or condition η in a physical law of Φ, such that,
> 1'. The range of values of σ or the condition η compatible with the existence of intelligent life (intelligent-life-permitting range) is much smaller than the range of possible values of σ or η;
> 2'. σ or η is within the intelligent-life-permitting range;
> 3'. Φ is intelligent-life-permitting.

For the statement 1', the range of σ or the condition η for intelligent life being smaller than the possible values of σ or η means that the probability of getting the intelligent-life permitting σ or η is very small. Therefore, the statement 1' can be restated as "the probability of getting the intelligent-life permitting range σ or η is very low". If a certain

GOD DOES EXIST!

condition is highly specific (i.e. many strict and specific requirements are needed), the probability of getting this condition by chance would be very low, and so this condition should be regarded as a fine-tuned condition.

The fine-tuning phenomena can be addressed from either of two worldviews: the theistic worldview and the naturalistic one. In the case of the theistic approach, God is seen as having created the universe within certain parameters such that life would be able to exist on earth. Therefore, the existence of God explains why the universe is fashioned as it is. This modern form of the design argument does not build on analogy, but on certain analytical and philosophical arguments. Richard Swinburne, for example, employs the confirmation principle to show that the fine-tuning phenomena can be best explained by a theistic worldview (cf. "Argument from Fine-Tuning").

According to the naturalistic approach, on the other hand, it is alleged that all of the fine-tuned values in our universe have been generated through purely natural mechanisms. Stephen Hawking (with Leonard Mlodinow, *The Grand Design*, 118), makes his case by arguing that the fine-tuning phenomena may be explained by means of the multiverse theory. This postulates the existence of many different universes, and so of many distinct space-time regions, characterized by different sets of values of the various parameters, and which might be conceived to arise physically in several ways. Obviously, however, the creation of multiple universes out of thin air is a highly speculative endeavor. No evidence whatsoever exists to demonstrate that they are more than merely a figment of a fruitful imagination. According to this view, the vast majority of these space-time regions will not be fine-tuned, but the supposed existence of the ensemble is taken to explain the existence of at least one that is (i.e. the one that we live in). The following arguments and unanswered questions have been lodged against the multiverse theory:

1. Are the infinitely many universes genuinely physically realizable?
2. Is the set of life-bearing universes actually of measure zero in the space of possible universes?
3. Is the infinitely many universes hypothesis testable?

The Fine Tuning Argument

4. Is the hypothesis simple, and therefore of high prior probability? This inquiry tests the hypothesis against the generally accepted and almost universally applied principle of Occam's Razor (Latin: *novacula Occami*) or the law of parsimony (Latin: *lex parsimoniae*). Usually paraphrased as, "the simplest solution is most likely the right one," this principle argues that in no case is it appropriate to choose a prediction that multiplies the number of assumptions essential. Multiplying the number of universes almost to infinity most assuredly complicates the scenario beyond the limits of what is necessary for a plausible solution. And all for what? Purely in order to avoid the option of theism. So, this hypothesis fails the test of Occam's Razor.

5. What is the nature of the explanation provided by the many universes hypothesis? Is it plausible, or does it merely avoid the inevitability of a competing solution? It would seem to be such as to explain literally anything by a shrug of the shoulders—"we just happen to be in a universe like that."

6. Why is there, in this universe, *more* fine-tuning than is required for Life? Probabilistically we would expect to be in a universe which had just enough fine-tuning for life. But that is *not* where we find ourselves. How is this to be explained?

7. Why does our universe occur *now* rather than much earlier, given that, as per this hypothesis, there have been many previous universes? Why does our universe occur *here*, rather than somewhere else, given an ensemble of coexisting universes? It is indeed surprising, and highly improbable, that our universe occurs when and where it does (i.e. *here* and *now*). That would be agreed to by everyone, whichever side of the controversy we are on. Hence, *that* universe, assuming it is one universe in this ensemble of coexisting universes, arbitrarily chosen as it was, has a very slim chance of being fine-tuned for life, and a much slimmer chance still of being the universe that produces us. So *that* universe has a very small chance of being *our* universe, i.e. *this* universe!

8. Why does the order necessary for life persist in this universe? Why not in some other instead? Is there an explanation for our extraordinary good fortune?

9. All current cosmological models involving multiple universes require some kind of mechanism for generating universes. Yet such a "universe generator" would itself require precisely configured

129

physical states, thus begging the question of its initial design. Where did this machine come from and how did it arise? In all currently worked out proposals for what this universe generator could be, such as the Oscillating Big Bang and the Vacuum Fluctuation models, the "generator" itself is governed by an intricate set of laws that allow it to produce universes. So, effectively, we have reasoned ourselves back to our same starting-point, except that we have added a feature that is itself unsubstantiated and lacking entirely in any evidence to justify it. Too, we have come to know a great deal from our experiences with machines that generate other machines. And all that we know tells us that a Designer is required in both instances. There are no self-originating or self-replicating machines. There is always at least one Designer, and sometimes there are a host of them. Clearly we have circled the block and are back to square one again.

10. All things being equal, we should always prefer hypotheses that are natural extrapolations from what we already know about the causal powers of various kinds of entities. Yet, when it comes to explaining the anthropic coincidences, the multiple-worlds hypothesis fails this test, whereas the theistic-design hypothesis does not. Robin Collins has illustrated this point by asking his readers to imagine a paleontologist who posits the existence of an "electromagnetic-bone-producing-field," as opposed to actual dinosaurs, as the explanation for the origin of large fossilized bones that he has discovered. While it could certainly be argued that such a field qualifies as a *possible* explanation for the origin of his fossilized bones, we have no experience of such fields or of their actually *producing* fossilized bones. On this account, the theory of the existence of such a field and its ability to produce fossilized bones of the sort he has found is purely hypothetical. It has no basis in experience, nor does it have a firm basis in logic. At the same time, we have observed animal remains in various phases of decay and preservation in sediments and even in sedimentary rock. Thus, most scientists rightly prefer the actual dinosaur hypothesis over the "apparent dinosaur hypothesis" as an explanation for the origin of such fossils. Similarly, we have no experience of anything like a "universe generator," that is not itself designed, producing finely tuned systems or infinite and exhaustively random ensembles of possibilities. At the same time, we have extensive experience with intelligent agents producing finely-tuned

The Fine Tuning Argument

machines and systems, such as Swiss watches. Hence, when we postulate the existence of a "supermind" (God) to explain the fine tuning of the universe, we are extrapolating from our considerable experience of the causal powers of known entities (in this case, intelligent human beings), whereas when we postulate the existence of an infinite number of separate universes, we are not (cf. Collins, "The Fine-Tuning Design Argument: A Scientific Argument for the Existence of God," 61; cited in Meyer, "Evidence for Design in Physics and Biology," 63).

11. For the many-universes theory to suffice as an explanation for anthropic fine tuning, it must posit an exhaustively random distribution of physical parameters and thus an infinite number of parallel universes to insure that a life-protecting combination of factors will eventually arise and persist for a time sufficient for intelligent life to thrive. Yet neither of the physical models that allow for a multiple-universe interpretation—Everett's quantum mechanical model or Linde's inflationary cosmology—provides a compelling justification for believing that such an exhaustively random and infinite number of parallel universes exists, but instead only a finite and nonrandom set, namely what prevails in our own (cf. Craig, "Cosmos and Creator," 23; cited in Meyer, "Evidence for Design in Physics and Biology," 64).

12. Use of the many-universes theoretical postulate in order to avoid the theistic-design argument betrays a kind of special pleading and metaphysical desperation on the part of its protagonists. As Clifford Longley suggested, "The [anthropic design argument] and what it points to is of such an order of certainty that in any other sphere of science, it would be regarded as settled. To insist otherwise is like insisting that Shakespeare was not written by Shakespeare because it might have been written by a billion monkeys sitting at a billion keyboards typing for a billion years. So it might. But the sight of scientific atheists clutching at such desperate straws has put new spring in the step of theists" (*London Times*, 1989; quoted in Meyer, "Evidence for Design in Physics and Biology," 65).

These are just some of the lingering questions and serious problems with the infinitely many universes hypothesis. Several others have been expressed elsewhere and are equally effective in undermining the legitimacy of this desperate antithesis to a theistic explanation (see

GOD DOES EXIST!

Holder, "Fine-Tuning, Many Universes and Design," 5-24). The ones we have provided above are certainly sufficient to respond to this highly speculative non-answer to what might be theism's most powerful ally in the present highly charged scientific era.

The Explanatory Filter: The Specified Complexity Test

William A. Dembski's insight, first elaborated in his scholarly monograph, *The Design Inference: Eliminating Chance through Small Probabilities* (1998), is that intelligent persons recognize design in the form of what he describes as "specified complexity" or equivalently "specified small probability." In other words, we apprehend design in highly improbable (complex) events that also fit some independently identifiable pattern (specification). In the book he sets out to establish the different approaches by which evidence of intelligent agency could be inferred in natural and social situations.

So, he distinguishes between three general modes of competing explanations in order of their priority: regularity, chance, and design. The processes in which regularity, chance and design are ruled out one by one until only one remains as a reasonable and sufficient explanation for any event, are what he then describes as an "explanatory filter." It is a method that attempts to eliminate competing explanations in a systematic fashion including when a highly improbable event conforms to a discernible pattern that is given independently of the event itself. His purpose was to replace an informal and somewhat unclear criterion (warranted attribution of design, usually by means of intuition, i.e. a thing "seems" or "appears" to be designed) with a more precise, mathematically defined one (specified complexity).

The evidence for the correctness of Dembski's epistemological theory is essentially inductive: he argues that his mathematical criterion agrees in extension with the informal one in all clear cases. Moreover, he defines the specification of an event in terms of the computational resources needed to characterize the event. An event warrants the inferring of design when it meets the dual condition of specified complexity: its probability must be sufficiently low (complexity), and the computational resources needed to define the event must fall below a certain level (λ). His answer to the question of where to set the improbability threshold is that it must fall in a range so low that such an event has a

The Fine Tuning Argument

less than one-half chance of occurring even once in the history of the world. In other words, it must be extraordinarily unlikely to happen in the absence of an intelligent agency.

Robert C. Koons granted that Dembski's model provides a good fit to our intuitive judgments about the conditions of unwarranted design inference, but went on to suggest that an event can be specified in many ways, but that three are especially prominent in this regard: by means of its causes, by means of its intrinsic structure, and by means of its effects. In most cases, he affirmed, if an event can be specified with few resources in terms of either its causes or its intrinsic structure, it will not be an extremely unlikely event. An event with simple causes or with simple internal constitution is an event that has a fairly high prior probability, given the essential connection between simplicity and prior probability. Thus, in general, an event will have specified complexity only when it is specified in terms of its *effects*. An event with a simple effect but with quite complex causes and internal structure can be improbable to any possible degree. Since agency is (by definition) that which orders complex events to a fixed effect, it is quite possible to have a simple effect combined with a complex cause, and for the complex cause to be highly improbable in the absence of a teleological explanation (since teleology is the only alternative to sheer coincidence in such a case (cf. Koons, "Are Probabilities Essential to the Design Argument," 12-13).

As noted above, there are several other interpretations of the fine tuning data that have been observed and have been applied so as to suggest the anthropic principle. One is the so-called "weak anthropic principle." This approach says that the facts assembled to define it do not require any explanation at all. They simply are what they are. Life has appeared and evolved in the universe as it is. Life has acclimated to the prevailing conditions of the universe with which it has had to deal, both in terms of its origin and its maintenance. We shall return to take a more in-depth look into this attempt at resolution of the problem of fine tuning momentarily.

A second approach attempts to explain the fine tuning in terms of the natural laws that prevail in the universe. They are as they are because natural law required them to meet the particular criteria that they did. They could not have been any other way than the way they turned

GOD DOES EXIST!

out. Natural law forced them into the parameters to which they conformed. Appeals to natural law have proven, however, to be the least satisfactory way of understanding the predominant conditions and parameters of the universe. The precise "dial settings" of the different constants of physics are specific features *of the laws of nature themselves*. For example, the gravitational constant G determines just how strong gravity will be, given two bodies of known mass separated by a known distance. The constant G is a term within the equation that describes the gravitational attraction. In this same way, all of the constants of the fundamental laws of physics are features of the laws themselves. Therefore, the laws cannot explain these features, being that they comprise the very features that we need to explain. Need we say that this attempt at explanation is an *argumentum ad circulum*? As Davies admitted, the laws of physics "seem themselves to be the product of exceedingly ingenious design" (*The Superforce*, 243).

Further, natural laws by definition describe phenomena that conform to regular or repetitive patterns. Yet the idiosyncratic values of the physical constants and initial conditions of the universe constitute a highly irregular and nonrepetitive ensemble. It seems unlikely, therefore, that any law could explain why all the fundamental constants have precisely the values they do. Why, for example, does the gravitational constant have exactly the value 6.67×10^{-11}? Why not something else? (cf. Meyer, "Evidence for Design in Physics and Biology," 58-60).

The third approach attempted by those who wish to "explain away" the evidence are those explanations based upon chance. As per this view, things turned out as they did because of a "grand roll of the dice" that turned out in our favor. Of course, we are not dealing here with a single roll of the dice, but of millions of them, with every one of them ending up in favor of the existence of intelligent life on earth. In all of these efforts, there is a denial that the fine tuning evidence is explicable on the ground that there was an intelligent agent superintending the process. For further discussion of this aspect of the question, we refer the reader to the next chapter where we deal with the extreme unlikelihood of that being the explanation of all of these physical constants coming together by chance.

The Fine Tuning Argument

Of the three approaches outlined above, the most popular has been the "weak anthropic principle" (WAP). At first it seemed very appealing to a great number of theorists, especially those who were dedicated atheists. Its popularity, though, has waned over time. Advocates of WAP argued that if the universe had not been fine-tuned sufficiently to allow for life, then humans would not be here to observe it. And so, as far as they are concerned, the fine tuning issue requires no formal explanation.

Of course, that is not a very satisfying resolution to the problem. It leaves us with more questions than answers. As a consequence, this approach has received severe criticism from philosophers of both physics and cosmology. John Leslie and William Lane Craig, for example, have insisted that such fine tuning does require some sort of explanation. They have argued that even though we humans should not be surprised to find ourselves living in a universe suited for life (by definition), we ought to be surprised to learn that the conditions necessary for life are *so vastly improbable*.

Leslie likens our situation to that of a blindfolded man who has discovered that, against all odds, he has survived a firing squad of one hundred expert marksmen. Though his continued existence is certainly consistent with the theory that all of the experts' bullets missed him, it does not explain why the marksmen *did* miss. Did all of the experts *intend* to miss him? Were all of the rifles loaded with blank ammunition? Did God perform a miracle in stopping all of the bullets from penetrating his flesh? Or, was he simply the luckiest man who has ever lived? Some explanation is demanded by the phenomenal circumstance in which he finds himself. A shrug of the shoulders and a, "So what?" does not seem to be an adequate response to so unlikely an event as he has experienced.

In essence, the weak anthropic principle wrongly asserts that the statement of a necessary condition of an event eliminates the need for a causal explanation of that event. Ordinarily, though, this is an unsatisfactory way to deal with data of any kind. Why should it be deemed adequate, or even tolerable for that matter, in this instance? Let us illustrate the point. Oxygen is a necessary prerequisite of fire. Fire cannot happen without it. But simply saying this does not explain either the

GOD DOES EXIST!

San Francisco fire of 1851 or the great Chicago fire of 1871. Many rather natural questions arise in an instance of such oversimplification. In fact, to simply say that the devastating fire that consumed the greater part of San Francisco in 1851 happened because there was an ample supply of oxygen present in the atmosphere at the time to permit such a horrendous event to occur, would only raise more questions than it answers. It would leave the hearer stroking his chin and perhaps scratching his head. Being that oxygen is almost always present anywhere on earth, we would be left to ask, "What does that have to do with it?"

Similarly, it is agreed by all that the fine tuning of the physical constants of the universe is a necessary precondition for the existence and maintenance of life. But that does not explain, nor does it eliminate the need to explain, the origin of the fine tuning that has been observed in such magnificent profusion in our universe. Where did it come from? Why is it present at all? We know that if we were not here to observe it and measure it, it would still be there, only unobserved and unmeasured. But that would not alter *the bare fact of it*. And it is the bare fact of it with which we must intellectually wrestle. So, we are left with the same queries, yet unanswered, if we deem the WAP a satisfactory response to it. Where did it come from? And, why is it present at all? The weak anthropic principle is not an answer to anything. In truth, it is rather an effort at avoiding the real issue raised by the bare fact of cosmic fine tuning.

Examples of Anthropic Coincidences

Up to this point we have only cursorily alluded to the anthropic coincidences that occur in nature. It is time for us to look at a few of them more specifically. While there are many examples, hundreds of them in fact, of claimed anthropic coincidences that can be found in the literature on the topic, the following ones are the most significant of the lot:

1. ***Electromagnetic and Gravitational Force Ratio.*** The electromagnetic force is 39 orders of magnitude stronger than the gravitational force. If they were more compatible in strength, stars would have collapsed long before life would have had a chance to exist (or evolve).

2. ***Vacuum Energy Density.*** The vacuum energy density (or energy density of space) of the universe is at least 120 orders of magnitude lower than some theoretical estimates. If at any time it were as large as these calculations suggest, the universe would have

The Fine Tuning Argument

quickly blown apart. Likewise, physicists have calculated that the value of the cosmological constant must be exact to 1 part in 10^{120}. Shortly before the cosmological constant (λ) was discovered, astrophysicist Lawrence Krauss noted that its addition to the Big Bang model "would involve the most extreme fine-tuning problem known to physics" ("The End of the Age Problem," 461).

3. **Cosmic Mass Density.** The cosmic mass density is critical to life. Physicists have calculated that for physical life ever to be possible in our universe, the overall cosmic mass density must be fine-tuned to a mere 1 part in 10^{60}.

4. **Electron Mass.** The electron's mass is less than the difference in the masses of the neutron and proton. Thus, a free neutron can decay into a proton, electron, and antineutrino. If this were not the case, the neutron would be stable and most of the protons and electrons in the early universe would have combined to form neutrons, leaving little hydrogen to act as the main component and fuel of stars.

5. **Neutron Density.** The neutron is heavier than the proton, but not so much heavier that neutrons cannot be bound in nuclei, where conservation of energy prevents the neutrons from decaying. Without neutrons we would not have the heavier elements needed for building complex systems such as life.

6. **Carbon Nucleus Energy Level.** The carbon nucleus has an excited energy level at around 7.65 million electron-volts (McV). Without this state, insufficient carbon would be manufactured in stars to form the basis for life. Using anthropic arguments, astronomer Fred Hoyle predicted this energy level before it was confirmed experimentally (cf. Hoyle, et. al., "A State in C12 Predicted from Astrophysical Evidence," 1095).

7. **The Speed of Light.** The constant of the speed of light, 299,792,458 kilometers per second, is critical to the existence of life. A faster speed would cause energy (E) to increase dramatically, burning up life on the earth. A lower speed for light would cause things to freeze.

8. **The Age of the Universe Conducive to the Possibility of Life.** The earth had to appear in the process of the formation of the universe, at a certain stage, or else life would have been impossible. Several generations of giant stars had to have fused enough heavy elements to allow for the proper earth chemistry. Also, the earth

had to be located in the proper spot in the galaxy for life to appear. Both conditions were met, and so life appeared and thrived.

9. **Small-mass and Large-mass Stars.** Both types of luminaries are required in order for life to exist in the universe. For this to be possible, the ratio of the electromagnetic force constant to the gravitational force constant (see point 1) must be correct within 1 part in 10^{40}. An increase or decrease in this ratio by only that factor would make life untenable (cf. Ross, *The Creator and the Cosmos,* 152-53).

In addition to these major considerations, as scientists have continued to probe more deeply and pursue this line of investigation, each year around 10 to 15 new critical parameters have been discovered. At this juncture there are far too many of them for us even to mention them here. One author recently noted that the list is up to around 152. Such matters as the following all have to be considered: earth's distance from the sun is suited for life, not too close and not too far away; the sun's location relative to the center of the galaxy, since it had to be born one third of the way out from the galactic center in order for life to be a possibility; the sun's mass is the key to energy distribution to the earth; the sun's short-term and long-term luminosity variability is in proper ranges for photosynthesis to be possible; the tilt of the planetary axis is essential for seasonality; the presence of all three forms of water (liquid, ice, gas) are essential to maximize life variables; the single moon circling earth is critical for tidal forces, but more than one would eventuate tidal instability; the ratio of oceans to continents must be correct to keep temperatures stable since land and water absorb heat at different rates; the position and mass of Jupiter relative to earth is significant because its gravity is critical to life on the earth; atmospheric transparency is important both for the rate of photosynthesis and the degree of energy transfer to earth; the carbon dioxide level must be within specific parameters for vegetation stabilization; the oxygen level parameters are important for ozone protection and amount of breathable air for animal life; chlorine quantity in the atmosphere is critical for developing electrolyte balance in living organisms; the level of phosphorus in the crust of the earth is important for health of bones and muscles in animals; selenium and fluorine in the earth's crust are critical for animal life; volcanic activity in the crust is necessary for spreading soil nutrients and creation of new land mass, but if it were out of balance it would

The Fine Tuning Argument

block out the sun's light and impede plant photosynthesis; quantity of forest and grass fires are necessary on the one hand for the destruction of undergrowth and dead trees and revitalization of nutrients in the soil, but in too great profusion, the smoke would block out critical sunlight. This list goes on interminably. But from this partial listing we are able to determine that the conditions of planet earth are anything but random. A variation of any one of them of only 10 percent, and in some cases as little as one-thousandth of a percent, would make life impossible. So many delicate balances and constants are clear evidence of planning and of intelligent agency.

Astrophysicist Hugh Ross applied probability theory to the 128 parameters that he listed as the most significant ones, and he summarized his findings as follows:

1. The probability of all 128 factors being found in any one planet is 1 chance in 10^{166}.
2. The maximum number of planets in the universe is 10^{22}.
3. Putting these together, there is only one chance in 10^{144} ($10^{166} - 10^{22} = 10^{144}$) that any other planet like earth exists.

That is an exceedingly small number. How small? One writer has likened it statistically to winning 21 lotteries in a row with a single ticket purchase for each one. It would be comparable to taking all the subatomic particles from almost two entire universes the size of ours and randomly picking a preselected particle (Ross, ibid., 198; Muncaster, *Dismantling Evolution*, 212-215). Essentially, it is like saying that it is impossible probability-wise. This is a hard-science based calculation. What it tells us is that design is evident in every aspect of life on earth. Design is proof that there was a Designer.

Conclusion

Stephen C. Meyer provides two quotations from noteworthy astronomers which offer insight into this interesting situation. This evidence is so powerful that its evidentiary force is irrefutable:

> As astronomer George Greenstein mused, "the thought insistently arises that some supernatural agency, or rather Agency, must be involved. Is it possible that suddenly, without intending to, we have stumbled upon scientific proof for the existence of a Supreme Being? Was it God

who stepped in and so providentially crafted the cosmos for our benefit? (*The Symbiotic Universe: Life and Mind in the Cosmos,* 26-27). For many scientists, the design hypothesis seems the most obvious and intuitively plausible answer to this question. As Sir Fred Hoyle commented, "a commonplace interpretation of the facts suggests that a super intellect has monkeyed with physics, as well as chemistry and biology, and that there are no blind forces worth speaking about in nature" ("The Universe: Past and Present Reflections," 16). Many physicists now concur ("Evidence for Design in Physics and Biology," 57-58).

Such admissions as these are not easily made in the present environment in the sciences. Still, these towering figures in science are being forced to admit what it is difficult for them to say. Similarly, William Dembski, in his book *Intelligent Design: The Bridge Between Science and Theology*, wrote specifically about discovery of some of these parameters and what they seem to be telling us:

> Anthropic coincidences signify all the prior conditions that need to be precisely satisfied and correlated for human life to be possible. . . . For example, the fundamental forces of nature have to fall within very precise tolerances for the basic constituents of the universe to support life. If the strong nuclear force were slightly stronger, hardly any hydrogen would form because its nuclei would be unstable. If, on the other hand, it were slightly weaker, no elements other than hydrogen would form. Similarly if the force of gravity were slightly stronger, stars would burn out too rapidly to support life on surrounding planets. If, on the other hand, it were slightly weaker, there would not be enough heavy elements with which to build surrounding planets.
>
> Such anthropic coincidences abound. . . . With the emergence and development of the universe, we are in the position of a cook confronted with a cake requiring hundreds of ingredients, each given in just the right amounts and all amounts being precisely proportioned so that any divergence, whether in the amount of the ingredients or in their relative proportions, results in total failure of the cake.
>
> Not surprisingly, scientists are asking themselves how all those "ingredients" needed to produce the universe came together in the first place. They offer two answers: chance and design. Of these, design has proven the only viable contender (265).

Alternative theories of how these intricate settings on so many different aspects of the known universe came to be programmed for in-

The Fine Tuning Argument

telligent life to exist have fallen flat at every turn. How phenomenally complex they are and how intrinsic they are to the warp and woof of the universe is indeed mind-boggling. As well, how little it would have taken at any point along the way to bring the whole thing crashing in on itself is hard to fathom. The tiniest miscalculation could have frustrated the possibility for intelligent life to flourish! And yet we all are here to contemplate these amazing realities and to appreciate the genius of the One who has been at the helm of the universe all the while, guiding it unerringly toward its goal.

Those scientists who have duly noted these features of the finely tuned universe and yet have doubted His intelligent agency and have opted, at all costs, to explain away the wisdom of the Almighty, are without excuse for their blindness in so doing. The average irreligious fellow, who has never been made aware of these phenomena, can plead ignorance because these facts are far above his head. But the academic and the professional cannot so plead. In our opinion, if they deny the work of an intelligent agency in this case, namely God, then their entitlement to the designation of objectivity must be forever surrendered. That is a claim that rings hollow in this instance. They are unbelievers for one reason only, and that is on account of their unwillingness to consider theism as a viable alternative to their atheism. I say this with full knowledge of how it may sound to some readers. But I say it because there is not anywhere, anything in all of God's repertoire of proofs for His involvement in the vast creation, that serves to demonstrate more profoundly or undeniably that He exists and is in control of the material cosmos even at the present hour.

Questions for Discussion

1. Who was Copernicus and what is he known for? What is the Copernican principle? How has it been abused over the years since it was first delineated?
2. Define the idea of a "fine tuned universe." What might that entail?
3. Why do many cosmologists and philosophers speak of an anthropic principle being at work in the cosmos? What does that word mean, and how is it employed to describe our universe? Are you comfortable with using such language?

GOD DOES EXIST!

4. Give some examples of the anthropic principle. Do you find the concept convincing?

5. What is the "weak anthropic principle," and what are some of its weaknesses?

6. What is the "many worlds" or "multiple universes" hypothesis? What is the reason for its being promoted? Do you find it compelling?

7. Are you familiar with the term "multiverse"?

8. What are some of the arguments that are lodged against the theory? Which one of those listed, if any, would you consider the most devastating to the viewpoint?

9. Can you explain the concept of a universe generator? How do you perceive the idea? Does it make sense to you, or would you consider the whole idea absurd?

10. List a few of the cases of cosmic fine tuning that you consider most impressive. How are they to be explained?

11. Dr. Stephen Meyer's story of the cosmic explorer who visits the control room of the universe is one of the most impressively simple but powerfully illustrative of any we remember. Can you summarize it? Retell it in your own words.

Chapter 7
The Probability Argument

For more than two thousand years many leading thinkers, from Plato to Aquinas to Newton, argued that the natural world manifests evidence of a designing intelligence, a preexistent mind, often referred to as "God," or simply as "the Creator." During the late nineteenth century, however, this general theory of origins was rejected by many scientists. Charles Darwin's theory of evolution by natural selection, and other materialistic theories of the origin of life, the solar system, and of the universe, portrayed nature as a self-creating and self-existent machine. It was argued that it does not show any evidence of design by a directing agency or superintending intelligence. The emphasis was being placed on the latter aspect of that description.

Of course, even Darwinists from the start have acknowledged that biological organisms do "appear" to be designed. As Richard Dawkins,

GOD DOES EXIST!

a leading spokesman for the Darwinian camp, has admitted, "Biology is the study of complicated things that give the appearance of having been designed for a purpose." He went on to say, ". . . the living results of natural selection overwhelmingly impress us with the appearance of design as if by a master watchmaker, impress us with the illusion of design and planning" (*The Blind Watchmaker*, 1).

Nevertheless, Darwinists have insisted that this appearance is merely illusory, since the mechanisms of natural selection can explain the observed complexity of living things. Thus, for most of the twentieth century, science seemed intent upon undermining the argument for design as well as the long-held belief that the universe and the life that is its crowning achievement was created (cf. M. Behe, W. Dembski, S. Meyer, *Science and Evidence for Design in the Universe*, 11).

So science gradually became the realm of the atheists. Most of their arguments began and ended with science. In recent years that has begun to change in a very serious way, however. Science has begun to be the first redoubt of a great many theists. As a consequence, many atheistic scientists have begun attempting to "explain away" simple scientific observations that do not seem any longer to support their cause. Clearly the tables have begun to turn in a most intriguing way. More about this momentarily.

The greatest challenge of the thoughtful and reflective is the question of ultimate origin. Where did the universe come from? How did it get here? Did it "stumble" into existence through a series of marvelous accidents, or was it designed and then created by an intelligent agency? As one protagonist inquired: "How did nothing become something and turn itself into everything?" How did life arrive on the scene? Was life designed? And, was *intelligent life*, the pinnacle of all life forms, created, or was it the product of wholly material laws and processes? These two main lines of inquiry have engaged the intellects and stirred the imaginations of the curious from ancient times to the present. Did God create the universe and its finest treasures (life and intelligence) or did they somehow develop through a series of serendipitous accidents? It seems that these two options pretty much exhaust the list of possibilities, even though there have been various suggested amplifications of the one as well as of the other. The universe began either by chance or by design. Life also began either by chance or by design.

The Probability Argument

Stating the Formal Argument

As we have done in the earlier chapters of this work, it is important to define precisely the nature of the argument, so as to see it clearly and then argue it accordingly. As in the earlier instances, the proof has to be stated in the clearest language possible. So, we shall do the same in this case. Since we are dealing with two potential solutions to the question of ultimate origins, it requires that we construct the syllogism in a slightly more complicated form than in some of the other arguments:

Premise 1: There are only two potential explanations for the origin of the universe and of the life within it.

Premise 2: One explanation is material evolution, which posits that natural law acting on the material substance of the universe, gave rise to the universe itself and of the life within it.

Premise 3: A second explanation is theism, which posits that God designed and created the universe itself, and then the life within it.

Premise 4: The materialistic explanation is statistically implausible.

Conclusion 1: Therefore theism is the only logically feasible explanation.

Conclusion 2: Therefore God must exist.

Premises 1-3 are simple statements about the problem itself and of the potential resolutions to it. One might quibble with precisely how they are stated, but in general it could be said that they are noncontroversial. Premise 4 is where the controversy heats up. And even though most atheists will agree that the odds are clearly against the possibility of the universe appearing and reaching its present form without being guided and superintended, they would still attempt to make the case for it having happened that way nonetheless. So this is where the battle must be fought. The first and second conclusions only follow if Premise 4 can be sustained. But if Premise 4 can be sustained, then both conclusions logically and necessarily follow. In our view there do not appear to be any other possibilities. The universe and the life within it either came to exist randomly by chance or else by the design of a Creator, and God is the only Creator that can be conceived. Therefore God must exist.

GOD DOES EXIST!

Random Universe or Universe on Purpose?

As this book is being written, the most commonly accepted state-of-the-art hypothesis for the origin of the universe is the "hot Big-Bang" theory. This viewpoint states that the universe has expanded from a primordial hot and dense initial condition.

The Big-Bang theory has been extremely successful in correlating the observable properties of the universe with the known underlying physical laws. How did we arrive at this level of our understanding of the physical processes that took place at the beginning of the present universe? How was this consensus arrived at? Perhaps a brief summary would be appropriate at this juncture.

In the early part of the twentieth century the law of universal gravitation was investigated and it was then possible to discuss the formation of the galaxies (and the stars within those galaxies) as an example of gravity acting to pull large masses together.

By the 1940s, science had learned enough about the atomic nucleus and the more common elementary particles to take another giant step. The process by which protons and neutrons came together to form the nuclei of hydrogen and helium, the raw material of the stars, was comprehended. This brought science within what was estimated to be about three minutes of the moment of creation.

By the mid-1960s, increasing insight into the structure and behavior of elementary particles (an insight gained through a tremendous effort on the part of a large number of experimental and theoretical physicists) allowed researchers to trace out the somewhat convoluted development of the particles that eventually condensed into nuclei.

By 1970 the boundaries of knowledge had been pushed back to within 1 millisecond (10^{-3} second) of the Big Bang. Spurred by the unresolved problems of particle physics, a new type of theory was born, one that resulted in an immense simplification of the seemingly complex subatomic world. Called *gauge theories*, these new ideas brought with them an entirely new way of looking at natural phenomena. Such theories attempt to explain the dynamics of elementary particles. In this overlapping area between high-energy physics and astronomy, the frontier of knowledge of the early universe has been pushed back

The Probability Argument

again, to somewhere between 10^{-35} and 10^{-43} second of the Big Bang, an interval so short that our concept of time itself may have to be redefined before science can proceed any further (cf. J. S. Trefil, *The Moment of Creation*, 3-5).

Yet this theory still cannot describe what came *before* the Big-Bang event or account for what happened during the first miniscule time-fraction after the initial Big-Bang, referred to as Planck time, named after Max Planck, founder of quantum theory. A unit of Planck time is the time it takes for light to travel, in a vacuum, a single unit of Planck length. These are physical units of measurement defined exclusively in terms of five universal physical constants: (1) the gravitational constant; (2) the reduced Planck constant; (3) the speed of light in a vacuum; (4) the Coulomb constant; and, (5) Boltzmann's constant. Ultimately, Planck time is derived from the field of mathematical physics known as dimensional analysis, which studies units of measurement and physical constants. They are often referred to by physicists as "God's units" because they represent an attempt to eliminate anthropocentric arbitrariness from the system of units, unlike the meter and second, which exist for purely historical reasons and are not derived from nature (cf. https://www.universetoday.com/79418/planck-time/). In general, any model of the institution of the universe that involves preliminary conditions or requires an initial state is incomplete since it lacks an explanation of what created these initial conditions.

A few theories have been put forward in accordance with this line of thought and in the hope of resolving some of these issues. Alexander Vilenkin suggested a cosmological scenario for the creation of the universe from "nothing" (the author's own words; cf. "Creation of Universes from Nothing," *Physics Letters B* 117.1 [1982]: 25-28). He opined:

> The standard hot cosmological model gives a successful description of many features of the evolution of the universe. However, it is not totally satisfactory, since it requires rather unnatural initial conditions at the Big Bang. One has to postulate that the universe has started in a homogeneous and isotropic state with tiny density fluctuations which are to evolve into galaxies. Homogeneity and isotropy must extend to scales far exceeding the causal horizon at the Planck time. In addition, the energy density of the universe must be tuned to be near the critical density with an incredible accuracy of $\sim 10^{-55}$ (ibid., 25).

GOD DOES EXIST!

His cosmological model has the universe created by quantum tunneling from literally nothing into a de Sitter space; after the tunneling, the model evolves along the lines of the inflationary scenario. His proposed reconstruction interacts gravitational and matter fields, and a symmetric vacuum state that has a nonzero energy density. Therefore, the initial state does not, in fact, represent an absolute, pure, "nothing."

Another perspective, put forward by E. P. Tryon, suggested that our universe was initiated spontaneously from nothing ("Ex Nihilo") as a "quantum fluctuation of some pre-existing true vacuum, or state of nothingness" ("Is the Universe a Vacuum Fluctuation?" *Nature* [London], 246.5433 [1973]: 396-397). Following this line of thought, the universe is a fluctuation of the vacuum in the sense of the quantum field theory. Therefore, the initial state is not property-less, and it requires an explanation of how fluctuations can evolve from "nothingness." In the same manner, those theories that support the emergence of the universe by quantum tunneling, from vacuum in quantum-cosmology or from the string perturbative vacuum, encounter the same limitations. Such views are plentiful. At any rate, several physical theories have suggested that the universe was created out of nothing, but while each defined "nothing" differently, this "nothing" was not free from substance or matter. So it was not really a creation "out of nothing," at least not in the strict sense of what that expression seems to imply for most people of ordinary intelligence.

As a response to these theories, and hoping to address and perhaps overcome their deficiencies, the "Creation *Ex Nihilo*" or CEN theory was proposed by Maya Lincoln and Avi Wasser, following the lead of J. Wheeler (1990), J. Bekenstein (2003), and V. Vedral (2012). It was aimed at describing the origin of the universe from "nothing" in information terms. The notion of bit-based information at the core of the universe's evolution suggests that the physical world "is made of information, with energy and matter as incidentals." Accordingly, information gives rise to "every it—every particle, every field of force, even the space-time continuum itself." Therefore, what we refer to as reality, "arises in the last analysis from the posing of yes-no questions." Vlatko Vedral, on the same line, claimed that information is the building block from which everything is constructed and that all natural phenomena can be explained in information terms: "The universe and its workings are the ebb and

The Probability Argument

flow of information. We are all transient patterns of information, passing on the recipe for our basic forms to future generations using four-letter digital code called DNA" ("Decoding Reality: The Universe as Quantum Information").

Maya Lincoln and Avi Wasser of the University of Haifa in Israel state their unique perspective on the theory as follows: "According to the newly suggested theory, CEN, in the beginning there was nothing—no material, no energy, no space and no time. This situation was fully symmetric with no entropy. Therefore, this initial state was allegedly static, with no motive for change." From a philosophical viewpoint they conceive the universe "as a self-excited machine" as follows. We can refer to the dynamicity laws in the universe platform as the "code of the universe" or "code of nature." In the beginning, the hypothetical Universe machine is self-ignited from "nothing." In the next phases, it "holds" at each time the current universe state (information), which encapsulates the probabilities of the next arrangement. An input of potentially additional NIEs (Nullifying Information Elements—information elements that co-exist simultaneously and cancel each other) triggers the "reading" of the code of the universe/nature. As a result, the code is executed, changes are "computed" and implemented—in terms of new relationships between NIEs, and as a consequence the machine "outputs" the next universe state (information) ("Spontaneous Creation of the universe *Ex Nihilo*," *Physics of the Dark Universe* 2.4 [Dec. 2013]: 195-199).

The viewpoint of these authors is that in terms of information systems, it is possible to present "nothing" as a system which consists of infinite information elements and infinite anti-information elements that coexist simultaneously and therefore cancel each other. Therefore, such a "nothing system" results in no material, no energy, and as a matter of fact, no physical existence of anything in terms of information. According to the theory, prior to the formation of the universe, this system was symmetrical, with infinite items of information and anti-information nullifying one another.

However, according to a commonly known phenomenon in physics, such systems are prone to a "Spontaneous Symmetry Break" (SSB), when the unequal number of bits at each bit group destabilizes the information balance. This breaking generates information which results in energy and

GOD DOES EXIST!

by that transforms the information system from a "nothing system" into a material system. At this point, then, the "Creation Ex Nihilo" (CEN) theory converges with the Big-Bang theory and other common theories in the field, from the stage in which the universe becomes material.

According to the authors, the newly innovative theory explains additional phenomena of theoretical physics, part of which have been considered unsolvable until today, such as the sources of the second law of thermodynamics, the phenomenon of matter and antimatter, and other phenomena these scholars intend later to explain (cf. Ilan Yavelberg, "How Was the Universe Created Out of Nothing?" *Innovations Report* (March 13, 2014).

This way of seeing the beginning of the universe may seem exhilarating for some physicists, especially those who are immersed in the new and dynamic field of information technology and computing, but for most average people this sounds like an "off the wall" notion that replaces God with a universal supercomputer. If we were to assume that this representation of reality is accurate, we are once again brought back to "square one." In other words, it reasons back to where we started. It motivates us to inquire: who or what made this universal supercomputer and who or what wrote the software that makes it perform its functions? If the answer is "God," then why do we need either the supercomputer or the instruction set to run it?

Gottfried Wilhelm Leibnitz, the famous German mathematician and philosopher, and one of the inventors of the mathematical technique of calculus, used the following logic in his proof of the existence of God. It was imminently simple. He found it surprising that something, rather than nothing, exists in the universe, given that nothing is by far the simpler state. If nothingness is the simpler state, then why did it not persist? The only reason he could find for something to exist at all is that an independent Being created that something. This for him was enough evidence, by itself, to suggest an external Influencer, that Influencer being God. To his way of thinking, therefore, God *must* exist.

So in a sense it could be said that even Leibnitz, like so many others who have shared his perspective on the matter, could find no better answer to the creation *ex nihilo* question, which is where we always

The Probability Argument

seem to end up after all, than postulating a supernatural being. Atheists, however, have tended frantically to look elsewhere, essentially anywhere imaginable, to answer this ultimate question of the existence of everything. It has been sought out through the search for a law or universal principle, or in the most recent example a universe made up of Quantum Information, which might have the potential to evade the existence of a Supreme Being.

The trickiness of having a law that explains everything without postulating a law (or some kind of general principle) in the first place, was addressed by Oxford physicist David Deutsch. On this issue, Deutsch reasoned as follows: If there were no all-explanatory physical principle P approachable by the methods of science, this would presumably mean that there exist aspects of the natural world that are fundamentally inaccessible to science. In other words, if we cannot find an overarching principle, then science cannot explain the universe and fails in its ultimate objective. Deutsch reasons that any inability to explain the universe through a single principle P would run directly counter to rationalism and "to our view of physics as the universal science, which has hitherto been the driving force behind progress in the subject and which we should be extremely reluctant to abandon." This is a heady admission for a physicist to make, but the associated reluctance of a rationalist to let go of this starting point is fully understandable. The problem, though, has not gone away in spite of its resistance to an easy answer.

However, as Deutsch goes on to point out, the flip-side of this is also problematic. If there were such an all-explanatory principle P within physics, its origin would be forever insoluble, given that no principle (or law) can explain its own origin or form. It would seem to be like asking an air-conditioner, "Why are you an air-conditioner and not a chair?" Clearly the answer lies outside of the air-conditioner, because the air-conditioner itself was just made that way. So, paradoxically, P, the ultimate principle in physics or the law that explains everything, just cannot be. It cannot be what it is intended to explain. Again, its origin must lie outside of physics. Physicist John Wheeler described deduction without principles as a "law without law." He reasoned that if we can explain laws of physics without invoking any *a priori* laws of physics, then we would be in a good position to explain everything. It is this view that is

GOD DOES EXIST!

the common take on the notion of "creation out of nothing," or *creation ex nihilo* (cf. V. Vedral, *Decoding Reality*, 1-13).

It should be evident to the reader that this argument involves circular reasoning. Ultimately it always leads us back to the Grand Originator or Creator of the universe itself. Whether we speak of the beginning in terms of a natural law, an ultimate principle P, the vacuum of tranquil nothingness, quantum vacuum, a hot Big-Bang, or whatever, it always takes us back to the question of who or what caused it to happen. Who or what got it started. Who or what went before it.

At the same time, we all understand the chances of something randomly deriving from nothing. *The chances are zero*. It did not happen because it could not ever happen. *Nothing ever comes from nothing*. On the simple level of the average person that is well understood. Only in the case of magic and miracle can an exception be made to this principle. And we explain most magic as being a ruse or sleight of hand trickery, and most miracle claims as mere frauds. We only entertain the notion of biblical miracles on the basis of the idea that it is God who made the laws of the universe, and God has the power to set them aside when He is minded to do so. Otherwise neither magic nor miracles happen. So, God is the only possible explanation for creation *ex nihilo*. This is precisely the declaration of Genesis and of the remainder of Scripture. God spoke it into existence. Prior to that, there was nothing, only God. God is the only eternal reality.

On the other hand, it is only in the environment of the "group think" of professional academics and elite intellectuals where atheism is the precondition of all discussions that it could be or would be reasoned that perhaps in this one particular instance, the greatest of all cases, there was an exception to this rock solid rule of our existence, "something came from nothing, and from that came everything." We say it again, *the chances are zero*. Only God could make that happen in an act of sheer creative energy. Before that happened, there was only God.

What Are the Chances of Life Appearing by Accident Rather Than by Design?

I remember when I was in an introductory Biology course in my freshman year at Wayne State University, that the professor spoke non-

The Probability Argument

chalantly about proteins forming in a "primordial soup" when life began on the planet. Proteins are, of course, the primary building blocks of life. All living things are composed of proteins. Those proteins which are said to have "formed" inexplicably in that ancient pool, according to his reconstruction of events, subsequently constituted the basis of all of the various life forms that are found on the earth today. He addressed the topic as if it was a simple and easy thing to happen. He spoke of it almost as if that sort of thing happens all the time. And, I suppose that he believed that they did, for that is precisely what would have been essential for it to happen that way at all. Not only so, but it would have had to occur repeatedly, as many times as it took, until a self-replicating strain of living things formed for the first time. That much is certain.

However, he did not deal with the question of *how* those original proteins actually formed or how they subsequently developed the ability to duplicate themselves and thus assure their continuance. Being that they were living things, they would certainly eventually die. So, at their inception they had to be capable of some sort of self-replication or reproduction. If they were not, then their death would spell the extinction of all life and end the whole experiment for at least millions, if not billions of years.

But, that represents quite a challenge, for as we all know, the process of reproduction is a very complicated phenomenon, even in regard to the most rudimentary forms of living things. Moreover, this fact suggests that not only would functional proteins have had to form once only, but many, many times in order for them to develop the mechanism and systems necessary for them to be capable of replicating themselves and thus passing on to another generation their genetic footprint.

So, whatever the unlikelihood of it happening in the first place, it would then have to occur not just once, but repeatedly in order to put all of the essential ingredients together at just the right moment for a functional and sustainable protein to appear. This raises the bar of probability to a level where the word "impossible" becomes entirely appropriate. And, we have not yet gotten beyond the stage of a single viable protein, let alone a creature that is composed of hundreds or even thousands of such proteins and the biochemical systems that employ them!

GOD DOES EXIST!

Truly, the good professor, like so many others of his ilk, was leaving out just a few things and oversimplifying the matter of origins in a way that is less than praiseworthy. He was able to escape careful scrutiny of his simplistic analysis that particular day by a group of seventeen to twenty-one year old students, but more and more these days such fellows are being called out on their speculative and unproven assumptions and oversimple reconstructions by their own peers in the scientific community, even if their students continue to sit reverently and listen respectfully without challenging them.

What Are the Obstacles to a Single Functional Protein Randomly Appearing in Nature?

Several hurdles must be gotten over before ordinary people will be able to believe that a functional protein randomly appeared in a natural setting on the primordial earth. Scientists often make reference to these obstacles as if they represented "no big deal" to them. But they *are* a "big deal" to those of us who are not confirmed atheists who are looking for any excuse at all to believe in the theory of unaided evolution of life by chance. It will take more to convince us than a shrug of the shoulders, a wink and a nod. In our view these hurdles are enormous and the odds of such events occurring in nature by chance alone are all but impossible. The following is a brief list of these difficulties, which will be introduced here and discussed in more detail later:

1. Odds of the random appearance of a single functional sequence of amino acids in nature, which would require a minimum of 150 amino acids, are exceedingly slim. Amino acids appear in two forms in nature, left-handed and right-handed. However, all living things are composed of left-handed amino acids. This is described as *the chirality problem* in biology. So, what is the probability that 150 left-handed amino acids might randomly appear in a row? Given that the odds of getting left-handed amino acids would be 50%, the probability of having 150 left-handed ones occur together is $(½)^{150}$ or 1 chance in 10^{45}. This is about the same likelihood as flipping a coin 150 times in a row and getting heads every time. Most ordinary people have difficulty being convinced that this could ever happen.

2. Assuming that you were able to collect 150 left-handed amino acids in one place, you would next have to bond them together

The Probability Argument

with peptide bonds. Peptide bonds hold the sequences of amino acids together in proteins; but not all bonds are peptide bonds in nature, hence the odds are 1 in 2 or 50%. Therefore, for a single basic protein the chances are 1 in 2^{150} that the proper peptide bonds will form, holding the sequences together in their proper order. Again, having all of these fall into place precisely as needed is comparable to flipping a coin 150 times and having heads appear all 150 times. This is what is called in biology *the bonding problem*.

3. Proteins also require that the amino acids appear in a very specific order on the string of molecules and that they be folded into a proper form for them to function as intended. Each amino acid must be placed exactly where it belongs on the string or it will not fold properly and it will not function in delivering the appropriate information to the system. This is described as *specified complexity*, or *specified information*, when it appears and functions as it should. This is even more daunting, numerically speaking, than the other two problems. The reason for this is that amino acids are comparable to a 20-character chemical alphabet. So, at each site on the string there are 20 different amino acids to choose from. (Many more appear in nature, but only 20 are useful to construct living organisms.) Therefore, there are 10^{195} total possible ways one could potentially construct a protein composed of 150 amino acids. That is a staggeringly large number of possibilities; but remember that like the letters in an alphabet, only certain very specific combinations form understandable "words" or decipherable units of information.

4. Given these possibilities, Dr. Douglas Axe at Cambridge University calculated that the chance of getting a functional protein from all of the possible proteins that could be randomly thrown together would be about 1 in 10^{74}. Thus, the overall chance of randomly producing a single functional protein is 1 in 10^{164}!

5. Having said all this, it must be kept in mind, however, that even though these odds are prohibitively unlikely in the case of a single functional protein, even the most rudimentary form of living thing requires not one, but hundreds of them. So these numbers must be multiplied by the minimal number of requisite proteins essential for the particular organism being formed.

6. Here is an even more thorny issue to consider: All living things are built from proteins. Where do proteins come from? They are

GOD DOES EXIST!

generated in little factories called ribosomes: these are RNA rich cytoplasmic granules inside the cell. What are ribosomes made from? Proteins! That is what we call a "chicken and egg" problem! Which came first?

The notion that mutations happen frequently in nature is encouraged by constant reference to the changes that occur in viral populations, such as influenza, human immunodeficiency virus (type 1; HIV-1), hepatitis C virus (HCA), as well as many of the plant viruses and viroids. Most people are not aware that unlike DNA polymerases, RNA viruses lack proofreading activity as an aspect of their structure. This is very problematic for the viral host because it makes it difficult for it to "keep current" on the present state of the viral intruder. It builds up antibodies against an ever-changing enemy. By the time the host has built up its defenses against a particular virus, it may have altered itself and it is almost as if a new invader has developed. But for the virus itself, this is an adaptation that is clearly in the favor of the viral population's long-term survival, in most cases. There are exceptions to this, however.

Because RNA viruses lack the proofreading activity of DNA polymerases, they have an error rate during replication that is very high. It has been estimated to be as high as 10^{-3} to 10^{-5} mutations per nucleotide per replication cycle. An acutely infected organism may include 10^9–10^{12} viral particles at any given time. With an RNA virus genome length of approximately 10^4 nucleotides, every possible single mutant and many double mutants are likely to occur by the time the population attains the size of many natural virus populations. Although combinations of multiple mutations may be rare, diversification of RNA virus populations clearly drives antiviral therapy response (Cf. E. Domingo, *Virus Evolution*, 389-421; E. Domingo, et al., "Viruses as Quasispecies: Biological Implications," *Current Topics in Microbiology and Immunology* 299 (2006): 51-82).

This unique ability of RNA viruses is something that is critical for the survival of these populations as they attempt to survive within their individual hosts. But it is not a capability that is shared with other organisms. DNA-based organisms are restricted from such virtually unlimited changes taking place by all of the roadblocks that we have discussed above. It should be understood that this survival mechanism in RNA viruses, however, can prove destructive to viral populations even for vi-

The Probability Argument

ruses of the RNA type. The cause for this is the well-known principle of genetics called "Muller's ratchet," which states: "The mean fitness of a population will always decrease." It describes a process in which recombination in an asexual population results in accumulation of destructive mutations in an irreversible manner. Sexual reproduction avoids this ratchet effect. But in asexual reproduction, best adapted genotypes are occasionally lost from the population through mutation, and as a result the overload of unfavorable mutations destroys the entire population. Andrés Moya, et al, observed, "When finite populations with high mutation rates are considered, a significant proportion of the mutants should be deleterious. If populations are asexual and small in size, mutation-free individuals become rare and can be lost by random genetic drift. In that case a kind of irreversible ratchet mechanism gradually will decrease the mean fitness of the populations. Chao provided the first experimental evidence for the action of Muller's ratchet in RNA viruses" ("The Evolution of RNA Viruses: A Population Genetics View" *PNAS* 97.13 [Jan 20, 2000]: 6967-6973; L. Chao *Nature* [London] 348, 454-455).

Chance of a Single Functional Protein Appearing in Nature: A Test Case?

"The probability that a functional protein would appear *de novo* by a random association of amino acids is practically zero. . . . creation of entirely new nucleotide sequences could not be of any importance in the production of new information" (François Jacob, "Evolution and Tinkering," *Science* 196 [1977]: 1161-1166). When Jacob wrote that "Nature is a tinkerer, not an inventor" in this famous essay, his point was that "evolution works only with material immediately at hand, not with the foresight of an engineer." He emphasized the role of gene duplication in creating new genes with new functions; while doing so, he strongly discounted the possibility that new genes could arise *de novo* from nongenic DNA sequence.

Amino acids are the building blocks for proteins. There are in nature 80 varieties of amino acids. Only 20 out of the 80 are found in living organisms. However, these molecules have an unusual trait about them: they would more readily react with other molecules than with each other. But, let us assume, for the sake of argument, that in this "primordial soup mixture" that evolutionists perennially dream about, all of

GOD DOES EXIST!

the chemical reactions necessary to form all 80 amino acids occurred. If that were to happen, it would qualify as a "long shot" in the first place. It would be about the same thing as assuming that a truck carrying groceries empties its supplies into a swimming pool; all the boxes, cans, bottles, and bags opened and their contents spilled into the pool. And out of this chaotic mess, we are able to separate 80 distinct varieties of soups.

Of course, this is an assumption so large that we cannot even attach a numerical probability to it; but this is precisely what we are supposed to believe in order to start the process of biochemical evolution and get it up and running. Then, the proper 20 amino acids somehow isolated themselves from all of the other chemicals in the mixture and began to bind to one another and form proteins. This is a huge assumption: it assumes that 20 specific left-handed-only amino acids randomly came together, randomly refused to react with other molecules which they have a natural tendency to react with, randomly excluded all right-handed amino acids (all amino acids form left-handed and right-handed versions of the same compound; these opposite forms are called enantiomers or optical isomers; this is a well-known problem in biology called the *chirality problem*), then randomly formed the correct peptide bonds, and finally randomly began to produce fully-formed proteins capable of producing other proteins.

Evolutionists would have us believe that amino acids, contrary to their nature, did not attach to other compounds nor did they form the racemates that they usually tend to form. Instead, they went right on linking to one another, forming peptide bonds, and making proteins and large biological molecules. This has been compared to one taking a handful of magnets and throwing them into a bowl of paper clips and shredded paper, and contrary to the nature of the paper clips, they are not attracted to the magnets. Rather, the paper clips are magically linked to one another, forming a chain of paper clips. Few of us would believe that such a thing could ever happen. And yet that is exactly the kind of thing that we are expected to believe, if we place our faith in those who espouse evolutionary biology.

What are the mathematical chances of this happening? The probability that a given amino acid in the sequence is one of the 20 preferred ingredients is calculated as 20/80 or 25%. Now, a 25% chance of something happening is pretty good odds. So that part is not out of reason.

The Probability Argument

But that is not the end of the story; this is where it gets complicated. It has been estimated that the minimum number of amino acids needed to produce a bio-protein is about 100,000. So if we were to assume that in this primordial soup, the right 20 amino acids somehow linked only to each other to form a simple bio-protein of 100,000 amino acid links, the odds of that happening would be calculated as $(20/80)^{100,000}$.

Unfortunately, it would require a thousand times the age of the universe for such an event to occur, even assuming for sake of argument that the universe is as old as it is sometimes estimated to be. *In other words, it did not and could not ever happen.* Evolutionists counter this statistical argument, not by attempting to make the case that the estimates are inaccurate, but by saying that these primordial proteins would not have had to be nearly so complex. Complex forms came later, they theorize, evolving from the simpler ones. Their problem is, however, that they have no evidence for the existence of proteins that are simpler than this, none at all. So the burden of proof lies with them to show that viable proteins *ever existed* that are less complicated than the ones we presently encounter in nature. It requires this level of sophistication to produce functionality. This is the most important "missing link" that they need to find (cf. D. Jappah, *Evolution*, 224).

But even that is not all that is required. One author has put in simple terms the rest of what is required in order to produce a finished product, namely functional and self-replicating proteins, the most basic and essential building-blocks of all living organisms:

> Before all of this started, DNA and rRNA, more complex than amino acids and proteins, randomly appeared (nobody knows from where), fully formed and well programmed (by whom or what nobody knows) to randomly direct protein synthesis from only left-handed amino acids out of all the chemicals in the primordial broth....
>
> We know, in real science, that DNA, itself a conglomerate of proteins, is responsible for protein synthesis. If DNA is responsible for directing protein synthesis in living systems, and the DNA itself is made of proteins, then where did the first DNA come from to direct protein synthesis? Which came first, DNA or protein?
>
> These left-handed proteins randomly isolated themselves from the rest of the broth and randomly formed enzymes that randomly assist-

GOD DOES EXIST!

ed in the creation of chromosomes, lysosomes, mitochondria, Golgi body, ribosomes, smooth and rough endoplasmic reticulum, cytoplasm, and other cellular structures. With all the chemical reactions going on in this primordial soup, the cellular structures were randomly isolated from everything else (by whom or what nobody knows), randomly enclosed within a membrane, and the enclosed system somehow developed a pulse and life spontaneously began (Daniel Jappah, *Evolution*, 226-27).

Clearly some of the above description is overly simplified and the processes truncated in order to serve the author's purposes, but the essence of it is absolutely accurate. This is exactly what the theorists expect for us to accept as having happened. They require that we accept their view that it all happened over hundreds of thousands of years, perhaps in some cases millions, but this is what they hope we will be convinced to believe. Is it any surprise that only the upper echelons of the scientific community, all of them rabid atheists, really accept this hypothetical reconstruction of events? It amazes us sometimes to hear them attempt to make light of the possibility of miracles in the context of religious belief, when they believe in millions of biological, chemical and microscopic miracles themselves.

The co-discoverer of DNA, Francis Crick, confessed, "The origin of life seems almost to be a miracle, so many are the conditions which would have been satisfied to get it going" (*Life Itself: Its Origin and Nature*, 88). It is little wonder that Anthony Flew, the famous atheist debater and apologist, when confronted with the information that was being uncovered on this topic, wrote a letter to Britain's *Philosophy Now* magazine and said, "Biologists' investigation of DNA has shown, by the almost unbelievable complexity of the arrangements which are needed to produce life, that intelligence must have been involved. It has become inordinately difficult even to begin to think about constructing a naturalistic theory of the evolution of that first reproducing organism." Pugnacious atheists tell us that we are silly to accept the biblical testimony about the resurrection of Jesus from the grave on the third day after His death. And yet, these same scoffers want us to accept this fanciful depiction of the origin of all living things! Resuscitation of a dead corpse would be, relatively speaking, a simple miracle by comparison!

The Probability Argument

Attempting to Prove the Impossible

Some recent authors, like C. M. Weisman and S. R. Eddy have attempted to make the case that, "New genes arise from pre-existing genes, but some *de novo* origin from non-genic sequence also seems plausible." In making their case, they went on to argue on the basis of a 2017 study that "25% of random DNA sequences yield beneficial products when expressed in bacteria ("Gene Evolution: Getting Something from Nothing," *Current Biology* 27:13 [July 10, 2017]: R661-R663). The study referred to was conducted by Rafik Neme and colleagues ("Random Sequences Are an Abundant Source of Bioactive RNAs or Peptides." *Nat. Ecol. Evol.* 1, 0127). Moreover, they claimed that, "In vitro selection experiments show that it is surprisingly easy to obtain functional RNAs and proteins from random sequence libraries (cf. A. D. Keefe and J. W. Szostak, "Functional Proteins from a random-sequence library." *Nature* 410, 715-718; and C. Tuerk and L. Gold, "Systematic evolution of ligands by exponential enrichment: RNA ligands to bacteriophage T4 DNA polymerase," *Science* 249.4968 [Aug. 1990]: 505-510).

Genomics has found widespread low-level transcription of many apparently non-coding and non-conserved RNAs, and these "non-coding" transcripts are often detectably translated at low levels to peptides. This being true, it appears that there is abundant raw material for nature to tinker with as it goes about the normal business of cellular routine. On this account, Anne-Ruxandra Carvunis and her coworkers introduced the concept of the "protogene," a gene born from non-genic sequence by random processes without selection (cf. Carvunis, et al., "Proto-genes and de novo gene birth," *Nature* 487 [2012]: 370-374). In order for such a protogene to form, three barriers must be overcome. First, a piece of random DNA sequence is transcribed, next the RNA transcript is translated (for protein-coding genes, anyway, as opposed to functional RNAs), and finally, the protein product must at least provide some beneficial function. Theoretically speaking, a protogene is the earliest stage of a *de novo* gene origin that has a beneficial phenotype that selection can begin to act on. Experiments using random sequences to investigate the possibility of *de novo* gene origin are viewed as attempts to measure one of the terms essential to this process (transcription, translation, and functionality).

161

GOD DOES EXIST!

Neme and his colleagues used random DNA sequences to address the third term, the issue of functionality. They cloned a library of synthetic random 150 nucleotide DNA sequences into an expression plasmid under control of a strong inducible promoter and ribosome binding site. They were working with *Escherichia coli* cells. *E. coli* is a rod-shaped anaerobic coliform bacteria. It is a favorite bacterium for researchers because it is well known and it has frequently been manipulated and it has a long history in the laboratory. Genus *Escherichia* is commonly found in the lower intestines of warm-blooded organisms. In addition, it has been widely used to synthesize DNA and proteins.

When induced, each plasmid expresses a ~500 nucleotide-long RNA (150 of which are random) encoding a 62 amino-acid protein (50 of which are random). Because the vector provides strong transcription and translation signals, the first and second terms of the protogene equation are bypassed. In contrast to *in vitro* selection experiments that select for specific functions, the experiment aimed at asking how many random sequences have "functions" in the sense of conferring a measurable growth-rate phenotype on the host bacterial cell. Out of a few thousand random DNA sequences that were analyzed, 75% were found to be differentially enriched or depleted over the course of competitive growth. To the surprise of the team, it was reported that 25% were enriched, and therefore seemed to have a beneficial effect on *E. coli* growth rate when expressed as RNA or protein. They were not surprised to find that the majority of cases (75%) were determined to be deleterious. Of course, most of such random sequences would be expected to be costly to the host.

However, it was the finding that 25% of random sequences were beneficial that was of interest to the investigators. This was unexpected. *E. coli* is a highly adapted organism. It had previously been determined that beneficial mutations occur relatively rarely in quantitative long-term *in vitro* evolution experiments in *E. coli* (R. Woods, et al, "Tests of parallel molecular evolution in a long-term experiment with Escherichia coli," *Proc. Natl. Acad. Sci. USA* 103 [2006]: 9107-9112). But in this case the opposite seemed to be true.

Reviewers dampened the enthusiasm of the team, however. They warned that if the experiment measured relative (normalized) frequen-

The Probability Argument

cy changes in competitive growth conditions, the change in frequency of a sequence would depend on its growth rate relative to every other random sequence in the pool. As well, even assuming that drift is negligible, as they argued, sequence enrichment does not mean that a sequence is beneficial relative to wild-type *E. coli*, only that it was better than other random sequence competitors. It could be that all of the random sequences are deleterious to *E. coli*, but some are less deleterious than others, and these would rise to higher relative frequencies. Other criticisms were leveled at the experiment as well, some too complicated for us to enumerate here.

The most devastating critique was to their ultimate conclusion, worded as follows, "Although we have reservations about the correctness of the conclusion of Neme, *et al.* that 25% of their random sequences have beneficial effects on *E. coli* growth rate. . ." (3). The reviewers were unconvinced by the arguments set forth by the panel of researchers who produced the study, even though they went on to compliment the project itself, and even went so far as to draw a similar conclusion from the research, saying: ". . . work from these and other authors does suggest that each of the three terms in the protogene equation are high enough to be measurable in laboratory experiments, and thus could easily be relevant on evolutionary timescales. François Jacob was correct that gene duplication and divergence is a dominant force in gene evolution, but his personal intuition about the odds of new genes arising *de novo* may have been simply wrong. Experiments studying the transcription, translation, and functionality of random sequences are proving to be fruitful territory, replacing Jacob's intuition with experimental data" (Weisman and Eddy, "Gene Evolution," *Current Biology* [July 10, 2017]: R663).

Reference to this particular study is offered as an illustration of the kind of research that is being done in the hope that the naturalistic theory of evolutionary development can be confirmed through laboratory experimentation. However, it should be noted by the reader that the entire process, in this case, is conducted with pre-existing strings of "prewritten code," pieces of DNA that have been split off from one another and then randomly "glued back together." Now that doesn't seem quite fair, does it? You see, the main problem that needs to be addressed is the origin of the code itself. How did the code come to be "encoded" in the first place? That is the real question. Research of this sort does not address that problem. But it shows the relative desperation of these convinced believers in the theory of gene evolution.

Interestingly, the team and their reviewers are themselves quite agnostic about the results of their experimentation, even though they seem hopeful. They are aware of its inherent weaknesses, but cannot figure out a way to avoid them. They recognize that looking at just one aspect of the organism (its growth) is not sufficient to provide a clear picture of what the real outcome of the experiment will be. There is more to any organism than merely its ability to grow, especially over the near future. (Cancer has a marvelous ability to grow, but is ultimately destructive to its host; most of us do not consider this a desirable quality!) Too, there are three terms that must be dealt with, as we explained in our remarks above, not just the final one as in this instance. There are three mechanisms employed by the cell to "weed out" bad or incomplete strands of DNA, and this experiment bypasses two-thirds of the process. Once more, their method of studying the issues involved is not challenging enough. It does not deal with the real problem of origination. How did these "data sets" that are encoded on the DNA strings get there in the first place?

The following is a more realistic plan for testing the theory that all of this arose by purely mechanistic means: Recreate the "primordial soup" as it would be expected to appear in nature at the beginning of time, and then see what happens. Mix together a chemical "stew" of all of the ingredients that are necessary to constitute the pre-encoded DNA, and then wait to see what comes of it. What are the chances that such a precise list of the exact ingredients would be found in nature? Probably not very high; but we might assume that somewhere and somehow in the history of the earth this group of specific chemical compounds could have been available in the precise amounts necessary. What would come of this "witches brew" of chemicals? How many strings of encoded DNA will arise from the "stew" after a certain period of time? How many proteins will randomly issue from it? We all know what the result of that investigation would be. Zero. Not a single string of DNA. Nevertheless, that would provide us with a much more realistic comparison with what

The Probability Argument

we are told by the theorists happened in nature when they claim life began. But, of course, they know that nothing would come of it. There are simply too many hurdles to be crossed. And that is why such an experiment would never be conducted in the first place.

Fiddling around with pre-written pieces of encoded information does not prove anything at all about the evolution of living things. DNA is often likened to computer code. Mixing up pages of pre-written computer code, and then jumbling them together again, might produce a software program with some functionality, but would that prove that the code itself merely happened in nature without the agency of some intellect behind it? Something or someone had to be the impetus behind it, the originator of it. An intelligent mind must first write the code before the experiment can begin. This kind of biological "tinkering" and recombining of pre-existing biological information might be useful in understanding how nature might alter and rearrange the information at the center of the living system so as to adapt to changing environmental circumstances, etc., but even that does not tell us anything about how one thing changes into another, a reptile into a bird, for example. That would require much new code to be written, and no explanation has yet been forthcoming to explain how that might have been done.

So, what are actually the chances of such a thing as this happening? Everyone recognizes and will admit that it is a "long shot" at best, and impossible at worst. François Jacob's quote above is illustrative of this point. He was correct when he said, "Nature is a tinkerer, not an inventor." But what are the real chances of this "long shot" actually having taken place? In point of fact there have been those who have attempted to put the matter into real numbers, so as to explain in real terms how long this "long shot" really is. Sir Fred Hoyle, for example, wrote, "In *Steady-State Cosmology Revisited* (University College Cardiff Press, 1980) I estimated (on a very conservative basis) the chance of a random shuffling of amino acids producing a workable set of enzymes to be less than 10^{-40000}. Since the minuteness of this probability wipes out any thought of life having originated on Earth, many whose thoughts are irreversibly programmed to believe in a terrestrial origin of life argue that the enzyme estimate is wrong. It is—in the sense of being too conservative" ("Reflections on the Universe," 4-5). This unfathomable

GOD DOES EXIST!

number, as extreme as it sounds, says Hoyle, is in his own words, "too conservative." Hoyle believed that the idea of chemical evolution was so ridiculous that he sought to display his ridicule by saying that the odds of all of these chemical reactions happening all by themselves are just as likely as a tornado hitting a junkyard and accidentally constructing a fully functional Boeing 747.

The probability of winning most major lottery games is about 1 in 4×10^6, that is 1 chance in 4 million. Some lotteries are much larger and have even worse odds than that. When you compare the probability of winning a major lottery, winning the lottery seems like a relatively sure thing by comparison with the possibility of biochemical evolution. That also means that you are considerably more intelligent to play the lottery than to believe in the theory of evolution. And few of us who know the odds consider playing it a particularly intelligent activity! Paleontologist Niles Eldridge admitted as much, when he wrote: "The pattern that we were told to find for the last one hundred and twenty years does not exist. There is now overwhelmingly strong evidence, both statistical and paleontological, that life could not have been started on earth by a series of random chemical reactions. Today's best mathematical estimates state that there simply was not enough time for random reactions.... to get things going" (Cf. G. L. Shroeder, *Genesis and the Big Bang*, 25).

The reason that most people are taken in by the convincing-sounding theory of the organic evolution of life is that the story of it sounds so incredibly *simple*. But the simple story of evolution is a deception. The more we learn about what is necessary to make life happen without an intelligent agent being behind it, the less simple the whole thing becomes. In fact, it would have taken nothing short of an actual miracle to make it happen.

Most proteins are very complex. There are no truly simple proteins. Scientists believe that the simplest form of life has a minimum of 250 to 400 proteins. The most basic of proteins contain ca. 100-150 amino acids; the average protein is closer to 300-400. So, a modest protein with 150 amino acids with 20 possible combinations at each site translates to 1×10^{195}! To illustrate the extreme unlikelihood of this combination of amino acids and proteins assembling so as to form a living organism, without outside assistance, it should be observed that there are only

The Probability Argument

10^{80} of elemental particles in the entire universe! And, for us to understand this number, it has been calculated that there have only been 10^{16} seconds since the beginning of the universe, i.e., the "Big Bang"! (And this assumes their own time-line is correct, something that we are not willing to concede.) This is precisely why dedicated researchers are "fiddling about the edges" of the theory in the vain hope that the general public will buy the narrative that their research is providing evidence that organic evolution produced life on the primordial earth. The evidence opposed to the theory is mounting daily, and statistically the odds are so heavily against its rational probability that only the most zealous believers are brave enough to address directly the issue of its likelihood.

To illustrate the point, in July of 2012 Harold S. Bernhardt composed an article for *Biology Direct* (7:23), entitled, "The RNA World Hypothesis: The Worst Theory of the Early Evolution of Life (Except for All the Others)." Now, Bernhardt is a convinced believer in the view that "while theoretically possible, such a hypothesis is probably unprovable, and that the RNA world hypothesis, although far from perfect or complete, is the best we currently have to help understand the backstory to contemporary biology." Which came first, RNA or DNA? He suggests that the answer to the question is RNA, while he also recognizes the extreme unlikelihood that two such different types of extraordinarily complex macromolecules arising simultaneously "would appear unlikely." (The reader should note that he admits the statistical difficulty with two such complicated macromolecules arising together, without admitting the extreme unlikelihood that even one of them should randomly arise alone!) In our view, that is an understatement!

The discovery that RNA possesses some rather limited catalytic ability provides for him the potential solution to the mystery of which came first in evolutionary development. Since both DNA and RNA possess replication abilities, the RNA had to be the first in line: "A single macromolecule could have originally carried out both replication and catalysis. RNA—which constitutes the genome of RNA viruses, and catalyzes peptide synthesis on the ribosome—could have been both the chicken and the egg!" (Note how heavily the "chicken and egg" analogy weighs on his consciousness.) Clearly he is a zealous proponent of the view he espouses. But what he expects for an ancient strand of rudimentary RNA is a tall order for it to fill.

And so, he frankly admits several very serious weaknesses of his view: (1) RNA, even though it is a single strand of nucleotides rather than a double one like DNA, is too complex a molecule to have arisen prebiotically; (2) RNA is inherently unstable since its major role in the cell is involved in the process of protein synthesis (translation) and its regulation; (3) Catalysis is a relatively rare property of long RNA sequences only; so, this property is only found on highly refined and developed sequences, not rudimentary ones as the theory would demand; and, (4) The catalytic repertoire of RNA is too limited.

All of these four criticisms are devastating to his theory, but he persists with the proposal that RNA was the first to develop irrespective of this. This study is typical of how the difficulties of such developmental stages are skated over by researchers intent on clinging to the theory of evolutionary development from simple to complex in spite of its very obvious weaknesses and the relative improbabilities involved.

Conclusion

This chapter has been about the question of probabilities. What is the likelihood of a given event taking place? It is always difficult to quantify anything that is complicated or sophisticated in the first place. But it is not impossible. Given that this is true, we have looked at the relative likelihood of proteins appearing randomly and spontaneously in a primordial setting as it is commonly believed that they did. And we have concluded that *this is not only highly unlikely, it is impossible.* Nevertheless, it is not always to be expected that even though something is out of the range of what is reasonable to believe, that people will give up on believing it. The theory of organic evolution is a perfect example of this type of belief. Evolution is faith based, it is not evidence based. Belief in evolution is tantamount to a sort of religious belief. Make no mistake about it, atheism is a religion. We all understand how difficult it is to divest a "true believer" of his unreasonable belief in something.

One very wise man wrote about this matter of how the mind works and treats questions and opinions that it is simply unwilling to give in

The Probability Argument

to, even though the logic and the probabilities are solidly allied against our proposition, and on the side of what we reject:

> If anyone were to ask me what probability one gave to the other, I should not try to answer by contemplating the propositions and trying to discern a logical relation between them, I should, rather, try to imagine that one of them was all that I knew, and to guess what degree of confidence I should then have in the other. If I were able to do this, I might no doubt still not be content with it, but might say, "This is what I should think, but, of course, I am only a fool" and proceed to consider what a wise man would think and call that the degree of probability. This kind of self-criticism I shall discuss later when developing my own theory; all that I want to remark here is that no one estimating a degree of probability simply contemplates two propositions supposed to be related to it; he always considers *inter alia* his own actual or hypothetical degree of belief. This remark seems to me to be borne out by observation of my own behavior; and to be the only way of accounting for the fact that we all give estimates of probability in cases taken from actual life, but are quite unable to do so in the logically simplest cases in which, were probability a logical relation, it would be easiest to discern (Frank P. Ramsey, "Truth and Probability," *Foundations of Mathematics and Other Logical Essays*, [1931]; recently in *Readings in Formal Epistemology*, 21-45).

"The object of reasoning is to find out, from the consideration of what we already know, something else which we do not know. Consequently, reasoning is good if it be such as to give a true conclusion from true premises, and not otherwise," said C. S. Pierce. The truth is what we should be after. Logic is only useful if it is used. Even the most honest person must check his or her personal beliefs at the door when dealing with questions of logic and especially in the area of probability. Ramsey was being brutally honest about his own personal tendency to see things in a certain way because "he always considers *inter alia* his own actual or hypothetical degree of belief." It is difficult if not impossible for us at times to "step outside of ourselves" and look at the *brutal fact* of a thing rather than seeing it as we have for so long.

W. F. Donkits is quoted as saying, "When several hypotheses are presented to our mind which we believe to be mutually exclusive and exhaustive, but about which we know nothing further, we distribute our

GOD DOES EXIST!

belief equally among them.... This being admitted as an account of the way in which we actually do distribute our belief in simple cases, the whole of the subsequent theory follows as a deduction of the way in which we distribute it in complex cases if we would be consistent" (cited by Ramsey, ibid.). Being consistent and honest is a great challenge where one is confronted with an issue in which he has heavily invested. Whether it is one's professional reputation, career, or self-esteem that has been invested in an opinion, or simply a long history of believing a particular thing, it is hard to give up on a perspective into which we have plowed so much of ourselves.

That is what is at stake in the present moment of scientific research and the introspection and self-discovery that goes along with it. A great many physicists have begun to admit that in regard to the concept of the original creation *ex nihilo*. Now that it is generally admitted that the universe, space, and time, had an actual beginning, they have had to come face to face with the hard objective reality that prior to that millisecond that started everything there had to be something or someone who initiated it. The chances that it somehow started itself are far-fetched and purely theoretical. And even if it is viewed in terms of an expansion/contraction process, it still only leaves us with all of the same unanswered questions as previously: who or what started it?

Likewise, as the structure and functioning of all living things has come to be better understood, in terms of their phenomenal complexity and interdependencies, it has come to be admitted by many of them that, even if they are right about genetic mutation and natural selection being responsible for the present diversity of living things, how the first living things came to be is incomprehensible from their standpoint. The odds are against their theory. And even if we allow them the 13.8 billion years of universe history (Lambda-CDM concordance model) that they generally argue for, that does not begin to provide them with a sufficient period of time to get them where they need to go. In fact, if they had a thousand times that amount of time it would not be enough. And many of them know this all too well, even though they proceed in their endeavors as if this were not so.

The Probability Argument

But, as Ramsey went on to say,

> We all agree that a man who did not make inductions would be unreasonable: the question is only what this means. In my view it does not mean that the man would in any way sin against formal logic or formal probability; but that he had not got a very useful habit, without which he would be very much worse off, in the sense of being much less likely to have true opinions.
>
> This is a kind of pragmatism: we judge mental habits by whether they work, i.e. whether the opinions they lead to are for the most part true, or more often true than those which alternative habits would lead to.
>
> Induction is such a useful habit, and so to adopt it is reasonable (Ibid).

It is preferable always to form the habit of believing what is true, and so, speaking what is also true. It is only thus that we will have true opinions. The notion that the universe has come about by a process of self-evolution is beyond absurd. It is against all that we would usually see as logical or sensible. No person who believes it, as long as he continues to believe it, will hold a true opinion of it. The same is the case with the organic evolution of life on our planet. Living things have not arisen on earth unaided. Probability-wise that is an impossibility. It is time for the atheist to give up the contention that this is what happened and that it is reasonable to say that this is what happened. No person who believes that, as long as he or she persists in holding to that opinion will hold a true or realistic perspective on the subject. For as Ramsey counselled, "Induction is such a useful habit, and so to adopt it is reasonable."

Inductive reasoning starts with experience and observation and synthesizes what we have learned in order to produce a general truth. This is precisely what we have done in this case. Evolutionists, on the other hand, employ deductive reasoning instead, beginning with the theory that life evolved from simplicity to complexity, and ignoring the fact that even the most "simple" life-forms are extraordinarily complex. They also neglect or else disregard altogether the question of probability. When the numbers are crunched to confirm the probability of the theory, it is found that there is not enough time in a thousand universes like the one we live in to allow for the working out of their hypothesis. But that does not distract them from their mission. They are in no wise

GOD DOES EXIST!

deterred, for they know that the only alternative to their theory is theism. It would be best for all of us to heed the advice of the sagely scholar Ramsey and adopt induction and follow the logic to its inevitable conclusion: "God *must* exist."

Questions for Discussion

1. What are the real chances of the universe appearing out of nothingness without any agent to make it happen? Do most people accept the notion that things come from nothing? Is it really sensible to believe such a thing, even if complicated arguments are employed to make the case for it?

2. State the formal argument for the existence of God from the perspective of mathematical likelihood?

3. What are some of the theories of how the universe came to exist? Almost all of them are associated with something besides nothingness, leaving one to inquire as to how what pre-existed the initial creation came to be. What is logically wrong with this picture?

4. Do you recall any of your teachers or professors making any assertions about the simple matter of life's appearance on the early earth. It is a common recollection for many students both in high school and in college or university.

5. Do you see the wondrous complexity of living organisms in a different light now that you have had the chance to see how extraordinarily difficult it would be to initiate any living thing from the raw materials alone?

6. How would you respond now to the implication that the whole of the living system could have somehow begun with a lightning strike in a tidal pool?

7. What are some of the obstacles to the random appearance of life on the earth? List them and describe how difficult these criteria would be to satisfy.

The Probability Argument

8. Life is made of protein. How complex are proteins? How are proteins made? Do you consider it possible for a protein to appear randomly in nature, let us say in a primordial soup of chemicals?
9. What are right-hand and left-hand bonds in biology? How do they play a part in the production of proteins?
10. One reason many people are taken in by the theory of the random appearance of life on earth and natural selection to alter it and bring it to its present status is that the story is deceptively simple. Is it really as simple as they try to make it sound?
11. The concept of computer code and of the software that causes a computer to perform a specific function is a useful means of illustrating how the inner workings of the cell performs its various tasks. Describe the DNA sequences in some detail and use the computer analogy to depict their complexity and how difficult it would be for a system of this sort to "randomly appear" in nature.
12. Expound on the notion that truth is the ultimate issue that is at stake in this whole matter of whether or not the universe began by a process of self-evolution or not. Do the same with the idea that life began by means or organic evolution. The atheist is persistent with his charge that theism leads to "pseudoscience." Who is being honest with the facts in this instance?

Chapter 8
The Moral Argument

Moral arguments for the existence of God represent a family of related proofs in the history of western philosophical thinking. Generally speaking, they reason from some feature of morality or the moral life to the existence of God. Christianity has embraced these arguments in their various forms, and many different Christian philosophers and theologians have formulated versions of these arguments. Some have thought them to be of preeminent importance, while others have deemed them worthwhile but have not seen them as compelling as some of the other proofs.

C. S. Lewis's *Mere Christianity* (1952) well illustrates this point. It is probably the best-selling book of apologetics in the twentieth-century. A key to its success is that Lewis's book utilizes this approach. The popularity of his book tells us that the general public considers this argu-

The Moral Argument

ment very compelling, even if many philosophers and theologians are not overly impressed with it. Although it is not a logical treatise and was written more for the general public than for philosophers or theologians, it takes the readers precisely where Lewis wants them to go. Importantly, it begins its thread of argumentation with a moral argument for God's existence. We will return to *Mere Christianity* momentarily. But for now it is best to fit it into its special category of apologetic works.

All of the writers who make their case from the perspective of the significance of morality follow these lines of reasoning toward the God-idea. Universally they have claims about the character of moral thought and experience in their premises, and affirmations of the existence of deity in their conclusions. In essence they all come down to a few basic points. They observe that there are objective moral values and duties that we experience in the world. Such values and duties are critical for human life to persist on the planet in a way that is meaningful and more or less pleasant for the majority of people. They then reason that behind these objective moral values and duties there must be some source.

Finally, they conclude that God, as the embodiment of the ultimate Good, is the source of the objective moral values and duties we experience. "Therefore, God must exist" is always the conclusion to which the argument directs the thoughtful.

Early Forms of the Argument

Plato (ca. 428-347 BC) insisted that things have goodness insofar as they stand in some relation to the Good, which subsists in itself. "One knows the form of the Good, a perfect, eternal, and changeless entity existing outside space and time, in which particular good things share, or 'participate,' insofar as they are good." Plato did not specifically identify this ultimate Goodness as God. Since he did not draw this conclusion from the argument, namely that God exists, it could not genuinely be said that he was making a moral argument for the existence of God. Christians propose, however, that, conceptually, this preeminent Good to which Plato made allusion, is God; God is good and ultimately He is the source of all goodness. Therefore it is asserted by them that God exists.

Another form of the argument was set forth by Thomas Aquinas (1225-1274). It should be noted that in his *Quinque viae* or "Five Ways,"

GOD DOES EXIST!

Aquinas argued for God's existence in his *Summa Theologicae* (a work intended as a primer for theology students) from the perspective of "natural theology" (a concerted attempt to discern divine truth from the order present in the natural world). The fourth of these "ways" or arguments had to do with a postulate for God from the perspective of value, or "degrees of perfection." He began with the idea that among beings who possess such qualities as are "good, true, and noble" there are gradations. Apparently he intended to say that even though there are many good things in our experience, some things are better than others. And among good people, there are some people who are better than all others. They are the best that life has to offer.

In so saying, Aquinas argued, we are, at least implicitly, comparing them to some absolute standard. But what is this standard? Is it simply an idealized concept of "the good"? He went on to assert that in his view this standard cannot merely be "ideal" or "hypothetical" in nature. It has to be something more. This gradation is only possible if there is some *Being* which has this quality to a maximum extent: "So that there is something which is truest, something best, something noblest and, consequently, something which is uttermost being; for those things that are greatest in truth are greatest in being. . . ." All imperfect beings approach yet fall short of it. He persisted in his reasoning by affirming that this being which provides the standard is also the cause or explanation of the existence of these qualities. He concluded by asserting that such a cause must be God. So, in Aquinas's system, God is that paramount perfection, therefore necessarily, He must exist.

Now, obviously, this argument like the one made by Plato could not be said to be the argument from morality in a "fully fleshed out" form, even though it just as obviously does encapsulate the essence of the proof. Nevertheless, according to many modern philosophers, because of its association with ancient Platonic thought and Aristotelian assumptions, which are no longer widely held to be true by most philosophers, "such assumptions would either have to be defended on modern grounds, or else the argument would have to be reformulated in a way that frees it from its original metaphysical home" (cf. C. Stephen Evans, "Moral Arguments," *Stanford Encyclopedia of Philosophy*).

The Moral Argument

In our view this critique is unjustified. Aquinas did share many things in common with Platonism and Aristotelian logic, but so do a great many of us. Obviously Aquinas did not believe everything that Plato or later Platonists did, but he held that many concepts pressed into service by Platonists were valuable and should not be dismissed without adequate cause for their rejection. The distinction between Platonists who affirm the existence of "abstract objects," which are asserted to exist in a third realm distinct from both the sensible external world and from the internal world of consciousness, and nominalists, who deny their existence, is a worthwhile place to draw a line of demarcation. In this sense, Aquinas was not a Platonist (except in the signification of Hebrews 9:23-24; the heavenly realm being the third plane), and neither are we. But Aquinas did not, "throw the baby out with the bathwater," and neither should we.

Platonic thought and Aristotelian logic are valuable on many levels, far too much so for us to enter into a discussion of either in the present context, but suffice it to say that we want to be counted as among those who side with Aquinas on this matter. At any rate, we consider ourselves to be in good company, for as one scholar rightly observed, "Today Neo-Platonism's influence can be felt almost everywhere from Art to Social Theory, from Set Theory and Category Theory to Ecology, from Charles Sanders Pierce to Alfred North Whitehead" (Vernon Kooy, "The Turn to Neo-Platonism in Philosophical Theology," 1).

Immanuel Kant

Immanuel Kant (1724-1804), an East Prussian lecturer at Königsberg (now Kaliningrad, Russia), was an intriguing character as regards his philosophical beliefs. Many consider him to be *the* central individual in modern philosophy. "He synthesized early modern rationalism and empiricism, set the terms for much of nineteenth and twentieth century philosophy, and continues to exercise a significant influence today in metaphysics, epistemology, ethics, political philosophy, aesthetics, and other fields" (Earlyn Alexander). He wrote three major critiques that continue to be important in those fields today: *Critique of Pure Reason* (1781), *Critique of Practical Reason* (1788), and the *Critique of the Power of Judgment* (1790), along with a host of other philosophical essays and books. In the area of metaphysics he is especially noteworthy.

GOD DOES EXIST!

He is an interesting thinker to explore because, on the one hand, he is primarily responsible for the modern version of the argument for the existence of God from the perspective of morality, yet on the other hand he was an opponent of the very popular ontological argument. He was unconvinced by it, and so rejected it and everything that was connected in any way to it. He famously argued that the "theoretical arguments" for God's existence were unsuccessful, but in their place presented what he described as a "rational argument" for belief in God as "a postulate of practical reason." It will be recalled that the "ontological proof" attempts to establish the existence of God through the determination of the concept of God.

As a consequence, he opposed the cosmological and physico-teleological arguments as well, at least insofar as they relied on the ontological proof in their affirmation of God's existence. Kant was firmly convinced that God exists. That was not the problem, as far as he was concerned. It is just that he was unmoved by this one argument in particular. This being an unusual position for a philosopher/theologian to take at the time, he established a reputation for himself on this account.

At the same time, he became a force to be reckoned with in regard to the argument from the concept of moral law. If the number of modern works that quote him and attempt to explain the various aspects of his writings are any indication, he may be also the single most influential writer in the field of philosophy in human history. It is therefore justifiable for us to spend a few pages exploring his special arguments on behalf of God from the perspective of morality.

The Kantian Version of the Argument

Before we proceed to deal with the Kantian approach to the subject in greater detail, it would be helpful briefly to summarize his argument. Kant held that a rational, moral being must necessarily will "the highest good," which consists of a world in which people are both morally good and happy, and in which moral virtue is the condition for happiness. The latter condition implies that this end must be sought solely by moral action. However, Kant held that a person cannot rationally will such an end without believing that moral actions can successfully achieve such an end, and this requires a belief that the causal structure of nature is

The Moral Argument

conducive to the achievement of this end by moral means. This is equivalent to belief in God, a moral being who is ultimately responsible for the character of the natural world (ibid.). So, from the perspective of this reasoned approach to the matter, according to Kant, God must exist. He is the ideological prerequisite to such a prevailing circumstance.

In the three *Critiques* and in another of his works, *Religion within the Bounds of Pure Reason* (1793), Kant enumerated his unique form of the moral argument for the existence of God. The basic structure of the argument has been expressed simply by the following syllogism:

Premise 1: The highest good is the necessary object of the moral law.
Premise 2: The highest good must be (believed to be) possible.
Premise 3: God is the condition of the possibility of the highest good.
Conclusion: Therefore, God must (be believed to) exist.

Kant's concept of "the highest good," and specifically the human being's need to affirm its real possibility, is the main point of the argument, and the one on which the argument as a whole stands or falls. The great philosopher explained what he meant by the highest good (*höchste Gut*) at the beginning of chapter 2 of the Dialectic of the second *Critique*. There he begins by noting that there are two different ways to understand the term "highest good." The supreme good (*das oberste Gut*) is highest insofar as it is unconditioned, that is, it is not desired for the sake of anything else. The complete good (*das vollendete Gut*) is highest insofar as it is not part of a better, greater whole, and thus, nothing could be added to make it better. The highest good combines these two senses of "highest" into one concept: it must be both supreme and complete good. He further explained that virtue is "the supreme condition of whatever can even seem to us desirable." But that does not mean that virtue exhausts our desires, for we can also desire happiness, although under the condition of virtue, and therefore perfectly proportioned to virtue. Further, we can desire not only our own virtue and happiness, but also that everyone should be virtuous and, on that account, happy. Thus, "happiness distributed in exact proportion to morality (as the

GOD DOES EXIST!

worth of a person and his worthiness to be happy) constitutes the *highest good* of a possible world," which is highest both in the sense of being supreme and in the sense of being complete.

Now, the highest good also has the character of an end. Kant also suggests in this case that we can understand the term "end" in two ways. First, it may be understood as an ultimate end (*letzter Zweck*), or an ultimate state of affairs in the universe, and also as a final end (*Endzweck*) or final *purpose* of our actions. So the concept of the highest good is to be understood as an intended purpose for our actions and not merely our prediction of their results. Nevertheless, Kant draws a distinction here between an action's intended *object* and its *motive*. The moral evaluation of our actions abstracts from the end intended and considers only the motive for which we do them. If the determining ground of my will is a moral maxim, adopted out of respect for moral law, then my action is moral. But the execution of moral actions, for humans, always involves reference to an end.

The third premise of the moral argument also depends on the nature of the highest good, insofar as it invokes God as the necessary condition for the highest good's combination of virtue and happiness. These two elements are heterogeneous, according to Kant, but we must also resist the temptation to read him as saying that they are somehow contradictory or that they come from different sources. The highest good is not the state wherein I seek happiness as long as the moral law lets me get away with it, abandoning the pursuit when it runs up against the categorical imperative. Rather, the moral law itself, in providing the highest good as its object, mandates the pursuit of universal happiness as part of what makes me virtuous. One and the same human nature in me is the source of both the determination of what makes me happy and the determination of duty according to pure practical reason. Kant believed that because of the way the human will works, we must set the highest good as our final end if we are to be moral people. Sometimes he expresses this by saying that we have a duty to pursue the highest good, but this does not mean that this is a duty with its own content, in addition to the other duties we know from the categorical imperative.

Rather, it is the concept of a final end that unites all of the objects that morality sets for the human being; pursuing it is therefore a duty

The Moral Argument

for me only insofar as it contains the concept of all my other duties put together (cf. Paul Guyer, *Kant on Freedom, Law, and Happiness*, 339-45; W. C. Duraney, *Kant's Moral Argument for the Existence of God*, 26-32).

In his argument on behalf of the highest good in his first *Critique*, Kant outlines the idea of what he describes as "a moral world" that pure reason provides for us. He says there is a connection of nature and freedom, a "system of self-rewarding morality," which would require the existence of God for its possibility, since nature does not offer the ground of such a systematic connection of virtue and happiness. After presenting the concept of the moral world and arguing that it would require the existence of God for its possibility, he argues that it is "a world into which we must without exception transpose ourselves in accordance with the precepts of pure but practical reason." Pure reason itself supplies us with this concept, abstracting from all inclinations toward self-gratification: happiness in proportion to virtue is the complete good that a rational being would choose if he were to disinterestedly distribute happiness among all others. The reason that we must think of ourselves as being in this moral world is that otherwise we would not be able to ground our actions in the world on moral maxims. Instead, the moral law would remain a mere idea without the ability to determine actions in history.

In the second *Critique*, he moves on to speak of the highest supreme good as the virtuous disposition of moral beings in that world, and so he posits that this must also be the condition for happiness insofar as these are combined in the highest complete good. This combination is, therefore, necessary and not merely by chance. Once he establishes the necessary connection between virtue and happiness in the highest good, Kant argues that this is a synthetic and *a priori* connection. This combination is synthetic, in that the concepts of virtue and happiness are of completely different species, and do not contain one another. What is more, since the concept of the highest good as the supreme and complete good does not come about through experience, it must be *a priori*. If the highest good is a synthetic *a priori* object as well, then the moral law commands me to pursue it. I *ought* to follow it. The precise meaning of this *ought* is not clear in the second *Critique*.

In the second *Critique*, Kant further argues from the concept of the highest good insofar as it is the supreme and complete good. But in the

GOD DOES EXIST!

third *Critique* he reasons from the nature of the highest good as an end: not merely as an ultimate end, or a final state of affairs in the universe, but as a final end or final *purpose* of our actions. In reasoning *a priori* about the final end, Kant states, we arrive at a subjective condition that we call "happiness" and an objective condition (worthiness to be happy) for setting a final end. Thus, he establishes the highest good as an *a priori* object of pure practical reason through the consideration of what it means to set a final end for moral action.

Kant's presentation of the argument for the highest good in the second *Critique* is considered to be the *locus classicus* for this argument, and for the moral argument for God's existence as a whole. In framing the argument, Kant repeatedly refers to the highest good as a duty or command of the moral law. To his way of thinking, the highest good is not another duty provided by the moral law, but simply the sum of all my duties taken together. With respect to its practical use, reason seeks not only the unconditioned determining ground of the will, which is the moral law, but also the unconditioned object, which is the highest good.

So, he argues for the highest good insofar as it is the unconditioned object of moral striving. And, because it is an *a priori* synthetic concept, whether considered under the aspect of the complete good or of the final end, the concept of the highest good is *necessary* for us in the sense of being a psychological necessity: our faculties demand that we think about the actions we carry out in experience (whether under a pragmatic or a moral law) in connection with the goods that are their ends. It does not, however, seem necessary that every human being think about the complete good or the final end with respect to morality in general, only that the moral law supplies a finite end here and now. But insofar as a person asks himself, "What end would be produced by a wholly moral life?" the answer is necessarily the highest good.

The central premise of the moral argument is the possibility of the highest good. From this it is clear that there is something persuasive about the claim that the highest good is the necessary object of morality. It forces a rational agent toward a belief that the highest good is possible in the world and that he or she *ought* to strive toward that end. As Frederick Beiser interprets this notion, the second premise of Kant's thesis sets forth the rationale "that if we assume we have a duty,

The Moral Argument

we must also presuppose the conditions necessary to act on it" (Beiser, "Moral Faith," 605).

This is frequently associated with the principle of "ought implies can" as being important for the second premise of the moral argument. Given this principle, the ought of *pursuing* the highest good cannot imply the can of *achieving* the highest good. The two are not the same. Objection to this argument is only fatal if it is taken as meaning that Kant conceives his reasoning to be proceeding from the practical claim that "I ought to pursue the highest good" to the theoretical claim that "the highest good is in fact possible for me."

Once again, the two are very different things. We can believe one without believing the other. So, in sum, the content of the moral argument's second premise has to do with the recognition of a rational relationship between a man undertaking a moral action and his affirming the possibility of the end to which it is directed. This is an affirmation of the real possibility of the end, which is implied at least in general by the very fact that it is represented as an end to be pursued in the world, but it cannot be theoretical knowledge.

Because of the systematic connection among moral ends, moreover, it follows that even the representation of a finite moral end that is a duty for a person is an implicit affirmation of the real possibility of the highest good. Said Kant: "Make the highest possible good in this world your own final end." This exhortation contains the *a priori* principle of the cognition of the determining grounds of a free power of choice in experience in general. To represent morality as possibly having an effect in experience, one must simultaneously implicitly represent the real possibility of the highest good. The concept itself of the highest good will yield a certain content for the conditions of its possibility, and one of those conditions is God's existence.

Kant's argument for God's existence, in its essence, is given most explicitly in the second *Critique*. The highest good demands the systematic connection between the virtuous disposition of moral agents and the happiness they enjoy. Therefore, the highest good requires some ground capable of effecting a systematic connection between the virtuous disposition of moral agents and the happiness they enjoy. Says

GOD DOES EXIST!

Kant, "Happiness is the state of a rational being in the world in the whole of whose existence *everything goes according to his wish and will,* and rests, therefore, on the harmony of nature with his whole end as well as with the essential determining ground of his will."

Therefore neither the moral law itself nor the acting rational agent could suffice as the ground of the highest good. It would be insufficient for the highest good if nature were merely designed such that when people do their duty, they become happy; it must be that doing their duty *because it is their duty* causes them to become happy. Therefore, the supreme ground of the highest good must be capable of the representation of laws of duty and of causality according to such representation.

In sum, Kant explains, "the highest good in the world is possible only insofar as a supreme cause of nature having a causality in keeping with the moral disposition is assumed." This means that the supreme cause is an intelligence, since it represents laws, and has a will, which is causality according to the representation of a law. So the supreme ground of the highest good must be "a being that is the cause of nature by understanding and will (hence its author), that is, God." Logically, then, he goes on to say, the real possibility of the highest good provides us with "a precisely determined concept of this original being," One "possessed of the highest perfection": omniscient, omnipotent, omnipresent, eternal, etc.

So the determinate concept of God yielded by the moral argument is determined by the concept of the highest good, "which is infinite" (Duraney, *Kant's Moral Argument*, 57-58). He describes this being in the following brief paragraph:

> Omniscience, omnipotence, omnipresence, etc., are requisite as the natural properties belonging to [the concept of a supreme author] which must be conceived as connected with and hence as adequate to the moral final end, *which is infinite, and which can thus alone* provide the concept of a *single author* of the world that is suitable for theology (Kant, *Critique of the Power of Judgment*, 5:481).

Kant's language at times is difficult to follow, as is his meandering reasoning. But the direction of his thought and the conclusion to which he takes the reader is abundantly clear. He is relentless in his movement toward that goal. There must be a God. He must exist. He is the only plausible explanation for the ubiquitous moral climate in the world. He

The Moral Argument

is the singular satisfying answer to the mystery of morality in human experience.

The Moral Law Within

And so, according to Kant, the concept of morality, of the reality of good and evil, implies the existence of a Being that is the embodiment of the ultimate Good, the source of the objective moral values we encounter in the world. As complex as the great philosopher's presentation may seem at times to the reader, in fact what we have set forth above, is a vastly simplified form of his overall argument. Kant cannot be read without the application of profound thought. His argumentation must be taken in slowly and reflectively in order for one to appreciate its persuasiveness.

One passage from Kant has been remembered for precisely the opposite reason, however, and will be so throughout the ages. It is remarkable in its unexpected simplicity and perhaps the one quotation from his pen that will always be associated with him and his thinking on the subject. It is found in his book *Critique of Practical Reason*: "Two things fill the mind with. . . admiration and awe. . . the starry heavens above and the moral law within."

In so saying, Kant was alluding both to what he described as the "uniform universe" as well as to the "sense of ought" within the human mind. This "sense of ought," a moral inclination within man, is not merely the result of the mores and customs of a particular culture. Rather, it is an innate capacity to know right and wrong, to designate them as such, and to know that some things are morally superior or inferior to others. John Henry Newman, in his 1870 book, *An Essay in Aid of a Grammar of Assent*, made excellent use of this argument to make the case for the existence of God. It is considered by many to be the preeminent statement of this aspect of the proof.

The quotation below is protracted, but beautifully written and indicative of the much longer and extraordinarily well argued case he made to justify his conviction about morality as a proof for the being of God:

> Half the world would be puzzled to know what was meant by the moral sense; but every one knows what is meant by a good or bad

conscience. Conscience is ever forcing on us by threats and by promises that we must follow the right and avoid the wrong; so far it is one and the same in the mind of every one, whatever be its particular errors in particular minds as to the acts which it orders to be done or to be avoided; and in this respect it corresponds to our perception of the beautiful and deformed. As we have naturally a sense of the beautiful and graceful in nature and art, though tastes proverbially differ, so we have a sense of duty and obligation, whether we all associate it with the same certain actions in particular or not. Here, however, Taste and Conscience part company: for the sense of beautifulness, as indeed the Moral Sense, has no special relations to persons, but contemplates objects in themselves; conscience, on the other hand, is concerned with persons primarily, and with actions mainly as viewed in their doers, or rather with self alone and one's own actions, and with others only indirectly and as if in association with self. And further, taste is its own evidence, appealing to nothing beyond its own sense of the beautiful or the ugly, and enjoying the specimens of the beautiful simply for their own sake; but conscience does not repose on itself, but vaguely reaches forward to something beyond self, and dimly discerns a sanction higher than self for its decisions, as is evidenced in that keen sense of obligation and responsibility which informs them. And hence it is that we are accustomed to speak of conscience as a voice, a term which we should never think of applying to the sense of the beautiful; and moreover a voice, or the echo of a voice, imperative and constraining, like no other dictate in the whole of our experience.

And again, in consequence of this prerogative of dictating and commanding, which is of its essence, Conscience has an intimate bearing on our affections and emotions, leading us to reverence and awe, hope and fear, especially fear, a feeling which is foreign for the most part, not only to Taste, but even to the Moral Sense, except in consequence of accidental associations. No fear is felt by any one who recognizes that his conduct has not been beautiful, though he may be mortified at himself, if perhaps he has thereby forfeited some advantage; but, if he has been betrayed into any kind of immorality, he has a lively sense of responsibility and guilt, though the act be no offence against society,—of distress and apprehension, even though it may be of present service to him,—of compunction and regret, though in itself it be most pleasurable,—of confusion of face, though it may have no witnesses. These various perturbations of mind which are characteristic of a bad conscience, and may be very considerable,—self-reproach, poignant

The Moral Argument

shame, haunting remorse, chill dismay at the prospect of the future,—and their contraries, when the conscience is good, as real though less forcible, self-approval, inward peace, lightness of heart, and the like,—these emotions constitute a specific difference between conscience and our other intellectual senses,—common sense, good sense, sense of expedience, taste, sense of honour, and the like,—as indeed they would also constitute between conscience and the moral sense, supposing these two were not aspects of one and the same feeling, exercised upon one and the same subject-matter (107-8).

At the last, Newman draws his conclusion:

Conscience too, considered as a moral sense, an intellectual sentiment, is a sense of admiration and disgust, of approbation and blame: but it is something more than a moral sense; it is always, what the sense of the beautiful is only in certain cases; it is always emotional. No wonder then that it always implies what that sense only sometimes implies; that it always involves the recognition of a living object, towards which it is directed. Inanimate things cannot stir our affections; these are correlative with persons. If, as is the case, we feel responsibility, are ashamed, are frightened, at transgressing the voice of conscience, this implies that there is One to whom we are responsible, before whom we are ashamed, whose claims upon us we fear. If, on doing wrong, we feel the same tearful, broken-hearted sorrow which overwhelms us on hurting a mother; if, on doing right, we enjoy the same sunny serenity of mind, the same soothing, satisfactory delight which follows on our receiving praise from a father, we certainly have within us the image of some person, to whom our love and veneration look, in whose smile we find our happiness, for whom we yearn, towards whom we direct our pleadings, in whose anger we are troubled and waste away (109-10).

Our terminology about such things constantly reveals this fact of human nature, about which Newman and a host of other authors have spoken. We use freighted words like murder, steal, rape, plunder, savage, and a whole host of others, to depict an action as morally wrong. These terms are shot through with moralizing overtones. In fact, this is a moral constant in our use of language. And yet, we understand that animals commit these same acts against their fellows all of the time, under generally similar circumstances, without our imposing moral strictures on them.

GOD DOES EXIST!

For example, a larger baboon takes away a piece of fruit from one of his smaller band (technically, a "congress") members, and we do not accuse him of "theft." He is merely doing what comes naturally to him as an animal. If he is the larger of the two, he does as he likes, and takes what he wants. But if a larger man takes from another person what he has worked for and purchased with his own money, we accuse him not merely of taking, but of "stealing." When a male great white shark forcibly copulates with a female of the same species, he is doing what nature has programmed him to do. But if a man forces himself on a woman or girl, he is considered guilty of "rape." The word with which we choose to describe his action is a term that has moral overtones. It connotes a form of immorality. He has not merely done what came naturally to him as the larger and stronger of the two persons, he has committed an immoral act, he has "stolen" from another or committed "forcible rape" (a legal term describing carnal knowledge of a female forcibly and against her will), but also a term of ignominy.

If an ox gores a man to death, he is not arrested, tried, and condemned to death by a jury of his peers in a court of law. Rather, we recognize the creature's inability to make moral judgments, confine him in a sturdier pen than formerly, and warn everyone not to come near him. He is a dangerous animal, but he is not a murderer. Those who are wise understand that any animal is capable of a similar act under comparable circumstances. When a man kills another man, however, his treatment is vastly different. The only reason for it to be different is that man has an ethical and moral sense of what is right and what is wrong, and that sense normally restrains him from doing things of this sort. If he does take the life of another under certain circumstances, we charge him with a violation of law, and call him a *murderer*. He has not merely killed someone, he has *murdered* him. Again, this word itself is a form of moral judgment imposed on the person who commits certain acts unjustifiably. Not only so, but we hold him accountable and punish him for his crime. His punishment is meted out relative to his ability to understand and be intellectually responsible for his actions. The greater his maturity and capacity for appreciation for the moral turpitude of his behavior, the stiffer the penalty imposed. We shall return to this notion momentarily, but for the present this is sufficient to illustrate the point.

The Moral Argument

That man has this capacity, and thinks about such things as he does, can hardly be explained unless there is a moral governor of the universe. It implies a moral Creator, God. Now, there is a related fact that needs to be introduced into the discussion at this point. It is universally observed that human beings attempt to convince themselves in every instance of action or belief that their own actions or beliefs are right and justifiable. In fact they sometimes do this in the most despicable instances, where they have behaved in a manner that is deplorable to everyone except themselves. It seems that they desire the approval of their own consciences, as well as the hoped-for approval of their fellow men. They hope against hope, that they will be able to convince the rest of us that what they did was understandable under the circumstances as they perceived them to be at the time.

This is one of the reasons that it is often said that "there are no guilty people in prison." They are virtually *all* innocent, accused wrongfully. The person that admits his crime is rare. Now, this is not to demean the fact that there are occasionally people who are wrongfully accused, and even actually innocent and therefore wrongfully imprisoned. That is not the point. The point is that even the most guilty offender sees himself as innocent on some level. He has been able to convince himself that this is so, even if no one else ever falls for his pitiful attempt at personal justification. This returns us to our original assertion: human beings want to justify their attitudes and actions, even when they are unjustifiable. They very much desire the approbation of their own conscience as well as the approval of their fellow men. Even the most violent and evil among us are so.

In the light of all this, is it unreasonable to assume that the presence of a moral nature in man is an indication of a moral governor? Why should man be concerned with the demands of conscience if he is nothing more than an animal or a chance combination of random atoms? (Cf. Baxter, *I Believe Because*, 45ff). Most of us would agree that if there is no God, then the presence of this moral nature of which we speak is an enormous inconvenience for us. To some degree it may be profitable in the sense that it forces most of us to conform to societal norms and expectations. It therefore dampens down the level of criminal behavior and general chaos that would ensue otherwise. That part is not arguable.

GOD DOES EXIST!

But all in all it is an aggravating quality in the human species, if that is all there is to it. It extends quite beyond the bounds of merely limiting excessive behavior and societal breakdown. This is something that is eminently personal and has the potential to be personally devastating, and in fact has often been so. Why should the responsible party lie awake at night, haunted by a guilty conscience, long after the fact of an action, when there is nothing to feel guilty about? Why should a person suffer in silent mental agony decades after having committed an infraction of the moral code, if it represents no more than a social convention intended to press us into conformity with societal norms? In that case, morality is merely a custom-based device which has been invented to force compliance with society's expectations but also frustrates the ends of evolutionary development. If God does not exist, then only the strongest and the most cunning *ought* to survive!

Social justice, indeed! Why do we invent such concepts in the first place, if indeed we do? Why do we concern ourselves with ideas like fairness, reciprocity, honesty, kindness, compassion, mercy, grace, forgiveness, humility, chivalry, politeness, good manners, etc.? Why do we attempt to domesticate the ravenous monster that lies hidden or dormant (but not always so) in the worst and sometimes even in the best of us? This goes far beyond the bounds of complicity with societal norms. It plumbs to the depths of the soul itself. It wreaks havoc on the human psyche and has frequently led to mental breakdowns. Why do our infractions against the moral code disturb us so deeply? Why does not even time assuage their injury? Why is haunting guilt a perturbation that is almost always tinged with dread and fear, even though we may have already escaped the temporal consequences of our actions?

The answer to these questions is simple: *it is because we believe in God*. We are convinced that He exists. Because we believe this, we know that He expects us to do better than the worst that we can do. And we are convinced that He will hold us accountable for our actions as well as the attitudes that have motivated them. *We have a moral nature, and we cannot escape it*. Try as we may, we cannot. As inconvenient as it can be at times, it is always there to condemn us when we do wrong. And the conscience follows in its wake, punishing us mercilessly unless we

The Moral Argument

suppress it with alcohol or drugs or repeated repetition of the action or forcing it into quiescence by means of radical self-justification.

This inner sense of right and wrong is referred to in the Scriptures. For example, Paul related the notion to unknowledgeable pagans who were devoid of understanding of God's law given to Moses, yet still had moral underpinnings on account of what God had "written on their hearts." In this same context he noted the participation of the conscience in addressing the problem of the human tendency to refuse or simply fail to conduct themselves in compliance with the expectations of this inner code:

> For when Gentiles, who do not have the law, by nature do what the law requires, they are a law to themselves, even though they do not have the law. They show that the work of the law is written on their hearts, while their conscience also bears witness, and their conflicting thoughts accuse or else excuse them. . . (Rom. 2:14-15, ESV).

Paul here freely admits that legitimate knowledge of God's will is available for men outside the direct revelation found in the Old Testament Scriptures. The concept of natural man's awareness of a universal divine law was an idea that was promoted by the Stoics. Epictetus was well known for his enumeration of the concept. In Cleanthes's *Hymn to Zeus*, a work of early Greek Stoicism, there is this notation: "And this the evil among mortal men avoid and heed not; wretched, ever desiring to possess the good, yet they nor see nor hear *the universal Law of God*, which obeying with all their heart, their life would be well. But they rush graceless each to his own aim." Even pagans knew well this concept.

In fact, it is worth mentioning that Paul in verse 14 employs exactly the same words when he speaks of certain men being "a law to themselves" that Aristotle does in his *Nicomachean Ethics* (cf. 4.8; and *Politics* 3.13.14; compare also Gal. 5:23). It seems that in the text from Romans Paul is saying that those who never knew of the Law of Moses would not be judged by that law which they had no opportunity to know, and even if they had known it were not subject to its dictates, but would be judged on the basis of their own sense of right and wrong, the law that God had "written on their hearts." They did not come to this knowledge by their own reflection, however. God initiated the process. Paul says that he wrote it on their hearts.

GOD DOES EXIST!

As R. L. Whiteside remarked about this passage:

> The Gentiles never had the law of Moses, but there are certain fundamental principles that inhere in the nature of our existence and in our relations to one another. Some things are right, and some things are wrong, within themselves. If a man never had a revelation from God, he would know that it was wrong to murder his fellow man, or to rob him of his possessions, or in any way to infringe on his rights. Cain sinned in killing his brother and felt his guilt, though we have no record that God had told him not to kill. God's moral law is the same to all nations (*Commentary on Romans*, 57).

Theoretically, on this assumption, it is possible that a man might not ever come to know and experience sin. If he were to live up perfectly to the best that he has the capability of knowing, then he would never become a sinner and so would never be lost.

However, we all know that this is all but impossible. The idea itself is nothing more than a theoretical postulate. No person can live up perfectly even to the most elemental moral and ethical code. Inevitably that individual will at some point violate his own sense of right conduct. When a man does this he becomes a sinner and is lost, or estranged from God. It is this reality, along with the practical demonstration of this principle made evident by the law of Moses (Rom. 2:12; 7:10-11), that sets the stage for the Christian understanding of "salvation," i.e. deliverance from sin, or forgiveness: "For we have already charged that all, both Jews and Greeks, are under sin, as it is written: 'None is righteous, no, not one; no one understands; no one seeks for God. All have turned aside; together they have become worthless; no one does good, not even one'" (Rom. 3:9-12).

For the modern secularist these words may sound harsh and judgmental, for that is precisely what they are. They are not too harsh or too judgmental. What they tell us about is the perspective of the one who wrote the code. He is not pleased with our rebellion. But the fact that some people do not appreciate the language employed to communicate this truth does not alter the logical necessity of what they tell us. In saying what he does in this passage, Paul was making the point that God had used the Mosaic code of laws in order to prove to the Jewish people that they were sinners in need of a Savior.

The Moral Argument

Absent that, the pagans and others outside the purview of that system of moral restrictions were left to the system of their own inner barriers God had imbued in them since the creation. And like the Jews, they also had proven themselves incapable of living up to the standard of their own inbuilt understanding of moral behavior. They were sinners too: "for through law comes a knowledge of sin" (as translated literally; Gr. *dia gar nomou epignōsis hamartias*).

Any legal code has the effect of accentuating the reality of law-breaking or transgression. The author is addressing specifically the flagrant transgressions of the Mosaic code by the people of Israel in the context, but the point is generally applicable to any comparable situation. Any legal system will eventually prove us to be transgressors, because we will eventually fail to live up to our own expectations for ourselves, not even to mention the divine anticipation of our obedience to His will. Once more, the bare fact of this inner code's existence is evidence that God made us.

In his book *Mere Christianity*, C. S. Lewis makes the case for the moral law within man and its proof for the existence of God. It is evident in the simplest and most uncomplicated ways in human nature. He wrote:

> Every one has heard people quarreling. Sometimes it sounds funny and sometimes it sounds merely unpleasant; but however it sounds, I believe we can learn something very important from listening to the kind of things they say. They say things like this: "How'd you like it if anyone did the same to you?"—"That's my seat; I was there first."—"Leave him alone; he isn't doing you any harm." —"Why should you shove in first?"—"Give me a bit of your orange. I gave you a bit of mine."—"Come on, you promised." People say things like that every day, educated people as well as uneducated, and children as well as grownups.... [One] is appealing to some kind of standard of behavior which he expects the other man to know about.... Nearly always he tries to make out that what he has been doing does not really go against the standard, or that if it does there is some special excuse.... It looks, in fact, very much as if both parties had in mind some kind of Law or Rule of fair play or decent behavior or morality or whatever you like to call it, about which they really agreed. And they have. If they had not, they might, of course, fight like animals, but they could not *quarrel* in the human sense of the word. Quarreling means trying to show that the other fellow is in the wrong. And there would be no

GOD DOES EXIST!

sense in trying to do that unless you and he had some sort of agreement as to what Right and Wrong are; just as there would be no sense in saying that a footballer had committed a foul unless there were some agreement about the rules of football.

Now the Law or Rule about Right and Wrong used to be called the law of Nature... they really meant the Law of Human Nature (3-4).

Sometimes it is argued that this point is not well taken because different societies have had different moral codes. But this is not actually the case. Minor differences have too often been overblown in our comparisons between various cultures. No matter what society is appealed to in history, even over vastly different historic periods, there has been a remarkable consistency about virtually everything. Stealing what is someone else's property has never been considered acceptable behavior in any society. Lying in court has never been justifiable. Committing fraud against an unwary victim has not been seen as good. Killing an innocent person has been criminal in every society we know anything about. These same behaviors and others similar to them are still condemned in the legal codes of every land.

Moreover, it is expected that visitors to any other country on earth will not need to be advised that murder is wrong and punishable in that particular jurisdiction. It is wrong everywhere; and everyone is expected to know this. Can you think of any situation where a visitor to any other nation has pleaded innocence on account of "ignorance of the law" in a case of first degree homicide? It could never happen! How "lame" would that argument sound in court: "I was not aware it was a crime to kill people in your country"?

Distinctions that relate to local practices, such as which side of the road is considered the wrong side to drive a vehicle on, are not relevant to this topic. There is nothing inherently moral or immoral about driving in the right or left lane. It does, though, have applicability in terms of whether or not one's action, such as driving under the influence of alcohol or drugs, or intentionally driving erratically so as to endanger the lives of others, might lead to the death or injury of an innocent person. Then, even so seemingly insignificant a matter as this could result in moral culpability for someone who ignores or disregards a purely local preference that has been written into law.

The Moral Argument

Some claim that the Moral Law of which we speak is simply our "herd instinct," something that has developed in *homo sapiens* like all of our other instincts. But is this true? We all understand what it is to be prompted by instinct, by the love of a mother for her child, or the sexual instinct, or the instinct to seek out and consume food or water. These are instinctual needs of the human body and the human psyche and they are rather easy for us to understand and explain. But others are more complex and are far more difficult to understand or explain.

For example, let us assume that a man is standing on the bank of a swiftly moving stream, and he notices someone floundering in the water, about to drown. When they call out to him for help, he is confronted with a dilemma. This is so because two different instincts or impulses immediately register in his mind. The first is the instinct for personal survival. There is no stronger one than this. It is the most powerful of all instinctual desires, simply to stay alive, to survive in the face of danger. That instinct recognizes that if we jump into the water, our own life is in peril and we may also drown.

The second is an instinct that tends to ignore the factor of danger or risk of personal injury or death. It is the desire to plunge into the stream in the hope that we may be able to save the life of another struggling human being, someone who wants to live just as much as we do. All of our heroes are people who have followed this second course of action, in spite of the potential for injury or death. Lewis continues his commentary:

> But you will find inside you, in addition to these two impulses, a third thing which tells you that you ought to follow the impulse to help, and suppress the impulse to run away. Now this thing that judges between two instincts, that decides which should be encouraged, cannot itself be either of them.... If two instincts are in conflict, and there is nothing in a creature's mind except those two instincts, obviously the stronger of the two must win. But at those moments when we are most conscious of the Moral Law, it usually seems to be telling us to side with the weaker of the two impulses (8-9).

This is a profound observation. But who cannot understand it? It depicts precisely the give and take that goes on in the mind of a person who is confronted with such a situation as is described. And it helps us to understand this mysterious something that causes a hero to become

GOD DOES EXIST!

a hero. It also helps us define cowardice. That person who risks life and limb to help another is universally recognized as the type of sacrificial individual that we would most want to imitate. We all hope that in similar circumstances we would be willing to do likewise. A fireman runs toward the danger of a burning building in hopes that he will save a helpless victim or salvage valuable property from being utterly ruined. He does so in spite of the fact that fear of fire is one of the most vivid of our human concerns. A policeman selflessly speeds towards a crime scene in order to rescue someone who is a victim of a merciless perpetrator. He does not know how strong or how large, nor yet how well armed the fellow might prove to be. He goes there anyway. A soldier runs in the direction of the gunfire, thoughtlessly doing what he was trained to do for his family at home and for his friends who run and fight beside him. Of course he is afraid of what he is running toward; but what he fears most of all is not doing his duty.

All of these are the actions of people who are doing exactly the opposite of the most powerful instinct within the human mind: the will to survive, the desire to live one more day. And they do not do it for their own benefit but for the benefit of others. They are heroes indeed. But they are more than heroes. They are perfectly illustrative of the principle which we are struggling here to understand. And that principle is more than merely a social convention. Heroism is not a social convention. Cowardice is not respected in any community of human beings. But bravery and heroism are admired and appreciated in every society on the planet.

What makes this so? As C.S. Lewis insisted, it is the impulse to do what is right and good and noble, even in the face of extreme danger. The Moral Law within the human psyche, installed there by the Creator, when it is followed and not thwarted, is a powerful force for good in the lives of those who do extraordinary things for the benefit of their fellows. Every act of self-sacrifice, heroism, courage, humble service, tender mercy, etc., is evidence that God, the ultimate source of what is good and noble, has made us like Himself.

The Contemporary Iteration of the Argument

In more recent times, a considerable number of philosophers from the perspective of the Christian Western tradition have explored questions related to whether or not this argument from morality has validity.

The Moral Argument

The cogency of the argument is taken for granted by a long list of scholars and writers, philosophers and theologians. Kant has continued to inspire imitators into the twentieth century. Many have written to perpetuate and further elucidate his ideas: W. R. Sorley (*Moral Values and the Idea of God*, 1918), Hastings Rashdall ("The Moral Argument for Personal Immortality," 1920), and A. E. Taylor (*The Faith of a Moralist*, 1930; and *Does God Exist?* 1945).

The books that the more recent crop of philosophers have produced are often described as "a revival of divine command metaethical theories." Robert Adams ("Moral Arguments for Theism," 1987), John Hare (*The Moral Gap*, 1996), and C. Stephen Evans (*Natural Signs and Knowledge of God*, 2010). In addition, several writers have defended slightly altered versions of the "divine command theory." Angus Ritchie (*From Morality to Metaphysics*, 2012), and Mark Linville ("The Moral Argument," 2009) have been responsible for works of this kind. But the standout in this regard is the book by David Baggett and Jerry L. Walls (*God and Cosmos*, 2016). This latter study of the subject offers a comprehensive form of the moral argument on solid philosophical grounds. It also extensively explores the underlying issues involved. The Introduction to their book provides an observation that is well worth our repeating here:

> *Moralistic* is one of the worst terms of disapprobation and derogation nowadays, and this whole notion of morality is often castigated as the deepest source of blame. Ethical relativists, to foster more tolerant attitudes and ostensible openness to those of opposing views, encourage us not to overreach by assuming that our convictions have any purchase on those outside our culture or subculture; postmoderns of various stripes eschew totalizing meta-narratives, assume a hermeneutic of suspicion, and, in the process, leave behind anything like objective moral truth. Some downright celebrate leaving morality and its judgments, condemnations, inconvenient behavioral strictures, suffocating sanctimony, and dire warnings about brimstone and hellfire altogether behind.
>
> We could not disagree more or demur with more adamacy. This book is based on the idea that morality matters deeply; that moral truth is real; and that it, in fact, offers us one of the clearest windows and veridical intimations into ultimate reality. This does not mean that we

cannot see the ways in which moral language and practice can be perverted, the way people have on occasion imposed their moral convictions in inappropriate ways, the way all manner of evils has been perpetrated under the cloak of morality. We can see that all those things have happened, but none of them provides any evidence to suggest that moral truth itself is to blame. In fact, most all of the abuses, perversions, corruptions, and various instances of cruelty, inhumanity, and meanness are best identified for what they are and denounced for being as bad as they are only by holding fast to the category of objective moral truth, without which we lose the resource to renounce them robustly (1-2).

Conclusion

Where then does objective moral value reside? Where can it be found? We know the answer to this question both from a positive and a negative vantage point. It is not in material things and not in animals. Moral value is associated with and has its reality in human persons. Non-personal things have only instrumental value in relation to persons. They are instruments that humans employ to accomplish various tasks and do work. Such instruments have no moral value intrinsic to their nature. Only persons have intrinsic value, because meaningful moral value requires purpose and will. This is the basis of the moral argument for God's existence.

In this world we find a graduation of values: some things are more good, more true, more noble, etc. Such comparative terms describe the varying degrees to which things approach a superlative standard: most good, most true, most noble, etc. Therefore, there must exist somewhere something or Someone who is best, and truest and noblest. *He does exist.* God is that most superlative standard of morality and good.

Stated simply, in syllogistic form, it would be put thus:

Premise 1: If God does not exist, objective moral values and duties do not exist.
Premise 2: Objective moral values and duties do exist.
Conclusion: Therefore, God exists.

Although the argument itself does not reach the conclusion that God is the basis of objective moral values and duties, such a claim seems to be implied in the first premise of the syllogism and will in-

The Moral Argument

evitably emerge in defense of that premise against any potential objection. Many philosophers have attempted to make the case that if God does not exist, then morality is ultimately subjective and non-binding. We might act in precisely the same ways as we do already, but in the absence of the idea of God such actions would no longer count as good or evil, right or wrong, since in the absence of God, descriptives such as these would no longer be appropriate because objective moral values and duties cannot exist.

"Moral" and "immoral" are both judgmental terms, so by their usage in a description of actions, they propose the existence of a being who is either pleased or displeased with the aforesaid actions. In the absence of that Being, morality terminology should be dispensed with. But, of course, whether or not this Being exists is exactly the question with which we are dealing in this proposition.

When we speak about moral values, we mean to designate something either good or bad. When we speak of moral duties, we are concerned with whether something is right or wrong. Now, right and wrong have to do with moral obligation, what one ought or ought not to do. Moral values, on the other hand, have to do with the intrinsic worth of something. It might be good for me to become a chemist, but it might not be best for me to become a chemist.

Either way, it would not be morally reprehensible for me to become a chemist. It might be good and it might be bad, but it is neither right nor wrong. This aspect of it has to do with its moral value. Other things are not of the same type, however. I have a moral obligation to tell the truth. To tell a lie instead is morally wrong. It is not right; it is an act that is morally evil.

However, when we say such things as this, we are employing terms of judgment. And terms of judgement assume the existence of an objective moral code. But if atheists are right in their position, then logically it cannot be sustained that a moral code exists. Therefore, lying is not wrong. Lying is morally neutral. Judging it as *wrong* may be itself morally repugnant because it might be considered to be *judgemental*. And so there you have it: that is precisely how we have gotten to the place where we are today! A great many have allowed for the appropri-

GOD DOES EXIST!

ateness of atheistic presuppositions in their approach to these things, even if they have done so subconsciously.

So, speaking of such things in objective rather than subjective terms is an important distinction. To say that something is objective is to express that it is what it is independent of what people think about it. By contrast, to say that a thing is subjective is to see it in terms of what public opinion might be about the matter. Thus, we mean to suggest that there are objective moral values and duties that are so in spite of what anyone (or even everyone) thinks about them.

Such values and duties could not exist in the absence of God. Without God, human beings have no objective moral value, and moral duties cannot exist. And, as a consequence, genocide is not morally wrong. Humans are of no more intrinsic value than cattle. We slaughter cattle regularly to consume them as food. Why would it be wrong to do something similar with populations of people that we do not favor? This is the necessary implication of atheism.

Richard Dawkins is one of the few of their number who will actually admit this, and so we quote him here: "The universe we observe has precisely the properties we should expect if there is at bottom no design, no purpose, no evil, no good, nothing but pointless indifference.... We are machines for propagating DNA.... It is every living object's sole reason for being" (*River Out of Eden: A Darwinian View of Life,* 155; cited in Craig, *Reasonable Faith,* 173-4).

Similarly, on the first page of his book *The Selfish Gene,* the same author declared: "We no longer have to resort to superstition when faced with the deep problems: Is there a meaning to life? What are we for? What is man?" These questions, he goes on to say, were given a final, unmistakably negative answer in 1859 with the publication of *The Origin of Species.* Interestingly, in his book *A Devil's Chaplain* (34), he admitted that "science has no methods for deciding what is ethical." At the same time, he fiendishly and feverishly in every book of which he is the author, makes the case that religion is evil and unethical. But how can this be? How can anything be deemed to be *unethical*? His atheism is not suited to determine what is or is not ethical empirically. This is so, by his own admission. What is this moral code by which he judges all religions

The Moral Argument

to be morally wrong? It is the moral code of his own devising. It is this and nothing more.

Another observation by C. S. Lewis may be appropriate in this context. When challenged as to the scientific validity of his Christian faith, Lewis once remarked: "I believe in Christianity as I believe that the Sun has risen—not only because I see it, but because by it, I see everything else" ("Is theology poetry?" 21). The world makes sense when we are people of faith. Everything about it is in perfect harmony with our understanding of God and His nature. It makes no sense at all when we are not. It is harsh and cruel and nothing about it is comprehensible. Atheistic thinking is therefore dissolute and perverse. Dawkins is a perfect illustration of this.

But, again, Dawkins is rare among atheists. He admits the truth on this matter. And he follows it to its logical destination. Most are in denial. On a naturalistic view of moral values, they are to be seen as mostly beneficial by-products of socio-biological evolution. As Michael Ruse, a philosopher of science, explains: "The position of the modern evolutionist... is that humans have an awareness of morality... because such an awareness is of biological worth. Morality is a biological adaptation no less than are hands and feet and teeth... ethics is illusory... Morality is just an aid to survival and reproduction,... and any deeper meaning is illusory" ("Evolutionary Theory and Christian Ethics," 262, 268-89; quoted in Craig, *Reasonable Faith*, 174). On the atheistic view, socio-biological pressures have caused development of a sort of "herd morality" which functions well in the perpetuation of the species. But there is nothing about any of this that makes morality objectively true. Human beings are not really special. To say so is "species-ism," an unjustified bias toward one's own species.

Therefore, if this view is taken to be true, there are certain logical and ethical conclusions that are unavoidable. For example, killing a person is no different than killing a cow or a pig. Exterminating a population of people whom we consider to be of little or no value is a question about which we may feel ambivalent. It is really little different from exterminating cockroaches from a house they have infested. Or killing off mice that have moved into one's garage space. The Holocaust was a morally neutral event. The Nazis certainly thought so. Marxists felt the

GOD DOES EXIST!

same in the Soviet Union and Communist China. Havens of atheism. Should we see it any differently? But, of course, this is only true if there is no God. Under this rubric a man has no obligation to do anything that we might call "right" or to demur from doing anything that we might refer to as "wrong." There is no such thing as "right and wrong." These are only social conventions. So to tell the truth, or to tell a lie, has only social conventions to commend the one and condemn the other.

Certainly many in our Western nations today have recognized the inevitable consequences of this viewpoint. They have bought into it "hook, line and sinker," so to speak. Politicians look at the cameras every day now and spew falsehoods, many malicious and patently untrue. People listen to their speeches and know that they are lying. But they do not consider what they are doing to be morally wrong because they are members of the same political party, and party affiliation is more important than anything else. This has bred the following "one liner": "How can you tell when a politician is lying? His mouth is moving." And we know this sad characterization is mostly accurate.

Public news outlets unabashedly spread what we sometimes describe as "fake news" in print and on national broadcasts. And they do so with relatively few repercussions from the public. They continue to buy their papers and magazines, follow them on Twitter and Facebook, and tune in to their reports in spite of it. Apparently a great many have wished away the moral code in the interests of party affiliation. "Thou shalt not bear false witness" means nothing to them anymore. They have lied until lying has become a practiced art with them. And, why should they not? What is there to distinguish between the true and the false if there is no God who is the standard of what is ultimately true and who is the arbiter of truth vs. error? But, again, this is only an accurate assessment of things if there is no God.

If atheism is true, then it is impossible to condemn any form of war, oppression, or crime as evil. It does not matter what we do if there is no *right* or *wrong*. Rape and incest may not be biologically or sociologically advantageous, but they are not *evil*. Remember, terms of this sort are all based in morality. They are words associated with moral concepts. And morality is associated with God.

The Moral Argument

Now, this is not to say that *belief* in God's existence is the key to the objective reality of moral values and duties. Rather, it is to assert that *God* is essential to their existence. Whatever one believes may be conducive to certain attitudes and behaviors, but belief is not the critical element in this case. It is the reality of a divinity who created mankind and imbued him with a sense of morality. The central question about moral and ethical principles concerns their ontological foundation. Where did they come from?

Our response to this question will determine whether we decide to live in harmony with a moral code or not. If they are neither derived from God nor anchored in some transcendent grounding, then they are purely ephemeral (cf. Kurz, *Forbidden Fruit*, 65; Craig, *Reasonable Faith*, 174-76). This is the problem with which the naturalist must contend. Precious few of them will admit this to be an accurate depiction of the situation, but in practice, in the daily conduct of our lives, it is extremely difficult for them to deny that this is so. Dr. William Lane Craig has stated the case against atheism on moral grounds in a convincing way:

> It seems that the atheistic humanist must simply insist, with the Dartmouth ethicist Walter Sinnot-Armstrong, that whatever contributes to human flourishing is morally good and whatever detracts from human flourishing is bad and take that as his explanatory stopping-point. But the problem is that such an explanatory stopping-point seems premature because of its arbitrariness and implausibility. Why, given atheism, think that inflicting harm on other people would have any moral dimension at all? Why would it be harmful to hurt another member of our own species? Sinnott-Armstrong answers, "It simply is. Objectively. Don't you agree?" ("There is No Good Reason to Believe in God," 34). Of course, I agree that it *is* wrong, since I am a theist. But I can't see any reason to think that it *would be* wrong if atheism were true. Sinnott-Armstrong thinks that rape is wrong, even though the physical activity that counts as rape among human beings goes on all the time in the animal kingdom—just as acts that count as murder and theft when done by one human to another occur constantly between members of other animal species—without any moral significance whatsoever. As Michael Ruse has argued, we can well conceive of extra-terrestrial rational beings for whom rape would not be immoral ("Is Rape Wrong on Andromeda?"). Were they to visit Earth, why should they respect the values that have evolved among *homo sapiens*? Had our own evo-

GOD DOES EXIST!

lutionary history gone differently, creatures with a different set of moral values might have existed here. All this underlines the arbitrariness of Sinnott-Armstrong's explanatory ultimate (*Reasonable Faith, 177*).

And, make no mistake about it, the non-Christian public sees where atheistic naturalism is leading them. An unfortunate number are marching in lockstep. Nihilism is the final stop on this highway of doom. A great many people have already arrived at the destination. Aimlessness, suicide, drug addiction, and conspicuous alcohol consumption is the end result for far too many. Others are awakening to the fact, almost daily, that this is where they are headed. Hopefully they will turn back from the chasm before they reach it. There is a better way. Recognizing the reality of God and acknowledging the legitimacy of His claim on us by living moral lives is the only hope for each of us personally, and for Western civilization for the long term.

God knows, and we also recognize by the hard business of everyday experience, that no finite person has ever fully realized all moral value or attended perfectly to every moral duty. All reasonable people recognize this simple truth. "All have sinned and fallen short of the glory of God" (Rom. 3:23). "There is no man who does not sin" (1 Kings 8:46; 2 Chron. 6:36). All of us are aware of and acknowledge our own personal and societal failings. We deal with them everyday. We admit the truthfulness of the burden of them when we say such things as the following: "To err is human, to forgive is divine." So, if the moral ideal is not realized in this physical world by any person or persons, it must be realized in One who is both personal and eternal, that is, God. That, dear reader, is the essence of the Moral Argument for God's existence.

Questions for Discussion
1. What are the main outlines of the various arguments based on objective moral values and duties to make the case for the existence of God?
2. Summarize the argument as it was framed by Plato. Did the ancient philosopher specifically identify "the Good" about which he hypothesized? What is it about his argument that has caused Christian philosophers and theologians to be drawn to it and embrace it?

The Moral Argument

3. Summarize the approach to "the fourth way" suggested by Thomas Aquinas. What are "degrees of perfection," and how do they point toward God?
4. Is it fair to criticize Aquinas for his general approach to morality as it points the mind toward God as the source of the moral code in man? Was he merely borrowing concepts from Plato and Aristotle, or was his approach sufficiently Christian in orientation to justify it as such?
5. Immanuel Kant is one of the most formative figures in the history of making arguments for the existence of God from the perspective of morality. Why is he so important? Can you frame his line of argumentation in just a few words? The conclusion of his argument was that "God must be believed to exist." Do you share this conviction? Why or why not?
6. How would you define "the highest good" in the philosophy of Kant? What did Kant mean by "the ultimate end" or "final end"?
7. Kant speaks of a "system of self-rewarding morality" as pointing toward some Being, some intelligent force, behind that system. Flesh out this concept in your own words. What is he talking about?
8. The concept of a "moral law within man" has been conceptualized by numerous authors throughout the history of philosophical speculation. Describe this notion in some detail, and discuss its implications. What is it and where did it come from? Is it taught in the Bible, and if so, where?
9. "Conscience... is something more than a moral sense," wrote John Henry Newman. How does the presence of a conscience in the constitution of a human being's mental architecture argue for the existence of God? In what way does it point us to God?
10. How do terms like murder, steal, rape, incest, etc., enter into the picture of a human being's tendency to "moralize" about certain types of human actions? Illustrate this notion by analyzing the distinction between "taking" and "stealing."

GOD DOES EXIST!

11. Different societies have various moral codes and have had throughout human history. Are there essential similarities between them all? Why is this so? How is this to be explained? How would you deal with some of the differences between them?

12. How would you state the moral argument for God in simple terms for a contemporary generation? Do you believe the argument has validity? What are some alternative explanations for morality in human communities? How would you answer these objections?

Chapter 9
The Intelligence Argument

In this segment of our study we plan to discuss the argument from the phenomenon we describe as intelligence. Intelligence is a trait that is unique to humanity. It is the ability to think abstractly and apply knowledge to manipulate one's environment. Animals do not exhibit a capacity for abstract thought. Moreover, the mechanism of how such thought works is no easy matter. This is true on several levels. After many years of attempting to work through the processes in order to apply them to artificial intelligence, Terry Winograd of Stanford, speaking of "Thinking Machines," said, "there is no reason but hubris to believe that we are any closer to understanding intelligence than the alchemists were to the secrets of nuclear physics" (Winograd, 1986). So this is not an easy subject, but to explore the topic in terms of the origin of intelligence is particularly important for our examination of the formal arguments for the existence of God.

GOD DOES EXIST!

Elusive Definitions

A wide range of different definitions appear in the literature that deals with this topic. As R. J. Sternberg is quoted as saying, "Viewed narrowly, there seem to be almost as many definitions of intelligence as there were experts asked to define it." Shane Legg and Marcus Hutter in their essay, "A Collection of Definitions of Intelligence" (in the 2006 book *Advances in Artificial General Intelligence: Concepts, Architectures, and Algorithms*, 17-24) listed 18 separate ways of defining it under the heading of "Collective Definitions," and 35 different ones under the rubric of "Psychologist Definitions." Our personal favorite is from J. Drever: "... in its lowest terms intelligence is present where the individual animal, or human being, is aware, however dimly, of the relevance of his behavior to an objective. Many definitions of what is indefinable have been attempted by psychologists, of which the least unsatisfactory are: (1) The capacity to meet novel situations, or to learn to do so, by new adaptive responses and; (2) The ability to perform tests or tasks, involving the grasping of relationships, the degree of intelligence being proportional to the complexity, or abstractness, or both, of the relationship" (*A Dictionary of Psychology*, 1952).

And so, in spite of a long history of research and debate, and many intelligent and helpful observations about it, there is still no standard definition of intelligence. This has led some to believe that *intelligence may be approximately described, but cannot be fully defined*. That fact, by itself, is suggestive of the notion that there is something about human intellect that goes beyond the natural. Anything that is this difficult to define cannot be merely "of this world."

In order to demonstrate how complex this problem is, it might be helpful to give a simplified definition of an intelligent cognitive agent in the area of artificial intelligence. The one below is from a collaborative article by Jose Hernandez-Orallo and Neus Minaya-Collado:

> An intelligent cognitive agent is an interested system with input/output devices for a complex environment and a contextual knowledge organisation [sic] and competing concepts governed by principles of short explanations and purpose related relevance ("A Formal Definition of Intelligence Based on an Intensional Variant of Algorithmic Complexity" 11).

The Intelligence Argument

Intelligent Machines and Their Makers

This should suffice to illustrate the fact that intelligence (whether human or artificial) is neither easy to define nor simple to measure. In human terms we tend to measure it in relation to IQ, or intelligence quotient. This is based mostly on induction and analogy. In the case of human intelligence, testing to measure it is highly controversial. Artificial intelligence (AI) is not an independent endeavor, however, it sets about the task of copying the human brain (psychologically or neurologically) with the implicit objective of resembling human behavior.

This is true even though, at this point at least, human behavior and machine behavior are worlds apart. But for purposes of definition it might be said that this mode of comparison is helpful, because, quite simply, we lack any other better option. Certainly no one would argue against the proposition that machine (computer) behavior in terms of modes of computational processing are created in such a way as to mimic, if not magnify, human ways of thinking and thus processing data.

That being said, we cannot resist the impulse to observe that the machine behaves as it does because it is made in the image of its creator. Man has made his machines in his own likeness. But, of course, this just as naturally leads us to inquire as to whether or not man himself, who is in this instance the creator of these machines, may not have been created by another Creator who, likewise, fashioned him after His own likeness?

We would never conclude that our own intelligent machines are the product of accidental development. And yet we recognize that these machines are mere shadows of our own capacity to think and reason. How is it then logical to argue that our computational machines were made in our own image and after our own likeness, but we ourselves, our brains and the minds that inhabit them, just happened accidentally as wonderful "freaks" of nature?

In our estimation, it makes no sense at all. It is illogical. The arguments made to attempt justification of the theory are implausible, and the only legitimation they have for those who embrace them is the fact that they allow their adherents to avoid the idea that God created human intelligence along with the brain that it resides in and depends on for external sensory perception.

GOD DOES EXIST!

What is the Origin of Mind, Thought, and Intellect?

Sometimes this mode of investigation into the issues that surround whether or not God exists is called the argument from reason. This notion is based on the fact that intelligence always derives from prior intelligence. Intelligent human beings get their capacity for high thinking from their parents, both in terms of their genetic predisposition toward intelligent existence, and their training from their parents and other humans with whom they interact and gain knowledge and various skills. They are taught to communicate and function in society through interaction with other intelligent beings. There are no exceptions to this rule.

And, once more, it is impossible to conceive of a situation where intellectual capacity had its origin in non-rational or irrational sources. All agree that an infinite regress of intelligent beings is not conceivable. Intelligence had to begin somewhere or with Someone. Materialists or "naturalists" proclaim that intellectual capacity is a product of an unintelligent source, namely biochemical processes within a highly developed mammalian brain.

Thought, then, is considered to be an advanced set of biochemical electrical processes of a sophisticated conglomeration of neurons, composing the nerve center or brain of *homo sapiens*. Few people who have thought "long and hard" about the matter are convinced that this is so, but it is the conclusion that is drawn by those who are disposed to deny that God is the origin of anything, mental capacity included.

The Argument for God from Intellect

In our view intellectual capacity in human beings is a powerful argument for the existence of an intelligent source for humanity's unique gift in this regard. Stated as a syllogism, the logic is impeccable:

Premise 1: Human beings possess high intelligence.
Premise 2: Intelligence derives from an intelligent source. There are no exceptions to this rule.
Premise 3: An infinite regress of intelligence is inconceivable.
Conclusion 1: Therefore, intelligence had to have its origination with someone or something intelligent.
Conclusion 2: God is the only intellectually defensible source conceivable: therefore God exists.

The Intelligence Argument

Human beings have cognitive faculties; the ability to think and reason; to make arguments and weigh possibilities. Intelligence is more than simply the ability to learn or understand or deal with new or trying situations in one's environment. Lower forms of animals do this sort of thing daily. It is not even the ability to apply knowledge in order to manipulate one's environment in such a way as to make survival possible. Animals also do this regularly, as when a gopher digs a hole in the ground to escape predators and when a bird builds a nest in a tree to raise its young. All would agree that human intelligence is of a higher order and of a different essential nature than any of these.

Abstract thought, for example, is illustrative. A romance novel would have no interest for a gopher. First, because the critter could not read it. But, secondly, because it has no capacity for abstract thought. It cannot comprehend the idea of love, romantic or otherwise. Human beings, on the other hand, have the capacity for both. They are able to read and have an understanding of the concept of romantic love. Therefore, some human beings read and enjoy romance novels. What this demonstrates is that the human brain is qualitatively different from that of a lower animal on both counts.

This brings up another and related matter. It has to do with a significant distinction that deserves to be recognized. The brain is different from the mind; brain matter is simply a grey jelly; now admittedly, that grey jelly is exceedingly complex. But the mind is much, much more. What it is, in fact, is unfathomably complicated, so much so in fact, that it is still not understood even though it has been studied for hundreds of years by thousands of researchers. Brain matter can be weighed and measured; it can be analyzed as to its content and chemical makeup; its structural components have been isolated and enumerated; its physiology is now fairly well known.

The human mind, on the other hand, cannot be treated in any sense in the various ways that the brain has been. Such means and methods do not pertain to that which is generally recognized to be in some sense of the term the "product" of that which resides within the human skull. Why not? Because the human mind is the most incomprehensible thing in the universe. The brain is part of the visible, tangible world of the body.

GOD DOES EXIST!

The mind, on the other hand, is part of the invisible, transcendent world of thought, feeling, attitude, belief, and imagination. The brain is the one physical organ of the body that is the most to be associated with the mind and consciousness, and yet the mind is not confined to the brain. This is part of the problem.

The Evolutionary View of Brain Development

According to the naturalist, evolution by random accidents or genetic mutations formed the brain; so it is the sum total of the biochemical reactions that occur inside the skull. And as marvelous as it may seem, it has its negative side for other species on the planet. Man's impact on the planet and other forms of life has been regrettable, according to current evolutionary thinking. We would suppose it would be the same if, let us say, giraffes had evolved into intelligent animals rather than *homo sapiens*. In fact, the whole grand experiment is to be regarded as a mistake, and a most unfortunate one at that:

> I believe that human intelligence is a mistake because it is completely out of proportion in respect to all the other species. This makes us less and less natural,—less animal. And this is why we are more and more isolated from nature, and for the same reason, we use and abuse it as if it were a tool, a means to satisfy our miserable and selfish human interests. The astonishing disproportion of our intelligence in comparison to other animals makes us feel "special"—and for many, the chosen ones of a god we created to also make us special—and this makes us think that we have the right to dispose of the rest of the planet for our own benefit. One of the regrettable inherits of Judaeo-Christian ideology was to justify the exploitation of nature under the direct orders of the temperamental architect-god of Genesis. This calms the devoted consciences of millions of believers who accept the use of other animals and the systematic ransacking of natural resources for our own comfort. Although it's obvious to say that our intelligence is also used to create beauty and useful and amazing inventions, we also use it to satisfy frivolous and unnecessary pleasures that only destroy the resources and habitats of other less fortunate animals. I hope my complaint is not confused with trendy ecological stances, or with an antiprogress or antitechnological feeling. I believe my accusation intends to go much further than that.

> When I say that human intelligence is an evolutionary mistake I obviously don't mean that evolution can be mistaken or correct in a te-

The Intelligence Argument

leological sense. We know very well that evolution does not have a predetermined course or an intentional direction. The use of the noun "mistake" must be understood in the sense of "unfortunate"; in this way our intelligence would be the result of an unfortunate direction taken in the aimless paths of evolution. To consider human intelligence as a mistake is certainly a value judgment, but I am not talking about a mistake as if there were a "correct" direction in evolution; this only means that in a hypothetical world the evolution of our intelligence could have taken a different direction, perhaps more in tune with the intelligence of other animals. This hypothetical position is founded on the fact that if our intelligence were more natural and modest, undoubtedly the other species and the whole biosphere would be much better off than they are now. With this I hope to have cleared away any possible misunderstanding of the evolutionary process considered as a teleological or intentional phenomenon (George Clark, "Human Intelligence: An Amazing Evolutionary Mistake," 1).

This must not be taken as a minority viewpoint in the community of believers in evolutionary development of the human species. The reality is that all evolutionary steps, whether forward or back, are considered merely accidental, and the evolution of intelligence is simply one part of that overall perspective.

Dr. David Barrowclough, Director of Studies Wolfson College, at the University of Cambridge, has very specifically suggested the route that evolution took in "creating" intelligence in the human species. Over the past sixty million years, Barrowclough says the Primates, including monkeys and humans developed into animals that lived in highly social groups. Group living requires that individuals develop an awareness of those with whom they live. It means being sensitive to friendships and rivalries, not just between oneself and the other group members, but also interactions between third parties.

Processing this web of information and remembering where each group member stands within the group hierarchy may well have driven the steady evolution of increased brainpower, according to his reconstruction of evolutionary events. He suggests that the common ancestor of humans, chimpanzees and gorillas, is an unknown extinct ape. In this ancestor (who lived between fifteen and ten million years ago), a gene called RNF213 began evolving rapidly.

GOD DOES EXIST!

This may have boosted the flow of blood to the brain by widening the carotid artery.

However, in humans, he admits, RNF213 mutations result in Moyamoya disease especially in Asian populations, in which the artery is too narrow. The disease causes transient ischemic attack (ministroke), stroke, or bleeding in the brain. Vision problems, movement disorders, and learning or developmental issues are the result. But in the case of the fortunate beneficial mutation of this gene, Barrowclough believes that it led to greater intellectual capacity.

He says that our ancestors split from their chimp-like relatives between thirteen and seven million years ago. Following this split both the ASPM and ARHGAP11B genes, and a region called HAR1 began to change. It is not completely clear what impact the changes had, but the HAR1 region and ARHGAP11P are involved in the growth of the cerebral cortex. This suggests that the gene mutations were linked to cognitive changes. Two other genes also mutated: SLC2A1 and SLC2A4. Both of these genes build proteins that transport glucose in and out of cells. The salutary tweaks made by these genetic changes may have had the effect of diverting glucose away from muscles and into the early hominid's brains. In the brain the glucose would have provided more energy boosting the capabilities of the brains of these animals and permitting them to enlarge.

Interestingly, research linked to intelligence in humans points to a gene called SRGAP2, which we are told was duplicated no less than three times. As a consequence, the ancestors of *Homo sapiens* had several copies of this gene, some of which appear to have evolved freely, or so the theory goes. One of the mutated copies turned out to be better than the original as it caused brain cells to extrude more spines, allowing them to form more synaptic connections, and thus increase cognitive ability. According to Barrowclough, these major changes would have allowed the human species to think as it does.

But many other changes would have been required for it to be able to speak, hold things and utilize tools, allow females to birth children with large heads, digest meat (meat being more calorically dense than plants and thus able to provide the essential energy for the brain to function), development of smaller jaws which would have freed up

The Intelligence Argument

space in the cranium for the brain to grow, etc. Actually, it would have entailed hundreds if not thousands of serendipitous and beneficial mutations in order to accommodate these major structural, biochemical and other changes. After all, the brain is only one of the major differences between Primates and humans.

Problems with the Evolutionary Picture of Human Brain Development

Each of these attendant changes are described as though they present no great difficulty for the theory, even though they would have required a host of other fortunate mutations in order to make them possible. All this, in spite of the fact that the vast majority of mutations that occur in nature lead to unfortunate results. That is a problem we all understand. We would never wish for a child to be born with a genetic mutation of any kind. All of us can name a number of instances where such mutations have led to birth defects and abnormalities. We cannot name a case where a child was born with an unusual birth anomaly that was fortuitous. Not one. And yet we are told that thousands upon thousands of such anomalies occurred in the history of life on earth, and in particular in the development of the "naked ape" that evolutionists claim us to be.

For example, unlike the great apes, humans do not have air sacs on their vocal tracts. In the great apes these sacs allow them to make loud bellows. However, the air sacs also make it impossible to produce different vowel sounds. We are told that it is only because our human ancestors lost these sacs that modern humans are able to talk. Moreover, a few people have developed mutations in a gene called FOXP2. This is the gene that is responsible for this aspect of ape and human anatomy. But they are not the better for it. As a result of this unfortunate mutation, they struggle to grasp grammar and pronounce words. This suggests that the FOXP2 gene in its present form is crucial to learning and using language.

It is surmised by evolutionary theorists that the modern FOXP2 gene evolved in the common ancestor of humans and Neanderthals, about half a million years ago, since this gene in Neanderthals is identical to our own. In our own view this suggests no more than that Neanderthals were humans. They were a genetically distinct group of humans, as

GOD DOES EXIST!

would be the case in the differences between major racial groups in our own time, but they were human nonetheless. If we were to discover the bones of ancient pygmies, and no vestiges of that racial minority were living today, undoubtedly some would have concluded that they were less than fully human in the way that Neanderthals have been viewed.

At any rate, is it not interesting that in spite of the well known fact that mutations are almost always deleterious to any form of animal or plant life where they occur, evolutionists persist in acting as if just the opposite were true? Moreover, they hardly ever seem to deal with the fact that they have not uncovered one single example of any mutation that has ever led to a new organ or organ system being created as the result. They talk as if this sort of thing happens all the time, even though they know that it doesn't and that this is a wholly unscientific claim, since they cannot prove what they allege.

DNA is biological information coded for each aspect of a living system and all of its parts. Where does new information enter the process? Where does it come from? Many new lines of genetic code are required in order to make any change of any significance to a living system. How were these lines of code written and who did the writing? Neither mutation nor natural selection have been proven to produce new living systems, let alone the complex of sequence-specific information-rich DNA, along with the proteins requisite to assure their self-replication into another generation. Theoretically speaking, everything is easy, but practically speaking everything we are talking about here is extraordinarily challenging.

The nucleus of the cell is a computational system that is run by the code that is fed to it through DNA and RNA. Any small change in the code will make changes in the final product, usually for the worse. It is rather like a stray line of code that accidentally (or maliciously) makes its way into a software program for a computer. Who knows what it will lead to? Who believes it will result in something beneficial?

Every software engineer can tell stories about their experiences in spending many dreary hours searching through hundreds of lines of code for that one offending line that must be corrected before a system will be able to function properly. Mutated genetic information, gener-

The Intelligence Argument

ally speaking, is no less destructive. Replication errors and DNA damage are actually happening in the cells of the human body constantly. In most cases, however, they do not lead to mutation, or cancer, or any other malevolent result, for that matter. The reason for this is simple. Cells are equipped with several levels of protective measures to assure that this rarely ever happens.

In point of fact, cells have a variety of "firewalls," mechanisms to prevent mutations or any other permanent changes in DNA sequence structure. During DNA synthesis, most DNA polymerases "check their work," repairing the majority of mispaired bases in a process described as "proofreading." If the polymerase (an enzyme that catalyzes the formation of DNA or RNA from precursor substances) detects that a wrong (incorrectly paired) nucleotide has been added, it will remove and replace the nucleotide right away, before continuing with DNA synthesis. Even so, occasionally a few will slip through the process.

Therefore, immediately after DNA synthesis, any remaining mispaired bases can be detected and replaced in a process called "mismatch repair." It can detect and correct small insertions and deletions that happen when the polymerase "slips," losing its footing on the template. This happens by means of a two-step system. First, a protein complex recognizes and binds to the mispaired base. Second, another protein complex cuts the DNA near the mismatch, and more enzymes chop out the incorrect nucleotide and a surrounding patch of DNA. Finally, a DNA polymerase replaces the missing section with correct nucleotides, and an enzyme called a DNA ligase seals the gap.

Also, if DNA is damaged (other than during replication), generally speaking, it will not be permitted to continue in this condition. It can be repaired by various mechanisms, including chemical reversal employing enzymes in the cell, nucleotide excision repair, and double-stranded break repair. The latter process uses two major pathways to accomplish its work: non-homologous end joining and homologous recombination. Both are used to repair double-stranded breaks in DNA, when an entire chromosome splits into two pieces.

In some cases, a cell can also fix DNA damage simply by reversing the chemical reaction that caused it. This is accomplished when an extra group of atoms get attached to DNA through a chemical reaction. Base excision repair is a mechanism used to detect and remove certain types of damaged bases. When this occurs, a group of enzymes called glycosylases play a key role in base excision repair. Each glycosylase detects and removes a specific kind of damaged base. Once the base has been removed, the "empty" piece of DNA backbone is also removed, and the gap is filled and sealed by other enzymes.

Double-stranded break repair is needed when environmental factors, such as high-energy radiation, cause a chromosome to split in two. When this happens, one of two processes is employed to repair the damage. In non-homologous end joining, the two broken ends of the chromosome are simply glued back together. This is a situation that sometimes produces a mutation, but such mutations are not helpful. Something is lost in the process rather than gained. In homologous recombination, information from the homologous chromosome that matches the damaged one (or from a sister chromatid, if the DNA has been copied) is used to repair the break. When this method is used, mutations seldom occur (cf. Alberts, B., et al., *Molecular Biology of the Cell*, 2002).

So, even though theorists often speak of alterations of the DNA information code as if this were an easy process, which happens constantly, and frequently advantageously, geneticists are well aware of the difficulties involved. Cellular DNA is powerfully resistant to change!

In addition, evolutionary theorists consistently ignore the relative chances of new and beneficial information being generated by whatever process, including mutation in the code. In reality, the chances are astronomical. Nevertheless, they speak about them as if they happen commonly in nature, in spite of the fact that they cannot name a single instance that is demonstrable where they have observed it happening. H. J. Muller, Indiana University evolutionist, in a lecture/article titled, "Evolution by Mutation," explains in mathematical terms how unlikely evolution by mutation actually is, even though he is convinced that it happened in precisely this way. He describes it as "fantastically unlikely," the changes that he supposes to have taken place as "preposterous anomalies," and on both counts in this regard, he is right:

The Intelligence Argument

Herein we shall attempt to assess how fantastically unlikely we and our fellow creatures are, and by what means such preposterous anomalies could have come about. The old-time philosopher still insists that such extravagances of organization could have arisen only by design, inasmuch as an accident cannot be expected to convert itself into order. However, a dispassionate examination of the rules of this game of life should throw some light on the question of how such a massive compounding of improbabilities may have taken place. . . .

Taking now the number 10,000, derived from flies, as a minimum estimate for the number of different genes in a higher organism (despite the fact that the higher organism contains a far larger total number of nucleotides), we see that there must have been at least 100 X 10,000, that is, a million separate successful mutations in the ancestry. Applying this million as an exponent to 100 (our conservative figure for the reciprocal of the probability that a mutation will be advantageous) we then get $100^{1000000}$ (or $10^{20000000}$) as the total number of trials that would have been necessary, in the absence of multiplication and selection, to obtain one combination as well organized as our own or as that of some other advanced organism.

Although so much smaller than our other estimate of about $10^{2400000000}$, based on the number of nucleotide pairs, the present more conservative number deserves some scrutiny, some comparison with more familiar things. In this connection we may ask, how much room would it have taken to contain this many combinations of genes at one time, in order that amongst them our own constitution might find a place as one of these random occurrences? A sphere having a diameter of six billion light years goes far beyond the most distant galaxies now detectable. For our present purposes, however, we shall call it, by a stretch of terminology, "the known universe." A little arithmetic will show that in this vast expanse there would be room, if they were all packed closely together, for about 6.25 X 10^{100} packets or skeins of nucleotide chains, such that each skein contained as many nucleotides as we have taken to exist in a mammalian sperm nucleus, namely, 4,000,000,000, the number that we previously found it necessary to employ 133 Webster's volumes to represent. Yet we see that this enormous number of packets, 6.25 X 10^{100}, is inordinately smaller than the number $10^{2000000000}$, that on our more conservative estimate could be expected, as a random event, to include a packet with a composition as select as our own. And even if we had some science-fictionist's method of reducing the size of a genetic packet to that of a proton, we could still get only about 10^{128} of them into the known universe (American Mathematical Society; Josiah Willard Gibbs Lecture, Cincinnati, Ohio, Jan. 28, 1958; pp. 137, 146).

Like Muller, all naturalists understand how exceedingly unlikely their theory of development by mutation and natural selection really is. They do not often admit this, and that is why Muller's lecture is so impressive. He recognizes and admits the phenomenal unlikelihood of the theory that he holds to be true. What amazing faith this man has!

In spite of these facts, Muller argues that the human species evolved into what it is today, with all of its brain power and the incomprehensible capabilities of its mental facilities. All of this, in order to avoid belief in a Creator! If more evolutionists were that honest, there would be far fewer people who would commit to the theory. And that is precisely why so few who believe the theory of evolution to be true will admit this factor into any discussion of the issues involved.

The Brain and the Mind

For the naturalist, who believes there is only the material world, the mind also represents an insuperable problem. Why is this so? Because it is an undeniably immaterial reality in a material world. René Descartes (1596-1650) is the single most influential figure in the philosophy of the mind. His expertise extended to the disciplines of science, mathematics, and of course, philosophy. He struggled to answer three main questions in his investigations of the material world with respect to the human mind:

1. What kind of thing, if anything, is a mind?
2. How do mind and the mental fit into the broader scheme of things, and in particular how do minds relate to the material world, especially those bits of the material world which "have" minds?
3. What are the mental characteristics—what is it to think, feel, imagine, and so on?

Simplistic answers to these three questions are elusive. Nevertheless, Descartes made striking contributions in providing answers to all three of these queries, and on account of his work in responding to them, the field of study that centers about the mind and the material

The Intelligence Argument

world will always owe him a debt of gratitude. He began his investigation by recognizing only two ultimate classes of things: those which pertain to mind or thinking substance (which he often referred to as "the soul"); and secondly, material things, i.e., those which pertain to extended substance or body.

Hence, he argued that a human person was an amalgam of two things: immaterial mind and material body, "which happen to be joined together but which could be separated in principle." He said that this separation might come about if the body were to die and decompose and the mind continues to exist, on earth or elsewhere. Being primarily a philosopher, and not a theologian, he showed little interest in defining what "elsewhere" might mean.

Even though Descartes's philosophical distinction between mind and body is less popular now than it was for many years, "this in-principle separability of the mind from the body it inhabits continues to be very common for a variety of reasons, even among those who are not fully-fledged Cartesian Dualists" (McCulloch, *The Mind and Its World*, 4). His view incorporates the claim that thinking and other intellectual activities involve mental items called ideas of which we have "inner awareness." And at least some of these ideas represent things distinct from themselves, such as items in the material world.

Thus, in his view, to think about Paris would be to entertain an idea of Paris, or the Paris-idea. But whereas the idea is mental, and thus in the mind, the city of Paris is a distinct thing, to be found, not in any brain or mind, but on the river Seine. So, in this case Paris exists on two levels: it has a distinctive existence in the mind that envisions it, and it exists as a material reality geographically on the river Seine. To make it more complicated still, if there were no such place as Paris on the river Seine, and a human mind envisioned such a place, it could be said that it exists only in the mind as a figment of the mind that imagines it.

But, how could that be? How could something exist in a world of imagination and not exist in the material world? And, what is a world of imagination, anyway? Where is that world? Obviously, this is a very complex problem without simple solutions. On this account, this view is today just as influential as Descartes's account of the mind-body distinction, and has survived rejection of many of the great thinker's specific doctrines.

In our day, probably the most dominant thesis among scientists and naturalistic philosophers is the Mind-Brain Identity Thesis. According to this view, the mind is just the brain. Under this rubric minds are things—brains—but not immaterial things; and material characteristics are considered to be aspects of the brain's complicated workings. Those who adhere to this view argue that mental damage and disorder correlate with neural damage and disorder. And thus, for them, the problem is settled. The mind is the brain, and the brain is the mind.

However, even though this is an aspect of the question that deserves to be considered, this does not actually settle the matter. It is admitted by everyone that the brain is *causally connected* to the mind as long as the body is alive. No one disputes this. And thus, any physiological issues that limit the ability of the mind to, let us say, access memories (as would be the case where Alzheimer's disease is an issue), would delimit the brain and so restrict the functionality of the mind. But that still would not prove that the brain is identical with the mind. An illustration will make the point. If a man is paralyzed and restricted to a wheelchair, he cannot walk or get around without the chair. If the chair is broken, he is immobile. The chair cannot move, so he cannot move. Are the man and the chair the same thing? No, they are not. The man is one entity and the chair is another entity altogether. One is a living being and the other is a simple machine. But he is yet immobile because the chair is broken.

It is the same with the brain and the mind. If the brain is injured or diseased, the mind is restricted in its abilities to function in the physical world. That does not signify that the brain and the mind are the same, however. The brain is one thing (an organ of the body), while the mind is an immaterial reality. The two are connected causally, and thus they are related to one another, but they are not the same.

And so, Cartesian Dualism, the approach taken by Descartes to deal with the brain-mind question, will not allow them to walk away from the problem nearly so easily. He challenges every alternative approach with questions that leave us without any easy answers. Epistemology is his strongest point of contention. He wrote:

The Intelligence Argument

> I saw that while I could pretend that I had no body and that there was no world and no place for me to be in, I could not for all that pretend that I did not exist. . . . From this I knew that I was a substance whose whole essence is to think, and which does not depend on any place or material thing in order to exist (127).

This is a profound observation. It can not and should not be dismissed without reflection. His argument may be summarized in the following way:

1. I can pretend that the material human René Descartes does not exist.
2. I cannot pretend that I do not exist.
3. So, I am not the material human René Descartes.

Again, obviously the body and the mind are causally related. Descartes admitted as much. Pain in one part of the body causes the mind to be aware of the pain. And the mind has the capacity to cause the hands to strike together in a clap. So, clearly the brain is that part of the body which integrates the body with the mind and the mind with the body. Sensations from any part of the body are transmitted to the brain which in turn registers those sensations, whether pleasurable or painful, or simply sensate, in the mind.

Additionally, "there occur within us. . . operations which we perform without any help from reason" (42). The physical brain carries out many functions without our conscious awareness of them taking place. This he likens to the operation of an animal's brain, which also carries out many functions without conscious awareness of them, "mechanisms which are no more aware or conscious of things than any other 'automaton, or moving machine'" (139).

Descartes was convinced that the present existence of a non-substantial self could not be contradicted, and found other reasons to support his view that this self was not material, persisted in time, was possibly immortal, and had a relation to its body which was merely contingent and with which it interacted frequently. Taking consciousness seriously, in his view, requires a non-material self. Most western traditional (theistic) philosophers have argued that the existence of consciousness requires some form of substantial non-material soul or

GOD DOES EXIST!

self. Both God and the self are non-material, but the self has a material component that God does not. So, it is the non-material aspect of man's nature that is made in the image of God.

There have been several varieties of non-material substantial souls in the thinking of Western philosophers past and present. Three prominent conceptions are the Platonic/Cartesian, the Aristotelian/Thomistic, and now there are also "emergent" dualists. All three are thought to be dead by the majority of contemporary philosophers of mind. But Cartesian Dualism is far from dead.

The Cartesian view of the self is derived from the examination of the mind and consciousness as we are aware of it directly, but does also have interesting relationships with Western theism. It is often claimed by its supporters that God is needed to explain the existence of souls, and, conversely, that the existence of souls provides important evidence to justify belief in a Western theistic God. That is our conclusion. Materialists have a theory for explaining the origin of physical being, and even though it is faulty from start to finish, at least it provides for them a hypothetical reconstruction of how living organisms like human beings came to be. But they have no explanation that accounts for a non-material mind.

Descartes: Can An Atheist Know That He Exists?

One of the most intriguing questions that Descartes wrestled with in his *Meditations on First Philosophy* has to do with what he describes as the "deceiver doubt". As he put it in the Second Meditation, "There is a deceiver of supreme power and cunning who is deliberately and constantly deceiving me." He goes on, ". . . if he is deceiving me; and let him deceive me as much as he can, he will never bring it about that I am nothing so long as I think that I am something. So after considering everything very thoroughly, I must finally conclude that this proposition, *I am, I exist (Ego sum, Ego existo)*, is necessarily true whenever it is put forward by me or conceived in my mind."

This existence of the thinking and conceiving *I*, the so called *cogito* (Lat. "I think"), has by many readers of the great philosopher been taken as the *first full certainty* found by Descartes, and considered to be a *foundationalist proof*. As Descartes is mostly read to liken full certainty to be

The Intelligence Argument

the result of indubitability, the fact that the existence of the doubter cannot be doubted, would make it fully certain.

In the Third Meditation, he proceeds further in his reasoning by saying that not only is the *cogito* certain, but every intuitively seen *clear and distinct perception* is certain as well. This would cover mathematical truths also. Intuition, and clear and distinct perceptions it offers, are therefore Descartes's remedy for skeptical scenarios. They are able to provide some propositions which are indubitable and therefore, according to the *cogito*-foundational reading, certain. Interestingly, he proceeds from this point to argue that the existence of God is essential to this formulation:

> But in order to remove even this slight reason for doubt, as soon as the opportunity arises I must examine whether there is a God, and if there is, whether He can be a deceiver. For if I do not know this, it seems I can never be quite certain (*plane certus*) about anything else.

Here he raises a very important question, one that has been challenged by a great many over the years since his statement of the principle, but one that is worthy of contemplation and serious reflection. What is the main force of his argument? Here it is in a nutshell: Let's say I am an atheist and I do not acknowledge the existence of a Higher Power. It does not matter whether I do not believe in God on intellectual grounds, or I simply do not recognize His being in a formal or informal way.

At any rate, no matter how hard someone tries to convince me, I do not acknowledge God. Can I then discover the seemingly (or so Descartes claims) intuitive truth of the *cogito*? Can an atheist be *absolutely certain* that he exists? In order to appreciate the force of this query, it must be understood that Descartes makes a distinction here between two different types of knowledge or certainty. This is key to his argument. His point is that because the "deceiver doubt" is not yet resolved, one cannot yet be sure that his clear and distinct perceptions actually correlate with anything that is true and real:

> And yet firmly included in my mind is the long-standing opinion that there is an omnipotent God who made me the kind of creature I am. How do I know that He has not brought it about that there is no earth, no sky, no extended thing, no shape, no size, no place, while at the same time ensuring that all these things appear to me to exist just as they do now?

GOD DOES EXIST!

His point is that he cannot know whether or not he is being deceived by all that he perceives to exist unless he concludes that he has been created by a God who is not a deceiver, who does not fool him into believing what does not actually exist. Moreover, even formally denouncing God does not release one from this doubt, but actually makes the case that much more fatal:

> Perhaps there may be some who would prefer to deny the existence of so powerful a God rather than believe that everything else is uncertain.... According to their supposition, then, I have arrived at my present state by fate or chance or a continuous chain of events, or by some other means; yet since deception and error seem to be imperfections, the less powerful they make my original cause, the more likely it is that I am also so imperfect as to be deceived at all time.

So, even if I am an atheist and believe that "I am here" by fate or chance, it would still not release me from the grips of the lingering doubt, since my nature has the propensity to be so imperfect and/or impotent that I might still be deceived by all (even by the clear and distinct perceptions that I experience) and therefore would not grasp reality as it is. As an atheist, how can one know that his nature is not so imperfect that when he thinks that he has counted correctly that $2 + 2 = 4$, he is not mistaken? The result of this reasoning is that there is a gap that exists between one's understanding of the world as it *actually* is. This is not to be seen as an attempt to bridge the gap on all clear and distinct perceptions, but that one piece of reality that seems to be the most intuitive and intimate of them all: one's own existence.

So, even though the atheist believes that he exists, perhaps he *actually* does not. If, according to Descartes, I cannot bridge this epistemic gap except by coming to the conclusion that God exists, is the author of my nature and is not a deceiver and therefore has authored my nature so that I *do* grasp true reality when using my native faculties correctly, then can I even claim this most intimate and intuitive knowledge with certainty? Descartes asserts that it cannot be done.

It was objected by some of his opponents that an atheist mathematician could still make correct deductions on geometry and mathematics without having to rely on God's existence, so that one's mind could still tell the deceiver in him that these things are true, even without a

The Intelligence Argument

knowledge of God. The assumption is that the Cartesian does not have any advantage at all in regards to the knowledge of his own existence over the atheist. Descartes took this objection very seriously, and so he responded to it at great length.

In summary, he stated that he did not deny that the atheist could clearly and distinctly be aware of, let us say, a triangle's mathematical features (that the three angles are equal to two right angles, meaning that their sum is always 180 degrees). But he nevertheless maintained that "this awareness (*cognitio*) of his is not true knowledge, since no act of awareness that can be rendered doubtful seems fit to be called knowledge (*scientia*)." Here he distinguishes between two states of "certainty": an isolated and momentary awareness of *p* (*cognitio*) and systematic and absolutely certain knowledge of *p* (*scientia*). The difference between these two seems to be that while *cognitio* can be rendered doubtful, *scientia* cannot. *Scientia* is the final goal of the inquiry taken in the Meditations, absolute certainty capable of surviving any attempts of even the most radical doubt.

So, the momentary awareness of anything for an atheist cannot offer the stability and lastingness required for true *scientia*. This is so because, as previously stated, an atheist cannot overcome the deceiver/imperfect nature of doubt in a satisfactory way. Everything he "knows" will always remain at least somewhat doubtful. Absolute certainty evades him. Why? Because he has no absolute standard of what is certain, namely God. "So he will never be free of this doubt until he acknowledges that God exists." The atheist cannot know who is the author of his nature and therefore cannot be certain that his knowledge is true metaphysical knowledge.

"I see," wrote Descartes, "plainly that the certainty and truth of all knowledge depends uniquely on my *cognition* of the true God, to such an extent that I was incapable of *perfect knowledge* about anything else until I cognized him." This implies that the atheist can indeed have *cognition*, which means he can be momentarily aware of some certainty which imposes assent, but he does not ever have true *scientia*, lasting and absolute (metaphysical) certainty of anything in his experience.

GOD DOES EXIST!

Thus, *cognition* is time-bounded (so temporarily limited) while *scientia* is timeless (temporarily unlimited), and therefore lasting. It could be said that it partakes in the eternal, which is the nature of God. This then is the ultimate advantage of the Cartesian over the atheist: his certainty is timeless and lasting, whereas the atheist's certainty is time-bounded and remains partly in doubt. By cognizing the existence of a non-deceiving God the Cartesian is able to fix the time-bound temporal persuasion and turn it into a metaphysical certainty—non-temporal and tenseless.

Consequently, for Descartes, knowledge of self and knowledge of God are intrinsically tied together. When I become aware of my own existence and begin inquiring further into my own nature and essence, I ultimately cognize in myself the concept of God, and by cognizing God I also cognize God's existence to be an intuitive and necessary truth. Consequently, if an atheist knows that he exists, he should also be aware of the concept of God, ultimately proving God's existence. By following the order of reasons, according to Descartes, no-one ever should be an atheist. To be so is to be counter-intuitive and adversative to the existence of ultimate truth (cf. Jan Forsman, "Can An Atheist Know That He Exists?"; M. Della Rocca. "Descartes, the Cartesian Circle, and Epistemology without God," 1-33; E. M. Curley, *Descartes Against the Skeptics*).

This argument, couched in different language but more or less the same one, has been made frequently in recent years by apologists in regard to the question of whether or not those who deny the existence of God, and therefore, objective moral truth, are capable of actually believing that *anything* can be acknowledged as objectively true. Relativism is close kin to atheism. It has frequently been observed that in Western thought in recent years "it no longer seems possible to rationally assess competing knowledge claims." As one writer bemoaned, "In the social sciences in particular, the fashionable post-positivist view is that any belief can be valid, depending upon one's perspective; that truth is simply a term of praise (or, alternatively, a display of power); and that there is in fact no such thing as a reality that does not belong in quotation marks" (R. Groff, *Critical Realism, Post-positivism and the Possibility of Knowledge*, 1).

Such fuzzy thinking is responsible for a host of logical curiosities in post-modern society. This whole confusing world of relativism is a

The Intelligence Argument

clear reflection of the consequential acceptance of the implications of Darwinian evolutionary theory in Western thought. When materialism is predominant and God is removed from the equation, an absolute standard of morality and truth has been subtracted from the discussion, and relativism has won the day. Nothing can be said to repulse this notion, even though it is totally divorced from common sense, as long as God remains subtracted from the process.

Consider for a moment what the word "knowledge" itself implies. Even though it has other potential aspects of its meaning that might be important, the key idea behind it is that something is true. We can only have knowledge of things in this sense if they *are* true. If they were false, we could not say that they are true, and we could not say that we have knowledge of them, if they were false.

Further, objective reality confronts us at every turn in our existence. But objective reality requires that we be able to perceive it as such and then communicate with words that have meanings that we all can agree to. Our perceptions and notions of things must be, at least at some rudimentary level, consistent with each other. If we approach such things from the perspective of subjectivity, as if each one of us had our own reality, *our own unique and personal truth*, so that my truth is different from your truth, then we live in a world that is chaotic and confusing to us all. What many people want today is to live in their own reality, having their own special universe, with them acting as god over their own unique province of cognizance and description.

To illustrate: One lady thinks that she is actually a feline. She believes that she was born into the wrong species. She looks human to everybody else, but she is convinced that this is true, that she is actually a cat. But is it *really true*? Another fellow believes that he should have been born as a lion, so he is gradually altering his body through surgeries and additions to look more like a lion. Further, a man who has the genitalia of a male perceives himself to be a woman in a man's body. Even though his general physical appearance tells everyone else that he is a man, and his genitalia agree with this proposition, he thinks the opposite. This fellow wishes to compete as a woman in athletic contests. Should his perception of himself allow him to compete with girls in spite of the testosterone that is coursing through his body and giving him the

GOD DOES EXIST!

strength of a man? Most of us would not think so. Our perception of the situation is different from his. But, in many places he will be allowed to do so, in spite of all of the obvious evidence to the contrary. And in some of those places it is considered to be a "hate crime" to tell this fellow that he is a man. This is truly a world gone mad!

In each of these instances the perception of the individual is permitted to be exercised, in spite of the fact that it is contrary to fact and flies in the face of the perceptions of others who are perfectly sane and reasonable. It is thought that this will bring these individuals happiness. But that is not what is happening. In fact, exactly the opposite is the case. When we are constantly at war with ourselves and those around us, the joy of life always flees from us. Welcome to the brave new world of relativism! It allows everyone to indulge his or her own sick fantasies as being true reality, while in the end making no one happy.

Inevitably also, situations of this sort challenge us to consider what is really wrong in those cases. Perception is confused with true reality. I cannot have my own reality, and neither can you. None of us can. It does not work that way. You see, the real issue here is that there is *no arbiter* to settle this disagreement between us, when we each have our own definition of words and ideas. If we cannot settle the issue of what a lion is, or a cat, or even a male and a female, we are "up a creek without a paddle," so to speak. Hence, the only possible way to resolve this issue ultimately is with force. Either you must yield to my perceptions or I must yield to yours. We cannot have it both ways. Relativism is a street that leads us all nowhere fast. It divides us from one another and forces us to go to war with each other. In some instances the State is called upon to force others to accept what they consider to be contrary to reality!

Some people these days think that if they can only get the Supreme Court to settle a matter in their favor, and so to be the ultimate arbiter between differing parties, that will resolve it forever. But that will only give one side satisfaction temporarily. Has anyone ever heard of *Roe vs Wade*? The Supreme Court of the United States did not solve anything when it overturned all previous decisions to favor the side of the abortionists. The majority of the judges of that court created out of whole cloth a new constitutional right. The judicial branch of government es-

The Intelligence Argument

sentially wrote legislation that the legislative branch could not have gotten passed and the administrative branch would not have signed. Since that time the anti-abortion element of society has worked diligently to get that decision overturned. (You see, no human agency that pretends to arbitrate an issue of this sort has the *final* say.) And the abortion lobby in America has labored just as feverishly to keep it as the law of the land. So, nothing has really been settled, has it? Evangelical Christians, Roman Catholics, and many judicial conservatives, who opposed this decision from the start, consider God to be the true arbiter of right and wrong, not the justices on the high court of the United States. They will never rest until they get it reversed.

So, where are we going with this? It should be obvious. *Knowledge is about what is inherently true, and thus objectively true.* Subjective truth does not qualify. Personal, individual truth will not work. Two stories illustrate this point, so that in our view it cannot be contradicted. The first is about a fellow who was discussing this question with his friend who was a radical skeptic. When he brought up the fact that $2 + 2 = 4$, he made the point that this was an "objective truth" and not a subjective one. His skeptical friend declared in response that there was no such thing as "objective truth." "Are you certain of that?" he asked. "I am absolutely sure of it!" he affirmed. "Is that an objective truth? I thought you said objective truth did not exist," he responded. This flabbergasted his friend. You see, he contradicted himself in the conclusion of his argument. Any argument that leads to an absurdity in its conclusion is invalid. Are those who make the case that absolute truth does not exist *certain* of their stance? If so, they have an inherent problem with their reasoning. That certainty of theirs assuredly seems to imply that they actually do in fact believe in some form of truth that is absolute, whether they will admit it or not!

The second story has to do with a debate between a skeptic and a Christian apologist. Once again, the subject being dealt with had to do with whether or not absolute, objective truth existed or not. In the course of the debate the apologist declared that God was that mind that was behind the objective truths of the universe, mathematical and otherwise. "All of those laws," he argued, "had to have had their origin in a mind somewhere. God is that spaceless, timeless, and immaterial mind of which we speak." With this point being made, the opponent perked up and responded with a question. He thought he had the other fellow on the ropes: "Name something else that is spaceless, timeless, and immaterial!" The inference he was leading to was that such things do not exist at all. He was surprised to hear the answer. The apologist said, "The laws of logic!" To this the skeptic had no answer. In other words, the very laws which this fellow was using to make his case were grounded in minds. That made them also, spaceless, timeless, and immaterial. God is that eternal mind from whence have arisen the laws of nature, the moral laws by which men ought to live, and the laws of logic itself. We utilize them everyday, whether we acknowledge God or not. And they are spaceless, timeless, and immaterial, just as the mind is.

One final point is appropriate in this regard. Those who argue that human intellect arose as a result of a series of wonderful accidents of nature, wholly without any assistance from a divine designer, are faced with an interesting conundrum. The very laws of logic and experimental proof so frequently employed by them in the sciences are grounded in the human mind. But all we can say of the human mind from their perspective is that it is an imperfect product of a hapless and unguided process. How can it deliver what we might describe as true *scientia*? The philosopher Descartes alleged that it can never do so. The best we can say of this process that we call "thinking" is that it is all about the firing of synapses within the brain, and nothing more than this, if what they say is true. If they are right, then there is no such thing as absolute, objective truth. Even scientific truth.

Exploring Cartesian Dualism

There is no doubt that the Cartesian argument for dualism has considerable weight, in spite of its being readily dismissed by the majority of modern thinkers. In our view the explanation for this is that its force as an argument for theism is what discourages more scholars from recognizing its value. Most people readily see the logical concomitant of it. But precious few are willing to take on the angry, apoplectic atheists of our time.

Nevertheless, as Frank Dilley of the University of Delaware has noted, "Recent philosophers of mind have been dismissive of Cartesian dualism, but when one looks at the reasons for its supposed demise, those reasons look rather lame, and have often been refuted decisively,

The Intelligence Argument

but apparently overlooked. Substance dualism is much more defensible than it has often been given credit for being..." ("Taking Consciousness Seriously," 136). A few arguments have been made against dualism, but the answers to these contentions are available and, in our view, respond to them in a way that will satisfy most of those who genuinely care whether or not dualism is reasonable and ultimately defensible. Here are a few of them:

1. Some contend that a Cartesian dualist is required to hold that in a disembodied state, without the brain's assistance, the mind is unable to think. But why would this be so? Why should the fact that the brain is working when the mind is causally connected with a body, imply that the mind cannot work in its absence? After all, the contents of thoughts and thinking activities as well as memories, beliefs, desires are mental, however much they are correlated with brain processes. An honest dualist admits that *some* functions of the soul depend on the operation of the brain (or a brain surrogate). Such operations are communicating with other minds, gaining information about the material world, and developing the structure of the soul by engaging in interactions with material bodies and through bodies with other souls.

Souls need bodies in order to gather information and to interact with other souls. And, it may well be that bodies are needed for souls to develop. Many theists from Plato onward have developed "soul-building" explanations for the soul's attachment to and even restriction to one body at a time. Obviously, the mind or soul is very closely "paired" with the body. However, an honest dualist should also say that activities such as thinking, feeling, remembering, and willing *do not depend* for their functioning on bodies or body surrogates. They often suggest that once the soul is unencumbered by the body, those activities might even be enhanced. That would certainly be this writer's contention.

2. Some philosophers say that the body/brain has a structure and that a structured non-material being is counter-intuitive. Actually, Cartesian philosophers have no problem at all recognizing this reality, and may even proceed to say (as does Frank Dilley) that the soul or mind must also have a structure. The mind is not at present a blank slate. Rather, our minds are slates that have been well written upon. Our present experience discloses to us that our souls are structured. Therefore, why

GOD DOES EXIST!

a particular existing soul *continues to be paired* with a particular existing body with which it mutually interacts has a rather simple solution. Dilley argues:

> Let us assume that Cartesian dualism is true. Let us grant that I have a mind, that my mind cannot be reduced to the brain or its products, that my mind interacts causally with the brain and body that I call mine, that my mind is contra-causally free, and that my mind has unity and persists through time. What else should I think about the mind? I propose that we need to add that my mind or soul has a definite structure which it has acquired over time.
>
> What does my experience suggest? Am I a pure subject? No, I find that my mind has certain definite features. My mind brings with it more or less integrated sets of memories, desires, and beliefs, all of which are, like my body, contingently related to my mind in the sense that I would be the person that I am even if my memories, desires and beliefs were quite different than the ones they in fact are, but which nevertheless are part of this me that exists now. The subject faces an internal given, in other words.
>
> How should we talk about these more or less integrated sets of memories, desires and beliefs that we each bring to the present moment? Swinburne offers the suggestion that we think of the soul as having a structure. What "I mean by claiming that the soul has a structure is very roughly that the determinants of change of belief and desire are in part soul-states, not mere brain-states; and that if body and soul were separated, some character would remain with the soul" (Swinburne, 262). He broadens his discussion of soul states to include perceptions, knowledge, memory, emotions and other mental states such as pleasures and pains (Swinburne, 236–241).
>
> What sort of thing is a structured non-material thing? Given the privacy of the mental subject and of its states, no external description of mental structures is available. To say that the self has a structure is simply to say that at any present moment there is a set of memories, beliefs, desires, perceptions, and other mental states present to the self which affect the set of memories, beliefs, and desires which develop in the future and which, to a great extent, influence what these future sets will be, but without determining them ("Taking Consciousness Seriously," 144-45).
>
> And so, as a practical matter, a soul needs a body which it has trained to accomplish its purposes in acting on and communicating

The Intelligence Argument

with other souls. A particular soul and its particular body have adapted to each other over whatever length of time they have been paired, and for a soul to think or communicate or act efficiently it must use the body which it has shaped. Bodies which are different would be to varying degrees intractable to that soul's use.

Of course we would have to imagine that there are degrees of intractability ranging from the bodies of identical twins raised in similar environments to bodies raised in cultures speaking a different language, utilizing different tools for realizing purposes, valuing different behavior more highly, and fostering quite different value choices.

Bodies would need to resemble closely the one with which the soul was used to interacting for efficiency of operation. It therefore could be said that the soul is both independent of and related to the life of its body. What it does causes modifications in the structure of the brain, and what the brain does affects the soul's structure, but the soul could continue to exist independently of its body, and could carry its structure into its disembodied state. In a disembodied state, it would not be encumbered by the existence of a body that distracts it, but the body has its uses as well. Plato did say that the body was the prison house of the soul, but he also recognized that in its relationship to its body, the soul works out its character (Dilley,"Taking Consciousness Seriously," 145-46 .

3. If Cartesian dualism is to be taken seriously as the truth about minds and their bodies, then both the problem of dependence and the problem of continuity need to be addressed in a way that exhibits the known facts as plausible consequences of the underlying metaphysical view. A string of ad hoc conjectures will not suffice (cf. W. Hasker, *The Emergent Self,* 37-49). Dilley mentioned this objection but did not deign to tackle it. Apparently he felt unqualified to do so, since his abilities lie in the area of Philosophy rather than in Theology.

For a Christian theologian, however, this is the easiest challenge of all. Moreover, "ad hoc conjectures" are unnecessary in responding to it. Christianity is, in its essence, a theological system that begins with the premise that God became flesh in the person of Jesus of Nazareth (John 1:1-3, 14). He was born of a virgin woman by miraculous conception (Matt. 1:18-23; Isa. 7:14). He was fully human and fully divine throughout His life on earth. He lived for some thirty-three and one half years, was humiliated, mercilessly beaten, and then executed by crucifixion on a Roman cross. On the third day afterward He rose from the dead and was seen by hundreds of people for the next forty days (1 Cor. 15:1-8).

Finally, in the presence of a group of His friends and supporters, He ascended to heaven to sit at the right hand of God in heaven (Mark 16:19-20; Acts 1:10-11). At the heart of this grandiose series of claims is the most important one of all: the conviction that Jesus was God in the flesh. As God, He "emptied himself, by taking the form of a servant, and being found in human form, he humbled himself by becoming obedient to the point of death, even death on a cross" (Phil. 2:7-8). Prior to His incarnation, He was a divine person (Phil. 2:6). The enfleshment of God in Jesus Christ is the central miracle of the New Testament. Even His resurrection from death pales by comparison.

Over the two thousand years since that seminal event, this uniquely Christian theological assertion has been tested endlessly in the crucible of controversy. Many different doubters, both inside and outside of the ranks of Christian believers, have put this proposition to the test from a whole host of different angles. As a result, and through these challenges to the concept of the incarnation of the divine Christ, "both the problem of dependence and the problem of continuity have been addressed in a way that exhibits the known facts as plausible consequences of the underlying metaphysical view." Hasker is not wrong to put forward this challenge to Cartesian dualism, but he needs to know that Christianity has met the challenge.

Literally, thousands of citations could be marshalled in response to this allegation, but a simple computer search for a listing of heretical claims about the deity and humanity of Jesus will satisfy most readers. In order to illustrate, however, that this is a never-ending challenge that must be perennially addressed by Christian theologians and apologists, let us cite just one article that is of recent vintage, and permit this to illustrate the ongoing challenges that have come to be a constant feature of the theological debate about this central question in Christian theology.

In the 2010 volume of *Faith and Philosophy: Journal of the Society of Christian Philosophers*, there appears an article by Luke Van Horn on "Merricks's Soulless Savior," about a writer named Trenton Merricks

The Intelligence Argument

who "recently argued that substance dualist accounts of embodiment and humanness do not cohere well with the Incarnation. He has also claimed that physicalism about human persons avoids this problem, which should lead Christians to be physicalists." In response, he argues "that there are plausible dualist accounts of embodiment and humanness that avoid his objections," and "that physicalism is inconsistent with the Incarnation" (330). Merricks's article is entitled, "The Word Made Flesh: Dualism, Physicalism, and the Incarnation" (in *Persons: Human and Divine*, eds. Peter van Inwagen and Dean Zimmerman, Oxford: Clarendon Press, 2007, 281-300).

At least three claims are advanced by Merricks: (1) That substance dualism does not cohere well with the doctrine that the Son is uniquely embodied in Jesus's body; (2) Dualism entails that a person can be human without being embodied, which is deemed objectionable; and (3) Physicalism about human persons avoids these problems and thus provides for a superior account of the incarnation. In his paper, Van Horn rebuts all three of these claims. Specifically, he argues that these objections to dualism fail adequately to consider alternative dualist accounts of embodiment and humanness. Furthermore, he points out that while physicalism does provide an account of embodiment that avoids Merricks's objections to dualism, its account of incarnation requires accepting so many counterintuitive metaphysical principles that it is not an appealing alternative to dualism.

Again, hundreds of such books and articles could be cited to illustrate that Christian theologians perennially have wrestled in a most meaningful way with the various profundities of these issues. It is not our purpose here to deal with its various exigencies, however, only to make the point that this is a well-worn pathway in Christian thinking. Orthodox Christianity believes that the man Christ Jesus, God in the flesh, possessed a human soul in a human body, and that it experienced all of the feelings and temptations of humanity, without committing sin of any kind. As such, he was perfectly suited to offer Himself as the supreme sacrifice for the sins of mankind (Heb. 4:15; 7:25; 10:10; etc.). Christianity has most certainly struggled with the issues raised by questions associated with dualism and has satisfied the minds of untold millions that its answers are both logical and reasonable.

GOD DOES EXIST!

Conclusion

In a world made up of space, time, and matter, you can produce a brain; but you cannot produce a mind. A human mind is the most complicated mechanism, if that is a proper term to describe it, that is found in the universe. Memories, recollections, emotions, relationships, capacity to think and reason, to love and hate, to laugh and cry, to forgive or hold a grudge, to be happy or sad, to rejoice and sing, all of these and so many more, can only be explained in terms of their being God's unique creative gift to humans. Genesis 1:27 says that "God created man in his own image...."

When God breathed life into the first human being (Gen. 2:7), the Bible says that, "God breathed into his nostrils the breath of life, and the man became *a living soul*" (*lenephesh chayyah*). Not only did the man *have* a soul, he in fact, *was* a soul. It was the essence of his being. It was what he "became" by God's creative fiat. So, he was made in the likeness of God as a living soul. When a person died, his or her soul departed from its physical home and went back to its Giver (Gen. 35:18; 1 Kings 17:21; Eccl. 12:7). That is the viewpoint of Genesis, and the overall biblical perspective, in the Old Testament as well as in the New.

We are still discovering how extraordinarily sophisticated this gift was that God gave us when He initially brought us into being as living creatures. And so, there is still much to learn about it. There may always be. But one thing is abundantly clear about it. This inexplicable reality that we call the mind did not come about as a result of a material process and so by means of organic evolution. Many years of refined human thinking and scientific research has still not produced a good working definition for it, let alone a definitive explanation for how it came to be.

Consequently, we are not at all concerned that in the years ahead anything about that will change. It cannot be explained in those terms, because it did not happen that way. We can think and reason and feel, and communicate those thoughts and feelings, because God Himself can think and feel and communicate, and because He decided to make us in His image. For most of humanity that will be the only explanation that will ever be convincing to us.

The Intelligence Argument

Questions for Discussion

1. What is intelligence? How does it work, and what is its relation to the brain?
2. Why is it so difficult to define intelligence in a way that is satisfactory to everyone?
3. How does this question of intelligence and how it is defined and understood, connected with what is today called "artificial intelligence" or "machine learning"?
4. How are our machines like us? Do they "think" in a way that is similar to the way the human brain works? What does this suggest about the thinking of human beings? Could their own manner of processing information be similar to that of their Maker?
5. Intellectual capacity in human beings is a powerful argument for the existence of an intelligent source for humanity's special talent in this aspect of its nature. State this argument in the form of a syllogism.
6. Abstract thought is a special feature of human intelligence. Romantic love illustrates the notion perfectly. This is a genuinely "human" characteristic; animals do not share it. Offer some illustrations of the idea.
7. Describe the evolutionary view of brain development. Why is human intelligence described as a monumental "mistake" by evolutionary theorists? Do you see it as an unfortunate error or as a divine blessing?
8. What are some of the reasons that the evolutionary view of brain development is faulty?
9. Are DNA mutations common in human beings? What are the processes that the body employs to assure that these mutations, when they do occur, do not persist and so are not transmitted to another generation?
10. What is "Cartesian Dualism" and how does it relate to the question of whether the physical brain and the non-material mind

are identical? What are the main objections lodged against it, and do you consider them persuasive?

11. Read Genesis 1:27 and explain it in terms of the intellectual and emotional nature of both God and man.

12. Read Genesis 2:7 and explain it in terms of humanity's unique and special place in the divine creation.

Chapter 10
The Consciousness Argument

Men have been conscious of the problem of consciousness almost since consciousness began. And each age has described consciousness in terms of its own theme and concerns. In the golden age of Greece, when men of wealth and leisure traveled about in freedom while slaves did most of the physical work, consciousness was as free as could be imagined.

Heraclitus, in particular, called it an enormous space whose boundaries, even by traveling along every path, could never be found out (Diels, *Fragment*, 45). His point was that a mind that is free from labor is also free to roam wherever it desires and engage in whatever mental activity it wishes. Meditation, contemplation, and imagining are the result.

A millennium later, Augustine, living amidst the caverned hills of Carthage, was astonished at the "mountains and hills of my high imaginations," "the plains and caves and caverns of my memory" with its recesses of "manifold and spacious chambers, wonderfully furnished with unnumbered stores" (*Confessions* 9.7; 10.26, 65). One should take note of how the metaphors of mind are the world it perceives and even the world that it imagines and dreams about (Jaynes, *Origin of Consciousness,* 2).

Easy but Hard

Someone has said that consciousness is "at once the most familiar and most mysterious aspect of our lives." All of us know what it is, but at the same time we find it difficult to put it into words. Thus, conceptually it is very difficult even to define.

At the most rudimentary level, of course, we think of it as "sentience or awareness of internal or external existence." It is an awareness of one's own existence, along with the sensations, thoughts, and the experience of our surroundings. Since each one of these things has to do with the mind, is consciousness then to be associated wholly with the mind itself? Or, is it simply an aspect of the mind? Is it, as some say, the "inner life" of a being, the world of introspection, of private thought, of imagination and volition? Beyond this, is it to include any sort of experience, cognition, feeling, or perception about the experience? Is it simply to be defined as "awareness" or even "self-awareness"? These are all questions that deserve exploration, and they have been explored by many intelligent people throughout history. A whole host of theories have been propounded in order to explain its many marvelous aspects, all without creating a satisfying consensus.

The dictionary defines it as "a sense of one's personal or collective identity, including the attitudes, beliefs, and sensitivities held by or considered characteristic of an individual or group" (*American Heritage Dictionary*). Note, that in the opening words of this definition it refers to it as being "a sense of. . . ." This seems to be the key ingredient. Obviously, consciousness stems from intelligence and is related very directly with it, and so it clearly has to do with the mind, even though the two concepts are not identical. A sentient being can only be conscious of anything, including itself, if it is first intelligent. So, intelligence is critical to understanding what it is, even though it could not be said that it is *merely* intelligence that defines it as such. Even though the two are intimately related, they are not the same.

The Consciousness Argument

How does this subject, when it is analyzed thoughtfully, touch upon the question of whether or not God exists? Precisely at the point where intelligence enters the picture. The two issues are almost "hand in glove" in their relationship to one another. They are not the same thing, of course, but they are definitely related. And so, intimately related to the argument from intelligence or reason is the argument from consciousness. What does the word consciousness mean in the present context? It is to be aware of and responsive to our environment. That is the simple answer. But we all know that it is so much more than merely this.

We are all *conscious* of the difference between a blue flower and a red one. We may experience a purple one differently, if purple is our favorite color. Hence, we may "feel" something special about the purple flower that someone else may not "feel." They are conscious of the fact that the color of the flower is purple, but they may not react to it in the same way. So their reaction to it, and thus their *consciousness* of it may be altogether different from our own.

One person may have a preference for daisies. Another for roses, if they are red. Someone else may love white roses. In each instance, feelings and sentiments may be associated with the particular favorite. The scent of flowers can make one individual feel "warm and fuzzy" inside, while the same scent may cause another to recoil because of a sensitivity to flower pollen. One person may be brought to tears, remembering the red roses that draped the funeral bier of his or her mother. Memories of that event may flood the mind if one sees red roses, or even thinks about them. Another person sees black roses and is stricken with fear on account of association of that color with death. All sorts of horrific fantasies and scary possibilities enter the consciousness.

A certain odor may bring to mind a particular place and time. One smell might take you back to Grandma's house when you were a child: a whiff of baked biscuits and gravy, of fried bacon and eggs on the platter. Another scent may transport a war veteran back to Vietnam, Cambodia, or Iraq, and send him into the dark world of PTSD, a most unfortunate state of mental consciousness. The thought of chocolate can make the mouth water. The sight of fresh donuts can do the same thing. The thought or the sight of the object of this desire has the potential to activate a craving for that food item and at times it may drive you to act

GOD DOES EXIST!

(to run down to the local baker and buy a dozen) in order to possess and enjoy the object of your obsession. So, consciousness includes a whole host of mental and physiological potentialities. Sights, sounds, touches, smells, all of the five senses may trigger them. It is multifaceted in every sense of the word. Too, it is complex, with all sorts of inputs and outcomes, nuances and special meanings, each of them dependent on the subjective and very personal perception of the individual involved. Consciousness is one of the most wonderful and amazing things about being human.

Theories of How Consciousness Came to Be

Julian Jaynes in his book *The Origin of Consciousness in the Breakdown of the Bicameral Mind*, wrote:

> O, what a world of unseen visions and heard silences, this insubstantial country of the mind! What ineffable essences, these touchless rememberings and unshowable reveries! And the privacy of it all! A secret theater of speechless monologue and prevenient counsel, an invisible mansion of all moods, musings, and mysteries, an infinite resort of disappointments and discoveries. A whole kingdom where each of us reigns reclusively alone, questioning what we will, commanding what we can. A hidden hermitage where we may study out the hidden book of what we have done and yet may do. An introcosm that is more myself than anything I can find in a mirror. The consciousness that is myself of selves, that is everything, and yet nothing at all—what is it?

And where did it come from?

And why?

Few questions have endured longer or traversed a more perplexing history than this, the problem of consciousness and its place in nature. Despite centuries of pondering and experiment, of trying to get together two supposed entities called mind and matter in one age, subject and object in another, or soul and body in still others, despite endless discoursing on the streams, states, or contents of consciousness, of distinguishing terms like intuitions, sense data, the given, raw feels, the sensa, presentation and representations, the sensations, images, and affections of structuralist introspections, the evidential data of the scientific positivist, phenomenological fields, the apparitions of Hobbes, the phenomena of Kant, the appearances of the idealist, the elements of Mach, the phanera of Peirce, or the category errors of Ryle,

The Consciousness Argument

in spite of all of these, the problem of consciousness is still with us. Something about it keeps returning, not taking a solution (7-8).

Where *did* this unique and mysterious power of the human mind come from? Why do we as humans uniquely possess it? Of course, the materialists have always searched first, and often only, in the physical realm for an entirely physiological and thus biochemical explanation for this amazing capacity of human psychology. Thus, the debate on how it has come to be has focused on two possibilities: physicalism and dualism. Physicalism holds that consciousness is an entirely physical process and nothing else besides. The following is a summary of the perspectives on these questions as set forth by a host of different theorists. This summary is gleaned from David Chalmers's 1996 book, *The Conscious Mind*.

Reductive or eliminative physicalist theories. Such theories deny that there is any gap of the suggested sort. They assert that once we have explained all the physical and functional properties related to consciousness—something which falls under the rubric of the "easy problems"—we have explained everything there is to be explained about consciousness. On this account, phenomenal properties—if they exist at all and are not merely illusory—supervene on and are reducible to physical or functional properties.

Non-reductive physicalist theories. Such theories accept that there is an explanatory gap—in the sense that the explanation of consciousness requires more than the explanation of physical processes and functions—but deny that there is any further gap of a metaphysical kind. They assert that phenomenal properties supervene on (and are grounded in) physical properties. The appearance of an explanatory gap is due to the fact that phenomenal properties are distinct from and irreducible to physical properties, so that, despite the supervenience relationship, explaining consciousness requires the use of concepts and categories distinct from those we use in physics or neuroscience.

Dualist theories. Such theories accept that there is both an explanatory and a metaphysical gap and assert that phenomenal properties do not supervene on (and are not grounded in) physical properties. In this picture, there is at most some weaker relationship between physical and phenomenal properties, such as one of nomological (rather than metaphysical) supervenience: relative to some contingent psycho-physical laws, phenomenal properties may depend on physical properties.

Idealist theories. These theories can be viewed as the mirror images of physicalist theories. They assert that there is a metaphysical dependence relationship between physical and phenomenal properties, but that physicalists have gotten their direction wrong, hence the appearance of an explanatory gap. It is physical properties that supervene on (and are grounded in) phenomenal ones, not the other way around. Idealist theories can also come in reductive and non-reductive forms, but this distinction is not important for our purposes.

Dual-aspect or Russelian monist theories. Theories of this kind assert that what we conventionally call "physical" and "phenomenal" properties are two different aspects of a single reality. More precisely, there is a single class of fundamental properties grounding everything, including the "physical" and the "phenomenal" aspects of the world. One way to develop this idea, though not the only one, is to suggest that physics and the ordinary sciences only ever study relational, extrinsic, or structural properties while being silent on any underlying categorical, intrinsic, and non-structural properties, but that consciousness has to do with the latter. Further, since there could not be anything relational, extrinsic, or structural if there wasn't something categorical, intrinsic, and non-structural, we can treat these latter properties as fundamental.

One group of theorists, labelled *identity theorists*, argue that no problem exists in this realm. For them it is simple. The mental is the physical, that is to say, the mental is nothing else than a particular physical situation that obtains given certain arrangements of atoms. In their way of thinking, consciousness is purely brain activity, purely physiological, entirely biochemical activities that happen in the 14-16 billion neurons of the cerebral cortex, and that is all.

Still another group of such folk are described as *functional theorists*. It is their view that mental states are constituted by the function or role they play in a given system. They see mental states as existing as causal relations to other mental states. Functionalism is especially popular with computationalists. They believe that the brain is merely a biologi-

The Consciousness Argument

cal implementation of a living computer system, and so is able to realize various mental states. Critics of this view have countered that their theory is insufficient to account for consciousness because the role a mental state plays does not explain why the state must be one that is conscious. Why would not all such mental states be processed unconsciously?

Dualism is the term that has come to be employed to describe the theory that consciousness somehow falls outside the domain of the physical. Dualism posits the existence of two separate realms: the physical and the non-material. The key to this approach to the problem of understanding consciousness is that it presupposes that understanding all aspects of the physical brain will not solve the riddle of what it is and how it works. The physical aspect of the brain is not the answer.

Several types of dualism have been suggested. One is called *Cartesian dualism*. It holds that there are both physical and non-physical substances and that consciousness is located within the class of those non-physical substances. We have dealt with this concept in the previous chapter and examined its strengths and weaknesses.

A second perspective is called *Property Dualism*. Those who maintain this approach say that consciousness is a non-physical property that emerges from the same things that give rise to physical properties. Property dualists believe that neural activity has both physical and non-physical properties. The physical properties include such things as electromagnetic potential, while non-physical properties include things like consciousness.

This latter group has been further subdivided into three sub-categories: fundamental, emergence, and neutral monist property dualism. Fundamental property dualists say that conscious properties are basic properties of the universe itself, similar to physical properties like electromagnetic charge. They see conscious properties as their own distinct fundamental entities.

So, according to this view, consciousness works just as electrical charges or any other physical property does. It may cause physical matter to transition among physical states and these physical states in turn may affect consciousness.

GOD DOES EXIST!

Evolution and Consciousness

Originally, the search into the nature of consciousness was known as the mind-body problem, heavy with its ponderous philosophical solutions. But since the theory of evolution, it has transitioned itself into a more scientific question. It has become the problem of the origin of mind, or, more specifically, the origin of consciousness in evolution.

A host of theories have been propounded since evolutionary thinking became the predominant mindset over recent decades. And, like everything else that has been touched by this overarching "holistic" approach to every conceivable discipline, both in and out of science, some theory of how consciousness evolved had to be developed that would explain how natural selection was responsible for this mysterious function within the human brain as well. On this account many attempts have been made, even though none has gained the ascendancy to the exclusion of all of the others. Julian Jaynes summarized the efforts under the following rubrics:

1. *Consciousness as a property of matter.* The most extensive possible solution is attractive mostly to physicists. It states that the succession of subjective states that we feel in introspection has a continuity that stretches all the way back through phylogenetic evolution and beyond into a fundamental property of interacting matter. The relationship of consciousness to what we are conscious of is not fundamentally different from the relationship of a tree to the ground in which it is rooted, or even of the gravitational relationship between two celestial bodies. Most scholars have rejected this approach, saying that it answers the wrong questions. We are not trying to explain how we interact with our environment, but rather the particular experience that we have in introspecting.

2. *Consciousness as a Property of Protoplasm.* This solution to the problem asserts that consciousness is not in matter *per se*; rather it is the fundamental property of all living things. It is the very irritability of the smallest one-celled animal that has had a continuous and glorious evolution up through coelenterates, the protochordates, fish, amphibians, reptiles, mammals and man. So, in a sense it could be said that all living things are, on some level or another, conscious. The problem, it seems, is the tendency on the part of many human beings to identify with the "feelings" of animals and thus to see them as almost human. And so if animals are be-

The Consciousness Argument

having such as we would in similar situations, so well are we trained in our human sympathies that it requires a particular vigor of mind to suppress such identifications when they are not warranted. The explanation for our imputing consciousness to protozoa is simply that we make this common and misleading identification. Yet the explanation for their behavior resides entirely in physical chemistry, not in introspective psychology.

3. *Consciousness as Learning.* A third solution states that consciousness began not with matter, nor at the beginning of animal life, but at some specific time after life had evolved. It seemed obvious to almost all the active investigators of the subject that the criterion of when and where in evolution consciousness began, was at the time of the appearance of associative memory or learning. If an animal could modify its behavior on the basis of its experience, it must be having an experience; it must be conscious. That was the thinking behind the theory. Thus, if one wished to study the evolution of consciousness, one simply studied the evolution of learning.

But consciousness is an actual space inhabited by elements called sensations and ideas, and the association of these elements because they are like each other, or because they have been made by the external world to occur together, is indeed what learning is and what the mind is all about. So learning and consciousness are confused and muddled up with that vaguest of terms, experience. In reality they are completely different phenomena. Learning is simply one aspect of what the human mind does in its functioning. It learns and remembers what it has learned, and that learning becomes an element of consciousness. But the two are not the same, and learning is not the explanation of consciousness.

4. *Consciousness as a Metaphysical Imposition.* The appreciation of the obvious discontinuity between the apes and speaking civilized ethical intellectual men has led many scientists back to a metaphysical view. But they are still wed to their theory of evolution by means of genetic mutation and natural selection, so this is often described as theistic evolution, but not always. The interiority of consciousness just could not in any sense be evolved by natural selection out of mere assemblages of molecules and cells. Therefore, it is argued, there has to be more to human evolution than mere matter, chance, and survival.

GOD DOES EXIST!

Something must be added from outside of this closed system to account for something so different as consciousness.

Alfred Russel Wallace, the co-discoverer of the theory of evolution by natural selection, held to this view. Wallace believed that man's conscious faculties, particularly, "could not possibly have been developed by means of the same laws which have determined the progressive development of the organic world in general, and also of man's physical organism." He felt the evidence showed that some metaphysical force had directed evolution at three different points: the beginning of life, the beginning of consciousness, and the beginning of civilized culture. But Wallace's perspective was not then, nor is it now, acceptable to the scientific establishment.

5. *The Helpless Spectator Theory.* Most materialists consider that there is nothing about consciousness that is all that special. It is just another factor about a wonderfully evolving living world. So in a sense consciousness is downgraded by these theorists from a higher order of being into an extraordinary development in the marvelous mechanical instrument called the human brain. In their view, animals are evolved over time and under the influence of multiple environmental and genetic factors; nervous systems and their mechanical reflexes increase in complexity; when some unspecified degree of nervous complexity is reached, then consciousness appears, and so begins its futile course as a helpless spectator of cosmic events. Hence, what we do and think and say is completely controlled by the wiring diagram of the brain and its reflexes to external stimuli. Consciousness is nothing more than the heat given off by the wires of the system of the functioning grey matter of the brain, a mere epiphenomenon.

6. *Emergent Evolution.* The doctrine of emergent evolution was very specifically welcomed into court to rescue consciousness from this undignified position as a mere helpless spectator. It was also designed to explain scientifically the observed evolutionary discontinuities that had been at the heart of the metaphysical imposition argument. Its main idea is a metaphor: Just as the property of wetness cannot be derived from the properties of hydrogen and oxygen alone, so consciousness emerged at some point in evolution in a way underivable from its constituent parts.

The Consciousness Argument

According to this view, all the properties of matter have emerged from some unspecified forerunner. Those of complex chemical compounds have emerged from the conjunction of simpler chemical components. Properties distinctive of living things have emerged from the conjunctions of these complex molecules. And consciousness emerged from living things. New conjunctions bring about new kinds of relatedness which bring about new emergents.

So the new emergent properties are in each case effectively related to the systems from which they emerge. In fact, the new relations emergent at each higher level guide and sustain the course of events distinctive of that level. Consciousness, then, emerges as something genuinely new at a critical stage of evolutionary advance. When it has emerged, it guides the course of events in the brain and has causal efficacy in bodily behavior.

7. *Behaviorism.* Behaviorism began as a theory in psychology, which was very popular between 1920 and 1960. But over time it became much more than simply this. Those who held to this perspective denied the existence of consciousness. Of course, that was easy in regard to animals. But with people it was more difficult. Each person has to deal with the problem of his or her own introspection. And for most people that is a hard thing to ignore. For those evolutionists who embraced it, this perspective was essentially an opportunity to ignore the subject of consciousness, even though none of those who pushed this perspective could have successfully convinced anyone that consciousness was not real. They themselves knew that they were conscious beings, and the experience of consciousness was a part of their everyday lives. So, in our day there probably are no behaviorists left to defend the cause.

8. *Consciousness as the Reticular Activating System.* Jaynes considers this to be the key to understanding how consciousness came to be. The other seven theories, in his estimation, are incorrect. In this way of approaching it, consciousness is a function of one part of the brain itself. As he puts it,

> All we have to do is to find those parts of the brain that are responsible for consciousness, then trace out their anatomical evolution, and we will solve the problem of the origin of consciousness. Moreover, if we study the behavior of present-day species corresponding to various

stages in the development of these neurological structures, we will be able at last to reveal with experimental exactness just what consciousness basically is. . . .

At the present, a plausible nominee for the neural substrate of consciousness is one of the most important neurological discoveries of our time. This is that tangle of tiny internuncial neurons called the reticular formation, which has long lain hidden and unsuspected in the brainstem. It extends from the top of the spinal cord through the brainstem on up into the thalamus and hypothalamus, attracting collaterals from sensory and motor nerves, almost like a system of wire-tabs on the communication lines that pass near it. But this is not all. It also has direct lines of command to half a dozen major areas of the cortex and probably all the nuclei of the brainstem, as well as sending fibers down the spinal cord where it influences the peripheral sensory and motor systems. Its function is to sensitize or "awaken" selected nervous circuits and desensitize others, such that those who pioneered in this work christened it "the waking brain."

The reticular formation is also often called by its functional name, the reticular activating system. It is the place where general anesthesia produces its effect by deactivating its neurons. Cutting it produces permanent sleep and coma. Stimulating it through an implanted electrode in most of its regions wakes up a sleeping animal. Moreover, it is capable of grading the activity of most other parts of the brain, doing this as a reflection of its own internal excitability and the titer of its neurochemistry. There are exceptions, too complicated for discussion here. But they are not such as to diminish the exciting idea that this disordered network of short neurons that connect up with the entire brain, this central transactional core between the strictly sensory and motor systems of classical neurology, is the long-sought answer to the whole problem (*The Origin of Consciousness*, 17).

So, from Jaynes viewpoint, consciousness is what happens in the reticular activating system of the brain. That and practically nothing more. This is the primary problem with making atheistic evolution the starting-point in any discussion of this issue. The end of the line for the study is always with some physical reality in nature, whether it is a particular law of physics, a biological mechanism in the cell or of a cellular system, a chemical reaction, or as in this case, an anatomical structure or physical feature of the brain. It cannot be otherwise, for their atheistic bias makes it impossible for them to look beyond the physical for answers.

The Consciousness Argument

It is clear from all of this that the field of study that encompasses consciousness is deeply divided and that consensus on the nature and origin of this quality of the human mind is virtually impossible to attain. In our view, and in the estimation of many others, this unique quality of the human mind is a magnificent gift the human being possesses based on God's gift to the human family at creation. The rest of the living creation was excluded from this special province that was supplied only to man and woman.

Anthony Flew, an outspoken atheist for most of his life, in fact one of the most radical and antagonistic of them all, was not a friend of theism. But in his book, *There Is No God,* he pointed to the existence of consciousness as a serious challenge for atheists. He was correct in his assessment of the notion. He was also being honest in appreciating the unique aspect of this special human trait. He saw consciousness as the quality or state of being aware on the primary level, but as a philosopher he understood it in another sense as well. In the philosophical sense it means to have mental processes that are self-directed and that provide a locus for subjective experience. Atheism cannot account for these aspects of humanity. The mind is more than the brain, and consciousness is more than the mind.

Miscellaneous Materialist Arguments

The arguments made by materialists in regard to the development of the human mind and especially of consciousness are, at times, rather ludicrous. Sometimes they border upon the absurd. Such intelligent people ought to know better than to reveal the depth of their biases, but it is their presuppositions that cripple their thinking.

Francis Crick, a person possessed of special talents and gifts, is a perfect illustration of this problem. The brilliant theoretician, best known as a Nobel prizewinner for his work on DNA, writes: "'You', your joys and your sorrows, your memories and your ambitions, your sense of personal identity and free will, are in fact no more than the behaviour [sic] of a vast assembly of nerve cells and their associated molecules" (*Astonishing Hypothesis: The Scientific Search for the Soul*, 5).

In the end he cheerfully admits that the evidence is not strong for his speculations about how the human mind developed (an obvious understatement), but claims that it might provide some new guidelines

GOD DOES EXIST!

for future research. Clearly the title of his book is no better than a slur against believers in God and the existence of the soul. Richard Gregory, a leading visual psychologist, after reading the book said that Crick was outside of his own field in saying such things, and could be regarded therefore as a "loose cannon" in the field of visual consciousness. There is some truth in this assessment of Crick's work. It is difficult to understand why he stepped outside of what was his own field of expertise and endeavor, in order merely to take what we consider to be a "cheap shot" at those who do not share his atheistic bias. But in doing so he clearly evidenced that he was "out of his element" as he did so.

This writer has a personal theory to explain such outrageous and incendiary comments coming from a man of such remarkable achievements as those for which he has been responsible. It is perhaps to be explained in terms of how his work on DNA had been utilized by theists as powerful evidence that materialistic processes alone could not have produced them. Certainly he was aware of this. As an atheist, perhaps he felt that he had to hit back at theists. He may have thought that he needed to strike a blow for atheism in order to atone for his sins, even if he must do so blindly and in a field unrelated to his own and about which he very obviously knew relatively little. That is our view on the matter, for whatever it may be worth.

Where is the proof for this heady allegation that he proffers? Are we "in fact no more than the behaviour of a vast assembly of nerve cells and their associated molecules"? The human mind and its powers are so vast and incomprehensible that most scientists will readily admit that they do not understand it on anything except a very rudimentary level. For one to be so bold as to declare that he has figured it all out and, at the end of the book, has explained it, is beyond supercilious. Being a scientist, Crick was someone who was fully aware that he was responsible, in this situation he had created for himself, to provide sufficient evidence to establish the veracity of such a broad statement as this one. And yet it is just as evident that his remarks were made without them being set forth in the context of proof. On his part there is no logical reasoning provided to explain his outrageous statement. It is purely the product of his personal bias grounded in materialistic presuppositions.

The Consciousness Argument

One reviewer of Crick's monograph, Bill Webster, observed that not even all materialists would agree with his assessment of the problem: "I imagine that Crick would tear his hair out if he read McGinn's (1994) argument that, while he takes a materialist view of the mind-body problem, he thinks that our very cognitive structures will prevent us from ever explaining consciousness" (*Psyche* 2.18 [July 1995]: 3). In other words, we do not have brains that are developed well enough for any of us to comprehend how the brain and the mind that resides within it functions!

Here is another illustration of the absurdity, and even outright preposterousness, of some of their abysmal arguments: Archaeologist Stephen Mithen presented his ideas about consciousness in the popular science book *The Prehistory of the Mind,* published in 1996. Essentially, this treatise is an attempt to study what archaeological evidence can say about the mind and how it supposedly developed. Mithen opens his work with a very honest admission:

> The human mind is intangible, an abstraction. In spite of more than a century of systematic study by psychologists and philosophers, it eludes definition and adequate description, let alone explanation (9).

With this insightful observation we are in full agreement. Would that he had settled with simply saying this and adding no more, or at least, that he had written the remainder of the monograph with this thought in mind. Nonetheless, he immediately contradicted what he said in this profound statement of reality. In fact, he stated on the next page, "Creationists believe that the mind sprang suddenly into existence fully formed. In their view it is a product of divine creation. They are wrong: the mind has a long evolutionary history and can be explained without recourse to supernatural powers" (10). Interesting; is it not? In the face of what he considers to be a theistic threat to his Darwinian model of gradual development, he claims to be able to explain what "eludes definition and adequate description, let alone explanation." Apparently he has taken on supernatural mental capabilities to enable him to accomplish his mission. His goal for the book is, then:

> I will be searching for—and will find—the cognitive foundations of art, religion, and science. By exposing these foundations it will become clear how we share common roots with other species—even though the mind of our closest living relative, the chimpanzee, is in-

deed so fundamentally different from our own. I will thus provide the hard evidence to reject the creationist claim that the mind is a product of supernatural intervention (16).

By the time he reaches his final chapter, he is confident he has done what he claimed he would be able to do:

> The human mind is a product of evolution, not supernatural creation. I have laid bare the evidence. I have specified the "whats," the "whens," and the "whys" for the evolution of the mind (215).

Of course, that is his assessment of what he has accomplished. Not everyone would concur. What is most interesting in this series of quotations is that Mithen contradicts himself in his initial admission. It is as if at the outset of this enterprise he admits that it has never been done, and then confesses that what he is about to do cannot be done. And then he sets out to do it. Afterward, he tells his audience confidently that he has done what has not been done previously. In fact, he has done no better than earlier theorists. He has set forth a theory devoid of real proof and then has proudly declared "mission accomplished!" As Kirsten Birkett observed in a review article in *Zygon*, his work is mostly a series of "creative speculations":

> Mithen perhaps overstates what he was able to "specify." His book is an interesting overview of the fossil evidence for human development with creative speculations as to the psychology of the different supposed stages of human evolution. He tells us how, for instance, human ancestor *Australopithecus* thought more than six million years ago, on the basis of some fossilized bone fragments, and even how the "missing link"—the theoretical common ancestor of humans and apes for which there is no fossil evidence whatsoever—thought. Even more surprising than the scientific overstatement is his assumption that any such study could prove that the mind was not created ("Conscious Objections: God and the Consciousness Debates," *Zygon* 41.2 [June 2006]: 252).

How can anything be proven on the basis of "creative speculations"? How does one know what our ancestors were thinking, or whether they thought at all, by examining fossilized bone fragments? How does one determine what a theoretical common ancestor thought, how their brain functioned, and at what point they developed a sense of consciousness of self—when we are not in possession even of the remains of their skeletal structures? How can we be sure such ancestors ever ex-

The Consciousness Argument

isted at all? Why are atheists so intent upon proving what is so obviously impossible for them to prove?

Simply because they recognize that consciousness is indeed thoroughly mysterious from a scientific viewpoint. They are accustomed to dealing with material realities and consciousness is not a material reality. Hence, they would very much like to simplify it so that it could be explained in purely materialistic terms, but they are frustrated at every turn because it lies outside of the realm that may be tested in the laboratory. They are sometimes referred to as "reductionists" on this account. They wish to define consciousness down to a point where it can be depicted as a thoroughly physical operation within the grey matter of the brain. They reduce an extraordinarily complex operation, challenging even to the most capable specialists among us, down to the simple functions that happen inside the skull.

Different atheists from widely divergent disciplines wish to explain it in terms of their own discipline, each in their own turn. The biologist considers it a purely biological matter. The biochemist sees it in terms of the biochemistry of the brain. The physicist, on the other hand, explains it in terms of natural physical laws. Obviously, each one of these scientific processes enter into the final product, but just as obviously, no one of them is capable of explaining it fully. Moreover, even when they all are taken together they are incapable of providing a complete portrait of what consciousness is in terms of the human experience of it.

In combination all these specialists view it as a system that is both complex and powerful. In spite of this, all of them together cannot begin to explain a thing so simple as a "daydream" being enjoyed by a teenager in a boring classroom setting in high school. After all, that ephemeral fantasy is capable of taking the boy anywhere in the universe, at any time in human history, to accomplish things that only the imagination is capable of picturing, and experiencing otherwise unknown worlds filled with creatures that have never existed at any time or place on this earth. These mental "adventures" are wide ranging and virtually limitless. If you do not believe this, then just take a look at the scribblings and drawings on the covers and pages of their notebooks for their classes at school. That will tell you all you will need to know about their secret thoughts and daydreams, i.e. their consciousness.

GOD DOES EXIST!

This kind of bias especially in the direction of physics, however, is in fact quite widespread, as any observer of science can testify. It follows a pattern in which physics is regarded as fundamental, the underlying basis of all other sciences to which all other sciences will eventually be reduced. Psychology can be explained by biology, which can be explained by chemistry, which can be explained by physics, which ultimately will give us the "Theory of Everything" (Steven Hawking).

One physicist in particular, Roger Penrose, is a case in point. Penrose, Professor of Mathematics at the University of Oxford, who worked with Steven Hawking on relativistic theories of gravity and made a huge number of contributions to mathematics and mathematical physics, stands alone with what must be seen as an entirely different approach to consciousness. Interestingly enough, he rejects the perspective on the subject that sees it only in terms of physical laws. He does not claim any particular religion in his writings, in fact, he is a self-described Platonist—he believes that there is a realm of absolute, eternal ideas that have specific instances in our world. At the same time, he also is a highly accomplished physicist and approaches consciousness, as he does everything else, in terms of physics. Physics is his bias, his presuppositional starting and ending-point. This ingenious author based his work on a variant of Kurt Gödel's theorem in mathematics. Gödel was a genius of unparalleled stature during his lifetime. He proved early in the last century that within certain closed logical systems there are statements that can be true but cannot be proved true by the axioms of the system alone.

From this, Penrose reasoned, we may conclude that there are certain mathematical problems that a computer cannot be programmed to answer. As an example, a computer cannot discover mathematical theorems in the way that human mathematicians do. Hence, Penrose argued, thinking must be a non-computational process. Therefore, the human mind cannot just be a living computer, composed purely of the biomechanical aspects of the brain, for it can do things that it is logically impossible for a computer to do. So it has to be more than simply the sum of its mechanical structures and their processes. Penrose insists that the problems of quantum mechanics and the problems of understanding consciousness are related. He avers that the bizarre and

The Consciousness Argument

counterintuitive properties of quantum physics can be used to solve the bizarre and counterintuitive problem of human consciousness. Therefore, it is his conclusion that when we understand quantum physics we will be in a position to understand consciousness.

Philosopher of science Nancy Cartwright, Professor of Philosophy at the London School of Economics and Political Science, disagrees with this perspective. Why, she asks, does Penrose think the ultimate answers are in physics rather than, say, biology? She thinks the resolution to this query comes down to the fact that we like to assume that the mind is not mysterious, that it can be explained in scientific terms; and, as science is now understood, that means it can be explained in terms of the laws and principles of physics. Without the kind of unity that physics gives, we are left with some kind of mysterious dualism. It is a basic physics bias that is found throughout science and philosophy of science. *And that boils down to a love of reductionist explanation.*

There apparently are a very, very large number of different properties at work in the world. Some are studied by one scientific discipline, some by another, some are in the intersection of different sciences, and a great many are not studied by any science at all. What legitimates the view that behind the appearances they are all really the same? Two things are responsible for this tendency to reduce the complex down to the simple, one size fits all, panacea: one is an excessive confidence in the systematicity of their interactions, and the other is an excessive estimation of what physics has accomplished. Both are clearly associated with a kind of scientific arrogance, an effrontery that disregards what any other discipline is able to contribute to the discussion.

Nevertheless, this kind of physics bias is widespread, as any observer of science can testify. It follows a pattern in which physics is regarded as fundamental, the underlying basis of all other sciences to which all other sciences will eventually be reduced. That takes us back to square one: Psychology can be explained by biology, which can be explained by chemistry, which can be explained by physics, which ultimately will give us the "Theory of Everything." Cartwright is of the opinion that this view flies in the face of empirical evidence. In practice, different sciences are not reduced in this fashion, and it would not help our understanding if they were. Biologists do not want to know about quarks, which have nothing to do with understanding how different cellular systems interact. Neither do psychologists. And neither do neuroscientists (cf. "Why Physics?," in *The Large, the Small, and the Human Mind*, 161–68; see also, Birkett, "Conscious Objections," 263).

Birkett is therefore correct to observe that in spite of the fact of many different competing theories of the origin and nature of consciousness, there is no such thing in the study of the topic as "settled opinion" or even a convincing theoretical reconstruction of how it came to be. This being true, it certainly could not be said that the existence of consciousness is somehow opposed to the notion that God exists and that He is the explanation for it:

> We still await the beginnings of scientific consensus on how consciousness is to be explained. There are not, yet, arguments between competing experimental models with testable outcomes. What we have is fascinating speculation, some more plausible than others depending on one's philosophical preference. There is no coherent theory, no substantial agreement between theorists, and no experimental program. There is not even agreement as to what kind of explanation should be sought. It is too early to conclude that consciousness studies prove Christianity, or any other religion, false. Materialist authors, as determined believers, can have a tendency to forget their scientific principles when arguing about religion. Debates about consciousness would do well to be freed from religious bias, either for or against religion (Birkett, "Conscious Objections," 265).

The Argument from Consciousness for God's Existence

As we noted previously, the existence of intellect in a human being is an indication of a creative Maker, who is Himself possessed of such an intellect, and who imbued His creature with intellectual capacity similar to His own. But consciousness goes even beyond this. Consciousness takes us far beyond the limits of simple intellect. It is as if consciousness employs intellect as only one element of its processing of information and experience.

At the same time, like intellect it suggests that the Creator Himself possesses this unique aspect of personal being. We are like our Maker in more ways than we can imagine (cf. Gen. 1:27). At the same time, He is greater than all of us in more ways than we can imagine. If the mind is not built by smaller parts (anatomical, physical, biological, or chemical)

The Consciousness Argument

and is in and of itself fundamental, then it must derive from a personal source which produces other persons.

The following is a summary of what is described as the "cosmic consciousness argument" for God. This argument has grown out of the revelations made available through the science of quantum mechanics, a fundamental theory in physics that describes nature at the most basic level, atomic and subatomic. It suggests that the mind plays an integrated role in the collapse of the wave function. Therefore, early thinkers like Eugine Wigner set forth an argument for the existence of God from this piece of data. Michio Kaku in his book, *Physics of the Impossible*, commented:

> One minority is there must be a "cosmic consciousness" reading the universe. Objects spring into being when measurements are made, and measurements are made by conscious beings. Hence there must be a cosmic consciousness that pervades the universe determining which state we are in. Some, like Nobel Laureate Eugene Wigner, have argued that this proves the existence of God or some cosmic consciousness (243).

In order to be able to better analyze this viewpoint, it would be helpful to place it in the context of a logical syllogism. In this instance the syllogism is in two parts:

Premise 1: Contingent minds either have a personal explanation or a natural one.
Premise 2: Quantum mechanics and other fields of science imply the natural universe is emergent from consciousness.
Conclusion 1: The natural universe cannot be the explanation of contingent minds.
Premise 3: The explanation of the existence of conscious minds is personal (1, 2).
Premise 4: This personal source is what we call God.
Conclusion 2: Therefore, God exists.

J. P. Moreland has stated the argument differently. His is a more simple syllogism, His argument is based on the irreducible nature of consciousness. The reductionist practice of breaking down a thought or concept to a point where it is explicable on the ground of physical law and biochemical processes has proven itself untenable. Thus he posits

GOD DOES EXIST!

this simple syllogism which argues for what he considers the most plausible explanation for consciousness:

Premise 1: Irreducible consciousness exists.
Premise 2: The best explanation for irreducible consciousness is either theism or naturalism.
Premise 3: Naturalism is not a plausible explanation.
Conclusion: Therefore, theism is the most probable explanation for the existence of irreducible consciousness.

David J. Chalmers, Philosopher and Cognitive Scientist, had this to say about the importance of conscious experience as a mysterious reality. He asked the famous question, "How does the water of the brain turn into the wine of consciousness?" He seemed not to know the answer. But he recognized that it is a phenomenon that we cannot fully explain: "Conscious experience is at once the most familiar thing in the world and the most mysterious. There is nothing we know about more directly than consciousness, but it is far from clear how to reconcile it with everything else we know. Why does it exist? What does it do? How could it possibly arise from lumpy grey matter?" He further remarks,

> Why should there be conscious experience at all? It is central to a subjective viewpoint, but from an objective viewpoint it is utterly unexpected. Taking the objective view, we can tell a story about how fields, waves, and particles in the spatiotemporal manifold interact in subtle ways, leading to the development of complex systems such as brains. In principle, there is no deep philosophical mystery in the fact that these systems can process information in complex ways, react to stimuli with sophisticated behavior, and even exhibit such complex capacities as learning, memory, and language. All this is impressive, but it is not metaphysically baffling. In contrast, the existence of conscious experience seems to be a new feature from this viewpoint. It is not something that one would have predicted from the other features alone.

> That is, consciousness is surprising. If all we knew about were the facts of physics, and even the facts about dynamics and information processing in complex systems, there would be no compelling reason to postulate the existence of conscious experience. If it were not for our direct evidence in the first-person case, the hypothesis would seem unwarranted; almost mystical, perhaps. Yet we know, directly, that there is conscious experience. The question is, how do we reconcile

The Consciousness Argument

it with everything else we know? (*The Conscious Mind: In Search of a Fundamental Theory*, 4-5).

Thomas Nagel, an atheist and naturalistic philosopher, had this to say about the question: "So long as the mental is irreducible to the physical, the appearance of conscious physical organisms is left unexplained by a naturalistic account of the familiar type. On a purely materialist understanding of biology, consciousness would have to be regarded as a tremendous and inexplicable extra brute fact about the world." Dr Nagel admits what many philosophers and scientists of our day know but refuse publicly to acknowledge. Consciousness *is* an "inexplicable extra brute fact about the world." This is true in spite of the fact that we have had all of human history to contemplate it.

In fact, in his book, *Mind and Cosmos,* he admits that the Darwinian approach to human consciousness is essentially flawed, and wrestles with the question, within the strict confines of his atheistic presuppositions, but in an honestly self-critical way that few are willing to do. Recognizing the shocking nature of his admissions for many other atheists, in the Opinionator, a page of *The Stone* (a web forum for contemporary philosophers and other deep thinkers), he wrote regarding the assumptions of the scientific revolution since the 17th century, that it depended on a crucial limiting step:

> It depended on subtracting from the physical world as an object of study everything mental—consciousness, meaning, intention or purpose. The physical sciences as they have developed since then describe, with the aid of mathematics, the elements of which the material universe is composed, and the laws governing their behavior in space and time.

> We ourselves, as physical organisms, are part of that universe, composed of the same basic elements as everything else, and recent advances in molecular biology have greatly increased our understanding of the physical and chemical basis of life. Since our mental lives evidently depend on our existence as physical organisms, especially on the functioning of our central nervous systems, it seems natural to think that the physical sciences can in principle provide the basis for an explanation of the mental aspects of reality as well—that physics can aspire finally to be a theory of everything.

> However, I believe this possibility is ruled out by the conditions that have defined the physical sciences from the beginning. The physical

sciences can describe organisms like ourselves as parts of the objective spatio-temporal order—our structure and behavior in space and time—but they cannot describe the subjective experiences of such organisms or how the world appears to their different particular points of view. There can be a purely physical description of the neurophysiological processes that give rise to an experience, and also of the physical behavior that is typically associated with it, but such a description, however complete, will leave out the subjective essence of the experience—how it is from the point of view of its subject—without which it would not be a conscious experience at all.

So the physical sciences, in spite of their extraordinary success in their own domain, necessarily leave an important aspect of nature unexplained. Further, since the mental arises through the development of animal organisms, the nature of those organisms cannot be fully understood through the physical sciences alone. Finally, since the long process of biological evolution is responsible for the existence of conscious organisms, and since purely physical process cannot explain their existence, it follows that biological evolution must be more than just a physical process, and the theory of evolution, if it is to explain the existence of conscious life, must become more than just a physical theory.

This means that the scientific outlook, if it aspires to a more complete understanding of nature, must expand to include theories capable of explaining the appearance in the universe of mental phenomena and the subjective points of view in which they occur—theories of a different type from any we have seen so far ("The Core of *Mind and Cosmos*," August 18, 2012, opinionator.blogs.nytimes.com).

Conclusion

These admissions reveal the soft underbelly of naturalism in regard to questions pertaining to non-physical realities like sentience, intelligence, and consciousness. Scientists are accustomed to being able to measure and quantify a thing, but in this case their usual methods and techniques do not apply.

Now that is strange, is it not? How could anything exist in a material universe that is not wholly material in nature and is not quantifiable by the tools and methodologies of science? Such a thing should not be. It is contrary to all of the regular assumptions of modern science. And yet, that is precisely what we have in this instance.

The Consciousness Argument

That being true, clearly this is a clue that may point us elsewhere, and so we need to explore further. For, it could very well be that we may be on to something that points us toward Something or Someone who lies outside the realm of the physical. Perhaps it is Something or Someone whose being and nature is "metaphysical" rather than merely physical? Is that even possible? Some would answer "no" at the outset of the inquiry.

But is that an objective way to approach what may be beneficial new information? From a scientific standpoint, we cannot know for certain at this point, but surely this is a matter that is worth our time looking into. Perhaps the philosophers and theologians are on to something that the scientists are just now beginning to discern?

Questions for Discussion

1. Why is it so difficult to find a consensus on how to define consciousness? What is there about it that makes it such a challenge as to accomplish so simple a thing as to provide a basic definition of it?

2. Describe the various aspects of consciousness. How do intelligence, memory, sensory perception, sights and sounds, etc., enter into the equation? The multifaceted nature of consciousness must be considered in order to describe it accurately.

3. What are some of the theories of how consciousness came to be? How are they influenced by their respective points of view: physicalism and dualism?

4. Proponents of evolution also have special theories that they have set forth in their various attempts at explaining the origin of consciousness by means of mutation and natural selection. What are some of the main ones?

5. Some of the explanatory rhetoric spouted by atheistic scientists on the problem of the nature and explanation of consciousness has proven to be downright outrageous. Certainly it is written or spoken outside of the context of scientific proof for their many claims and explanations. What do you think is the reason that they are frequently given to such frivolous allegations, unsubstantiated assumptions and unproven affirmations?

GOD DOES EXIST!

6. Could it have anything to do with how helpless they must feel in the face of something so inscrutable and mysterious as the mind and its many clearly immaterial aspects?

7. What is the "physics bias" and how does it have to do with Steven Hawking's "Theory of Everything"?

8. Summarize the argument for God's existence from the existence of human consciousness.

9. What are the main points in the syllogism that makes the case for God's existence from the perspective of consciousness? Can the natural universe be the originator of consciousness? Or, is the universe emergent from consciousness? Explain your answers to these two questions.

10. What is the soft underbelly of naturalism in regard to questions pertaining to non-physical realities like sentience, intelligence, and consciousness? Could they be dealing with a phenomenon that lies out beyond the limits of their capabilities?

Chapter 11
The Science Argument

The argument from science is a complex one, perhaps the most difficult one of all in the current scientific and philosophical climate. That is not because of a lack of evidence or on account of the nature of the evidence itself, which is both significant and weighty for those willing to open their eyes to it and give it careful consideration, but because of the present state of mind within the elite scientific community. That group is populated with atheists, and not just run of the mill unthinking atheists, but hardcore anti-religion haters of the God-idea.

That is an issue that we plan to deal with momentarily, but for now it would be best to set forth the general argument from science as it should be stated in as simple a syllogism as can be formulated. In this case, simplicity is quite a challenge:

GOD DOES EXIST!

Premise 1: If the material universe were the creation of some outside force or entity, such as God, it would most likely bear the marks of its Creator, and thus give some indication of how and by what means it was produced.

Premise 2: Science, being that it is, by definition, the disciplined study of the various aspects of the material universe and of the living organisms within it, would be the primary means of ascertaining whether or not there are signs of a Maker's work.

Premise 3: There have been numerous indications uncovered by scientific research that the material universe, and living entities within that universe, could not have produced themselves and could not have been produced by any wholly material mechanism, but must have been created by Something or Someone possessing incomparable intellectual prowess and unimaginable power, outside the material realm.

Conclusion 1: God is the only plausible solution to this mystery of origins.

Conclusion 2: Therefore God exists.

The first two premises are not subject to debate. They are merely precursors to the third premise and explain the reasoning behind that premise. If the third premise is correct, then the conclusions as stated necessarily follow. So, it is the third premise that is really the issue here. It is the one that must be proven to the extent that it satisfies the mind of the reader to a degree where he or she may feel confident that the stated conclusions are justified.

Absolute certainty may be fleeting in the present environment where the sciences are so overpopulated with hardcore atheists, their presentiments making objectivity impossible for them, but the evidence is so overwhelming that plausibility is possible even in the present situation. So, after we have discussed the problem of atheism in the ranks of the scientific elite, we shall turn to an examination of the evidence for God from science.

Science and Atheism

How did atheism become the dominant ideology among scientists? Association of scientific endeavor in the nineteenth century and beyond with atheism usually is traced to the work of the brilliant French scholar

The Science Argument

Pierre-Simon, marquis de Laplace (1749-1827). In his five volume work *Celestial Mechanics*, published between 1799-1825, he restated and developed what has come to be called "the nebular hypothesis" of the origin of the solar system. He was also one of the first scientists to postulate the existence of black holes and the notion of gravitational collapse. Whereas Sir Isaac Newton had concluded in his *Philosophiae Naturalis Principia Mathematica* (1687) that divine intervention was necessary to guarantee the stability of the solar system, since he considered it inexplicable otherwise, Laplace dispensed with this hypothesis altogether, opting rather for a purely mechanical and naturally occurring series of physical processes. Since the work of Laplace, science has never been the same again. Skepticism with regard to religion in general and the God hypothesis in particular had found a lasting home in the scientific community.

Whether Laplace was in fact an atheist or not (he is usually considered a deist), is beside the point. His theory was that the processes which produced the universe were entirely of a mechanical nature. They were explicable in terms of mathematics and science, and God was not needed anywhere in his reconstruction of events. In his thinking, mathematical formulations and scientific observations were entirely satisfactory to explain all of the processes involved. He accounted for the origin of the solar system strictly through natural gravitational forces.

Subsequent research has questioned many of his initial conclusions. But the name of Laplace has become synonymous with the notion that any allusion to God in relation to science is to be automatically labelled "pseudoscience." And from that point on the die was cast in terms of removing God from any aspect of the explanation of the solar system, the arrangement of the planets, or even of the origin of the material universe. Another factor must also be added to the mix, however. The time was ripe for this. The cultural milieu was friendly toward this change in scholarly thinking. God represented a tremendous inconvenience, morally speaking, to modernizing societies generally. The age of pietism was over in more places than merely the various fields of science. So, for a great number of scholars it was relatively simple for them to exclude a higher power from the realm of possible options. And even though this element is seldom considered in the determined effort to keep God out of the conversation, it should not be ignored.

GOD DOES EXIST!

God, therefore, seemed not to be required anywhere in the process since godless naturalism represented such a convincing ideology, so a predominant atheism displaced the God hypothesis and a great many scientists virtually ignored the evidence for design for many years afterward. As a result, since the time of Laplace, science has largely discounted the notion of design in the universe and attempted to explain every phenomenon encountered scientifically by means of reference to some particular natural law, blind chance, or the conjectural passing of vast eons of time. When these three factors are taken together, they represent a powerful combination, potentially capable of explaining, albeit shallowly, virtually everything that is encountered in the material universe.

Further, the English philosopher Sir Francis Bacon (1561-1626) had already contributed significantly to the theoretical methodology of this new regimen. His work had provided the grounding for this change. He is credited in large measure with developing the modern scientific method. In his writings he had adamantly opposed including "formal and final causes" within the category of what should be described as science, since he considered formal and final causes to be associated with metaphysics and not science. Science, according to Bacon, needed to restrict itself to "material and efficient causes," thereby freeing science from "the sterility that inevitably results when science and metaphysics are conflated" (*Advancement of Learning*, 30).

This identical line of reasoning is championed into our own day by many scientists, interestingly, atheists and a host of theists as well. Some readers may find this to be surprising, but it is true nonetheless. For example, Jacques Monad in his book, *Chance and Necessity: An Essay on the Natural Philosophy of Modern Biology* (1971), made the case that chance processes and deterministic laws alone suffice to account for every aspect of the universe. A Biologist and outspoken atheist, Monad explicitly denied any place for purpose in science. "The first scientific postulate is the objectivity of nature: nature does not have any intention or goal," he stated authoritatively. Even though many things seem to indicate purposive existence, and some processes clearly have the appearance of purposiveness, this notion ought to be rejected, he argued. Chance and physical law account, he was convinced, for every case of

The Science Argument

such seeming purposiveness. He also opined, "Man at last knows that he is alone in the unfeeling immensity of the universe, out of which he emerged only by chance. His destiny is nowhere spelled out, nor is his duty. The kingdom above or the darkness below; it is for him to choose." There is nothing unexpected about any of these claims for an avowed atheist.

Stanley Jaki, though, is another matter. He touted himself as a theologically conservative historian of science and a Roman Catholic priest. He was a lecturer at Oxford, and penned over two dozen books that dealt with the relationship between science and Christianity. He was a formidable figure, a towering intellectual. Yet, in spite of all this, he was in perfect agreement with Monad and other atheists on this matter (Chesterton, *A Seer of Science*, 1986, 139-40). His view was that purpose and design should be excluded from the study of science and ought to be seen only in terms of metaphysics. Such writers as Jaki provide at best a reductive account of Aristotle's formal causes, and leaves no room whatever for Aristotle's final causes (Dembski, *Intelligent Design*, 122-24). In his way of thinking, reference to design and purpose in nature only confuses the scientific process, introducing theology into what should be an entirely naturalistic endeavor. Science and theology should be kept separate.

Dr. Jaki is representative of many tentative believers who work in the scientific disciplines. To their way of thinking, even though they stumble upon an instance of utterly inexplicable complexity, having no possible natural explanation for the development of its several parts, it ought not to be seen in terms of design by an intelligent agent. According to Jaki and others like him, science should always wait a while longer for a possible naturalistic explanation. For them, the naturalistic explanation is always to be preferred. But is this preference a logical requirement, well established by scientific precedent, or is it simply a surrender to the prevalent worldview? From our perspective, it is the latter.

Stephen C. Meyer is correct in his observation that ultimately it was not the arguments of the philosophers that expunged the design argument from scientific thinking ("The Return of the God Hypothesis," 4). Instead, it was the emergence of increasingly powerful and logically compelling materialistic explanations of "apparent design." Such

GOD DOES EXIST!

features, as per this approach, are more apparent than real. They only demonstrate a semblance of design, not actual planning or purpose. In the wake of the convincing argumentation of Darwin and others, the leading philosophers of the time quite simply followed the direction of the scientists into the new world of Darwinian thought.

Darwin made the case in 1859 (*On the Origin of Species*) that living organisms possessing amazingly complex features of design and function, which had previously been seen as the most obvious examples of God's creative power, only *appeared* to be designed. Later genetic research seemed to confirm the inferential possibility of such developments over time, even though it could not point to any specific examples of the phenomena occurring in the natural realm at present. It was, of course, possible to demonstrate changes in the size and color of plants and animals, and that sort of minor alterations and adaptations of pre-existing life-forms. But new organs and organ systems, let alone new life-forms, could not be shown to be produced by that means. What was observable was essentially a rehash of that which was already known through the well understood practice of selective breeding. From this meager evidence was constructed a theoretical postulate of immense proportions, the evolution of life "from amoeba to man."

Over the years since this was first posited as a means to the end of developing such systems, additional research has only complicated the issue. Protein and DNA investigations have shown how extraordinarily difficult it would be to accomplish such a feat. Virtually all of the statistical studies of the potential of the phenomenon have declared that on the basis of blind chance alone, such a development is practically impossible. The reply that has come from stubborn promoters of chance is that over vast periods of time the highly unlikely will inevitably occur. To which it has been responded that there has not been near enough time since the beginning of the universe to make the case for blind chance as a reasonable answer to the problem.

But this objection has not been taken seriously, either then or now. Darwinian thinking in Biology was here to stay. This trend was reinforced by the emergence of other fully naturalistic origins scenarios in the fields of astronomy, cosmology, and geology. Philosophers tended in this case to follow the lead of the theoreticians in the arena of science.

The Science Argument

And so, for a period of years scientists generally either asserted that science contradicts theistic belief or denied that science has any religious or metaphysical implications whatsoever. Most philosophers followed along in tow, generally denying that the testimony of nature lends any support at all to a theistic worldview (cf. Meyer, ibid., 5-6).

Science Employed as a Weapon against Theism
In our time science has been turned into a cudgel with which the atheists attempt to destroy the faith of believers. It is firmly held by hostile and aggressive atheists that science has proven beyond any question that God does not exist. This is a misrepresentation, of course, but one that atheists are all too willing to encourage nonetheless. A great number of books have been produced lately by such outspoken atheists in the hope that they may be able to browbeat the ignorant masses with their high-sounding and arrogant claims. Such publications have appeared in recent years in great profusion: Daniel Dennett (*Breaking the Spell: Religion as a Natural Phenomenon*), Richard Dawkins (*The God Delusion; Outgrowing God: A Beginner's Guide; The Blind Watchmaker*), Victor Stenger (*God: The Failed Hypothesis—How Science Shows That God Does Not Exist*), Taner Edis (*The Ghost in the Universe*), Sam Harris (*The End of Faith*), Christopher Hitchens (*The Portable Atheist*), etc.

Most scientists are aware that science itself does not touch the area of metaphysics. The two disciplines do not overlap, and they recognize that. At the same time, several atheistic scientists have stepped outside their area of expertise in an effort to share their own faith about whether or not God exists. Some have given the impression that the real, hard evidence is clear on this point, and clearly on the side of the atheists. Coming from different branches of the various sciences, Dawkins, Stenger, Edis, Emile Zuckerkandl, Peter Atkins, Steven Weinberg, and others, have argued that it is the unanimous verdict of science that the proof is overwhelmingly against the God hypothesis.

Religion, in the thinking of these individuals, is a dangerous and repressive ideology, even at its best. Sam Harris, for example, reminds his readers that the Catholic Church was guilty of horrific crimes against humanity during the Spanish Inquisition. He blames religion in general for these evil acts, not the wicked men who committed them. These were isolated acts in the long history of Christianity. Others could be found, of course, but the fact that they are so few in number and difficult to discover should be taken as evidence that Christianity is not by nature an evil influence in society. Most scholars would agree in fact that just the opposite is true. The influence of Christianity in civilization has been almost entirely wholesome and salutary.

The Christian Crusades frequently have been offered as evidence against the Church, but it seems to be forgotten by some historians that those armies were sent into Christian regions where Muslims had been fighting continuous wars of conquest (*jihad*) for the better part of two hundred years. Do Christians have no right of self-defense? Are they simply supposed to bare their necks for the sword, and to do so without opposing or confronting their murderers? Are they expected to allow their brethren to be slaughtered in their millions without attempting to come to their aid? That is precisely what they did, and that is all they did, historically speaking! That does not mean that the Crusaders did not at times act out of revenge, kill innocent civilians, commit cruel acts, etc.

To admit that this is true, however, does not alter history. They were not the aggressors. The Muslim invaders were. It is a false charge to allege that Christian Crusaders had no right to fight against marauders, bandits, pirates, kidnappers, and invaders! Perhaps at times they overreacted to Muslim provocations, but who are we in the safety of our comfortable modern democracies to second-guess their actions to save their own lives and those of their fellows? But I digress. The point is that this is a false charge that is being made against Christianity and it should not be taken seriously.

At the same time, in regard to such matters, Harris neglects to mention that the twentieth century was hardly to be described as an age of faith and religion, and yet it produced such amoral and murderous figures as Lenin, Stalin, Hitler, Mao, Idi Amin, Pol Pot, and a host of others like them. Not one of these figures could be counted among the Christian religious leaders of mankind! Moreover, thousands of their atheistic cohorts were participants with them in these large-scale bloodlettings. They were certainly not men of deep religious conviction. Rather, many of them were anti-religion in their convictions, often so fierce in their animosity toward alternative views that they attempted to erase religion from among those within their grasp and under their power.

The Science Argument

So, make no mistake about it, atheism has its own dark history, which its adherents and proponents systematically ignore as they go about their destructive task. "Atheism had nothing to do with their crimes against humanity," we are told by those who wish to avoid the implications of their heinous actions. Hundreds of millions of rotted corpses seem to suggest otherwise. Only the comparable hundreds of millions of victims of violent expansionist Islam over the ages (thought to total around 200 million, and counting) can aptly compare.

Moreover, it would be impossible to argue that the indescribable horrors of the twentieth century were unanticipated. Although they came as a shock to most civilized people, they were in fact no surprise. In his work *The Brothers Karamazov*, Ivan Karamazov exclaimed that if God does not exist, then everything is permitted. Hence, throughout the nineteenth century, as religious conviction seeped out of the institutions of Western culture, poets and philosophers had the uneasy feeling that its withdrawal might signal the ascension of great evil in the world. And in this they were right.

A Hypothetical Syllogism

David Berlinski, in his excellent book, *The Devil's Delusion: Atheism and its Scientific Pretensions*, sets forth a hypothetical syllogism to put the agenda of these proud atheists into its proper logical context. We have altered Berlinski's syllogism slightly in order to make it more explanatory in nature. But on its own, it is a powerful piece of logical reasoning. Atheists are like the proverbial "pot calling the kettle black" in their charges against Christianity as being the culprit in much of the mayhem that has happened in civilized societies. His syllogism has two premises, whereas ours has three. This is their view in a nutshell:

Premise 1: If God does not exist, then everything is permitted.
Premise 2: If science is true, then God does not exist.
Premise 3: If science is true, then everything is permitted.
Conclusion: Science is true, and God does not exist, therefore everything is permitted.

Premise 1 must be accepted at face value. Few would argue with it. For if God does not exist, then there is no reason at all to be concerned with what is right or wrong, other than the material and physical con-

GOD DOES EXIST!

sequences that may follow upon our actions, i.e., we may be permitted to do a thing, but it may potentially pose a hazard to our life and well-being. Moreover, some things that certain aberrant individuals may like to do or want to do could well land them in prison, but that would not suggest that their desires are morally reprehensible. It would just mean that they are illegal. Serial killers like Ted Bundy and John Wayne Gacy may enjoy brutally murdering other human beings, but in a sense all they are doing is exploring an alternative lifestyle choice if some actions are not to be styled as morally repugnant. Who are we to judge their actions? If God is not in the picture somewhere then morality is not a factor. If God does not exist, then everything is permitted.

Now, of course serial murderers and spree killers cannot be allowed to walk free in any civilized society, for the safety of one and all. Where moral judgements are absent there are notable exceptions, however. Some of those have been men held in great renown. It must be remembered that Chairman Mao (ca. 65 million victims of his cruel experiments with socialism alone) and Joseph Stalin (ca. 20 million victims) lived out their lives as free men and died of natural causes, in spite of their many crimes against humanity. Both died of ordinary heart attacks. Where atheism is the dominant ideology, it seems that even the wholesale slaughter of one's political and ideological enemies is not to be viewed as "immoral"! If God does not exist, then everything is permitted. Even murder and mayhem. If you can get away with it, that is. And so, it is plain that Premise 1 is not arguable.

Premise 2, however, is the one that must be proven. It is here that the dogmatic atheists must make their stand. But this is where they face an insuperable difficulty. Scientific "facts" (as opposed to theories), simply do not say anything at all in any direct way about the subject of metaphysics, and thus, whether or not God exists. Facts of course may bear indirectly upon the topic, and so may have the potential to weigh in upon a conclusion that might be drawn, whether for or against. But they simply do not have the propensity to settle matters of a metaphysical nature. Physical facts and physical laws do not touch the realm of the metaphysical (the realm that has to do with what is beyond or outside the scope of the physical).

The Science Argument

Think of it this way: What scientific "fact" or natural law or even a combination of them establishes that God could not possibly exist? There is none. Not one of these writers knows of a single fact that may be brought forward that will establish the truthfulness of this unproven allegation, which they so confidently set forth. And yet, as all know well, they stubbornly persist in making this unprovable argument anyway. Now this is not a small conclusion to draw, it is in fact, as one fellow cleverly said, "the whole burrito." If the argument from science must be seen in those terms, as any fair minded observer would have to admit, then provable, demonstrable, repeatable scientific fact (as opposed to theory or hypothesis) is not on the side of atheists or anti-religion skeptics.

Premise 3 therefore proves absolutely nothing because genuine science has nothing helpful to contribute to questions of ethics and morality. Scientific particulars must be brought forth, evidence sufficiently weighty to prove that God does not exist and could not exist, not philosophical or even theological ramblings about what science might mean or could imply. What are these "scientific facts" about which they so confidently pontificate? March them out before us in their legions, if they exist at all! Such ruminations and baseless contentions as they persistently proffer are not sufficient to establish this proposition. It is mostly "bluff and bluster."

The Conclusion of this syllogism therefore fails, since Premises 2 and 3 will not stand. We would of course agree that "science is true," that is to say, the demonstrable facts of scientific research proven in the laboratory and repeatable in the same, are accurate. That which may be measured and quantified is not arguable. Everything does not fit into such categories, however. But that does not lead us to the inevitable conclusion that "everything is permitted" because science has not in fact proven that God does not exist.

Furthermore, it is not within the purview of science ever to be able to do so. God may very well exist, in spite of all of their high-sounding claims. If great numbers of well-educated and intelligent people, excepting the atheistic intelligentsia, count for anything then assuredly believers outnumber unbelievers many times over. Certainly the vast majority of intelligent humans have concluded that God is the most ra-

GOD DOES EXIST!

tional answer to the question about how we got here and why, in spite of the harangues of an elitist element of the scientific community that has set off on a mission to purge from the minds of the unwashed masses their comforting faith in an "astral deity."

Once more, which law of the natural realm is there that is against the idea that there could be a God who resides and has His base of operations outside the material world? We allege that there is none. How has science shown us anything at all that implies there could not exist a reality or "dimension" different from our own? If such a proof had been discovered, you can be certain that you would already have heard about it. And you would be constantly hearing about it. But of course you have not heard about it and will not hear about it. That is because it does not exist.

It is whether or not God exists that matters in this discussion. If God exists, then everything is not allowed. If God exists, then nothing that God has forbidden is morally acceptable. And, if God exists then we are accountable for our actions in regard to such things as these. It is just that simple. Our actions are subject to divine approval or disapproval. And disapproval carries with it consequences that are not to be desired or ignored: "It is a fearful thing to fall into the hands of the living God" (Heb. 10:31).

From this frank admission about the inability of science to speak in regard to matters having to do with the immaterial world, the erudite mathematician David Berlinski adjudges militant atheists like Richard Dawkins, Sam Harris, Daniel Dennett, and Christopher Hitchens as guilty of peddling "dangerous foolishness" rather than true science. Berlinski then draws the eminently logical conclusion: "Whereupon there is a return to a much older, vastly more somber vision of life and its constraints, one that serves to endow the phrase *bestial indulgence* with something more by way of content than popularly imagined" (20).

His book is a masterpiece of antithetical response to the heady arrogance of some atheistic scientists who are so absolutely sure that the present status of science has shown beyond all doubt that God and the metaphysical world do not exist and are merely the vestiges of a prescientific worldview. What makes him particularly irksome to the atheistic

The Science Argument

elites is that he is a secular scholar himself. He is different from the militant atheists because he freely admits the limitations of true science. He has not lost his grasp on reality. He understands that science can only go so far in its capacity intelligently and authoritatively to comment in regard to such matters. And he confesses that these radical atheists have stepped outside their roles as scientists in making the outrageous and unprovable claims that they do.

"Dangerous Sexual Repression?"

Christopher Hitchens, prior to his death in 2011, was one of the most rabid of these religion-hating atheists, arguing that religion is dangerous because, in his words, "it is the cause of dangerous sexual repression." With tongue firmly in cheek, to this bitter allegation David Berlinski responded by saying, "Short of gender insensitivity, what can be more dangerous than dangerous sexual repression?" (18).

Hitchens went on to suggest that the original Ten Commandments ought to be replaced with more modern ones, and among them should be the command "to enjoy their own sex lives as long as it damages nobody else." Clearly he has reached these impressive conclusions from the perspective of solid and indisputable scientific knowledge! This is so because scientific research is replete with evidence that contributes to our understanding of such things, and thus establishes the unquestionable soundness of this "scientific" declaration!

It is good, however we view such observations, that Hitchens revealed to the reader the not-so-hidden agenda which he wished to promote in his polemical writings against God and religion. It is easy to see from this that science represented little more for him than a stage prop to support his lifestyle choices. His argument and its justification was little different than that which was espoused by the flower children of the nineteen-sixties, the "hippies" who practiced "free love" and sex devoid of commitment. But clothing bestial indulgence with the garb of scientific approval and with the justification of scientific "proof" will not make this philosophy anything different from what it appears on the surface of it to be. From a practical perspective this is not a workable way to conduct one's life. There are both "pragmatic and prudential factors" that require to be considered prior to certain lifestyle choices being made. Just ask any good philosopher:

GOD DOES EXIST!

Whether a particular sexual act or a specific type of sexual act provides sexual pleasure is not the only factor in judging its nonmoral quality: pragmatic and prudential considerations also figure into whether a sexual act, all things considered, has a preponderance of nonmoral goodness. Many sexual activities can be physically or psychologically risky, dangerous, or harmful.... Thus in evaluating whether a sexual act will be overall non-morally good or bad, not only its anticipated pleasure or satisfaction must be counted, but also all sorts of negative (undesired) side effects: whether the sexual act is likely to damage the body, as in some sadomasochistic acts, or transmit any one of a number of venereal diseases, or result in an unwanted pregnancy, or even whether one might feel regret, anger, guilt afterwards as a result of having engaged in a sexual act with this person, or in this location, or under these conditions, or of a specific type. Indeed, all of these pragmatic and prudential factors also figure into the moral evaluation of sexual activity: intentionally causing unwanted pain or discomfort to one's partner, or not taking adequate precautions against the possibility of pregnancy, or not informing one's partner of a suspected case of genital infection... can be morally wrong. This depending on what particular moral principles about sexuality one embraces, the various ingredients that constitute the nonmoral quality of sexual acts can influence one's moral judgments ("Philosophy of Sexuality: The Dangers of Sex," in *Internet Encyclopedia of Philosophy*. www.iep.utm.edu/sexuality).

Hitchens was wrong in giving such permissive advice. What he urged upon his readers was nothing short of dangerous, in practical terms. That much is generally conceded by the vast majority of medical professionals. And yet, all of this concern for physical and psychological danger leaves out the greatest complication of all: God. If God exists then we are accountable to Him in all of our behaviors and actions. If we have an eternal soul, then such unbridled sexual practices and destructive moral choices as he gives encouragement to may well imperil the souls of those who follow his advice for eternity.

Unfortunately, Hitchens was not and is not alone in this. He was not much different than any other fellow who has a god-complex. He knows nothing of metaphysics. He thinks because he has a strong opinion, a ready wit, and some talent as a writer, that he is an expert in absolutely everything. And so he pontificates about things with which he was not

The Science Argument

very familiar but about which he has settled opinions. Sadly, he also clearly had "a dog in the fight" in that he did not want his sexual appetite restricted in any fashion.

Therefore it should be concluded that he is less than objective in his approach to the topic. His prideful disdain for those who disagree with him is most unbecoming of a genuine philosopher or a true scientist. Not only was his philosophical and scientific arrogance foolhardy, but it was and still is destructive. When asked about his own heavy drinking and smoking, he replied: "I don't want to live forever." He admitted being a heavy drinker from his teen years on. He died at age 62 of pneumonia which was a complication of his esophageal cancer (a disease that has been linked to heavy alcohol consumption).

Frontal Assault on Religion

The following is a forceful illustration of our point. In the year 2007 a scientific conference was held on the topic, "Beyond Belief: Science, Religion, Reason, and Survival." It was called in order to provide a frontal assault on religious thought. If this sounds something akin to your personal experience in your university course in Biology, Botany, Anthropology, Physics, or one of the other sciences, where the professor waxed eloquent in his deliberations on metaphysics, then you would be right to see it so. Clearly this is the same group of arrogant snobs who know absolutely nothing about either philosophy or metaphysics but who despise the rest of us "ordinary folk" because we believe that God exists and that there are moral absolutes and imperatives by which we ought to live.

At any rate, the physicist Steven Weinberg delivered an address at the conference. As one of the authors of the theory of electroweak unification, for which he was awarded a Nobel prize, he decided to express himself on a topic about which he knows little or nothing. (Most of us "ordinary folk" have good enough sense to discern that an expert in electroweak unification is not particularly well qualified to preach at us about our belief in a Higher Power!) "Religion," he affirmed, "is an insult to human dignity. With or without it you would have good people doing good things and evil people doing evil things. *But for good people to do evil things, that takes religion*" (italics added). For these remarks he was warmly applauded by this assemblage of elite scientists. It should

GOD DOES EXIST!

be observed that if there is no God, then there is no such thing as "evil," and we should not use a judgmental term like this if we do not accept that there will be a Judgment to right those wrongs, but then again, I digress. Obviously he was speaking to an audience of listeners who were especially friendly to this strain of thought. Had he walked a block away from that building and asked the people on the street what they thought of what he had to say, he would likely have received a very different reception and response! Most ordinary people do not take too kindly to arrogant fellows like this insulting their religious convictions. We suggest that he take that speech on the road and deliver it in Islamabad, Tehran, Riyadh, or Kabul, and see how well it is received.

Amazingly, he failed to apply this identical principle to his own area of *actual* competence, namely science. Who was it that imposed on the suffering human race advancements like firearms, poison gas, barbed wire, high explosives, experiments in eugenics, euthanasia, abortion pills and clinical methods, the formula for Zyklon B, heavy artillery, pseudo-scientific justification for mass murder, cluster bombs, attack submarines, napalm, intercontinental ballistic missiles, military space platforms, nuclear weapons, etc." David Berlinski tops off his own version of this interrogatory with the following exclamation: "If memory serves, it was not the Vatican" (*The Devil's Delusion*, 21).

All of these modern horrors are products of the scientific endeavor. Science has brought us many time-saving and even life-saving machines and other beneficial inventions. But it has also refined the machines of war and of death to a point where it is now possible to visit our enemies (and even at times our friends) with merciless devastation. Berlinski remarks further:

> One might think that in the dark panorama of wickedness, the Holocaust would above all other events give the scientific atheist pause. Hitler's Germany was a technologically sophisticated secular society, and Nazism itself, as party propagandists never tired of stressing, was "motivated by an ethic that prided itself on being scientific." The words are those of the historian Richard Weikart, who in his admirable treatise, *From Darwin to Hitler: Evolutionary Ethics, Eugenics, and Racism in Germany*, makes clear what anyone capable of reading the German sources already knew: A sinister current of influence ran from Darwin's theory of evolution to Hitler's policy of extermination. A generation

The Science Argument

of German biologists had read Darwin and concluded that competition between species was reflected in human affairs by competition between races.

These observations find no echo at all in the literature of scientific atheism. Christopher Hitchens is prepared to denounce the Vatican for the ease with which it diplomatically accommodated Hitler, but about Hitler, the Holocaust, or the Nazis themselves he has nothing to say. This is an odd omission for a writer who believes that *religion* poisons everything... (ibid, 27).

Of course, Darwinism is only a theoretical construct of how and in what manner it is thought by some scientists that biological life may have developed into its vast diversity and amazing complexity at the present time. It is only a theory and nothing more. Honest scientists are willing to admit that the whole reconstruction of the process of evolution of living things from molecules to man is purely hypothetical. It is no more "scientific" than the account found in the book of Genesis! Undoubtedly it rankles some of the more contentious of their numbers to hear this suggested, but the facts of the case bear it out.

Why are we able to make this claim without any concern that it can be overturned either logically or scientifically? It goes to the heart of both science and true knowledge. Proof of what is believed in science is demonstrated to be so in the laboratory by means of experimentation, of trial and error. That which can be shown to be true is then repeated and thus shown to be universally so. Not one repeatable laboratory experiment has ever proven any part of the Darwinian model to be so. This is in fact the case after almost a century and a half of wishing and hoping by atheists for something solid to hang their convictions on. So, true science is not the friend of Darwinism. Over time, in fact, it's hopes have only been persistently and continuously dashed by the light shed upon the subject by additional scientific discoveries. It is no more "proven" now than it was when Darwin first published his *Origin of Species*. In fact, if anything, the evidence against it is now many times more convincing than it was when the book first appeared.

This explains the general public's aversion to acceptance of what most naturalist scientists have been trying to sell now for one hundred years. No doubt the scientific community has been baffled by its failure

GOD DOES EXIST!

to convince the general public to believe in evolution, and this explains the fact that they have such meetings as these where they lambast the *hoi polloi* for their tenacious continuance in faith and religion in spite of all that they have said and done in science and the science classroom.

There is little wonder: despite their massive educational efforts, including a pitch for evolution on every public television program that deals with nature, the state of public opinion has not changed very much over the past several decades. Polls persist in showing that less than ten percent of the American public believes in the official scientific orthodoxy, which is that humans and other living things were evolved by a materialistic evolutionary process in which God was in no way involved. The American public remains unconvinced and unmoved by all that has been and is being thrown at it. The remaining ninety percent is more or less evenly divided between biblical creationists and theistic evolutionists (who believe that evolution was God-guided).

How could this be true? The answer to this dilemma is in fact pretty straightforward. The general public has long suspected that what is being presented to them in the public schools and universities, and elsewhere, is pure propaganda, an atheistic ideology devoid of any scientific basis whatsoever rather than the "scientific fact" that it claims to be. In this they are absolutely correct. And they are right to be suspicious and even downright skeptical of their pretentious scientific "superiors." It is plain even to most of their students in the university classrooms (in spite of the fact that they are reluctant to confront their professors and suffer academically for their efforts) that their teachers are stretching the evidence beyond the limits of reasonableness. Moreover, they can see when a purely theoretical reconstruction of events is that and nothing more. Molecules to man evolution is precisely that: purely theoretical.

What Is Science, Anyway?

Natural science is to be defined as a system of knowledge concerned with the physical world and its various phenomena. It has to do primarily with those general truths or the operation of the general natural laws especially as obtained and tested by the scientific method. This being true, in the course of scientific inquiry one wonders whether at multiple junctures in the process there may be indications that an intelligent agent was responsible for the natural world? Or, on the contrary, is the

The Science Argument

natural world easily explicable on its own terms, without the initiative or assistance of a supervisory power, a Designer and Prime Mover?

These are the primary questions with which the philosophy of science must wrestle. Science itself may say little directly about the subject, but some scientists, especially of the atheistic bent, are ready at a moment's notice to let the rest of us know what they *think and believe* about the matter. They are also prepared at the drop of a hat to pour derision on the head of and expel anyone from their ranks who disagrees with their conclusion. After all, how could anyone be a *true* scientist who actually believes in God?

The argument from science as it has been articulated by a good number of modern thinkers might be summarized in the following way: "The evidence from science is against belief in God." Assuredly there are a great number of people who believe this. And those who represent this point of view are in most instances absolutely certain that this is the proper way to frame the question and elicit an answer to it. (Notice that the question mark is noticeably absent: to their way of thinking the question has long since been answered in the negative). Science is firmly on the side of atheism. That is their declarative affirmation.

But is this really true? Is science, at its heart, squarely on the side of atheism? Or, is it simply the case that numerous outspoken atheists have populated the ranks of several of the scientific disciplines and attempted by their semi-official pronouncements to give the impression that science *per se* is atheistic? We believe it is the latter and not the former. There have always been scientists who were believers and there are a great number of them now who are. Only the most courageous will say so. Many of them are not outspoken on the subject, for fear that their reputations and careers will be ruined if they let the wrong people know it. But they are out there in far greater numbers than the leading lights of the scientific disciplines could ever imagine.

To begin with, looked at historically, this is an argument which makes almost no sense at all. The Bible, and therefore Christianity, sets forth the notion that this world that we live in is a rational place. It runs by fixed and predictable laws and it is for this reason that it can be studied, investigated, and analyzed with the firm assurance that what is true

GOD DOES EXIST!

today will still be true tomorrow. In fact, science, music, and the arts, to name just three fields of study, had their greatest advances in the Christian West where an environment conducive to inquiry and experimentation was cultivated. This understanding of the history of scientific thought is well understood and generally appreciated. The birth of modern science was mainly due to the creationist convictions of its founders, as explained by Dr. Loren Eiseley, who is a professor of anthropology and an evolutionist:

> It is the Christian world which finally gave birth in a clear articulated fashion to the experimental method of science itself. . . . It began its discoveries and made use of its method in the faith, not the knowledge, that it was dealing with a rational universe controlled by a Creator who did not act upon whim nor inference with the forces He had set in operation. The experimental method succeeded beyond man's wildest dreams but the faith that brought it into being owes something to the Christian conception of the nature of God. It is surely one of the curious paradoxes of history that science, which professionally has little to do with faith, owes its origins to an act of faith that the universe can be rationally interpreted, and that science today is sustained by that assumption (*Darwin's Centenary: Evolution and the Men who Discovered It*, 62).

Science was not born in an environment created or controlled by atheists. Science was inaugurated in the Christian West. If it had not been for Christianity being the predominant influence in the West, science as we know it would never have come to be. Pagan religion would never have given rise to science, nor could it have allowed it to germinate. Religions of that stripe were typically animistic or pantheistic, treating the natural world either as the abode of the divine or as an emanation of God's own essence. The most familiar form of animism holds that spirits or gods reside in nature. Glens and groves, rocks and streams are alive with spirits, sprites, and demons. Nature teems with sun gods, river goddesses, astral deities, etc. Belief in the reliability of nature is a fundamental premise of a biblical worldview that ultimately contributed to the rise of modern science. Nobel Prize-winning biochemist Melvin Calvin (1911-1997) made this very point when he said, "As I try to discern the origin of that conviction, I seem to find it in a basic notion discovered 2000 or 3000 years ago, and enunciated first in the Western world by the

The Science Argument

ancient Hebrews: namely, that the universe is governed by a single God, and is not the product of whims of many gods, each governing his own province according to his own laws. This monotheistic view seems to be the historical foundation for modern science" (*Chemical Evolution*," 258).

Alfred North Whitehead wrote similarly: "modern science must come from the medieval insistence on the rationality of God. . . . In Asia, the conceptions of God were of a being who was either too arbitrary or too impersonal for such ideas to have much effect on instinctive habits of mind. Any definite occurrence might be due to the fiat of an irrational despot, or might issue from some impersonal inscrutable origin of things. There was not the same confidence as in the intelligible rationality of a personal being" (*Science and the Modern World,* 18-19). This notion is widely recognized as true, so much so that a host of quotations could be marshalled to prove it.

C. S. Lewis also said, "Men became scientific because they expected law in nature and they expected law in nature because they believed in a Legislator" (*Miracles,* 169). Not only is the nature of God important, but so is the nature of the created order itself. The claim that nature in and of itself is corrupt and evil (an ancient pagan claim) is in opposition to what God described as being a "very good" creation when He formed it (cf. Gen. 1:31; 1 Tim. 4:4-5). Christian belief in the goodness and integrity of the physical universe played an incalculable part in transforming the ancient worldview into what we today refer to as a "scientific" one. It destroyed the Platonic and Aristotelian idea that matter is, if not evil, the raw material of corruption and unreality and the source of disorder in the universe, and it also ruled entirely out of consideration the pessimistic views of nature that emanated from the various dualist sects such as the Manicheans and Gnostics, thereby anticipating the material reality of the universe for serious scientific attention (cf. Torrance, *Divine and Contingent Order,* 67).

The advice of Stanly L. Jaki in his often quoted essay, "The Biblical Basis of Western Science," in regard to what he referred to as the "linear perspective" that made the practice of modern science a possibility is most instructive:

> Whenever we find this linear perspective we find the Bible in the background. This is best appreciated if we take a look at the cosmic view

GOD DOES EXIST!

of all great ancient cultures. They are all dominated by the belief that everything will repeat itself to no end, or by the idea of eternal returns. Only on occasion does one hear about this. One hardly ever hears that this belief was responsible for the fact that science suffered a stillbirth, indeed a monumental stillbirth, in all ancient cultures.

I coined the phrase, the stillbirths of science, about thirty years ago. The phrase certainly did not catch on in secular academia. The reason is obvious. Nothing irks the secular world so much as a hint, let alone a scholarly demonstration, that supernatural revelation, as registered in the Bible, is germane to science—it made the only viable birth of science possible.

That birth took place in a once-Christian West. Still today it is that birth that fuels neocapitalism that not only needs free markets, but also merchandise to bring to market, and needs that merchandise in ever larger quantities. Only science can deliver them. The rise of that science, so crucial for Western man, and for the modern world, has distinctly biblical origins insofar as the Bible is a record of the Christian faith.

Whether modern man would be willing to learn in detail about the dependence of science on the Bible is strongly doubtful. But Christians will overlook those details only at grave peril in a great cultural contestation where science plays such a prominent role (*Crisis Magazine*, Oct. 1, 1997).

Moreover, by and large, the leading lights in science in the early years were, almost all of them, believers. It is a historical fiction, urged on the public mind by certain skeptics, that religion has been a deterrent to scientific discovery and advancement. The overreach of the Roman Catholic authorities are, of course, well known in regard to the discouragement of many of the early scientists. Naturally then, their opposition to some of the conclusions of the earliest thinkers and researchers is set forth as demonstration of the allegation that science and religion always have been and always will be irreconcilable. But those (few and far between) incidents are not the full story. It is not accidental that modern science arose in the Christian West and not elsewhere, and never previously in another environment. Historically speaking, this is generally recognized, even though some modern scientists are loath to admit it. Rodney Stark sets the record straight in this regard in his book *How the West Won*:

The Science Argument

Science arose only in Christian Europe because only medieval Europeans believed that science was possible and desirable. And the basis of their belief was the image of God and His creation. This was dramatically asserted to a distinguished audience of scholars attending the 1925 Lowell Lectures at Harvard by the great English philosopher and mathematician Alfred North Whitehead, who explained that science developed in Europe because of the widespread "faith in the possibility of science... derivative from medieval theology." This claim shocked not only his audience but Western intellectuals in general when his lectures were published (Stark, *How the West Won*, 315).

The facts do not coincide with the view which states that religious people are generally opposed to science. Quite the opposite, in fact. Most religious people have great respect for true science. At the same time, however, they are decidedly wary of the overstated claims of those who "have an axe to grind" in pushing their own personal belief system on others, and use their scientific credentials and their official positions to beat down and silence those who may not accept their pretentious generalizations about origins and other things about which true science does not actually speak.

Naturalism, Empiricism, and Good Science

Naturalism, as opposed to the notion of the supernatural (that which has to do with God), is an important key to understanding what is the essence of true science in the thinking and general worldview of the modern scientist. Anything else is simply unthinkable. Thus says Isaac Asimov:

> Science is a process of thought, a way of looking at the Universe. It consists of the gathering of observations which can be confirmed by others using other instruments at other times in other ways. From these confirmed observations, consequences, and conclusions can be reasoned out by logical methods generally agreed upon. These consequences and conclusions are tentative and can be argued over by different people in the field and modified or changed altogether if additional, or more subtle, observations are made. There is no belief held in advance of such observations and conclusions except that observations can be made, that consequences and conclusions can be reasoned out, and that the Universe can, at least to a degree, be made comprehensible in this fashion. (If these assumptions are not true, then there is no way of using the mind at all). (*In the Beginning*, 7-11).

GOD DOES EXIST!

Interestingly, Asimov describes science and the method of doing science as if it were a philosophical endeavor. That is, in fact, what "a process of thought, a way of looking at the Universe" should be taken to be. Science and the methodology of doing it correctly has taken several centuries for humans to develop as it is presently understood. Scientists have had to learn by a process of trial and error what sorts of questions can be addressed to nature, how to put those questions into nature's language and how to read nature's answers to those questions. It could rightly be said that humans have had to learn slowly from nature itself how to investigate nature. Hence, the historical scientific process has involved not merely discoveries about nature but also discoveries about how to investigate nature.

As one would therefore expect, conceptions of science and of the scientific method have sometimes changed historically, and at times rather radically, just as scientific theories themselves have changed over time. Gradually, several principles have risen to the top among the major practitioners of science. These principles now form a protective fence about all of its many separate disciplines. Those who dare to step outside of this protective barrier ("think outside the box") must be punished. They cannot be knowingly credentialed. And if they already are, their careers must be limited to undesirable positions, and any chance at all of their being given grants or government funding for their research has to be cut to a bare minimum.

What Are Some of These Governing Principles?
First, there is the principle that science ought to be thoroughly objective. It should function totally free of human speculation, choice, politics, preference, emotion, bias, and preconception. Leading figures in science demanded that philosophy, metaphysics, and in particular religion not be allowed to have any influence within the processes of science. The more mechanical the procedures of science could be made, the better. This was one of the first and most important guiding principles that has persisted in the various scientific disciplines, at least in terms of a theoretical understanding of how research *ought* to be done.

Now, of course, this is merely a principle that governs those outside of the mainstream of scientific research. Those elite scientists who tow the party line are free to force upon the scientific community a plethora

The Science Argument

of unproven, and even unprovable, assumptions, so long as they stay within certain accepted ideological parameters.

Objectivity is indeed a worthy goal in any serious endeavor, scientific or not. But to affirm that any discipline is objective in orientation while strapping it perennially with the neo-Darwinian model of development, from molecules to man, is not to be taken seriously as an effort toward that end. So, even though this is supposedly the theoretical operational principle behind science today, anyone who is experienced in the realities of the various fields will know that science has become as doctrinaire as religion has ever been. Anyone who has the audacity to question the unproven assumptions of Darwinian thought will know what one went through who was considered to be a religious non-conformist in the days when the papacy ruled in Medieval European society! There is little wonder that the claim of absolute objectivity, when it is made by the scientific community, falls mostly on deaf ears. Reality belies the claim.

Second, science was supposed to be empirical. It ought to be grounded, we are told, on empirical data and empirical data alone. According to this way of seeing it, data that is empirical in nature seemed to be ideally suited to serve as the foundation of an objective science. This is so because, supposedly, observation was purely neutral, purely objective, reproducible and shared, in the sense of being the same for all similarly situated observers.

Thus, if science was based on empirical data, then we all had a common set of touchstones dictated by nature itself, and if we insisted that our theories grow out of and conform to those nature-dictated data, then nature itself—not human beings—had the final say in the theories about nature and its workings. Having theories about nature controlled by nature seemed to be the ultimate in objectivity.

But is this really true, or is it merely a way of closing the door to any type of research that does not begin and end with naturalism? A great number of contemporary thinkers are beginning to realize it is the latter instead of the former. Has it been demonstrated by means of the scientific method that empirical data is the only type of proof that is worthwhile? Or, on the other hand, is this rather a philosophy of science

GOD DOES EXIST!

that has been legitimized by certain leaders in the various disciplines of science and has not been effectively challenged until recently?

If data that is discovered in the natural world seems to point to sources and causes that lie outside the natural world, should it be ignored or rejected out of hand because it does not meet the strict criteria of naturalism? Has naturalism been allowed to become a confining and constraining force within the series of potential options that might answer some of the most important questions (causation, purposiveness, design, etc.) that bare science leaves us with at the conclusion of our investigations? If it is only a presupposition, unproven because it is untestable, then why should it be permitted to obstruct and delegitimize what could be the only possible answers to some questions?

Clearly it has become a sacred cow of sorts for some members of the scientific community! Hence, if the natural world and its observable and measurable features cannot provide the solutions to such problems, then there is no answer that can be given. And there are a great many scientific minds that are starting to awaken to the reality that in some areas of research we may not be far from where this restrictive methodology is beginning to run out of viable possibilities.

Third, science was to be totally rational. In this way, the processes of theory construction, theory evaluation, theory testing, and eventually theory acceptance, had to be protected from the infection of human subjectivity, bias, blindness, distortion, and dishonesty. Philosophy and religion (theology and Scripture) were considered to be the main forms of infection. So they needed to be systematically excluded from the processes of science.

So, according to the strategy of modern scientific endeavor, data that is collected by scientists is utterly independent and objective. They are gathered and assembled into theoretical constructs by individuals who are encumbered with no preconceptions, prior theories, or anything along those lines. As Isaac Asimov puts it: "There is no belief held in advance of such observations and conclusions...."

Of course, we all understand that this is not the real world that any of us actually lives in. Pure and simple, it is a fantasy. On the surface of it, these platitudes sound as if they are the way that good science

The Science Argument

ought to be conducted, but in reality, they are merely clichés and little else beyond that. What we have come to know as modern science has become mired in its own guiding philosophy (naturalism and empiricism) is that it is up to its neck in an exclusivist religion of its own making (atheism). At the same time it eschews philosophy of every other sort, and despises religion of every other kind. It is very idealistic on the one hand, but it is hypocritical on the other. Only the "true believers" see modern science as genuinely living up to these high ideals and rigorous standards.

So, in truth, these working definitions of the scientific method do not mesh with what we see and hear in the scientific community. At work behind the scenes, and only occasionally mentioned by the principals involved, is a working hypothesis that excludes and declares "out of bounds" anything other than naturalism as an explanation for anything, no matter how totally inexplicable it may be in naturalistic terms. Under this rubric, a major driving force underlying the current system is the conviction that proper science can make no reference to, no appeal to, and no explanatory use of anything beyond the purely natural. The supernatural, the miraculous, is strictly out of bounds in science.

As Dr. Del Ratzsch stated it, "Doing science properly, on this view, requires that one formulate methods, concepts, and strategies that would be appropriate for a universe in which there was no supernatural domain, whether or not one has rational grounds for believing that there is a supernatural domain and even whether or not one *knows* that there is a supernatural domain. Science is *"forced* to function as if there is no such thing as a supernatural" (*The Battle of Beginnings,* 162).

As the term "forced" in this quotation indicates, this policy of confining science to the natural world and to it alone is not proposed as a polite suggestion to those who work in the various disciplines of science. In their view the very definition of science prevents any scientist from offering God's intervention as the cause of anything. If they wish to explain something, it must necessarily be explained in terms of potential natural causes. To their way of thinking, science as practiced in modern times is *necessarily* naturalistic; explanations founded on miracles *cannot be allowed.*

GOD DOES EXIST!

Indeed, some writers take any "supernatural explanation" of any phenomenon to be what they would consider to be a "contradiction in terms" (Stephen J. Gould). But why is this particular restriction considered so essential to doing modern scientific research? There are two standard answers to this question, and it would be helpful to examine both of them briefly.

To begin with, it is frequently claimed that science, with its empirical methods, has no way of dealing with the supernatural, the super-empirical or anything of that sort. And, since it would be pointless for one to attempt to handle anything for which one's methods were utterly inappropriate, science has no choice but to restrict itself to the natural. This is said to be so because the natural is the only realm that is empirically investigatable. Therefore, in their way of thinking science must behave as if the supernatural did not exist, *even if it does exist*!

But, as Dr. Ratzsch has countered, "if limitations on science grow out of the limitations of empirical methods, why restrict ourselves to empirical methods?" (*Battle of Beginnings,* 163). Why not show ourselves willing to explore the possibilities outside of our present, and rather obviously limited purview? If the region of the heavens we wished to investigate lay out beyond the power of our telescope lens, would it not be appropriate to attempt to create a more powerful telescope? If a particular living organism were so small that it could not be analyzed with our present microscope, would it not be wise to try to manufacture a microscope capable of detecting and analyzing what is smaller than what we have now? We know the answer to these questions, and we know also that if we have drawn boundaries around the scientific enterprise that will not permit it to explore that which (or He who) could be the real explanation for these phenomena, we ought to enlarge the borders of our search beyond what we have allowed up to now.

One historically influential answer to this challenge to their guiding assumptions is that by definition knowledge must be based on empirical interaction with reality, and that whatever might be produced by any other approach ends in confusion at best, and nonsense at worst. This doctrine of empiricism, that only what is ultimately based on sensory experience can be known or rationally believed or, in some versions, even thought about, has a long and influential history going

The Science Argument

back perhaps as far as ancient Greece. Their approach to reality sees the "universe" in terms of "what can be observed and described by humans with reasonable assurance and general agreement that what is being observed exists as some recognizable form of matter or energy" (Arthur Strahler, *Science and Earth History*, 1).

Thus, what humans cannot observe is, quite simply, not a part of the universe. Or, what we do not currently have the concepts to describe is not part of the universe. The astute reader will see that this is a case of decreeing the universe down to our very limited empirical and conceptual size. Strahler goes on to suggest that while empirical science is in the domain of knowledge, religion goes into the realm of belief. He later simply defines religion in terms of "faith without evidence." He further argues that the idea of "reasoned faith" is in his view, "another contradiction in terms."

Now, as popular as this kind of thinking has been over recent decades, naked empiricism faces serious difficulties logically. The doctrine itself is a philosophical declaration, not an empirical one. Too, if it were accepted as true, it would create severe difficulties for itself. The major issue could be stated in the following way: What empirical observations could be cited as indicating that anything outside the domain of the empirical is necessarily beyond the realm of the rational? The question is valid because, on this view, the empirical would be totally blind to that whole realm to begin with. The claim seems arbitrary at best, if not simply self-defeating.

Beyond even this, any strong form of empiricism would systematically create very serious, if not fatal, problems for science itself. This is true because science cannot operate without a variety of philosophical, nonempirical principles. Unfortunately, such philosophical principles do not seem to be matters of human observation, at least not directly so. Based upon empiricism as a starting point, such principles would be forbidden.

Furthermore, since as the arch-empiricist Hume himself observed, matters of *necessity* are beyond the scope of empirical reality (because necessity is a determination of the mind), that would pose an insuperable hurdle for the scientist. This is so because it is claimed that science

GOD DOES EXIST!

is "necessarily naturalistic." If it is *necessarily* naturalistic, then that puts it out beyond the ability of humans empirically to assess its worth. Clearly they cannot have it both ways! They therefore have a "contradiction in terms" which acts as one of the most rudimentary of the operating principles of modern science.

The second answer that is proffered in response to the question of why the nonnatural (supernatural) must be barred from science is the claim that as a practical matter of fact, purely natural, and so primarily empirical, methods are the only ones that have demonstrated any promise of success historically. It is argued that nonnatural standpoints have such a dismal record of unbroken failure that the best plan going forward is to continue doing science as if naturalism were true and to ignore the possibility of supernatural intervention in the world's processes. Even though this perspective is frequently expressed as if it were a truism, with all sorts of evidence to back it up, it is nonetheless uncritical and logically indefensible.

It is obvious to anyone that what we have here is a claim that is historical in its essence. All those who make the claim need, therefore, is historical data to show its validity. Hence, in order to establish its truthfulness or else falsify it, an enormous amount of historical study would have to be done. But that is not what we are given. Rather, a few isolated instances are cited.

The most noteworthy case that is usually discussed is the geocentric theory long held to be true by many theists and perennially seen as a case in point, maybe their only case in point. Many theists hundreds of years ago reckoned that the earth was flat and that it was the center of the material universe. This is true but it proves little. It seems not to be noticed by such critics that this antiquated view is not believed by any reputable theist doing science today. It is a view that was once held to be true but after it was disproven it has been completely discarded and is believed by no one any longer. It is only one of a great many discarded theories that could be enumerated. Why is this particular one given so much attention? Because it was once held by some theists.

Moreover, it is odd that views held by non-theists that have gone the way of the dodo bird are not usually mentioned, when over the

The Science Argument

course of the years there have been many. In fact, they are a regular aspect of scientific investigation. They are generally depicted as "fruitful failures" (and that is an appropriate description for them, since they have offered to the scientific community an opportunity for learning from its mistakes) whereas for theistic scientists they are enumerated in order to indicate an intrinsic stupidity about their methodology.

A relatively recent example of scientific error is provided by advances made in superconductivity. For almost three decades it was generally accepted that superconductivity was best described by the so-called BCS theory of 1957. For this theory Bardeen, Cooper, and Schrieffer received the Nobel Prize in 1972. In this theory, superconductivity results from the pairing of electrons in solids through their interaction with lattice vibrations (in technical terms, through the exchange of virtual phonons). Although the theory itself does not give any clear prediction of an upper bound to the critical temperature, T_c, above which superconductivity will not take place, it was generally thought that the BCS mechanism could not lead to superconductivity at a temperature as high as that of the boiling point of liquid nitrogen (77 K).

Early in 1987, reports came out of detecting superconductivity at temperatures above 90 K. It was not long before theorists came up with plausible mechanisms, different from that of BCS, to explain the new results, and the theory of superconductivity was enhanced considerably beyond its state before these discoveries. Thus the discovery of results that the BCS theory failed to explain led to advances in the theoretical understanding of superconducting mechanisms, advances that undoubtedly would have come much more slowly, if at all, than would have been the case had observations of superconductivity continued to fit nicely into the original BCS framework. So, for three decades the (mostly atheistic) scientific community operated on a theoretical basis regarding superconductivity that was dead wrong.

Now, the atheism of these researchers played no part at all in their incapacity to appreciate the true nature of this aspect of scientific truth, but apparently it also did not make them immune to scientific errors. Had they been believers in Deity, it would not have helped them either. In point of fact, it would not have changed anything either way. And that is exactly the point. In most aspects of scientific research faith plays

GOD DOES EXIST!

no part at all in how good science is conducted. But occasionally there are some areas of investigation where it would at minimum be beneficial for a scientist to have an open mind to the possibility of a Creator and a willingness to concede that at least some things in our universe are not explicable on the basis of naturalism alone.

The so-called "steady state theory" of cosmology provides another excellent example of fruitful failure in contemporary science. This theory, proposed in 1948 in one form by Bondi and Gold and in a somewhat different form by Hoyle, differs from the cosmological theory provided by general relativity in that the latter has the universe evolving from a "big bang" (a singularity in the geometrical structure of spacetime) at some finite time in the past, whereas in the former the universe is viewed as having existed infinitely in more or less its present form. According to standard Big Bang cosmology, known as the Friedman-Lemaître-Robertson-Walker (FLRW) model, the universe thus began in an unimaginably hot, dense state about 13.8 billion years ago. Matter, energy, space, and time came into existence at that point (often labeled as $t = 0$).

As noted above, the standard FLRW model predicts that the initial state of the universe was a *singularity*—described as a point of infinite density, infinite pressure, infinite temperature, and zero volume. "At this singularity, explained John Barrow and Frank Tipler, "space and time came into existence; literally *nothing* existed before the singularity, so, if the Universe originated at such a singularity, we would truly have creation *ex nihilo*" (Barrow and Tipler, *Anthropic Cosmological Principle*, 442). In other words, says Michael Heller, "all histories of photons and particles emerge from nothingness" (Heller, *Creative Tension*, 83). While the standard FLRW model of the cosmos predicts such a singularity, what actually happened in the beginning is beyond the observational limits of science. As Stephen Hawking and George Ellis explain, "the results we have obtained support the idea that the universe began a finite time ago. However, the actual point of creation, the singularity, is outside the scope of presently known laws of physics" (Hawking and Ellis, *The Large Scale Structure of Space-Time*, 364).

If there was such a singularity from which the cosmos emerged from nothing, as is depicted in this hypothetical reconstruction, it is veiled by what is known as the Planck epoch, a phase of the universe that lasted

The Science Argument

only a fraction of a second (from $t = 0$ to 10^{-43} seconds after the hypothesized singularity). The Planck epoch was a period of extremely high temperatures (about 10^{32} degrees Centigrade) where the physics of space-time as known today—along with the standard Big Bang model—breaks down. Before Planck time (10^{-43} after $t = 0$), all four fundamental forces (gravity, electromagnetism, the strong nuclear force, and the weak nuclear force) were one unified super force. Describing this super force is beyond our current capacities and, explains astrophysicist Larson, the details "await a successful theory of quantum gravity" (Larson, *Cosmology 101*, 116).

Because the universe was so small at this point, quantum physics would play a central role. In order to describe this period of cosmic history adequately, a new physics of quantum cosmology is needed, one that can provide a quantum treatment of space-time and gravity (Stoeger, *The End of the World and the Ends of God*, 176). Very little is known about this very brief and mysterious period, and notes Larson, "we currently lack the information to trace the history of the universe all the way back to the absolute beginning" (Larson, *Cosmology 101*, 116). Consequently, says cosmologist Guth, "the true history of the universe, going back to '$t = 0$', remains a mystery that we are probably still far from unraveling" (Guth, *The Inflammatory Universe*, 87).

While the cosmic veil of the Planck epoch may forever preclude cosmologists from glimpsing the actual physical beginning of the universe, a theorem developed in the 21st century—known as the BGV Theorem—by physicists Arvind Borde, Alan Guth, and Alexander Vilenken has shown that the universe must have nevertheless had a beginning. According to Vilenkin, the BGV Theorem demonstrates "that any inflating model that is globally expanding must be geodesically incomplete in the past" (Vilenkin, *Quantum Cosmology and Eternal Inflation*, 660). The BGV Theorem shows that if a universe is (on average) everywhere expanding, then the histories of particles cannot be extended to the infinite past. This means that any process undergoing gravitational inflation necessarily had a beginning (cf. J. Moritz, *Theology and Science: From Genesis to Astrobiology*, 351-353).

Since the expansion of the universe, which is accepted as being a true feature of the universe in both theories (steady state and Big Bang),

GOD DOES EXIST!

would otherwise necessarily lower the average density of matter in the universe, the steady state theory has matter being continually created throughout the universe. Although both the Big Bang and steady state theories were viewed by at least a significant fraction of the scientific community as viable possibilities for a good many years, ultimately most scientists agreed that the preponderance of the evidence weighed against the steady state theory, and it has been relegated to the dustbin of scientific investigation, as yet another instance of "fruitful failure."

At the same time, even though this popular theory of origins was a total failure over the long term, it spawned the present, generally accepted view of the formation of the heavy elements. This is the "fruitful" aspect of the now failed and therefore defunct theory. Interestingly enough, it could be argued that the Big Bang approach to cosmology has always been more in line with the concept of creation *ex nihilo*, and thus is consistent with the idea of the universe being the work of a Creator God and even with the first verse of the book of Genesis.

Not to say that it would be the only possible way it could have happened, but certainly it is more or less what we would have been expecting to find if we were operating under the assumption that the God of Jewish and Christian Scripture created the universe. And so, what was discovered is what the believer would have been expecting to find all along. Non-believers would have opted for the steady-state approach. But they would have been wrong, both in theory and in fact. So, it is safe to say, at the very least, that in this instance the believer's presentiment was not wrong, and in the end it turned out to be correct. Moreover, the reflexive view of many atheists turned out to be erroneous. Some may find it difficult to make this admission, but the truth of it is not really up for debate. It is a part of the history of science.

On the other hand, the historical argument against religion in science cannot be made without a recognition of the fact that, as we noted earlier, had it not been for Christianity there would be no science as we know it. Various mindsets and principles arising out of Christianity were essential to the birth of modern science in the first place, and this is well acknowledged (cf. Reijer Hooykass, *Religion and the Rise of Modern Science*; M. B. Foster, "The Christian Doctrine of Creation and the Rise of Modern Science," *Mind* [October, 1934]: 446-68; [October, 1935]:

The Science Argument

439-66); [January, 1936]: 1-27). Most atheists are loath to admit this, but facts are facts.

Conceptually it is well understood why this is so. Why, for instance, can *rational* investigation of nature be successful? Because nature is a creation of a Person who thinks, acts, and creates in the rationally orderly way of persons. Why must our investigation of nature be empirical? Because nature is a creation of a *free* Person who could have created in any of an unlimited number of ways. But the way that He chose to create was structured and logical, not chaotic and irrational, precisely as one would expect an intelligent being to make anything that is a product of intelligence. Yet, at the same time, we cannot reconstruct reality just by pure reason. More is required. We are obligated to investigate in order to see which option this free Person chose in any particular instance. In a sense, in doing good science we are simply "thinking God's thoughts after Him." We are learning how He created the universe and in what way He caused it to function.

But there is more to be considered here than merely validating a proper starting-point for the scientific endeavor. Many of the most important scientists in the history of its various disciplines were motivated by their belief in God and they worked in the light of that faith and not just in spite of it. Many very respectable men of science deliberately built theological constraints into their scientific theorizing. Newton, for example, postulated absolute space and absolute time largely for theological reasons. It has been argued that the structure Maxwell gave to his field theories was influenced by his views concerning the Trinity. Boyle rejected the medieval idea that nature abhors a vacuum because he thought he could show that such an idea was morally pernicious and subverted true Christianity. Newton's views concerning both the character and quality of matter in the universe had a theological basis. Pasteur rejected spontaneous generation in part on theological grounds. Also, Hershel's theories concerning the nature of nebulae had direct links to his theology. And yet such theorizing was frequently both productive and fruitful, and whether it started out as either good science or orthodox theology, it turned out to be correct.

Impetus theory, which was a crucial step on the road to modern views on inertia, was introduced in the fourteenth century by Jean Bu-

GOD DOES EXIST!

ridan. It was primarily intended to provide a better explanation of motion continued by a heavy body after loss of contact with a mover than given by either of the two theories that were mentioned by Aristotle. Both the older explanations relied on a supposed action of the medium surrounding the body. Impetus theory substituted the action of an impressed force imparted to the body by its mover. Consideration of a special case enabled Buridan to account also for the acceleration of a freely falling body in terms of increments of impetus occasioned not by external force but by speeds successively acquired. A mathematical rule for this process put forth by Albert of Saxony was accepted widely until the end of the sixteenth century. The theory itself was defended early on in part on grounds having to do with the character of the sacraments of the church. Similarly, early forms of some conservation principles in physics were initially defended on partially theological grounds (cf. D. Ratzsch, *Battle of Beginnings,* 164-66).

Even most modern Christian scientists would question the validity of some of these approaches today. As methods of investigation, and modes of proof, some are highly suspect; but their results cannot be questioned when they turned out to be right. We might even posit in some instances that they started out on the basis of wrong assumptions, but ended up being correct because they allowed the evidence to take them to their final destination. Hence, the notion that naturalism in science can be justified through the history of science is no more accurate than the idea that theism in science ought to be the preferred working hypothesis. There is a place for both.

It is fair to say that naturalism is a helpful starting point in most instances in regard to doing good science. But there are also points all along the way where naturalism will not and never will answer our ultimate questions about matters such as origins. Over one hundred years of scientific research in a host of different disciplines has demonstrated this.

Therefore, the mind of the good scientist is going to have to admit that room must be left for God and the metaphysical in responding to many queries of this sort. He is the only reasonable rejoinder to a whole host of such mysteries, matters that after many years of intense investigation continue to baffle the minds of armies of inquisitors. When naturalism is shown to be impossible, then it is time to quit looking to natu-

The Science Argument

ralism for the solution. There is a point where the confirmed naturalist must give in and reckon with the inherent weakness of his approach: it does not leave room for God. How is it to be deemed fair or reasonable for his methodology to exclude from the outset the only other possible answer to so many of our seemingly unanswerable questions in the sciences? And, make no mistake about it, that juncture has been reached in a whole host of different areas of scientific endeavor.

Evidence for God from Science

Such researchers as Dr. Stephen C. Meyer have been making the argument that the last 50 years have produced a significant number of major discoveries that have, on account of the unique nature of their findings, taken science back to the "God hypothesis." That is where it started out, as we have shown above, and to the chagrin of the atheistic element of the scientific community, that is precisely where it is returning. It needs to be appreciated that each of the following instances are based on particular discoveries made in specific fields of science and they all lead us back to God. Not one of them is considered a mere theoretical postulate. These are all established and accepted science. Each is taken from a separate field of scientific knowledge.

This is exactly what a believer would expect to happen. You see, the believer is convinced that God made the natural world, and that it exists and functions precisely according as the divine Mind planned it all and continues to regulate it throughout. The believer has little use for accidents. He knows that when they do happen, nothing good comes of them. He knows that only careful planning and intelligent design and capable manufacturing lead to success in the real world. He therefore has no faith at all in the Darwinian model of the origin of species or of the theory of evolution from molecules to man. He simply does not find any aspect of the theory especially convincing.

And, make no mistake about it, this is where the problem lies. It is not because he is ignorant or undereducated, and it is not because he is superstitious or even overly religious. Many of those who have cast doubt on this approach are not very religious at all. It is the weakness of the predominant theory itself. That is the problem. The hypothetical construct that it represents is just plain unbelievable! It challenges the limits of the imagination at every turn. Frankly, we consider those who do find

GOD DOES EXIST!

it appealing to be downright naive. If they are able to believe such absurdities, even though they are stated in the most scientific sounding terms, then they could be convinced of most anything. That is how the ordinary believer in God as Creator sees the matter. And even many unbelievers feel similarly. There is little that commends Darwinism, except the fact that for some skeptics, creationism is the only genuine alternative to it!

Why are there so many who respond to their claims in this fashion? Why has the elite scientific community been unable to move the general public in their direction after all these years of constant propagandizing? The answer lies in both the number and the astonishing nature of the discoveries from science itself. Science has become the best evidence against the prevailing ideology of scientists. Most of the disciplines in recent years have produced notable examples of information and observations that are very hard to square with the prevalent sentiment. In the paragraphs that follow, we will offer a sampling of the type of collected data that has troubled the general public for years, and has recently begun to cause consternation in the minds of some leading researchers and thinkers.

1. *Evidence from Astronomy and Physics.* The General Theory of Relativity, Hubble's redshifts, Penzias' and Wilson's universal background radiation, black holes, quantum cosmology, inflationary theory, and a host of other ideas and discoveries have led to a grand scheme of universal origins referred to as the "Big Bang theory." In the view of many physicists, this remarkable cosmological hypothetical reconstruction of events points to a singular "creation event" as well as an antecedent ordered unfolding of the universe to bring it to its present state.

A simple statement of the Big Bang theory is that everything in the observable universe is the remnant of a huge explosion dubbed the big bang that took place in the remote past, estimated to be about 13.7 billion years ago. Cosmologists believe that they have a fairly good overall picture of the history of the observable universe since this explosive episode occurred. What, if anything, may have happened *before* the big bang and what may exist out beyond the limits of the observable universe (beyond the horizon of what can be seen from our unique earthly perspective in the universe) is the subject of much speculation, some of it reasonable and some being highly improbable. At any rate, the gener-

The Science Argument

ally agreed upon overall picture of what has happened within the observable universe since the big bang is sometimes called the "standard" model of cosmology.

According to this model, space-time is described by Einstein's theory of gravity, which is called "General Relativity." As per his model, space-time is a four-dimensional manifold, which acts somewhat like an elastic medium. It can stretch, warp, and vibrate. When cosmologists say that the universe is expanding, they do not simply mean that objects within the universe are flying away from each other *through* space, they mean that *space itself* is stretching. Galaxies that are very distant from each other are getting farther apart, not because they are moving through space (which is a relatively small effect), but because the space in between them is getting stretched out.

All of this stretching of space is described by Einstein's theory. How space-time stretches and warps is determined by the matter and energy filling the space and how it is distributed. In the vicinity of a massive object like the earth, for instance, space-time is warped in such a way that objects moving near the earth have their trajectories affected, and they seem to be attracted to it by the force of gravity. In the Big Bang theory, the fact that the galaxies are flying apart from each other is explained by the space of the universe expanding. As one looks back in time, the galaxies were closer together, because there was actually less space! The farther back one looks, the smaller the distance between galaxies was.

Extrapolating all the way back then, one can deduce that all of the matter in our observable universe would have been in the same place at the beginning of this process. In fact, they had to be in the same place, because the volume of space of our presently observable universe at that point in time was either zero or very close to zero. As per this view, all the matter that we observe now was compressed into a fantastically dense, hot mass, which exploded and thus flew apart at an incomprehensible speed. The Belgian physicist, Georges Lemaitre, fathered the earliest form of this theory.

This theory was opposed in its earliest stages on account of its similarity to what might be expected from a reconstruction of a "creation" event. That of course would involve God, and for a great many scien-

GOD DOES EXIST!

tists this was simply unacceptable. Some evidence at first did not seem to square with it. But most of those "kinks" were worked out over time, and it was discovered that the calculation of the recession speed of the galaxies (a major problem for the theory at first) had been in error by a significant factor, and so the most important objection was resolved.

The breakthrough came in the year 1964 with the work of Penzias and Wilson in their findings related to the so-called Cosmic Microwave Background Radiation. The characteristics of these electromagnetic background noise pulses (strongest in the microwave region of the radio spectrum) were consistent with its being the residual light from the Big Bang explosion, once very intense, but now made very faint and red-shifted into microwaves by a prolonged period of cosmic expansion. Very precise measurements and refined mathematical analyses of this radiation (and, in particular, of the tiny fluctuations in its intensity in different parts of the sky) show a complex structure that is in remarkable agreement with the predictions of the Big Bang theory. Also, calculations based on the Big Bang theory correctly account for the relative amounts of the smaller elements (especially hydrogen and helium) in the universe. As well, there are other pieces of confirmatory evidence, so that at this juncture there is little doubt that some grand event comparable to the Big Bang did in fact occur.

The simplest version of the standard model of cosmology assumes that it describes the whole of the universe. In other words, first it assumes that there was no universe "before" the big bang, and second that the part of the universe that lies out "beyond our horizon" looks essentially the same as the part within our observable horizon. No empirical evidence at this point has been marshalled against either of these assumptions. Therefore, in this Standard Big Bang Model, the big bang itself was the beginning of time, and of space as well.

Thus, in this reconstruction of events, it is meaningless to ask what went on "before the big bang" because there was no "before." This is so because time is a feature of the physical universe. It is something physical, just like atoms and light. Time and space form a manifold that, as we earlier noted, has the capacity to stretch, warp, and vibrate. Since time is just a physical part of our physical universe, it follows that if the physical universe had a beginning, then time and space themselves began then also.

The Science Argument

It is worth noting that the first thinker to set forth such a prediction regarding this matter was not a physicist, nor even a scientist, but a theologian! Augustine of Hippo (AD 354-430) was the first to state this view. The circumstances that led to his statement of this perspective on time and space are as follows: Ancient pagans had taunted both Jews and Christians for positing that the universe had a "beginning." They mocked the notion of a beginning, asking what God might have been "doing" for the infinite time preceding the creation of the universe. Why did He wait so long to get started, they inquired.

Augustine responded by saying that there was no time "before" the Beginning. Interestingly, his answer was theological rather than scientific, but it parallels almost exactly the argument of modern cosmologists. Time, said Augustine, is something that was created. Since it is not God, it is something that was created by God. He further argued that it was meaningless to inquire as to what God was "doing" prior to the beginning because there was no "before." Augustine wrote: "Do not ask what [God] was doing 'then', there was no 'then' where there was no time." Hence, as a physicist at the University of Texas, Steven Weinberg, noted, it is common in research papers on quantum cosmology in recent years to quote the very prescient comments made by Augustine in his famous discussions of time.

Hugh Ross, an astrophysicist, had this to say in his 2001 book *The Creator and the Cosmos*:

> By definition, time is that dimension in which cause and effect phenomena take place. If time's beginning is concurrent with the beginning of the universe, as the space-time theorem says, then the cause of the universe must be some entity operating in a time dimension completely independent of and pre-existent to the time dimension of the cosmos. This conclusion is powerfully important to our understanding of who God is and who or what God is not. It tells us that the Creator is transcendent, operating beyond the dimensional limits of the universe. It tells us that God is not the universe itself, nor is God contained within the universe.

Now, of course, it must be recognized that, unlike philosophy and metaphysics, science cannot deductively prove either a creation or a God who caused it. This is true because natural science deals only with the physical universe itself and the natural laws that are obeyed by the phenomena within it. And since God is not an object or phenomenon or regularity within the physical universe, science cannot say anything about God directly.

Moreover, science is an empirical and inductive discipline. As such, science cannot be certain that it has considered all possible data that would be relevant to a complete explanation of particular physical phenomena or of the universe itself. It must always be open to new data and discoveries which could alter its explanation of any particular phenomena as well as of the universe generally. Revisions made to the Big Bang cosmology over the years (of which there have been many) are illustrative of this fact.

So then, these limitations being true, what is science able to do for us in this realm? It has the potential to identify, aggregate, and synthesize evidence. And the data gathered by the scientific method may be interpreted as indicating the finitude of past time in the universe as we currently know it to be or conceive that it could be. Science can also identify the exceedingly high improbability of the random occurrence of conditions necessary to sustain life in the universe as we presently know it to be or conceive it could be. We will have more to say on this later on.

Thus, the arguments that suggest the finitude of past time, i.e. that time had a beginning, are basically of two types. First, there are those arguments that concern the possible geometries of space-time. And then there are those that have to do with the Second Law of Thermodynamics. Both of these kinds of arguments have been persistently powerful justifications for this approach and so they have "respectable probative force" in any full discussion of this topic. Until such time as they are shown to be invalid or inapplicable to empirically verifiable characteristics of our universe, they should continue to be considered as justifying the conclusion that it is at least highly probable that the universe had a beginning.

Now it has been argued by Stephen Hawking and James Burkett Hartle, in spite of all the evidence that has been forthcoming in recent years, that the universe has neither beginning nor end. It has been de-

The Science Argument

scribed as the "no boundary proposal." In their argument (popularly called the Hartle-Hawking state, or wave function of the universe) they make time imaginary, and by this questionable means they attempt to prove their terribly restricted model that the universe has neither beginning nor end. The flaw in this approach to the issue, of course, in this exercise in logic, is that the authors never go back to real time.

Thus, the notion that the universe has neither beginning nor end is something that exists not in real time but in mathematical terms and thus in theoretical physics. So, in terms of real time, to which we as humans are necessarily attached and in which we have our very being, the argument has no true validity. Hawking's use of imaginary time, is not the actual world. It represents only an imaginary construct, the stuff of empty chatter and of unreal worlds, a discussion topic of science fiction and not of science fact. In the real world there is always a beginning for everything. And so there had to be a beginning of time.

In Stephen Hawking's 1988 book, *A Brief History of Time*, he actually concedes this point: "When one goes back to the real time in which we live, however, there will still appear to be singularities. In real time, the universe has a beginning and an end at singularities that form a boundary to space-time and at which the laws of science break down" (first edition, 144). It appears that Hawking himself did not take the perspective all that seriously. Else, why would he be inclined to make such an admission? Dr. Henry F. Schaefer, III critiqued the Hartle-Hawking view with the following devastating counterpoints:

First, the theory is a mathematical construct that has no unique empirical support. Second, the theory makes no verifiable scientific predictions that were not achieved earlier with simpler and more persuasive models. And, third, the theory generates no significant research agenda. The primary purpose of the theory seems not to be particularly earnest scientifically. Rather, it appears to be a semi-flippant attempt at evading the cosmological argument for the existence of God via the unwarranted claim that nature is self-contained and effectively eternal. Only if we lived in imaginary time would we encounter no singularities. In actual time and in the real world, the universe had a beginning and time itself had a real beginning-point (cf. Henry F. Schaefer III, "The Big Bang, Stephen Hawking, and God," 1-23).

GOD DOES EXIST!

Another perspective on this question has been popularized by Princeton physicist Robert Dicke (1965). His famous paper also effectively makes the universe eternal. It views the universe as infinitely oscillating. Since the hypothesized period between the present big bang and its imagined "big crunch" would be just one of an infinite number of such periods postulated by this scenario, any problems relating to the time scale that might be needed for evolution are resolved by the conclusion that our interval might be "just right." In reality, this issue was effectively resolved for most cosmologists in 1983 when a critical paper was presented by Alan Guth, who is best known for his pioneering work on the inflationary features of the Big Bang Theory, that appeared in the journal *Nature* (vol. 302, p. 505). The title of Guth's article tells the story: "The Impossibility of a Bouncing Universe." In his paper he showed that even if the universe contained sufficient mass to halt the current expansion, any collapse would end in a thud, not a bounce. Incidentally, the weight of opinion among cosmologists has shifted over recent years to the position that, short of direct intervention by God at some point, the universe will continue to expand infinitely.

When we speak of a beginning (a point prior to which there is no physical reality), we stand at the threshold of physics and metaphysics (that which lies beyond physics and the physical). Even though science cannot be validly used to prove a metaphysical claim (such as the assertion that a Creator or God exists), it can be used to maintain as highly probable a limit to physical reality (such as a beginning). And so, the scientific data for a beginning can be combined with the metaphysical premise (such as the statement "from nothing, only nothing comes") to render a metaphysical conclusion that there must be something beyond physical reality which caused physical reality to exist. This would be, necessarily, a transcendental cause. It would obviously transcend the natural, time and space, and would on account of what Robert J. Spitzer called "the accumulation of converging antecedent probabilities" drawn from the convergence of a multiplicity of probabilistic evidential bases, lead not to absolute certitude, but to a powerful if not undeniable formal deduction that God exists and was the Creator of the universe (*New Proofs for the Existence of God: Contributions of Contemporary Physics and Philosophy*, 14-23).

The Science Argument

Ernan McMullin ("How Should Cosmology Relate to Theology?" in *The Sciences and Theology in the Twentieth Century*, 17-51) said that, "If the universe began in time through the act of a Creator... it would look something like the Big Bang that cosmologists are talking about." Pressing the matter even beyond this seemingly radical admission, Arno Penzias made the point that the best data that we have concerning the Big Bang and the cosmological approach that has grown out of this theoretical postulate "are exactly what I would have predicted if I had nothing to go on but the first five books of Moses, the Psalms and the Bible as a whole" (quoted in M. W. Brown, "Clues to Universe Origin Expected," *New York Times* [12 March 1978]: 54).

An abductive syllogism helps to explain why this reasoning seems to follow from the evidence that we have:

Premise 1: If theism and the Judeo-Christian view of Creation are true, then we have reason to expect evidence of a finite universe.
Premise 2: We now have considerable and very convincing evidence of a finite universe.
Conclusion: Therefore, theism and the Judeo-Christian view of Creation may be true.

This represents a terrifying prospect for some scientists who are settled in their atheism. Their house of cards may come crashing in on them in the decades ahead! And, it is on account of this mounting evidence that a number of important scientists have made statements in recent years that have upset the atheistic monopoly in science. Some have been shocked by these embarrassing admissions by figures of such prominence in the academic and research community. Others are not at all surprised. They have known for years that many of these leading lights have been doubting the "party line" for decades now. The evidence is simply too substantial and inarguable for them to ignore.

For example, science historian Frederic B. Burnham, had this to say: "The God hypothesis is now a more persuasive and respectable hypothesis than at any time in the last 100 years." "Persuasive and respectable" is not how most atheistic scientists would have it to be viewed! Physicist Fred Hoyle also wrote as follows: "A common sense interpretation of the

GOD DOES EXIST!

evidence suggests a superintellect has monkeyed with physics, as well as with chemistry and biology, and that there are no blind forces worth speaking about in nature" ("The Universe: Past and Present Reflections," *Annual Review of Astronomy and Astrophysics* 1982 [20:1-35]: 16).

As well, Allan Sandage, well-respected Astronomer, wrote:

> This argument is not scientific, but through scientific cosmology we come perhaps as close to theology as science can come and still remain science. Because the "creation" event is outside science, it is only through the supernatural that the mystery of existence can be understood. . . . I do not believe that the universe can create itself. Typical attempts to provide a scientific answer to the question, "Can the universe create itself?" implicitly start with a "first" universe, out of which other universes are generated. It is here that I would ask Andrei Linde where his first universe came from that spawns his multiple baby universes *ad infinitum*. . . . Yet "creation" is nonetheless outside the realm of science. To say that the universe was created out of nothing by a "quantum fluctuation in the false vacuum" is simply promiscuous use of smoke and mirrors; it is empty speculation with no experimental basis except that the universe does exist. Scientists who say that "we do not need to invoke a higher power" simply mandate away any possible explanation outside the exceedingly narrow precepts of reductionist science. (What indeed is the origin of the false vacuum?). . . . Of course, *ab initio* creation itself is, by any definition of the boundaries of science, supernatural. To put the onus of creation on an unknown creator is seen by atheists as the height of absurdity; but for others, the alternative of believing that the universe created itself out of nothing is even more absurd (*Science and the Spiritual Quest: New Essays by Leading Scientists*, 58ff).

One of the most often quoted remarks in recent years, is this statement from astronomer Robert Jastrow's book:

> This is an exceedingly strange development, unexpected by all but the theologians. They have always accepted the word of the Bible; In the beginning God created heaven and earth. . . . It is unexpected because science has had such extraordinary success in tracing the chain of cause and effect backward in time. . . . For the scientist who has lived by his faith in the power of reason, the story ends like a bad dream. He has scaled the mountains of ignorance; he is about to conquer the highest peak; as he pulls himself over the final rock, he is greeted by

The Science Argument

a band of theologians who have been sitting there for centuries (*God and the Astronomers*, 116).

Stephen C. Meyer has made the case, therefore, that Big Bang cosmology provides a kind of confirmation of the Judeo-Christian understanding of Creation and is entirely consistent with its theistic worldview (cf. "Return of the God Hypothesis," 24). He moves beyond the Big Bang theory, however, to deal with the fact that it has been noted in recent years by a great many astronomers, physicists, and other scientists that the laws and constants of the universe give the appearance of having been uniquely fine-tuned to permit life. Some have described this as "the Anthropic Principle." Martin Rees of Cambridge said recently, "The possibility of life as we know it depends on the values of a few basic, physical constants and is in some respects remarkably sensitive to their numerical values. Nature does exhibit remarkable coincidences."

While some deny the need to explain these fine-tuning coincidences, and see them only as remarkable accidental occurrences and nothing beyond that, others have sought to formulate various naturalistic explanations for them. Of these, appeals to natural law have proven the least popular for a simple reason. The precise dial settings of the different constants of physics represent specific features of the laws of nature themselves, just how strong gravitational attraction or electromagnetic attraction will be, for example. These values represent contingent features of the fundamental laws themselves.

Therefore, the laws cannot explain these features, they are (or possess) the features that require explanation. As Davies observed, the laws of physics seem themselves to be the product of exceedingly ingenious design (*The Superforce*, 1984: 243). Further, natural laws by definition describe phenomena that conform to regular or repetitive patterns. Yet the idiosyncratic values of the physical constants and initial conditions constitute a highly irregular and non-repetitive ensemble.

It seems unlikely, therefore, that any law could explain why all the fundamental constants have exactly the values they do and why, for example, the gravitational constant should have exactly the value of 6.67 Newton-meters per kilogram and the permittivity constant in Coulomb's law the value of 8.85×10^{-12} Coulombs per Newton-meter, and

GOD DOES EXIST!

the electron charge to mass ratio 1.76×10^{11} Coulombs per kilogram, and the speed of light 3×10^8 meters per second, and Planck's constant 6.663×10^{-34} Joulesseconds, and so on (Halliday and Resnick, *Physics: Part Two*, 1978: A23). The mass of the electron, or derived scientific parameters such as the dipole moment of the water molecule, are critical factors for life.

If any one of these or other such important constants were changed only slightly, that would make the earth uninhabitable by human beings. These values specify a highly complex array. As a group, they do not seem to exhibit a regular pattern that could in principle be subsumed or explained by natural law alone. So there must be another explanation. And that explanation is God.

Another and more recent attempt at evading the theistic and logical consequences of the fine-tuning of the universe (anthropic constraints) is the proposal that there are potentially an infinite number of universes. Martin Rees is largely responsible for this viewpoint. His book titled, *Just Six Numbers*, was published in 2000 and made the following set of arguments. He began by conceding the point that a universe like our own is overwhelmingly improbable. The numbers show this plainly at every turn. Secondly, he argued with certainty that God does not exist, or else if He does, He had nothing whatever to do with the design of the universe.

Third, he suggested that there must therefore be an infinite number of universes in existence in order for this one to have happened. The chances of such a universe as this one to have come about are so remote that this conclusion must be drawn necessarily. Finally, he made the case that our universe just happens to be that one wherein all of the circumstances are exactly right for human life to exist within it.

Now of course, the major objection that could be levelled against this hypothesis is that there is absolutely no evidence at all for the existence of any other universe, let alone an infinite number of them. They exist only in the fertile imagination of Martin Rees. It is entirely appropriate to say that this perspective is "far fetched" in the truest and most applicable sense of the expression. Rees is obviously making an argument which has only one purpose, to avoid the essential inference of

The Science Argument

theism. The God hypothesis is a much more convincing explanation to the greatest number of intelligent people.

2. Evidence from Geology, Paleontology, and Paleobiology. If evolution actually happened as it is assumed to have by most leading scientists, the evidence for it should be plentiful in the various layers of rock in the earth's crust. Since there are hundreds of thousands of living things on the earth, there ought to be (at the very least) hundreds of examples of transitional forms between the different kinds of biota.

If, on the other hand, living things were created by God, as is taught in the Bible and believed by Jews and Christians, then examples of all sorts of once-living creatures should appear suddenly in the strata of the planet's sedimentary rock, without being preceded by any less well developed ancestral forms. Thus, the question of whether life evolved or was created should be resolvable on the basis of a close and careful examination of the earth's sedimentary layers.

When Charles Darwin wrote the *Origin of Species*, however, he noted at the time that there was a fundamental problem with the theory he was putting forward in his book. The twin pillars of his theory were the ideas of universal common ancestry and natural selection. The first of these pillars, universal common ancestry, represented his theory of the history of life. It asserted that all forms of life have ultimately descended from a single common ancestor somewhere in the distant past. He argued that "all the organic beings on this earth have descended from some one primordial form." It was his view that this primordial form gradually developed into new forms of life, eventually producing, after many millions of generations, all of the various complex forms of life we see in the present. Hence, biology textbooks today customarily depict this idea with a great branching tree. We have all seen it many times. It is described in terms of what scientists call "universal common descent."

When the *Origin* first appeared, Louis Agassiz of Harvard, the greatest living expert on the fossil record, read the book with great interest, but concluded there was a serious flaw in the theory. The fossil record, he said, and in particular the explosion of Cambrian animal life, posed an insuperable difficulty to Darwin's reconstruction of events. He had other criticisms of the theory, but his main one had to do with the abrupt ap-

GOD DOES EXIST!

pearance in the fossil record of the Cambrian fauna. To produce truly novel animal forms, Agassiz argued, the Darwinian mechanism would require not only millions of years, but untold generations of ancestors.

Thus, even the discovery of a handful of plausible intermediates allegedly linking a Precambrian ancestor to a Cambrian descendant would not come close to fully documenting Darwin's picture of the history of life. If Darwin's theory is correct, he reasoned, then we should find not just one or a few missing links, but innumerable links shading almost imperceptibly from alleged ancestors to presumed descendants. Geologists, however, had found no such myriad of transitional forms leading to the Cambrian fauna. Instead, the stratigraphic column seemed to document the sudden appearance of the earliest animals. The Cambrian period had been given its name in 1835 by Adam Sedgwick from the Roman name for Wales (Cambria) where phenomenal deposits from that period had been discovered and thoroughly studied.

Of these earlier (Precambrian) life forms, Agassiz inquired, "Where are their fossilized remains?" Far from dismissing the objection of the Harvard professor, he conceded that his argument carried considerable force. He had noted in the *Origin* that his theory was greatly threatened by the missing evidence in the stratigraphic record: "The abrupt manner in which whole groups of species suddenly appear in certain formations has been urged by several paleontologists, for instance by Agassiz, Pictet, and Sedgwick, as a fatal objection to the belief in the transmutation of species. If numerous species, belonging to the same genera or families, have really started into life all at once, the fact would be fatal to the theory of descent with slow modification through natural selection" (302). In answer to the objection he suggested that the fossil record might be significantly incomplete. But he took seriously the argument against his theory, admitting the force of the evidence against it: "To the question why we do not find rich fossiliferous deposits belonging to these assumed earliest periods prior to the Cambrian system, I can give no satisfactory answer.... The case at present must remain inexplicable, and may be truly urged as a valid argument against the views here entertained" (307).

Fortunately for Darwin and his theory, in the years immediately following the publication of his book, many of Agassiz's and other naturalist's concerns were swept aside as public and scientific fascination with

The Science Argument

Darwin's ideas grew in importance and influence. But the objection itself has not disappeared, and as additional study of the Precambrian and Cambrian sediments have added to the overall understanding of the eras represented, the concerns have not been alleviated but in fact have grown deeper. As previously noted, the primary work on those periods in the time of Darwin and Agassiz had been done in the British Isles in the Swansea Valley in southern Wales. It was thought by Darwin and his supporters that if other comparable sediments could be found elsewhere, they would provide the missing evidence.

The years since then have produced a number of major discoveries, beginning in the Canadian Rockies of British Columbia in 1909. Charles Doolittle Walcott discovered the Burgess Shale during that year, a rich treasure-trove of Middle Cambrian fossilized rock. Walcott's site provided more evidence of the identical "Cambrian explosion" of life, the abrupt appearance of a veritable "menagerie of animals as various as any found in the gaudiest science fiction" (Quoted in Meyer, *Darwin's Doubt*, 31). During this explosion of fauna, representatives of about twenty of the roughly twenty-seven total phyla present in the known fossil record, made their first appearance on earth based on the evidence from the Burgess Shale. In fact, the fauna of the Burgess Shale is so prolific in its profusion of forms that are represented in the sediment, that it has come to be described as the "Burgess Bestiary."

In 1930 Harvard professor Percy Raymond initiated a second excavation of the Burgess Shale, and then later paleontologist Harry Whittington of the University of Cambridge, along with his students Simon Conway Morris and Derek Briggs worked there as well. Dr. Whittington, a trilobite expert, published the first comprehensive taxonomic review of the Cambrian biota at Burgess. In so doing, he reemphasized the morphological disparity present in the Burgess animal biota and, in the process, deprived the evolutionary biologists of one part of Walcott's two-part strategy for minimizing the Cambrian problem. By lumping all of the Burgess animals into existing phyla and classes, Walcott had seemingly diminished the problem of disparity by reducing the number of novel phyla for which connecting intermediates were required.

Also, by recognizing the disparity that was clearly evident in the Burgess Shale, Whittington at least partially undercut Walcott's supposed "solution" to the Cambrian mystery and highlighted what would become its central unsolved problem, namely, the origin of novel biological forms. Where did they come from, and how did they get there? Stephen Jay Gould later characterized many of the Burgess Shale creatures as being so exotic that they defy affinity in classification with any modern groups. Many of these animals manifest such unique anatomical structures and arrangements of body parts that it is difficult to fit them into any previously known forms of life (Collins, "Misadventures in the Burgess Shale," 952-953). Hence, it is difficult to explain them by any known naturalistic hypothetical reconstruction of their development.

Dr. Stephen C. Meyer characterized the "puzzling pattern" as follows:

> Over the years, as paleontologists have reflected on the overall pattern of the Precambrian-Cambrian fossil record in the light of Walcott's discoveries, they too have noted several features of the Cambrian explosion that are unexpected from a Darwinian point of view in particular: (1) the sudden appearance of Cambrian animal forms; (2) an absence of transitional intermediate fossils connecting the Cambrian animals to simpler Precambrian forms; (3) a startling array of completely novel animal forms with novel body plans, and (4) a pattern in which radical differences in form in the fossil record arise before more minor, small-scale diversification and variations. This pattern turns on its head the Darwinian expectation of small incremental change only *gradually* resulting in larger and larger differences in form (*Darwin's Doubt*, 34).

Another major discovery of Cambrian-era fauna occurred near the town of Chengjiang in the Kunming Province of southern China in the year 1995. A paleontologist named Xian-Guang Hou first discovered the deposit in June of 1984 while prospecting for fossilized samples of a bivalved arthropod called a bradoriid. Renowned Chinese paleontologist J. Y. Chen wrote several widely read papers on the finds at the location, announcing evidence of a profusion of novel life-forms at the site. It is now recognized that the trove of early Cambrian fossils represent the most exquisitely preserved Cambrian fossils in the world.

As a result of the very fine, small-grained sediments in which they were deposited, the Chengjiang fossils preserved anatomical details with a fidelity surpassing even that of the Burgess fauna. This shale also

The Science Argument

preserved an even greater variety of soft-bodied animals and anatomical parts than the Burgess Shale had done. It is widely acknowledged that it surpasses even the legendary Burgess Shale in terms of its extensiveness and significance. These fossils from the Maotianshan Shale (as they have come to be designated) provide an even greater variety of Cambrian body plans from an even older layer of Cambrian rock than those of the Burgess. As of this writing, at least 16 phyla, plus a variety of enigmatic groups, and about 196 different species have been documented. Being that this is a site that is being actively studied, the various numbers associated with it are continually changing.

Thus, what has been found at Chengjiang contradicts the bottom-up pattern that Neo-Darwinism expects. The site does not show the gradual emergence of unique species followed slowly but surely by the emergence of representatives of ever higher and more disparate taxa, leading to novel phyla. Instead, precisely as in the Burgess Shale, it shows body plan-level disparity arising first and suddenly, with no evidence of a gradual unfolding and ranging through the lower taxonomic groups. Moreover, fossilized remains of two small Cambrian fish, testifying to the existence of both fishes and vertebrates (a class of chordates), both of which had been previously thought to have arisen much later in the Ordovician period, were discovered in Cambrian sediments. In any case, the discovery in China of chordates, and of other previously undiscovered phyla in the Cambrian, only serves to accentuate the puzzling top-down pattern of appearance that other Cambrian findings had previously established (cf. Hou, *The Cambrian Fossils of Chengjiang, China*, 130; Meyer, *Darwin's Doubts*, 74-76).

The most interesting aspect, for our purposes here, is that the Chinese fossils also helped to establish that the Cambrian animals appear even more explosively than had been previously realized. Speaking about his discoveries in Seattle, WA, at the Discovery Institute, as he highlighted the apparent contradiction between the Chinese finds and Darwinian orthodoxy, he was asked by one professor from the University of Washington whether he might be nervous about expressing his doubts about Darwinism so freely. To this question he responded adroitly: "In China we can criticize Darwin, but not the government. In America, you can criticize the government, but not Darwin."

GOD DOES EXIST!

In all of these sedimentary deposits representing the Cambrian era, the basic animal groups appear suddenly and without any evidence whatever of evolutionary ancestors. What is even more intriguing is that the evidence for Darwinian macroevolutionary transformations is most conspicuously absent precisely where the fossil evidence is most plentiful—among marine invertebrates. Such animals are plentiful as fossils because they are so frequently covered in sediment layers upon death, whereas land animals are more often than not exposed to and therefore consumed by scavengers and otherwise destroyed by the elements. If the Darwinian model were correct, and if the proper explanation for the difficulty in finding ancestors were the incompleteness of the fossil record, then the evidence for macroevolutionary transitions would be most plentiful where the record is most complete. The fossil record is most complete in regard to marine invertebrates. And yet the evidence for macroevolutionary transformations is entirely absent in the Cambrian deposits.

Now, various scientists have dealt with this in different ways, other than merely to suggest that those missing transitional forms will be discovered at a later date in another deposit somewhere else. Even some convinced evolutionists have given up the argument. Lynn Margulis of the University of Massachusetts, highly respected for her theory that mitochondria, the energy production mechanism in plant and animal cells, were once independent, bacterial cells, commented that history will ultimately judge neo-Darwinism harshly, in fact, as "a minor twentieth-century religious sect within the sprawling religious persuasion of Anglo-Saxon biology" (quoted in Behe, *Darwin's Black Box*, 26).

Niles Eldredge, one of the world's leading experts in invertebrate fossils, described the situation thus: "No wonder paleontologists shied away from evolution for so long. It never seems to happen. . . . When we do see the introduction of evolutionary novelty, it usually shows up with a bang, and often with no firm evidence that the fossils did not evolve elsewhere! Evolution cannot forever be going on somewhere else. Yet that's how the fossil record has struck many a forlorn paleontologist looking to learn something about evolution" (*Reinventing Darwin*, 95) Now, Eldredge is far from a creationist. Anyone who has followed his

The Science Argument

writings (such as his 1982 book, *Monkey Business,* and his 2000 work, *The Triumph of Evolution and the Failure of Creationism*) will be fully aware of this. Instead, he is a practitioner of an alternative theory of evolution called punctuated equilibria, the theory that states that evolution happened by means of sudden and radical changes in life forms (see his book, *Time Frames: The Evolution of Punctuated Equilibria*; 1985). But his admissions on this count are devastating.

This curious viewpoint has been forced upon the scientific community by study of the Cambrian fossils. Eldredge and Stephen Jay Gould argue that for long periods of time most species undergo little observable change, and then when it does occur, it is rapid and concentrated in small, isolated populations. If this happened, they reckon, then fossil intermediates would be hard to find. And this would square with the fossil record as we have it. Thus, they believe in common descent as do other evolutionists, but think that a mechanism other than natural selection is needed to explain rapid, large-scale changes. They do not know what this mechanism might be.

However, by opting for "hopeful monsters," as they are sometimes called, they are complicating the process even worse. At the genetic level, it is difficult to explain miniscule changes taking place without their being destructive to the plant or animal involved. Not one of us would ever hope to have a child with a "genetic mutation." There is a very good reason that this is so. Mutations are almost always harmful, and more often than not lead to the death of the organism involved. As we shall see, the chances of beneficial mutations are prohibitive in these minor instances. What they suggest has happened repeatedly in nature is beyond phenomenal. To hope for system-wide, radical transformations all at once, as Eldredge and Gould imagine, involving multiple coordinated mutations that are beneficial, cannot be accounted for in any naturalistic approach to the problem. Nothing short of theistic evolution would explain what they advocate must have occurred. The neo-Darwinian model encounters clear probabilistic limits if the structures needed require more than two coordinated mutations in multicellular eukaryotic organisms (which they always and inevitably do). If this is so, and it has been demonstrated to be so by research over many decades, then there is very little hope at all for their "hopeful monsters."

GOD DOES EXIST!

In regard to the fossil record itself, Eldredge is merely stating the facts of the case. Uncomfortable facts they are, but because of them a good number of theorists have begun to look for alternative ways of explaining what has been found to date, reckoning that there is little chance that time or additional discovery will make much difference in the picture of the Cambrian. The discoveries at Chengjiang are so prodigious in their extent and the quality of the evidence that searching elsewhere and later on is not likely to turn up anything that will change the current picture. Eldredge goes on to acknowledge that on this account "many a forlorn paleontologist" has been led to construe a curious fossil as an ancestor of another or else as an evolutionary transitional. Certainly there has been much of this that has gone on through the years, but the fact remains that the evidence for macroevolution is entirely missing, and the Cambrian explosion is the best evidence for this.

A number of different solutions have been attempted by various scientists to resolve what has come to be called the "Cambrian conundrum." A recent effort, published in the journal *Science* (334.6059 [Nov. 2011]: 1091-1097) tried to explain the "early divergence and later ecological success in the early history of animals." The standard scenario as set forth by these researchers is that the Cambrian creatures did not evolve until about 500 million years ago. In contrast, it is suggested that animals were actually alive and evolving around 800 million years ago.

But, of course, the fossils do not back up this picture of their history. The precursors and their intermediates are entirely missing from the deposits. Their answer to this problem is to ignore the fossils themselves and emphasize instead what they describe as "molecular clocks." When the idea of a molecular clock was first conceived, researchers believed that DNA bases change at a steady rate over time, and thus they "tick" like a clock at a reliable and thus predictable rate. Theoretically this was seen as the mechanism of change that led to the broad diversity of plant and animal life on the earth at the present. However, after a decade or so of research into this matter, it was concluded that DNA base change rates are not steady at all. And they certainly do not tick like a clock. That was wishful thinking instead of demonstrable and reproducible science. Rather, DNA base change rates are restricted to mutational "hot spots" and non-lethal changes that are different for various genes.

The Science Argument

For these reasons, and because most molecular clock-based evolutionary histories are markedly different from fossil-based ones, researchers routinely "calibrate" molecular clocks to the fossils of supposedly "known ages." According to these writers, the molecular clock estimates in this particular *Science* study were adjusted to 24 fossil-based "ages." And so, thus tuned, the researchers' clocks indicated that "the last common ancestor of all living animals arose nearly 800 million years ago." This falls within the range reported by Stony Brook University's Barry Levinson, who noted in *Bioscience* (58.9 [Oct. 2008]: 862) that the molecular-based histories constantly contradict the fossil-based histories of life on earth.

This leaves us with a very intriguing question: If the molecule-based age of 800 million years is true, then how did all of those animals avoid fossilization for some 300 million years or so? This, like all of the other efforts at explaining away the evidence from the Cambrian explosion of life on the earth, is illogical in the extreme and begs the very question it is supposed to answer.

Using this "molecular clock" methodology, some advocates of Darwinian evolution have attempted to explain the absence of the Cambrian predecessors in an even more radical fashion. Looking at the problem from the perspective of what they call "deep divergence," they theorize that the extent to which genetic sequences differ from one another between different kinds of animals is reflective of the amount of time that has passed since those animals began to evolve from a common ancestor. To determine exactly how short or long, these studies estimate the mutation rate by analyzing genes in two species or taxa that are thought to have evolved from an ancestor whose presence in the fossil record can be discerned and dated accurately.

For example, many molecular-clock studies of birds and mammals are calibrated based on the age of an early reptile thought to be the most recent common ancestor of both. Gregory Wray and others produced a study in 1996, entitled, "Molecular Evidence for Deep Precambrian Divergences among Metazoan Phyla" (*Science*, 1996). They argued that seven different data sets (differences between the amino-acid sequences of seven proteins from seven different modern animals) suggest that invertebrates diverged from chordates about a billion years ago, about twice as long ago as the Cambrian is theorized as having been deposited.

GOD DOES EXIST!

Hence they implied that the common ancestor of these animal forms lived 1.2 billion years ago, further implying that the Cambian animals took some 700 million years to evolve from this "deep divergence" point before first appearing in the fossil record. 700 million years with no evidence in the fossil record for them! Most people would consider that quite a stretch! But "true believers" are capable of spanning that enormous gap quite readily. They attempted to explain the absence of the fossil ancestral forms during this period of time by postulating that Precambrian ancestors existed in exclusively soft-bodied forms, rendering their preservation unlikely. The main problem with this theory, of course, is that plenty of soft-bodied life-forms are preserved in the Cambrian-era sediments. If they were preserved there, why not before?

Moreover, this manner of approach also points out a rather obvious flaw in the procedural methodology of those who go about the task of doing "science" in this way. Only a "true believer" in the theory behind their approach to these issues would permit such a presuppositional methodology to be employed in the search for an answer in the first place. The fact that these authors calibrated their clock to predetermined fossil ages proves from the outset that their clock is just as unreliable and lacking in objectively verifiable data as the prior clocks that the authors intended to replace. The Cambrian evidence cannot be ignored, and it cannot be explained away with a wave of the hand or "sleight of hand" methods that lead to a predetermined conclusion. Objective observers see through methodologies of this sort just as we see through clear glass.

Charles Darwin understood how devastating the Cambrian materials potentially were for his theory. Unlike modern Neo-Darwinists, he was even willing to admit as much. He hoped that what he considered the missing connections would be filled in by subsequent discovery. In fact, additional information and fantastic new Cambrian discoveries have only added to the problems for his theory. The Cambrian explosion, in all of its profusion, diversity, and unexplainable complexity, has led to the Cambrian conundrum for Neo-Darwinists. That problem will not be resolved for them in the near future.

3. *Evidence from Biology, Biochemistry, Genetics, Population Genetics, and Probability Mathematics.* The prevailing theory in academic circles states that all of the complex systems present today in

The Science Argument

the biological world came into existence gradually over vast epochs of time. This happened via the mechanism of natural selection acting on randomly arising, small-scale variations and mutations. It is believed that this evolutionary mechanism necessarily transforms organisms gradually, with modifications parceled into increments "as a sort of continuous change, where one structural condition melts gradually into another" (T. H. Frazetta, "From Hopeful Monsters to Bolyerine Snakes?" *American Naturalist* 104 [1970]: 62-63).

Frazetta, however, in his study of bolyerine snakes found on the island of Mauritius in the Indian Ocean, ran across what for him at least was a logical *non sequitur*. His boa-like snakes enjoy an anatomical specialization that is found in no other vertebrate. Their maxilla, the tooth-bearing bone of the upper jaw, is divided into two segments, linked by a flexible joint and serviced by many specialized nerves, extra bones, tissues, and differently arranged ligaments. This unique trait allows the snakes to bend the front half of their upper jaw backwards when they attack their prey. He wondered how this complex system of bones, joints, tissues, and ligaments could have evolved gradually. He wrote: "A movable joint dividing the maxilla into two segments seems to have a presence or absence, with no intermediate to connect the two conditions" (63).

Frazetta was making the point that either the maxilla occurs as one bone, as it does in every other vertebrate, or it has two segments with all of the accompanying joints, bones, ligaments, and tissues necessary to make it work, as it does in these unique snakes. He further puzzled: "I thus find it difficult to envision a smooth transition from a single maxilla to the divided condition seen in bolyerines" (63).

As he contemplated the problem further, however, he came to realize that this larger issue extended well beyond the peculiarities of rare snakes. He knew that almost any biological structure of interest, the inner ear, the amniotic egg, eyes, olfactory organs, gills, lungs, feathers, the reproductive, circulatory, and respiratory systems, as well as highly refined and closely coordinated biochemical processes, all possess multiple necessary components. This is true both morphologically and biochemically. To change such systems in any way requires altering each of the many independent parts upon which their functions are based.

GOD DOES EXIST!

Complex biological systems depend for their proper function on at least tens and in some cases hundreds of such independent, yet jointly necessary parts.

Five years later, as his thinking matured on this topic, he penned his most important work, a book called *Complex Adaptations in Evolving Populations* (1975). He wrote that when modifying the design of a machine, an engineer is not bound by the need to maintain a real continuity between the first machine and the modification. But in evolution, he argued, transitions from one type to the next presumably involve a greater continuity by means of a vast number of intermediate types. So, not only must the end product, the final machine, be feasible, but so must all of the intermediates. The evolutionary problem is then, in a real sense, the gradual improvement of a machine while it is still running! Too, he understood that another level of complexity is related to the DNA code and how it "maps" out these higher level complex morphological structures, how they work and how they work together in the overall system.

Thus, altering the anatomical structure of the mammalian ear or the vertebrate eye, for example, would involve altering the genes that code for its constituents, which implies, most implausibly, that *multiple* coordinated mutations would occur virtually simultaneously. He went on to say that "Phenotypic alteration of integrated systems requires an improbable coincidence of genetic (and hence, heritable phenotypic) modifications of a tightly specified kind." Yet the extreme specificity of the fit of the components and the functional dependence of the whole system on this fit imply limits to allowable genetic change. Genetic change affecting any one of the necessary components, unless matched by many corresponding, and thus vastly improbable, genetic changes, will result in functional loss and often death.

So, his conclusion was that researchers are still left with the unabating need to explain evolutionary changes in systems that have the operational integration characteristic of things we recognize as "machines." What Frazzetta had noted about such systems was truly important, but it was not recognized as such at the time because most evolutionary biologists assumed that mutation and selection had nearly unlimited creative power (cf. Meyer, *Darwin's Doubt*, 230-33).

The Science Argument

Research since that time has had a tendency to modulate those expectations, and to do so in a major way. It has come to be understood that genes are not merely complex adaptations, as they were once thought to be. Rather, building new genes and proteins is a process that would require multiple coordinated mutations, all at once. And that is a huge order to fill! The day when theorists could merely wave questions away blithely as if it was "no big deal" for a single mutation to be conceived of as possessing the power to produce a new trait in a biological system had passed and gone.

Frank Salisbury of Utah State University was one of those biologists who doubted the ease with which those types of transformations could take place. In 1970 he penned an article in *Nature* that raised questions about whether random mutations could explain the specificity of the arrangement of nucleotide bases necessary to produce functional proteins. Salisbury worried that the probability of random mutations generating functional arrangements of bases or amino acids was prohibitively low. According to his calculations, "The mutational mechanism as presently imagined could fall short by hundreds of orders of magnitude of producing, in a mere four billion years, even a single required gene." Maynard Smith, a convinced Darwinist, responded to Salisbury's concerns with a simplistic analogy and that seemed sufficient at the time. Later on these concerns would be reiterated and the problem revisited, but it would take nearly three decades for this to take place.

It was not until the first decade of the twenty-first century that biologists began once more to confront the challenge of making a rigorous quantitative analysis of the plausibility of protein-to-protein evolution. In 2004 Michael Behe (biochemist, Lehigh University) and David Snoke (physicist, University of Pittsburgh) published a paper in *Protein Science* that returned the attention of researchers to this problem once again. Behe and Snoke sought to assess the plausibility of protein evolution in the case that it does indeed require multiple coordinated mutations. They applied standard neo-Darwinian modes of analysis derived from population genetics to make their evaluation. They considered the plausibility of the main neo-Darwinian model of gene evolution in which evolutionary biologists envision new genes arising by gene duplication and subsequent mutations in the duplicated gene.

GOD DOES EXIST!

On this basis, they attempted to assess the need for multiple coordinated mutations, not only as a theoretical or potential problem for evolutionary biologists, but as a quantifiable difficulty. They observed that many proteins, as a condition of their function, require unique combinations of amino acids interacting in a coordinated way.

For example, ligand binding sites on proteins (places where small molecules bind to large proteins to form larger functional complexes), typically require a combination of several amino acids. It was observed that in such instances the combinations of amino acids would have to arise in a coordinated fashion since the capacity for ligand binding depends on all the necessary amino acids being present together.

Hence, a series of separate mutations could not generate a ligand binding function in a protein that previously did not have this capacity, since individual amino-acid changes would initially confer no selectable advantage on the protein lacking function. Instead, evolving ligand binding capability would require *multiple coordinated* mutations. They further observed that a number of other processes, like ligand binding, would likewise require multiple coordinated mutations.

Next, Behe and Snoke calculated on this basis that mutation and selection could generate two coordinated mutations in a mere 1 million generations. But this was in a population of 1 trillion or more multicellular organisms. However, this is a number that exceeds the size of the effective breeding populations of practically all individual animal species that have ever lived on the earth at any given time. Conversely, they found that mutation and selection could generate two coordinated mutations in a population of only 1 million organisms, but only if the mechanism had 10 billion generations at its disposal!

In 2007 Behe published *The Edge of Evolution*, a follow-up to his 2004 paper with David Snoke. Utilizing public health data about a single genetic trait, resistance to the antimalarial drug chloroquine in the single celled organism that causes malaria, he provided another line of evidence and argument to support the conclusion that multiple coordinated mutations are often necessary to produce even minor genetic adaptations.

Looking at the data, he determined that resistance to chloroquine only arises once in every 10^{20} malaria causing cells. By investigating this

The Science Argument

mutation Behe hoped to be able to explore what he described as "the edge of evolution," that is to say, the limitations of the creative power of mutation and selection at the genetic level. What he described as the "chloroquine complexity cluster" (CCC) was a simple adaptation, but he wondered what the chances of two coordinated traits, each as complex as CCC, might prove to be.

Using the principles of population genetics, he demonstrated that multi-mutation traits of that complexity would require many more organisms, or else vastly more time than was reasonable, given the history of life on earth. He calculated that the waiting time would increase exponentially with each additional coordinated change. A mere two coordinated CCCs would require many more organisms or vastly more time than was reasonable given the history of life. The square of the original amount for a single adaptation would apply here, and it would necessitate 10^{40} organisms. But given the present assumptions as to the history of the planet, it is reckoned that only 10^{40} organisms have ever existed on the earth. This implies that the entire history of the earth would barely provide enough opportunities to generate a single trait of this complexity!

Behe went on to point out that the problem of such coordinated mutations was particularly acute for longer-lived organisms with small population sizes, as is the case with mammals and human beings. His calculations demonstrated that two coordinated mutations in the hominid line would require hundreds of millions of years. Yet we are informed by neo-Darwinists that humans and chimps diverged from a common ancestor only 6 million years ago.

When two Cornell University mathematical biologists (Rick Durrett and Deena Schmidt) revisited Behe's calculations, they estimated that it would require only 216 million years to get one such complex adaptation. Thinking that they had corrected his numbers and upset his hypothesis, unwittingly they had confirmed Behe's analysis. Even if it takes "only" 216 million years to produce a single adaptation of this complexity, it is not long before one runs out of time for Darwinism to work its magic and change a pre-human hominid into a fully functional human being.

GOD DOES EXIST!

Remember that under their own rubric they have only 6 million years to work with. So, what they concluded was that it would take 36 times the amount of time they have allotted to themselves to produce a human from a hominid in order to produce a single beneficial adaptation. Obviously, producing a human being would require hundreds of such adaptations.

But, going back to our original problem: the issue of life arising during the Cambrian era in the "explosion" of various living organisms becomes especially thorny in the light of such calculations. It must be remembered that the Cambrian fossils represent most of the known marine life-forms on the earth today, along with others that are now extinct. Using their own numbers, the problem is simply incapable of a resolution given neo-Darwinian assumptions. As Stephen C. Meyer has remarked:

> An analysis by MIT geochronologist Samuel Bowring has shown that the main pulse of Cambrian morphological innovation occurred in sedimentary sequence spanning no more than 6 million years. Yet during this time representatives of at least sixteen completely novel phyla and about thirty classes first appeared in the rock record. In a more recent paper using a slightly different dating scheme, Douglas Erwin and colleagues similarly show that thirteen new phyla appear in a roughly 6 million year window. As we've seen, among these animal forms were the first trilobites, with their lens-focusing compound eyes among other complex anatomical features. The problem of explaining how so many new forms and structures arose so rapidly in the first explosive period of the Cambrian remains, whether or not one decides to include within the designation "Cambrian explosion" other distinct events (*Darwin's Doubt*, 73-74).

How did so many different highly complex creatures appear on the scene so abruptly as the fossil record suggests? Whether we accept the dating system of modern geology or not, the problem still remains. Advanced life forms appear in the record without any evidence of their having developed over long periods of time, with no evidence whatsoever of intermediates being present in the record. How did they get there in the first place? No theory of development is capable of accounting for their appearance, suddenly or otherwise. The mechanism of mutation and natural selection does not have the creative power attributed to

The Science Argument

it by evolutionists. If it did, we would all know about it because they would be shouting it from the rooftops.

Theistic evolution is one possible way of dealing with this problem of mechanism. Such evolutionists argue that God is responsible for accomplishing what mutation and natural selection never could. But it must be remembered that this is only one element of the process. It could account for the problem of innovation. Yet, facing the difficulty squarely, the evidence seems to be against the notion that evolution took place at all. The fossil record is no more friendly to theistic evolution than it is to Darwinian evolution. The sudden appearance of complex life-forms on the planet militates against both views.

The epigenetic information essential to life in its varied complexity on the earth is not explained by either perspective. New animal body plans with new biochemical processes in all of their amazing profundity could not have arisen in any of the ways postulated by materialistic scientists. And theistic evolution, which is essentially God-guided evolution, assumes that life on earth evolved from rudimental forms to more complex ones. Thus, it also assumes the very thing that evolution in all of the years of its history has been unable to demonstrate. So it is not the answer either. Neither theory is plausible.

Malcolm Muggeridge was correct when he observed:

> I myself am convinced that the theory of evolution, especially the extent to which it's been applied, will be one of the great jokes in the history books in the future. Posterity will marvel that so flimsy and dubious an hypothesis could be accepted with the credulity that it has (*The End of Christendom*, 59).

This brings us to the only genuinely plausible answer to the problem of origins: Intelligent Design. Simply put, all of the other ways of viewing the origin of the universe and of life within it, not to mention explaining the incredible complexity of life as we know it, are essentially dead-end streets. They lead nowhere. For those who wish to argue that life arose as a result of self-organizing properties intrinsic to the material constituents of living systems, these rather elementary facts of molecular biology have implications. The most obvious place to look for self-organizing properties to explain the origin of genetic information is in the constituent parts of the molecules that carry the information.

But biochemistry and molecular biology make clear that forces of attraction between the constituents in DNA, RNA, and proteins do not explain the sequence specificity of these large information-bearing biomolecules. We know this because of the multiplicity of variant polypeptides and gene sequences that exist in nature and can be synthesized in the laboratory. The properties of the monomers constituting nucleic acids and proteins simply do not make a particular gene, let alone life as we know it, inevitable. Yet, if self-organizational scenarios for the origin of biological information are to have any theoretical import, they must claim precisely the opposite. And they often do. One scientist said that the processes that generated life on earth were "highly deterministic," arguing also that life's appearance was therefore "inevitable," given "the conditions that existed on the prebiotic earth" (C. de Duve, "The Beginnings of Life on Earth," *American Scientist* 83 [1995]: 437).

But is this so? In fact, it is far from true. It is no more likely than a pile of rocks and bricks coming together to form the palace of Versailles or the Taj Mahal! If we were to imagine the most favorable prebiotic conditions on the early earth, they would surely include a pool of all four of the DNA nucleotides and all of the other necessary sugars and phosphates together in close proximity to one another. But would those essential ingredients for life being together at one place and at one point in time in a natural setting necessitate that a particular genetic sequence would assemble together precisely as needed to form a living organism?

Even given all of the necessary monomers, would any particular functional protein or gene, let alone a specific genetic code, a replication system, or signal transduction circuitry—all essential for the persistence of an organism once it was formed—have to arise on account of that unique pool of precisely the right ingredients for life? Frankly, it is only wishful thinking to believe so.

We all recognize that monomers of the kinds that we have surmised to have been in that primordial "soup" are merely building blocks for life. The fact that they are present in a particular place at a particular time does not guarantee that a living thing will arise from that special situation.

The Science Argument

Building blocks can be arranged and rearranged in innumerable different ways. The properties of blocks do not determine their arrangement in the construction of buildings. It is the builder who decides such things. He intelligently puts all of the right parts in all of the proper positions in order to construct his buildings. Similarly, the properties of biological building blocks do not determine the arrangement of functional polymers.

Instead, the chemical properties of the monomers allow for a vast ensemble of possible configurations, the overwhelming majority of which have no biological function whatsoever. Functional genes or proteins are no more inevitable given the properties of their building blocks than the palace of Versailles, for example, was inevitable given the properties of the bricks and stone used to construct it (Cf. Meyer, "Evidence for Design in Physics and Biology," 87-88) .

Such building blocks for life have no concern as to how they are arranged. They do not assemble themselves together in a logical and purposeful fashion. It is up to the builder to plan for their assemblage. It is up to the builder to arrange them precisely as they must be brought together for a functional living organism to appear at the end of the process of its creation. If a single functional protein had appeared in such a situation, so what? If a number of building blocks were to fall together in just the right proximity to one another to form a step, the house is still very far from built. We are still very far away from having the Taj Mahal!

Moreover, a functional protein is a part of a system, and it only has usefulness as it participates in the common life of its host organism. That protein could not even feed itself. It could not replicate itself. It would be dead soon after its accidental assemblage, and that would be the end of it!

All up and down the line of dealing with such matters we seem to end up at the same point, namely, asking who this builder was. Who was the builder who so intelligently assembled all of the necessary parts to create living things? God is the only credible answer to these questions. Being that He is wise beyond our meager understanding of intelligence, He was savvy enough to assemble all living things and build them in such a way as to make them capable of sustaining themselves and replicating themselves. Such mechanisms are inexplicable otherwise. For, without them how would life persist beyond its origination if it was not at first capable of performing both of these complicated functions? Being that He is timeless, He was there when life started. God is the de facto beginning of everything. It could not be otherwise. As the Bible says, "In the beginning, God..." (Genesis 1:1).

Since the dawn of the human race on earth men have seemed to understand this basic truth. Sometimes their notions about it were strange and far afield from reality. But it was something that was seldom denied. Most of the ancient philosophers and wise men believed it. It is only in recent years that great numbers of people have been persuaded that it could have been otherwise. But it must not be believed that this is a logically defensible position for us to take. Science, like all of the rest of the evidence, is clearly on the side of God as the builder and maker of all things (Heb. 11:10).

Conclusion

It is our settled conviction then, that the evidence for confirmation of the third premise of our original syllogism is solid. It will be recalled that it was the only one of the three original ones that was contested. The others were merely preliminary to it. That premise stated: "There have been numerous indications uncovered by scientific research that the material universe, and living entities within that universe, could not have produced themselves and could not have been produced by any wholly material mechanism, but must have been created by Something or Someone possessing incomparable intellectual prowess and unimaginable power, outside of the material realm."

What we have offered in this chapter are brief summaries of the kind of evidence that has been forthcoming from the scientific research that has led a great many incredibly bright people to conclude that Almighty God has indeed left His marks upon His creation. The material universe and the living systems within it have been slow to yield many of their secrets. Some of them have been extraordinarily difficult to unravel. But much work, considerable time, and the coordinated efforts of thousands of scientists throughout the world have brought forth a plethora of information from a host of different scientific disciplines. A great many things are yet unknown. But the amount of the evidence

The Science Argument

that has been uncovered, and is known now that was not known previously, has been cumulative and impressive indeed.

Analysis of this data has been faith strengthening to those who are willing to allow it to speak for itself. Our account of the evidence then led us to the inevitable conclusion that: "God is the only plausible solution to this mystery of origins. Therefore God exists." The universe around us and the life within it that we know about had its origin somehow. Neither one came about under its own power or by a means attributable to material sources and forces alone. Moreover, Laws are regulative, not creative. The evidence is foursquare against that. So we are left with God as the only reasonable, logical, and convincing answer to the question.

Why then are the atheists so loud in their protestations, you may ask. The answer is, precisely on account of the mounting evidence that is persistently making their case sound devoid of substance and their arguments hollow. The more vociferous they sound, the more obvious is their desperation. The voices of the newly awakened, heard from within the scientific community itself, is what is most frightening for them. It seems that the stranglehold that atheism has for so long held on the throat of the fellowship of scientists is being broken and the dogmatic acceptance of neo-Darwinism is losing its grip. So, we may expect to see in the years ahead more of their unproven claims and unsubstantiated statements as they desperately try to call their wayward children back into the fold. It will be interesting to watch.

Questions for Discussion

1. Can you state, in a simplified form, the syllogism for evidence from science for the existence of God?
2. Has atheism always been the dominant ideology of science? When did it become so, and how did that process develop to its current status?
3. Does science speak at all about metaphysics? Why are so many scientists so eager to set forth their opinions on matters of philosophy and religion? Are they experts in these fields? Does the study of science fit the scientist for investigation into philosophy and theology?

GOD DOES EXIST!

4. Scientists often argue that religion has been a rich source of evil in the world. Has science been utilized only for good in the world? Or, has it at times been the source of many different evils in the world? Give some examples of this.

5. When scientists argue that there could not exist another realm (of the spiritual, where God is), the heavenly, are they consistent when they speak of "many possible universes" and of other "dimensions" unknown to us, and other such concepts?

6. Christopher Hitchens and other naturalists and religion-hating atheists, have spoken of the "dangerous sexual repression" of Christianity and Judaism. Why are they wrong about this matter? Is it logical at times to repress sexual feelings and not express them? Give some examples that illustrate this perspective.

7. Why has the general public rejected evolution as the explanation for the origin of the human race? Is it because most of us are not as highly educated and intellectually sophisticated as the scientists are? Or, are there other reasons?

8. Explain the essential nature of science? What is its basic methodology? Why is it not possible to say that science is against the proposition that God exists? Could it have anything at all to do with the material world with which the scientific endeavor has to do?

9. Did the Christian world have anything at all to do with the beginnings of science? To hear many scientists tell the story, it would seem that scientists began their work as rebels, rejecting the Christian environment wherein they carried out their original experiments? Was this the case? Or, is there another back-story that they are not telling, that perhaps ought to be told in order to be fair to Christianity? In other words, did science start out in an atheistic world, comparable to skepticism of our own day? If not, then perhaps the "brave new world" into which the atheists and agnostics are launching us is not as sweet and grand as they give us the impression it will be. What are your thoughts on that? What will that world devoid of religion be like?

The Science Argument

10. What is empiricism? Why is it seen as the necessary basis of modern science? What is wrong with the present assumptions about empiricism?

11. Many scientists will argue that science in our time is utterly objective, and that objectivity is essential to doing science properly. But is this really true? Is it truly being objective to approach the scientific endeavor with the neo-Darwinian model of beginnings, and all of its accompanying assumptions, as the working hypothesis for all that they encounter? Is it objective to interpret everything they see and experience in their methodology as having its explanation in terms of a book written over one-hundred years ago (*The Origin of Species*)?

12. Offer some examples of discoveries made in recent decades that appear to lend credence to the proposition that science is on the side of believers, and not against their most cherished beliefs.

13. What is the testimony of the fossils from the Cambrian era in geology? Why is the phenomenon known as the "Cambrian explosion of life"? How have Darwinians attempted to explain the phenomenon?

Chapter 12
The Argument from the Existence of Evil in the World

The Problem Stated

This is considered a negative proof. It is said to show that God could not exist. The fact that evil exists in the world is often seen as *the* major problem with the existence of God. Certainly this is the most frequently mentioned charge that is made against the God hypothesis. Usually an atheist or agnostic parades a long list of the most horrendous crimes that have been perpetrated against humanity, or else he lists numerous and horrible natural calamities that have taken many lives and destroyed the homes and livelihoods of thousands of people, and then makes the point that no God could exist and permit such terrible evil to happen in His world. And, if it were consistent with His nature, then He could not be the good God of Christians and Jews. This is the line of reasoning that is commonly used by most skeptics and critics of theism.

The Argument from the Existence of Evil in the World

How could a perfectly good Creator permit evil to occur in His world? Our reply to this oft-made allegation may surprise some readers. We are convinced that the existence of catastrophic events as well as inhumanity and gross wickedness on the part of some elements of humankind is not only entirely consistent with the being of God, but absolutely essential to life in a physical universe where human persons enjoy the liberty to decide their own fates and choose either good or evil.

How Can There Be "Moral Evil" without God?

In fact, it is our contention that God is the one best explanation for the existence of the idea of evil. Like it or not, the liberal-thinking social justice warrior (who is frequently anti-religion or even anti-God) is a toothless, weaponless crusader without the intellection of God somewhere in the picture. God is what defines moral evil in our common vocabulary. In our view, the concept cannot exist in the absence of the idea of God. Simply put, if God did not exist, there would be no such abstraction as objective moral evil in the world.

There would just be what happened. No moral judgments could be or would be made about the unfortunate facts of the case. The degree or extent of the moral depravity of the wicked is beside the point. They are what they are. We do not pontificate about how ferocious lions are. We make no judgments about the cruelty of Bengal tigers. When ravenous bears attack campers or hikers we do not speak of how "evil" bears are or how "morally bankrupt" they must be. When a crocodile or alligator eats a child along the water's edge, we mourn the loss but we do not judge the animal. More often than not these days, we defend the right of these massive predatory beasts and wonder why humans "invade the territory" of the creatures.

Similarly, if there is no God, moral judgments of various human behaviors are impossible. And if they are made in spite of a lack of belief in God, then to our way of thinking they are vacuous. Mass slaughter under communist regimes where atheists have been in control are the best illustrations of how these anti-God men and their ruthless governments work. Moral judgments are deemed worthless where there is no ultimate accountability. And, make no mistake about it, if there is no God there is seldom any accountability. Decades after many of these genocides have happened, there still has not been any justice at all

GOD DOES EXIST!

for the victims of most of these dictators and despots. Either God will someday make an accounting of such unthinkable horrors, or else it will never happen in most cases.

Epicurean Denial of God

The Greek philosopher Epicurus of Samos (341-270 BC) argued the point that the existence of moral evil in the world was his main objection for believing in any deity. He made four points that he felt made the case. His logic flowed in the following way:

1. If God is willing to prevent evil but not able, then He is not all-powerful.
2. If He is able to prevent evil but not willing, then He is not good.
3. But if He is both willing and able, how can evil exist?
4. If He is neither able nor willing, why call him God?

The argument from the modern atheist is very similar to the line of reasoning pursued by Epicurus. As a syllogism, it would go something like this:

Premise 1: It is irrational that God would permit innocent suffering and evil.
Premise 2: It is impossible that God and evil could co-exist.
Premise 3: Suffering and evil both exist in the world.
Conclusion: Therefore God does not exist.

Hidden Assumptions

It should be noted that even though these propositions sound convincing on their face, there are certain hidden assumptions at work in the reasoning of the atheist in the course of pursuing an answer to the dilemma of human suffering in this fashion. These assumptions ought to be uncovered and examined more carefully in order to assess the relative value of these basic premises and the illogical and therefore unjustified conclusion that is drawn from them. Any argument that is based on uncorroborated postulates will lead inevitably to indefensible conclusions. That is the case in this instance.

For example, it is assumed that if God is all-powerful, He can, by virtue of this, create any world that He wants. This is the most important assumption underlying such reasoning. And it is false on the face of it.

The Argument from the Existence of Evil in the World

God would not and therefore could not ever do anything that is inconsistent with the nature of His being. Therefore, the world that He created must be congruous with the essence of His person. Interestingly, Scripture declares that when God had finished His work of creating, He pronounced the work of His hands, including man, to be "very good" (Gen. 1:31). It was not bad, it was good. Not merely or only *good*, but *very* good. It was not until later that His perfect work was spoiled and defaced, and that by the poor choices of His creatures and the inevitable consequences of those choices (Gen. 3:14ff). The world that we live in is like it is because of us, not because of God. Even the atheist must admit that human beings are guilty of murder, mayhem, and moral madness. Newspaper headlines testify to this fact daily. Can anyone believe that there will not be repercussions for such sordid behavior? It is common for people, believers and unbelievers alike, to speak of *karma*, the principle of cause and effect in regard to the attitudes and actions of sentient beings. Our deeds today will come back to haunt us in the days ahead.

We speak of such things, not because we believe in Hinduism or any of the other religions that accept this notion as a spiritual concept in terms of bad rebirths, but in the sense that we know our actions have inevitable consequences in this world. Most of us have had experience with those repercussions on a personal level, whether in our own lives or as a witness to it in the lives of others. We also strongly suspect that they may have aftereffects in the next life. If there is a life beyond this present state, how could they not?

In Epicurus's argument it is the word "innocent" that raises eyebrows, and, of course, questions and issues. We all understand that deserving people often suffer, many as a direct or indirect result of their own actions. But when those who are themselves innocent of any wrongdoing are caused to suffer on account of something or someone else, it gives us pause. Especially little children. If a small child is raped and murdered, we cannot ever justify such evil. We are repulsed by the very thought of such a thing happening. And, yet, we know that it does.

When a beautiful child is diagnosed with terminal cancer, an excruciating death, we find it difficult to reconcile this with the idea that God is just and equitable. There is no sense in which it could be said that a child "deserved" to experience its acquaintance with the dreaded dis-

GOD DOES EXIST!

ease. In all such situations, we tend to ask the question, "How is that fair?" And from this starting-point we proceed to draw the conclusion that God must be unfair to permit such things to occur in His world. Or, it is concluded by some that He must not exist at all. For, it is reasoned, if He did exist He would fix this problem or else He would never allow it to happen in the first place.

So, if we assume that God is all-powerful, may we also assume that God could create a world where innocent people could not experience pain or suffering? This is what the atheist confidently alleges. But is this really so? We would aver that it is not. It is important to recognize that certain aspects of God's own nature must be honored in order for Him to create anything at all. What God creates must be consistent with His being. It may not end up that way, but that is the way that it started out.

In other words, God would not make anything that was, in its own essence, a dishonor to Himself. God cannot lie (Titus 1:2) is a doctrine about God which is consistent throughout the Bible. It might be argued, though, that God made men who are liars. Indeed, God created all men. But God did not and could not create anyone a liar by His own hand. He created them in a state of innocence, and they learned to lie by hearing others do it and by practicing it themselves. Newborns are called "innocents" in Scripture (Jer. 19:4).

The atheist and the skeptic charges that if God is all-loving, He prefers a world without suffering. Again, is this really so? Clearly the theist does not think so, for he opts to argue for the existence of God despite his admission that our world does exhibit suffering and death as an enduring condition, and despite the fact that he readily acknowledges this is so. The atheist argues as he does because this is his own way of seeing things. He surmises that God is at liberty to make the world any way that He wants. But this assumes that it is realistic and workable to have such a world.

We shall attempt to show in the paragraphs below that this is not true. God does not want the world to be so, for He did not make it so. And He did not make it so because it was inconsistent with His nature and with the nature of the kind of men and women with which He planned to populate His world. He created free men and women, people who are

The Argument from the Existence of Evil in the World

at liberty to choose either to love Him or not. And with this came all of the other possibilities that we see in our world, good and bad.

And so, neither of these assumptions is true; other considerations need to be brought into the discussion in order for us to understand these concepts in their fullness. It needs to be recognized that some things are possible but not feasible in any conceivable world that God might have created.

When C. S. Lewis wrestled with the notion of omnipotence, he wrote in regard to our usage of the term impossibility and in terms of a thing, if it is self-contradictory being impossible in an absolute sense, thus:

> The absolutely impossible may also be called the intrinsically impossible because it carries its impossibility within itself, instead of borrowing it from other impossibilities which in their turn depend upon others. It has no *unless* clause attached to it. It is impossible under all conditions and in all worlds and for all agents.
>
> "All agents" here includes God Himself. His omnipotence means power to do all that is intrinsically possible, not to do the intrinsically impossible. You may attribute miracles to Him, but not nonsense. There is no limit to His power. If you choose to say, "God can give a creature free will and at the same time withhold free will from it," you have not succeeded in saying *anything* about God: meaningless combinations of words do not suddenly acquire meaning simply because we prefix to them the two other words "God can." It remains true that all things are possible with God: the intrinsic impossibilities are not things but nonentities. It is no more possible for God than for the weakest of His creatures to carry out both of two mutually exclusive alternatives; not because His power meets an obstacle, but because nonsense remains nonsense even when we talk it about God (*The Problem of Pain*, 27-28).

Lewis was correct in his assessment of this foolish charge that is so frequently alleged against belief in God during troublesome times. Logical absurdities are at the heart of all such allegations. For example, as we have already noted, God could not create a round square or a married bachelor; by definition these are impossible logically or infeasible physically. Similarly, God could not create a world where all men chose right always and still give them absolute moral choice. So, where there is moral choice, there is always the potential for bad moral choices. And where that potential exists, eventually someone will choose evil over good. Evil is, then, inevitable in a world where there is liberty. Moreover, innocent suffering is the inevitable concomitant of that. Innocent suffering then, as uncomfortable as it may seem to us, is completely consistent with the existence of a just God.

Physical Existence and Its Inherent Dangers

In addition, it should be observed that any physical world has intrinsic dangers that are associated with it: fire to cook and warm a man could potentially burn him; water that he drinks could drown or choke him; the wind that cools his face on a summer day may blow down his house on top of him, etc. So, creating a physical world without danger and the consequent pain and suffering that follows in its wake is inconceivable.

Two things are also true here. And although we may not have thought the matter through previously, the logic of both are unassailable. Take a moment to consider them, and you will surely say that we are right about this:

First, God could not have created a world with as much good but less suffering than the actual world. The claim made by skeptics that He could have done so and should have done so, is implausible. Philosophically speaking, good is as important as evil in this discussion. Atheists argue only about the existence of evil in the world. They concentrate on the fact that some people make terrible decisions, and so, bad things happen. They may suffer and others may suffer with them because of this. But God is also concerned with good. For there to be so many good choices and "happy endings" there must also be the potential for bad choices and unhappy endings. Both realities are critical to a universe where mankind enjoys freedom of choice.

Second, even though we may not always be able to understand how this could be true, God apparently has morally sufficient reasons for permitting the suffering that exists. We all know of some instances where unimaginable horror has characterized human history. Ancient history is filled with periods of such hideousness. Modern history has its own share as well. It is difficult to imagine that any of these incidents, either ancient or modern, should be permitted to occur. But they did. And in all probability things like this will happen again.

The Argument from the Existence of Evil in the World

So, once more, God if He exists, must have sufficient justification for permitting it. It is beside the point that some skeptics cannot believe that He exists in the light of this ugly reality. God does not have to explain Himself in every particular to those whom He has created.

"If I Were Running Things, It Would Be Different"

We sometimes think that if we were running things it would certainly be different. This is assuredly the view of the skeptic. But is this so, and is it really possible? Can it even be imagined? Frankly, we do not see how it could possibly be so, given all of the variables that have to play a part in this schema that we call our material existence. Believers have the ability in a real sense to make the world a better and more pleasant place through their application of righteous principles in their lives. They often have done so. Atheism and atheists, on the other hand, frequently have made the world a more unpleasant place through their oppression and persecution of those who disagree with them. Atheistic communism is the best illustration of this. Of course, this is not to say that all atheists are bad people. They are not. But all too frequently they have been the source of godless philosophies that have ended in some of the worst horrors of our recent past. That cannot be denied.

In our wrestling with these troublesome issues it would be helpful to remember that our intellectual powers are quite limited. This is true for even the most brilliant among us. If you believe this to be an overstatement, then ask yourself the following questions: Are you able to repair your own car when it breaks down? Are you able to fix your computer when it stops working? What about your refrigerator? Your television set? Your air conditioner or heating unit in your home? Very few of us, even if we know philosophy or theology intimately, have knowledge of the workings of any of these appliances or technological gadgets that are now so much a part in the lives of us all!

We may come to have impressive mastery of our own area of expertise, but the more this is true, the less we know about everything else in life! The point is this: just because I cannot comprehend why human suffering might be necessary in our world, that does not mean that it is not understood by God.

GOD DOES EXIST!

Job and Suffering

In the book of Job in the Hebrew Bible, it will be recalled that this was precisely the issue in question. Job demanded that God explain Himself on this matter. He wanted to know how his personal suffering could be justified. What had he done wrong? How could a man who had for so long tried so diligently to please God be allowed to suffer so unjustly?

The Lord's response to him was silence, stone-cold silence. God did not attempt to explain Himself. He never responded to Job's proud demands. He simply and methodically asked him a long series of questions which the patriarch could not answer. They were about things he did not know and could not explain. They were beyond his comprehension. All of them. Over the course of the conversation Job began to see how inappropriate and disrespectful it was for him to challenge the wisdom of the omniscient One. Finally, the humbled sufferer said, "I have uttered what I did not understand, things too wonderful for me, which I did not know. . ." (Job 42:1-6). Matters of this kind were beyond Job's level of intelligence and understanding.

Such things are too complicated for any mere human to understand. Putting such labyrinthine and sophisticated knowledge into a human brain would be like trying to stuff a basketball into the plastic shell of a ping pong ball. It would never fit! On a small scale, however, we can get a grasp of some aspects of the problem. We know from common experience that there are times when short-term pain is preferable to other non-suffering alternatives.

Types of Suffering

Let us say that your foot had developed gangrene, but you were far from civilization. You know that the foot must be removed but there is nothing available to alleviate the pain. Would you be willing to suffer the pain in order to save your life? Even though the operation would be excruciatingly painful, you would probably endure it in order to live. The pain would likely be only temporary, but you might be able to live a long and useful life afterward. It would be worth the trade, would it not? You see, at times suffering is justified in the course of one's life just as it is at times during the course of human history. Certainly we deem it justifiable for men to suffer and die in wartime to save the national life.

The Argument from the Existence of Evil in the World

Suffering of the kind that we commonly experience can be divided into two categories. The first is what we might describe as natural suffering. When I sprain my ankle or break my leg, that is the type of suffering which is endemic to a natural, physical world. How is God to be blamed for my clumsiness or misfortune? He did not trip me up or cause me to stumble. That was my own doing. Surely we can take responsibility for at least some of our own foolish decisions!

In this same category of suffering, however, there is another type which is much more difficult to wrestle with. It is illustrated by a case of childhood cancer, or some other disease that a child might contract. The child is completely innocent and yet suffers terribly and without any seemingly valid explanation. This shows us how the human mind deals with such things on two different levels.

Intellect and Emotion

Sometimes we deal with difficulties on an intellectual level and at other times on an almost entirely emotional level. Sad to say, but our emotions kick into gear and our brains no longer work. When children and innocent people whom we care about are hurting, we handle it emotionally. When we see injustice and abuse of the powerless, we wonder that such things are allowed to happen at all. We struggle to comprehend how God would permit such things to happen in His world. We readily admit that we do not have the perspective or the omniscience essential to understand how suffering of this sort could be justifiable. This does not suggest that it is not. It simply says that we are not qualified to make judgments about matters so profound as this. They are beyond our intellectual or emotional powers.

Skeptics argue that God could not possibly have any valid reason for permitting such suffering to occur in the world. But do they really know this for certain? Do they have unlimited knowledge? Are they intelligent enough to consider all possible variables? Do they have the ability to think in terms of hundreds of years and multiple generations and what the implications might be in those terms? Make no mistake about it: by proffering the claims that they do, they are saying that they possess a level of knowledge and understanding that is equivalent to God's! Most of us recognize that there are times when other people have understanding of some issue that we are not privy

GOD DOES EXIST!

to. Could not the omniscient God be privy to some things that we do not know?

The second category is suffering that occurs because of the bad moral choices that most everyone makes, and then live to regret, or else die or suffer injury on their account. Now, such decisions to engage in wrongdoing may be my own choices or those of someone else. When one person decides to commit murder, there is always at least one victim, but there may even be many. When a thief determines that he will steal something, there is always a victim who experiences loss. A large family may suffer grief and loss because of the choices of a single member. How is God at fault for the bad moral choices made by such a perpetrator of evil? He did not murder anyone or take away what was the property of another. He did not force anyone to do what he or she would not otherwise have done. Clearly, God is not guilty, even though some skeptics want to place the onus on Him.

How do we explain these phenomena in terms of potential divine responsibility? What part does God play in either of these two? The first type of suffering happens as the natural result of living in a physical world. Such things as floods, droughts, tornados, accidental injuries, and so forth, might appropriately qualify in this category. If I bang my knee on a table because I am walking and not paying close attention, I will inevitably hurt myself. However, God is not at fault because of my inattention or carelessness. Why blame Him for what is my own responsibility?

As we all know, at times terrible consequences sometimes follow in the wake of the most seemingly unimportant of such events. One thing leads to another and soon a situation is out of control. A cascade of events, where at any juncture a simple adjustment could have altered the ultimate outcome, leads to frighteningly life-shattering final chapters to certain people's lives. Why attempt to shift the blame off the party involved?

The second variety of this category of suffering is the direct result of human freedom of choice gone awry. In this classification there would be such things as thefts, murders, drunken driving incidents, etc. A man may suffer terribly in prison on account of his decision to rob a bank and was caught and sentenced for a long stay. In this instance, God is not

The Argument from the Existence of Evil in the World

to be blamed for the wicked actions of evil individuals. God does not make people rob banks! They are responsible for their own decisions and whatever may result from them. They suffer because of their own wrongdoing.

Moreover, the family of the perpetrator may endure lasting harm on account of the foolhardy choice made by the thief. How is it fair to shift the blame away from the wrongdoer and say that God is somehow responsible? Since the Garden of Eden we humans have been given over to the habit of committing this logical fallacy. As a popular song goes, "People are strange, God only knows..."

Suffering As Discipline

Now, this is not to say that God never uses such things to discipline mankind. Sacred Scripture has many examples of such things being employed as a punitive measure to bring judgment upon rebellious men, from the explosive phenomenon that destroyed Sodom and the cities of the *kikkar* or circle of the Jordan (Gen. 19:24ff), to the locust plague in the book of Joel (1:4ff), to the Roman destruction of Jerusalem and of the Jewish economy and homeland in the war of AD 66-71 (Matt. 24:1ff; Mark 13:1ff; Luke 21:5ff). But these facts do not equate to the conclusion that God is responsible for any and every incident that causes pain and suffering to any part of the human race. It is wrong-headed and unfair to the God of Abraham, Isaac, Jacob, and Jesus to blame Him for any particular case of human suffering that He has not directly taken credit for.

So, the world that God has created is the only truly possible world that permits these two necessary things to co-exist:

1. Human free will and free moral choice.
2. Human capacity to choose right and do good as well as to choose badly and commit evil.

If God had wanted to create a world without human free will and free moral choice, He could have done so. Had He done so, however, those persons who would have inhabited that world could not have chosen to do right, because of course they could not have such a choice without also having the option to do that which is wrong.

GOD DOES EXIST!

This is the very real conundrum we find ourselves in once we travel down this road, logically speaking. The implications are thus the same for both wrongdoing and rightdoing. There are no real choices unless both options are involved. There is no such thing as free moral choice unless the subject can choose either good or evil.

What about the Good?

Man could never do as much good as he has done throughout the ages if other men did not have the choice to do as much evil as they have done. Consider for a moment the implications of this. If we were to challenge you to make a list of all of the good people you have known in your life and to make a mental note of all of the good things that they have done that you have seen and heard done by them, that list might be quite extensive. It would probably begin with your loving parents and extend into the present with your spouse and other family members.

But there would be others as well. Think about, for example, the neighbor who brought you food when you or someone in your family was sick. Or, the friend who loaned you money when you lost your wallet or left your purse at home. What about the kind words spoken to you when a loved one passed away? Remember what it felt like when you hurt yourself and your mother held you tightly and reassured you that everything would be OK soon? Remember the loving words of encouragement that your father said to you when you felt depressed or lonely? How many kindnesses have there been that you have received from friends or family, and even at times from complete strangers?

For most of us the number would be staggering, if we were even able to count them at all! There is a lot of good in this world, in spite of the fact that we fully understand that there is also much evil. All of us would agree, though, that there is far more good in the world than there is evil. There may be times in our lives and even times in human history when it seems the other way around, but on balance the ledger is always more full on the side of good. And none of this would be possible if it were not for the possibility of evil.

Occasionally we hear a line like this one: "The peace and quiet of this friendly small town was disturbed last evening by a terrible murder, an act of unthinkable evil. The last time there was a killing in this lovely little

The Argument from the Existence of Evil in the World

hamlet was over fifty years ago. . . ." During that period of five decades innumerable acts of kindness, generosity, neighborliness, and charity went unnoticed by the rest of the world. But when a single act of evil caught the attention of the national media, people at last took notice of this tiny place and its beautiful people. This diminutive community where the unthinkable happened late one night illustrates perfectly the concept which we are trying to explain.

In order for there to be so many years of good, and such an unbroken string of kindnesses, there has to be the option for evildoers to work their occasional mayhem and madness. This is the world that God has created. For the one to be present, the other must be conceivable and even possible. Make no mistake about it; it could not have been any other way.

Free Choice

Know this, then, good and evil is all about one thing: choice. Choices are at the heart of both. Every time a good deed is performed by any one anywhere in the world, a choice has been made by someone. They have chosen to sacrifice their time, money, ability, or effort to help someone or something else.

Likewise, if an evil deed is done by someone, a choice has been made by some other person who may not even have thought through the ultimate consequence of what they have chosen. They have freely chosen selfishness and elected to place their own wants and wishes ahead of the needs of others. Bad choices are frequently evil choices. Morally reprehensible choices. Sometimes they are unlawful choices.

What follows in the wake of those decisions may be equally as painful for the wrongdoer as it was for the victim(s). A person who steals what another has worked to pay for might spend time in prison to "pay his debt to society," or may even pay with his life if he attempts to take from an armed man. Our choices and consequent actions are not without repercussions.

When God granted men the capacity for free will He understood that there had to be an option for evil or else the choice itself would be meaningless. And when evil is chosen, responsibility for that choice brings about what are sometimes exceedingly harsh consequences. The one follows the other just as the night follows the day. Alvin Plantinga

GOD DOES EXIST!

succinctly states what he calls the "free will defense" of God in the presence of evil in the world:

> A world containing creatures who freely perform both good and evil actions—and do more good than evil—is more valuable than a world containing quasi-automata who always do what is right because they are unable to do otherwise. Now God can create free creatures, but He cannot causally or otherwise determine them to do only what is right; for if He does so then they do not do what is right *freely*. To create creatures capable of moral good, therefore, He must create creatures capable of moral evil but He cannot create the possibility of moral evil and at the same time prohibit its actuality. And as it turned out, some of the free creatures God created exercised their freedom to do what is wrong; hence moral evil. The fact that free creatures sometimes err, however, in no way tells against God's omnipotence or against His goodness; for He could forestall the occurrence of moral evil only by removing the possibility of moral good (*God and Other Minds,* 132).

Moses therefore warned the Israelites about how important it is to make such choices as they encountered with great circumspection and careful consideration of what the consequences might prove in the end to be:

> Today I am giving you a choice. You can choose life and success or death and disaster (Deut. 30:15, 19).

"You can choose life and success or death and disaster." That says it pretty well! No choice is more thoroughly a life and death decision! This passage states that which is the general teaching of the Bible. The ancient prophetic voice set before men the alternatives and possibilities of the future. It said to men, on many occasions we might add, that you may go one way or the other. You have the choice. The choice is yours, and yours alone. But whichever way you choose, there are going to be consequences.

Now that concept is not foreign to us whether we believe in God or not. We understand the idea of the inevitability of consequences. They confront us at every bend in the road. All of our actions lead us eventually toward some inevitable destination. The only conceivable way to avoid the destination is to take the right route in the first place. As the

The Argument from the Existence of Evil in the World

old saying goes: "The road to hell is paved with good intentions." Once you are on the road to that destination, your intentions matter little.

How Did Man Go So Wrong?

Scripture gives an explanation for seemingly-gratuitous evil in the world. In fact there are several. God is not like a man who cannot see past the next corner. A human being must wait to round it in order to get a perspective on what awaits him there. God sees the end before the beginning. Time does not matter at all to Him. For mankind it is measured by the revolutions of the sun and moon. Both of these heavenly luminaries, along with all of the stars in the sky, are part of the physical universe. God created them but stands apart from and outside of them. He is timeless, existing beyond space and time. And since He created both space and time, they are subject to the whims of His creative power and alterable at His command.

Where did man go so wrong? How did his moral status become so utterly twisted and frighteningly tainted? What has taken him from the *imago dei* or image of God (Gen. 1:27) to the point where he is capable of virtually anything, no matter how vile and disgusting: mass murder, raping and pillaging, enslavement of human populations, brutality and torture, and even racial and ethnic genocide? How could men stoop so low? What brought us to this point?

The Holy Bible tells the story of the degradation of mankind even though some readers do not wish to give it any credibility and pretend that the narrative is nothing more than myth and legend. But, like it or not, it is hard to explain our present depraved and broken condition without giving it some credence. It all began with a heart problem. As the prophet Jeremiah noted, "The heart is deceitful above all things, and desperately sick; who can understand it" (Jer. 17:9; see also Mark 7:21-23; John 3:19). The heart issue derived from a tendency toward rebellion against God's original purposes and plans for us (Gen. 3:1-24). Pride and independence of spirit, along with simple curiosity and a limitless imagination, wrought all sorts of thankless attitudes in the human ego. Over the long ages, the issue became increasingly worse to the point where it was virtually universal in the human family, as Paul explained: "None is righteous, no, not one..." (Rom. 3:10-18).

GOD DOES EXIST!

At the same time, the creation itself seems destined at every turn to frustrate all of man's efforts at peaceful coexistence with his fellow creatures along with the environment itself. It is as if the entire creation "was subjected to futility, not willingly, but because of him who subjected it" (Rom. 8:20). With its extremes of cold and heat, tidal waves, tornadoes, cyclones, tropical storms, volcanoes, floods, droughts, bacteria and viruses, and such things, it appears that the planet itself is at war with all of us, and hastens to assure our extermination. The whole realm really and truly seems to be cursed (Gen. 3:17ff)! On this account, earth can never be confused with heaven. Perhaps this was the intention all along? The apostle further explained that it is as if the whole created order was "groaning and travailing" in its present state of corruption, looking forward to the doom of the current order while anticipating the revelation of the next one (8:21-22).

But in Christ Jesus this whole sorry mess was attended to in the only way it could be while the present order yet stands. In the life and vicarious suffering of the Messiah Jesus, deliverance from the sin issue became not only a very real possibility, but a *fete accompli* (Rom. 6:16-22; Eph. 2:1-3; 1 Cor. 2:14). "God was in Christ reconciling the world to himself" (2 Cor. 5:19).

Man in his rebellion against his Creator has descended into the depths of depravity and evil. Often the very people who object so tenaciously to the notion that God exists are the same ones who argue most vociferously against the idea of divine law and human accountability to it. At the heart of all such thinking is rebellion against divine authority.

The destination that such reasoning takes the wayfarer toward is entirely predictable. In fact, there is almost nothing that some men will not do. Jude likened them in their aberrant behaviors to brute beasts (Jude 10). In point of fact, they are much worse than mere beasts. The cruelty and viciousness of human predators is seldom equaled by the most savage of animals. But the depth of their depravity is beside the point. In fact, it can prove to be a distraction from that which is the main issue involved. Paul wrote that "all have sinned and fallen short of the glory of God" (Rom. 3:23). If we are not careful we may want to compare ourselves with the worst of the lot and think that we are somehow better off. Whether we are alienated from God a little or a lot, though, the

The Argument from the Existence of Evil in the World

result is the same, and so we must not be motivated to measure our own circumstances with theirs and take solace that our transgressions are not as bad as those of others.

Is There a Solution?

Jesus explained that repentance was the only appropriate response for mankind in the face of this unfortunate development in the divine-human relationship (Luke 13:3). "Repentance" is just a word in the vocabulary of religion, as far as most moderns are concerned. We may wish to pass it off as antiquated terminology from a bygone era. But it is more than simply this, you can be assured.

Certainly this is true on God's side of the equation. Let us illustrate the point. If you were to have a dear friend for whom you had done many favors and made frequent sacrifices over a lifetime, and this person on one day thoughtlessly embarrassed and humiliated you and then the next day acted as if nothing had happened—would you not expect from him some kind of explanation and apology for his actions prior to resuming the relationship as previously? Frankly, in most cases it would be the end of that friendship unless some meaningful explanation was forthcoming or at least a sincere apology given. Why would we expect it to be any different with God than it would be with any other friend? A shattered relationship requires certain expected actions to be taken for it to be repaired before it can go forward.

In our time most folks consider the idea of divine indignation to be verboten. Somehow they consider it to be beneath the dignity of God to be angry at human evil doing. But they ignore His own revelations about His personal nature in Scripture and seem not to notice how like Him we truly are, even if imperfectly so. Croatian Protestant theologian Marslav Volf, professor at Yale, writing about how personal experience shaped his notion of this harsh but essential reality, commented thus:

> My people (were) shelled, day in and day out, some of them brutalized beyond imagination, and I could not imagine God not being angry... Though I used to complain about the indecency of the idea of God's wrath, I came to think I would have to rebel against a God who wasn't wrathful at the sight of the world's evil. God isn't wrathful in spite of being love. God is wrathful because God is love (*Free of Charge*, 139).

GOD DOES EXIST!

God is angry at us at times because in His truest essence He is love. That must not be forgotten or ignored. Anger and love are not inconsistent realities. Wrath and punishment are entirely appropriate responses to certain human behaviors, in spite of what progressives would have us think. Current progressive thinking on such matters is a fad that will eventually pale into obsolescence because it is impractical at every level. It is also inconsistent with human nature as well as with the divine nature.

The god that is venerated by many liberal thinkers in our time is no different than Baal or Asherah or Moloch in the Old Testament. It is a false god of their own making. They have concocted it of the stuff of their own thinking. It suits their way of life and approves of their cherished beliefs. That is why they adore it and give it what homage they do.

Why So Much Evil?

Why is there so much evil in the world? The answer to this question is really quite simple. This is so because there are so many people, so many sinful humans! Again, Scripture explains this whole sordid conundrum. God has permitted our wickedness to run its full course, so that man could realize what life without Him is like (Rom. 1:24, 26, 28). In the cross God, who loved His own creatures in spite of all of their flaws and spiritual maladies, went so far as to rescue them personally. He entered the human experience, and even went to the extreme of suffering and death to deliver them from their own self-destructive ways (cf. Rom. 5:8-10; 8:18; Rev. 21:5).

Conclusion

For the faithful Christian, pain and suffering has a special meaning in our lives, given God's clarification of the doctrine in the case of the apostle Paul's "thorn in the flesh" (2 Cor. 12:7). He explained that it was on the one hand a messenger from Satan and on the other an opportunity to learn more about the grace of God:

> And lest I should be exalted above measure by the abundance of the revelations, a thorn in the flesh was given to me, a messenger of Satan to buffet me, lest I be exalted above measure. Concerning this thing I pleaded with the Lord three times that it might depart from me. And he said to me, "My grace is sufficient for you, for my strength is made perfect in weakness." Therefore most gladly I will rather boast in my infirmi-

The Argument from the Existence of Evil in the World

ties, that the power of Christ may rest upon me. Therefore I take pleasure in infirmities, in reproaches, in needs, in persecutions, in distresses for Christ's sake. For when I am weak, then I am strong (2 Cor. 12:7-12).

From this text, we learn that there are times when human pain and suffering are used by the Almighty to teach and train those whom He loves. Who knows whether at other times He may be employing it as a vehicle to train those outside of the family of God as well? Certainly it suggests to us that there may be a great many reasons as to which we may have no clue, but where God has some rationale behind it that is invisible or even incomprehensible to us from our current this-world orientation.

Also, our limited intellectual powers may preclude us from ever seeing the justification while we dwell in this fleshly body, but that does not mean that it is unjustified or even unjust. And, whereas the skeptic has no trust in God under such circumstances, the Christian generally lives by faith in Him and so does not require that every particular be explained to him. As Job said, "Though he slay me, yet will I trust in him" (Job 13:15).

Questions for Discussion

1. How is God the best explanation for the concept of moral evil? Is it possible to speak of moral evil without having the notion of God and accountability to Him somewhere in the picture?

2. Why do we not make moral judgments about Bengal tigers when they eat humans? Why do we fail to judge grizzly bears when they kill and consume people? Why not? Why do we judge and condemn people who do the same thing? Is it right to do so?

3. Are there inherent dangers to existence in a physical world? Would those same dangers exist in a non-material, spiritual world?

4. Is it important to recognize the importance of potential good in the world as well as potential evil? In your own experience can you say that there is more good or evil in the world?

5. In the matter of choice for good or evil, how is this idea significant in an understanding of the presence of so much moral depravity in the world?

GOD DOES EXIST!

6. How did the human race get it so wrong for so long? What explains the depravity of the human condition?

7. How does God's love explain His anger at so many evil actions taken by wicked men and women? Does God love the victims of genocide or mass extermination? If so, would it be right and proper for Him to ignore their pain and suffering? Would it be just for Him to reward or else fail to punish those who have perpetrated such evil in the world?

8. Romans 8 deals with the brokenness of the world system as it currently stands. How does it characterize it, and with what language does it depict the end result? To what does the writer look as the eventual righting of all wrongs and correcting of the system?

9. How does Christ in His life and death on the cross provide us with at least one magnificent instance of suffering that led to broad-based, even universal, good? What does the New Testament mean when it says that "God was in Christ reconciling the world to himself"? What did suffering have to do with that?

10. How did Paul's "thorn in the flesh" illustrate for us the possibility that pain and suffering might be employed in our own lives in order to teach and instruct us? In such a case, would it be better for us to grouse and complain, or give God thanks for His discipline and instruction?

Chapter 13
The "Hiddenness" of God Argument

The Problem Stated

Why is God so hidden from us, our eyes, ears, and our other senses? Why does He not merely speak with us and say, "I am here!" Beyond this, why does He not communicate with all of us on a regular basis? The skeptic tells us that if any God at all exists, this is the way that it should be and this is what He ought to do.

Why does He not make His existence more obvious to us than He has? Why is He seemingly invisible to us in the physical world? Why can we not hear His voice with our ears or see His visage with our eyes? One notable atheist was asked what he would say to God if when he died he found out the deity did actually exist all the while. To this question he replied: "I would ask him why he did not make His existence more apparent to me." It seems as if the existence of God is more clear to some than

GOD DOES EXIST!

it is to others. This is owing to the nature of the evidence proffered. But it is also dependent upon the openness of the observer to the conclusion to which it leads. Belief in a personal God has important ramifications.

Often I have attempted to feed my dog a pill that was prescribed for him by the veterinarian. He is both stubborn and smart, however. If the pill is concealed in his food, he will notice it and slosh it around in his mouth until he has swallowed the good stuff and then he will spit out the pill by itself. I have wrestled him down and tried to force it down his gullet, but somehow he will lead me to believe it went down and then I will discover it on the floor later. He does not like pills and he refuses to take them. His obstinacy is maddening! People are sometimes like my Boxer. Let's face it, some human beings are not going there, no matter the force or weight of the evidence! God is a pill that they cannot tolerate and will never swallow.

Too, there are other questions that also occur to certain inquiring minds. For example, why does He not "step in" at certain critical times to defend His own honor? The skeptic sometimes screams at heaven and even curses God, demanding that if He is "up there" He ought to react in some way in order to prove Himself and show that He is real. This is yet another important question that is posed by a few non-believers in order to challenge the idea that God exists but chooses not to behave as they expect He should. For our part, believers could wish that He would do so at times, violently if necessary, in order to convince deniers of His reality and power. But that is His decision and not ours to make.

The next question touches the heart for those who justly deserve relief and rescue from pain and suffering. Why does He not "step in" to defend the helpless and the innocent? By definition God has both the power and the capacity to do so. Why does He not?

These are the kinds of questions the skeptics ask regularly to challenge His existence.

Atheist J. L. Schellenberg states the case this way:

Premise 1: If there is a God, he is perfectly loving.
Premise 2: If a perfectly loving God exists, reasonable nonbelief does not occur.
Premise 3: Reasonable nonbelief occurs.

The "Hiddenness" of God Argument

Conclusion 1: No perfectly loving God exists (from points 2 and 3).
Conclusion 2: Hence, there is no God (from 1 and 4).

This argument, stated as it is, assumes that each person must be presented with sufficient evidence so that God could not be denied. In fact, there are serious difficulties with this approach to the evidence.

This also assumes that every human is perfectly reasonable and would be convinced if the right evidence were presented to him. But is this true? Do any of us really believe that? In fact, as fallible human beings we often dismiss evidence in order to hold to what we desire to be true. In the case regarding the existence of God this is a particularly troubling proposition. To admit that God exists has life changing implications. Under certain modes of thought about it, it requires accountability to a sovereign Maker and implies the possibility of judgment. Under every conceivable approach to the subject these would not necessarily be inevitable implications, but the potential for them is certainly there in others.

Many skeptics therefore harbor the sincere hope that there is no God. And a few will gladly confess this is so. One particular atheist even said as much. Thomas Nagel wrote: "I hope there is not a God! I don't want there to be a God; I don't want the universe to be like that..." (*The Last Word*, 130-131). For such people this is not an attempt at ascertaining what the truth of the matter might be. They have already predetermined the outcome. Their mind is and always has been made up. The very thought of God is something that makes them uncomfortable. It is therefore hard to imagine that they would give what evidence there is a fair and impartial hearing.

Aldous Huxley is another who wrote candidly on this matter. He said: "The philosophy of meaninglessness was essentially an instrument of liberation. The liberation we desired... from a certain system of morality. We objected to the morality because it interfered with our sexual freedom..." (*Collected Essays*, 366).

Again, the evidence for God must be given in conjunction with the freedom of man not to believe and not to love and serve God. The God of creation will not force one to believe in Him any more than He will

GOD DOES EXIST!

require people to love and serve Him. In each and every case, the free choice of a self-reliant and independent individual is determinative of an acceptable relationship with the Creator. That is the clear teaching of the Hebrew Bible and of Christian Scripture. God has no desire to have fellowship with robots or automatons. Had He made that choice, He would have enjoyed total compliance with all of His commands. But robots are not capable of free choice. So it is not possible for them to love Him or choose to thank, praise, or worship Him. Only beings with the liberty not to do so can make the choice to do that. And that is what He is after. That is what He wants and who He wants.

Forcing people to believe would violate their freedom. So, what type of evidence could God offer, besides what He has offered, that would not remove or somehow violate human freedom? That is the critical factor which must be considered. Thus, human freedom of choice is the key idea in the entirety of the relationship between God and man. Human persons enjoy the unbridled liberty either to praise or to curse their Creator. That is not to suggest that there will not be repercussions to follow, whichever direction is selected. Regardless, the latter is the easier and less demanding option.

Consequently, one does the first while another does the second. And even though this freedom is not unlimited or without further implications, the present status of things in the material world is unaltered by either response. That is exactly the way that God intended it. On this account many skeptics are further encouraged to renounce God at every turn. Believers, on the other hand, are undeterred in their resolve to love and serve Him. They understand that their liberty to do either one is the reason that God wants them for His own. In a world where men and women can select either to love Him and serve Him, or not, their free and fully conscious choice is to have God in their hearts and lives.

Again, in a world where many around them are skeptical and unbelieving, believers freely choose to accept the abundant and compelling proof that the Sovereign God has chosen to submit for their intelligent consideration and embrace it as both convincing and assuring. That is what is meant by the term "believer" on the question of whether or not God is.

The "Hiddenness" of God Argument

Coming to Know God on His Terms

At the same time, human beings do not have the right to know God on their own terms. Making demands of their Maker is a task that is "above their pay grade." Being that He is the Creator and we are His creation, it is His choice as to how and in what ways He will make Himself known. As the prophet Isaiah said, "You have no right to argue with your Creator. You are merely a clay pot shaped by a potter. The clay doesn't ask, 'Why did you make me this way? Where are the handles?'" (Isa. 45:9 CEV).

So, we must come to know Him on His terms. The evidence, of the kind and sort that He has elected to provide, will have to suffice. It is all there is or ever will be on this side of eternity. It goes without saying that on many occasions in the past atheists and agnostics have pointed out that the evidence which has been presented to them is not of the kind that they require in order for them to be convinced. This reminds us of some hardcore jurors in a murder trial who demand an eyewitness to the event itself in order for them to agree to convict the killer. They seem not to recognize that the majority of murderers are smart enough to choose a time and place where there are no witnesses to see the crime being committed. They therefore make an unrealistic or impossible demand for the prosecutor.

Circumstantial evidence will have to do, in a startling number of cases, because that is all there is. In addition, most prosecutors will tell us about the ineffectiveness of certain eyewitnesses as well as the powerful potential of a few kinds of circumstantial evidence. Any prosecutor will tell you that he or she must use what evidence he or she has. Wishing and hoping for a different kind of proof than what is available will not suffice. They will go to court with what they have. And if the corroboration is strong enough, of whatever nature it may be, they will be validated in their conviction that the perpetrator is guilty by the fact that the jurors are convinced by the case that is made.

We do not have the freedom to choose what sort of evidence God is going to provide in order to establish that He exists. That is what the old timers called "whittling on God's end of the stick." God made that choice at creation. As the Creator, He left His own personal "fingerprints" on the product of His innovative and extensive creative work. As investigators might look for fingerprints and DNA evidence that establishes

GOD DOES EXIST!

the prior presence of a suspect at a crime scene, it is up to us to look for marks of the Creator's genius and imaginative technique in His creation. Moreover, as we have seen, the evidence is plentiful and varied. All that is needed is an objective juror who will hear the case devoid of bias.

Selfish Demands

But one thing needs to be understood by all who call themselves "investigators." The path to God cannot possibly start with the selfish demand that He reveal Himself in a particular way to us or else! Assume for a moment that God does exist and that someone laid out terms of that kind. If you were God in such a situation, how would that make you feel? It would be very much like a small child standing before his parents stamping his feet and demanding that the father or mother explain their actions on a certain point, and that they do so "here and now!" Not many parents would take that kind of insolence lightly. Most would be angry and some would react by giving a child of that sort a good tongue lashing or even a painful paddling. And such punitive measures would be richly deserved.

How "Hidden" Is He?

Even so, all of this *assumes* that God is as truly hidden as is generally claimed. But, is this actually the case? Is God really as "hidden" as atheists and "God hypothesis" skeptics have frequently maintained? We would argue that in point of fact, exactly the opposite is true. If the arguments we have set forth in these earlier chapters of this book are valid, then God has not "left himself without witness" (Acts 14:17). Instead, He has made Himself known in a whole host of compelling ways.

However, it must be recalled that, in the first place, God is a spiritual being and not a part of the material creation. As such, He exists quite apart from that which is the product of His manufacture. Pantheistic religion argues that God is a part of His creation or perhaps even "one" with what He has caused to exist. But there is no indication from the universe itself that this is an accurate depiction. And no compelling argument can be made logically to that effect. Certainly the Bible teaches the exact opposite.

God's Revelation of Himself

The three great monotheistic religions which claim divine revelation as their source of information on the subject of origins are unani-

The "Hiddenness" of God Argument

mous in declaring the opposite to be true. God made the universe. But God exists outside of this realm and away from this physical mode of being. This being true, in order for any sort of acknowledgement to take place or communication to occur, some sort of abridgment of the two realms must occur.

In other words, there must be some kind of "miracle" for this to happen. The ordinary state of affairs will have to be altered for a moment in time. The regular will have to be replaced for an instant by the extraordinary. At that point the communication will be cleared for its occurrence. Until and unless that happens, the wall of separation between the two realms (assuming for the sake of argument that both realms actually exist), no transmission of information from the one to the other is conceivable.

In order to get some sense of the problem involved in this whole thing, there has to be some recognition of the utter separateness of the two realms of which we speak. The physical and the metaphysical are poles apart, in fact, worlds apart. And since we as human beings live in only one of those realms and have but the faintest notion of the other, it is hard for us fully to understand the difficulties and challenges of bridging the enormous gap between them. Certainly we as humans are incapable of venturing beyond our own circumstances in this physical realm in order to explore the other.

Seeing Is Believing?

When skeptics acknowledge their inability to know God or perceive that other reality, they are simply admitting the obvious. They can only see that which is in front of their eyes. But when they deny that God and the metaphysical exists, then they are failing to recognize or admit their own very real limitations in this regard. Most of us have not visited the moon or any of the planets in our solar system, but we readily admit their existence. Alpha Centauri is the nearest star to our own, and no human has ever traveled there other than in dreams or fantasies such as science fiction stories, yet we unanimously recognize its reality as such. The fact that we have not personally experienced these heavenly bodies by visiting them does not lead us to deny what the evidence tells us about them.

GOD DOES EXIST!

Some men have been to the moon and have returned with evidence of their visits. Moon rocks and moon dust and photographs are their proof. Most of us are not skeptical of their claims or doubtful of the proof they have shared with us. However, I knew a man once who disputed their claims and doubted their evidence. He argued that the photos and films of the landings were all created on a film set in Hollywood, California. He could not be convinced otherwise. He lived and later died while skeptical of that which most of us take for granted as fact.

Most of us would consider his beliefs to be ridiculous. We watched as those astronauts took off from the earth in front of a fiery inferno of rocket fuel, and we saw their re-entry craft as it floated down and then splashed in the ocean. Not to mention the scenes we beheld as they bounded from place to place on the surface of the moon. Could the whole thing have been faked by the government for some untoward reason? Certainly it could. But we cannot think of a plausible reason to think that is the way the thing went down. On this account, most of us consider NASA's various moon landings, six in all so far, to have been real history and not Hollywood fantasy, in spite of the arguments from naysayers like my dear but deluded friend.

I have never seen or experienced Moscow in Russia, but I have never been so foolish as to deny that the place exists or that others may have been there and experienced it. Friends of mine have gone there, and I have seen pictures of it. Therefore, the considerable evidence that there is such a place seems overwhelming to me. Likewise, even though I have not seen God with my eyes or spoken with Him directly, I would never be so foolish as to deny that He exists, especially since He has provided me with so many undeniable proofs of His spiritual reality.

Many people would find it surprising to know that the present complete preoccupation with the things and the outlook of this world has not always been the case. The widespread acceptance of atheism, or at least of agnosticism, is a new thing in human history. Emil Brunner observed that the special claim of Christianity to be a religion of revelation long has been an accepted concept generally in all previous societies where the Christian religion flourished, and was even so in the pagan cultures of the Greco-Roman world. The notion that God might have chosen to reveal Himself to humanity was not at all foreign; in point of

The "Hiddenness" of God Argument

fact it was virtually omnipresent in all of those earlier societies. It took many different forms, but it was always there:

> The most characteristic element of the present age, and that which distinguishes it from earlier periods in history, is almost complete disappearance of the sense of transcendence and the consciousness of revelation. In the ancient world in which the Christian Church first arose, the idea of revelation, and the belief that there was such a thing as revelation, was something that belonged to life as such; it was taken for granted. "Revelation," it is true, stood for a variety of conceptions: for primitive mantic practices of divination in order to discover the will of the gods; for oracles, seers, theophanies, and divine signs and wonders; or again for the teaching of thinkers who claimed to have received supernatural "illumination" in a state of ecstasy. But in whatever way revelation took place, and whatever its content may have been, the fact that revelation, as the proclamation of divine mysteries to man, did take place was generally believed. In the last resort all religion is based upon supposed or genuine revelation; moreover, in the ancient world the phenomenon of irreligion, and skepticism concerning the reality, or even the possibility, of revelation, was at first completely unknown, and even in late antiquity it was still exceptional. In the Middle Ages Christianity became dominant in the Western world. The revealed faith was the Christian faith, and this faith had practically axiomatic validity. Even a person who had not the slightest intention of being really religious, and of bringing his life into accordance with his faith, did not doubt that, as a whole, that which the Church proclaimed, about the divine revelation in the Holy Scriptures was the truth.
>
> Since the Renaissance, however, at first in the minds of the more daring spirits and then increasingly in wider and wider circles, a new mentality has gradually emerged: that of complete preoccupation with the things of this world, and an immaterial philosophy. For the first time in world history there is a mass atheism, and a completely secular culture; hand in hand with this there goes a kind of religion of "this world only," in which the very conception of revelation has no place. People come to believe that this universe which is evident to the senses and to the understanding is the sole reality. . . no one has any desire for a "revelation," either in the sense in which it was understood in the ancient world, or, still less, in the Christian sense. . . . Whatever cannot be proved scientifically is either not quite true or not quite certain. All that lies beyond the perception of the senses and the conclusions of logic, all that cannot be proved and verified experimentally, is "subjec-

GOD DOES EXIST!

tive," "hypothetical," or improbable and incredible. The Christian claim to revelation stands in the sharpest possible opposition to this conception of truth. For here the Church proclaims as absolute truth that which can be neither proved by the intellect nor verified by experience. Hence the Christian doctrine of revelation is regarded with the greatest mistrust (*Revelation and Reason*, 4-6).

It is fair to say that recent generations, and those within Western society in particular, represent the first in human existence to deny broadly this widely-held conviction. The reader would do well to remember this fact. It is always difficult for a person to divorce himself or herself from the *Zeitgeist* (i.e., the ideas and spirit of the time) of any particular age. Pressure from peers and professors is real and powerful. Ours is clearly an age of skepticism and agnosticism, if not of outright atheism, and that must be recalled. All around us there are people who sneer at the notion of God's existence, and of the idea that there is another realm besides this physical one. Likewise, they scoff at the suggestion of divine revelation. Some of you who are reading this book may be doing so also.

But let us remind the reader of how especially arrogant this claim sounds: in all of human history this is the first time that any large number of people have doubted the existence of God, have disputed that there is a realm beyond this material world, and have denied the reality, or even the possibility, of divine revelation! For some reason or other, every age of mankind before us has clung to these ideas, and yet the fact that a substantial number of elite professors and professional scientists in our own time, claim that these notions are impossible and that they ought to be given no consideration at all, seems to us to be enormously pretentious! And to be motivated thoughtlessly to follow their imperious lead in such matters seems downright uncritical.

Beyond this, the biblical narrative suggests that God has revealed Himself often in human history, and in a great variety of different ways. Some may deem this to be an uncritical source of information. But it must be remembered that, for some reason or another, for many centuries people have looked to these ancient written works as a rich source of wisdom and of valid information about how to conduct a successful life.

The "Hiddenness" of God Argument

According to the epistle to the Hebrews there was a logical progression in His approach to revealing His true nature and the fullness of His will to mankind. Gradually over hundreds of years He progressively gave to the human family a deeper and successively more profound knowledge of Himself, until at last He commissioned His own Son to provide the most personal look at Himself that could ever be possible for a spiritual entity. The author of the letter explains it thus: "God who at various times and in various ways spoke in time past to the fathers by the prophets, has in these last days spoken to us by his Son..." (Heb. 1:1-2).

He revealed Himself through the prophets and then through His own Son. The Hebrew prophets were the media through whom God made Himself known in the earliest stages of the process. They preached and taught the people of their own particular generations and ultimately formed a continuous line of conduits revealing the divine mind.

Their disclosures were at first only paltry and simple. But over the many generations among whom they labored and to whom they spoke, the accumulation of their combined wisdom became quite formidable. The cumulative effect of their hundreds of prophetic utterances which predicted events and persons mightily attest that the invisible hand of God was using them for His own purposes. As Peter said, "No prophecy of Scripture comes from someone's own interpretation but men spoke from God being carried along by the Holy Spirit" (2 Pet. 1:21).

And so, thirty-nine written compositions were the lasting literary legacy of these courageous spokesmen, plentiful evidence that God wanted to be known and loved by His creation. They today constitute the Hebrew Bible. They are a miracle not only in the mode of their revealing, but also in the fact that they have persisted over the many centuries since they were first given. They have done so in spite of many attempts by hateful rulers and despots to erase them from the earth. Both aspects are further proof that God desires to be known by us. Thus, the notion that God has hidden Himself from His creatures is falsified thirty-nine times over!

And as significant as these marvelous documents were in their own right, they were only a prelude to the most significant aspect of this revelatory progression. The birth of a tiny babe, laid in a manger in Beth-

GOD DOES EXIST!

lehem of Judaea, was the ultimate realization of many centuries of preliminary work toward the fullness of the divine revelation.

"God with Us"

The prophet Isaiah had signaled hundreds of years prior that this particular child was to have a special designation. He was to play the most important role of all in this brilliant divine plan. The epithet chosen for Him was *Immanuel* or "God with Us" (Isa. 7:14). It was not accidental that this particular term was selected for usage in His particular case. Later in Isaiah He is called "Mighty God" along with several other very special names (Isa. 9:6). His divine nature was signalled through these interesting epithets. They declare that He was not a mere man. He was God in the fleshy body of a man (Gal. 4:4; Phil. 2:5-8; Col. 2:9).

For those who have either neglected or rejected His prophets and His Son, He has not left Himself without witnesses. He has revealed Himself in the artistry and genius of the material creation (Psa. 19:1-4; Rom. 1:20). His untold kindnesses to the human family over the millennia also attest His love and care (Acts 14:17).

The life of Jesus Christ was punctuated by hundreds of "miracles and signs" which proclaimed Him to be in deed and in truth "God in the flesh" (John 20:30-31). All four of His contemporary biographers attest to this fact. No other human being ever had such eye-witness claims made about Him. Both in number and in nature they were impressive. But His greatest feat of metaphysical power was realized in the final chapter of His life.

Jesus died by crucifixion, a cruel means of torturing and killing criminals at the time. But that was not the end of Him. He conquered death. The resurrection of Jesus proves to be the most powerful of the many evidences for God's power and might. Paul said that there were many, in fact over 500 people at one time, who saw Him after His resurrection (1 Cor. 15:4-8). It represents a divine intrusion into history in an impressive way intended to arrest the attention of any and all who will give attention.

Moreover, the nature of it was such that it gave confirmation to all that Jesus taught and certified every claim He made about Himself and God while He walked among men. As well, it established that He will someday sit as judge over all people:

The "Hiddenness" of God Argument

> The times of ignorance God overlooked, but now he commands all people everywhere to repent, because he has fixed a day on which he will judge the world in righteousness by a man whom he has appointed; and of this he has given assurance to all by raising him from the dead (Acts 17:30, 31, ESV).

What was all of this about, then? Of course, the answer to this question is, like love, "a many-splendored thing." There are a whole host of true answers to it. Scripture attests to this in a number of places in the Gospels and later also in the Epistles of the New Testament. But one of the main reasons that God went to the trouble and effort to send Jesus to earth was in order, more fully, *to reveal Himself!* As John explained in the first chapter of his gospel:

> No one has ever seen God. The only begotten Son, who is in the bosom of the Father, he has declared him (John 1:18).

In the case of this intriguing verse, most of the manuscripts and versions have "only begotten Son," following the *Textus Receptus,* the "received text" form prepared by the scholarly Erasmus (2nd edition, 1519), as it is rendered here. But the three oldest and most widely respected uncial manuscripts, which are of the Alexandrian text-type, have "the only God," "unique one, God," or "only begotten God" (the two substantive terms taken together, *monogenes theos,* may be read and has been read any of these ways). Two others of great antiquity and value also have "only-begotten God." A. T. Robertson judged that "this is undoubtedly the true text" of the passage. The RSV, NASB, ESV, and ISV translated it as they did on this account.

Interestingly, Origen cites this passage in *Contra Celsum* 7.21, penned about AD 248, with a Greek phrase that is appropriately rendered as, "the one and only (Son), being God." This is especially important to take notice of, for our purposes here, given that this reading of the text clearly provides very early attestation that the ancient church unequivocally held that Jesus was a divine person, and not a mere prophet or rabbi. Moreover, this view of the passage is entirely consistent with John's introductory Prologue. At 1:1c, he states, "And God was the Word" (*kai theos ēn ho logos*). Even though it is most often rendered as, "And the Word was God," the Greek phrase says the opposite. Why is this important? Because *theos* is clearly placed in "rhetorical exposure" in the Greek sentence. In other

GOD DOES EXIST!

words, the intention of the author is to accentuate this concept in the line. The divinity of Jesus as the Word of God is his primary stress.

Consequently, it is our firm contention, and that of an army of others like us, that this theological conclusion was not an interpretation of His nature forced upon the majority of Christianity by much later theologians. The *early* church believed and taught it. In fact, the *earliest* church was convinced of it. It is an unproven and unhistorical theory devised by a number of very liberal theologians that suggests otherwise. There is no proof for the actual existence of a period of church history wherein its writers and thinkers did not believe that Jesus was God. In reality, it was the belief that Jesus was divine that created the church and made Christian theology a distinctive body of religious opinion.

In another passage from the Gospel of John, when Philip suggested that Jesus show the Father (God) to him, he responded thus: "Whoever has seen me has seen the Father" (John 14:9). So, John says that Jesus came to "declare" God. Moreover, he asserted that Jesus claimed that if someone had seen Him, he had envisaged the Father God. In so saying He was not claiming to be God the Father, but as Paul would later explain, He was "the image of the invisible God" (Col. 1:15). Moreover, "in him the whole fullness of Godhood dwells bodily" (Col. 2:9). As the writer of the epistle to the Hebrews said, He was "the radiance of the glory of God, and the exact imprint of his nature" (Heb. 1:3).

A significant aspect of His task while on earth then was to reveal the true nature of deity. So, when we today encounter the Jesus of the New Testament narratives, we also have come to know God in the very way that Jesus was sent to earth in order to express. References that attest to this truth in the New Testament are plentiful. God was revealing Himself to the human family in the person, words and work of Jesus Christ.

Therefore, any argument that alleges that these foundational concepts reflect a later stage in the life of the ancient church cannot be taken seriously. Hundreds of Christian martyrs from the earliest years of the church would not have sacrificed their lives on behalf of a philosophical belief that Jesus of Nazareth was a brilliant philosopher or rabbi whose teachings guided their minds toward a nebulous "higher knowledge" but nothing more than that. They died for Him because they believed

The "Hiddenness" of God Argument

with all their hearts that He was God in the flesh. They were convinced that His victory over death presaged their own.

Of course, there are people who are convinced of this idea the Jesus legend grew with the passing of the years, and that He was not seen in those terms until later generations had expanded upon His original reputation. Critical scholarship holds that this is the explanation for the miracle stories told about Him in the four Gospels. At the same time it is acknowledged by one and all that this is nothing more than a hypothetical reconstruction of events. The initial stage or stages of the literature about which they speak so confidently are hypothetical in nature. There is no proof that they ever actually existed. All we really have is the documents as they presently stand.

Furthermore, this is not a popular view, even among Bible scholars, and it is not likely ever to be, and the vast majority of ordinary Christian believers will never be persuaded to buy into that notion! There is good reason behind their skepticism. The early Christian martyrs are the best evidence against this theory. Great numbers of intelligent human beings could not have been persuaded to suffer an agonizing death over high-sounding platitudes alone! The martyrs died for their faith in Jesus because they were certain that He was the Son of God, Almighty God incarnate, crucified for the atonement of their sins, and risen victorious from the grave. Nothing less will suffice to explain their willingness to suffer and die for Him.

Conclusion

It is our contention that God has not really hidden Himself at all. As Paul the apostle said so keenly, "He is not far from any of us, for in him we live, and move, and have our being" (Acts 17:27-28). He has disclosed His being and nature at every turn throughout time. The "hiddenness of God" is a myth. The reality is quite different from this common delusion.

What then may we conclude from all of these facts when they are taken together? The God who exists in another realm from our physical one is deeply concerned for His creation and intensely interested in the conduct of every person's life. He not only made us, but He is intent upon seeing us through to our ultimate destiny, whatever we choose for that to be. If we choose selfishness and alienation from Him, then that is our own choice to make. It should be recognized, though, that by choosing that now, we are choosing it forever. If we would prefer to spend an endless eternity in the bosom of His love, then that is our choice as well. By choosing communion with Him now, we are also making an eternal choice.

The life that we live while here on this earth, from a Christian perspective, is a proving ground of sorts that sets the stage for a superior realm, the likes of which we have not heretofore deigned to imagine. We believe this because we believe that God exists. We are convinced that the weight of the evidence is on the side of the believer. God has spoken in His own defense in a whole host of ways. If we decide to deafen ourselves to the sound of His voice, we ignore it to our own hurt. Hence, we must see to it that we do not refuse to hear Him who has spoken (Heb. 12:25). See that you refuse not Him who is speaking. . . .

Questions for Discussion

1. What questions do atheists and agnostics pose to believers in order to challenge the notion that God exists and has revealed Himself in nature and Scripture?

2. Is it reasonable to expect that God has revealed Himself or will reveal Himself in such a way as to satisfy the curiosity of every single person who decides to investigate whether or not He exists?

3. Why must God's revelation of Himself be accepted on His terms rather than on our terms?

4. In what way does Isaiah 45:9 apply to this issue?

5. Skeptics argue that God is hidden from human perception in every way. Is this argument convincing to you? If not, how would you respond to it?

6. What is the evidence that God has revealed Himself in this world, and thus is not nearly so "hidden" from our view as some have maintained?

7. Ought we to be skeptical of anything we have not personally seen, heard or experienced? Is this how we customarily treat places we have not visited or things we have not seen with our own eyes?

The "Hiddenness" of God Argument

8. How does John 1:18 and John 14:9 help us to comprehend the place Jesus plays in the revelation of God to the human family?
9. How important were the miracles and signs of Jesus in establishing His place in the divine plan to reveal God's nature and will for men and women? How does His resurrection from death play a part in the divine purpose? How significant was it in the plan, and why is this so?
10. Explain the distinction between the two realms represented by this world and the metaphysical one. How does it explain the reason that God is not visible to human eyes or audible to human ears?

Bibliography

Adams, Robert. "Moral Arguments for Theism," in *The Virtue of Faith and Other Essays in Philosophical Theology*. New York: Oxford University Press, 1987.

Alberts, B., Johnson, A., Lewis, J., Raff, M., Roberts, K., and Walter, P. (2002). "DNA Repair," in *Molecular Biology of the Cell* (4th ed.). New York: Garland Science. Retrieved from http://www.ncbi.nlm.nih.gov/books/NBK26879/#_A840.

Anderson, C. Anthony. "Some Emendations of Gödel's Ontological Proof." *Faith and Philosophy* 7 (July, 1990): 291-303.

Asimov, Isaac. *In the Beginning*. New York: Crown, 1981.

Baggett, David, and Walls, Jerry L. *God and Cosmos: Moral Truth and Human Meaning*. Oxford: Oxford University Press, 2016.

Bibliography

Barrow, J. D. "Cosmology, Life, and the Anthropic Principle." *Annals of the New York Academy of Sciences* 950.1 (2001): 139-153.

———. *New Theories of Everything.* Oxford: Oxford University Press, 2007.

Barrow, John D., and Tipler, Frank J. *The Anthropic Cosmological Principle.* Oxford: Oxford University Press, 1986.

Barrowclough, David. *A Short Guide to the Evolution of Human Intelligence: A Timeline for the Evolution of Homo Sapiens Over the Last Sixty Million Years.* Cambridge: Red Dagger Press, 2015.

Behe, Michael J. *Darwin's Black Box: The Biochemical Challenge to Evolution.* New York: Free Press, 1996, 2006.

Behe, Michael J., Dembski, W. A., Meyer, Stephen C. *Science and Evidence for Design in the Universe.* The Proceedings of the Wethersfield Institute 9. San Francisco: Ignatius Press, 2000.

Beiser, Frederick C. "Moral Faith and the Highest Good," in *The Cambridge Companion to Kant and Modern Philosophy.* Paul Guyer ed., 588-629. Cambridge: Cambridge University Press, 2006.

Benzmuller, Christoph, and Paleo, Bruno Woltzenlogel. "Automating Gödel's Ontological Proof of God's Existence with Higher-order Automated Theorem Provers." *ECIA* 2014. IOS Press. page.mi.fu-berlin.de/cbenzmueller/papers/C40.pdf.

Bettini, Stefano. "Anthropic Reasoning in Cosmology: A Historical Perspective." *Academia.edu.* https://www.academia.edu/922214/Anthropic_Reasoning_in_Cosmology_A_Historical_Perspective?swp=rr-rw-wc-4594964. Accessed 5/23/2020.

Birkett, Kirsten. "Conscious Objections: God and the Consciousness Debates." *Zygon* 41.2 (June 2006): 249-266.

Bondi, Hermann. *Cosmology.* 2nd edition. Mineola, NY: Dover Publications, Inc., 1960.

Brown, Malcolm W. "Clues to Universe Origin Expected." *New York Times* (12 March 1978): 54.

Brunner, Emil. *Revelation and Reason: The Christian Doctrine of Faith and Knowledge.* Translated by Olive Wyon. Philadelphia: Westminster Press, 1956.

GOD DOES EXIST!

Calvin, Melvin. *Chemical Evolution: Molecular Evolution Towards the Origin of Living Systems on Earth and Elsewhere.* Oxford: Clarendon Press, 1969.

Cartwright, Nancy. "Why Physics?" in *The Large, the Small, and the Human Mind*, ed. Roger Penrose, 161–68. Cambridge: Cambridge Univ. Press, 1997.

Chalmers, David J. *The Conscious Mind: In Search of a Fundamental Theory.* Philosophy of Mind Series. New York: Oxford University Press, 1996.

Clark, George. "Human Intelligence: An Amazing Evolutionary Mistake." *Academia.edu.* https://academia.edu/1022747/Human_intelligence_An_amazing_evolutionary_mistake?sm=a

Collins, Desmond. "Misadventures in the Burgess Shale," *Nature* 460 (2009): 952-53.

Collins, Robin. "The Fine-Tuning Design Argument: A Scientific Argument for the Existence of God," in *Reason for the Hope Within*. M. Murray ed. Grand Rapids: Eerdmans, 1999.

Copan, Paul, and Flannagan, Matthew. *Did God Really Command Genocide? Coming to Terms with the Justice of God.* Grand Rapids, MI: Baker Books, 2014.

Copan, Paul. *Is God a Moral Monster? Making Sense of the Old Testament God.* Grand Rapids, MI: Baker Books, 2011.

Craig, William Lane. *Apologetics: An Introduction.* Chicago: Moody Press, 1984.

———. *The Cosmological Argument from Plato to Leibniz.* London: Macmillan, 1980.

———. *The Kalām Cosmological Argument.* London: Macmillan, 1979.

———. *Reasonable Faith: Christian Truth and Apologetics.* 3rd edition. Wheaton, IL: Crossway, 2008.

Craig, William Lane, and Smith, Quentin. *Theism, Atheism, and Big Bang Cosmology.* Oxford: Oxford University Press, 1993.

Crick, Francis. *Life Itself: Its Origin and Nature.* New York: Simon and Schuster, 1981.

Bibliography

———. *The Astonishing Hypothesis: The Scientific Search for the Soul.* London: Touchstone, 1995.

Curley, E. M. *Descartes Against the Skeptics.* Cambridge, MA: Harvard University Press, 1978.

Davies, Paul. *The Cosmic Blueprint.* New York: Simon and Schuster, 1988.

———. *The Superforce.* New York: Simon and Schuster, 1984.

David, J. J. "The Design Argument, Cosmic Fine Tuning, and the Anthropic Principle." *Philosophy of Religion* 22 (1987): 139-50.

Della Rocca, M. "Descartes, the Cartesian Circle, and Epistemology Without God." *Philosophy and Phenomenological Research* 70.1 (January 2005): 1-33.

Dembski, William A. *The Design Inference.* Cambridge: Cambridge University Press, 1998.

———. *Intelligent Design: The Bridge Between Science and Theology.* Downers Grove, IL: Intervarsity Press, 1999.

Dicke, Robert H. "Dirac's Cosmology and Mach's Principle." *Nature* 192 (1961): 440-441.

Dilley, Frank B. "Taking Consciousness Seriously: A Defense of Cartesian Dualism." *International Journal of Philosophy of Religion.* 55.3 (June, 2004): 135-153.

Domingo, E. "Virus Evolution," in *Virus Evolution.* D. M. Knipe, et al., eds. 5th edition. Philadelphia, PA: Lippincott Williams and Wilkins, 2007.

Domingo, E., et. al. "Viruses as Quasispecies: Biological Implications." *Current Topics in Microbiology and Immunology* 299 (2006): 51-82.

Duraney, William Charles. *Kant's Moral Argument for the Existence of God.* Thesis. Washington, DC: Catholic University of America, 2015.

Eisley, Loren. *Darwin's Centenary: Evolution and the Men Who Discovered It.* New York: Doubleday, 1961.

Eldredge, Niles. *Reinventing Darwin.* New York: Wiley, 1996.

C. Stephen Evans, "Moral Arguments for the Existence of God." *Stanford Encyclopedia of Philosophy.* https://plato.stanford.edu/entries/moral-arguments-god/.

———. *Natural Signs and Knowledge of God: A New Look at Theistic Arguments*. Oxford: Oxford University Press, 2010.

Forsman, Jan. "Can An Atheist Know That He Exists? *Cogito*, Mathematics, and God in Descartes's *Meditations*." *International Journal for the Study of Skepticism* 9.2 (June 2019): 91-11.

Giberson, Karl W. "The Anthropic Principle." *Journal of Interdisciplinary Studies* 9 (1997): 63-90.

Greenstein, G. *The Symbiotic Universe: Life and Mind in the Cosmos*. New York: Morrow, 1988.

Groff, R. *Critical Realism, Post-positivism and the Possibility of Knowledge*. Routledge Studies in Critical Realism. London: Routledge Taylor and Francis Group, 2004.

Guth, A. *The Inflationary Universe: The Quest for a New Theory of Cosmic Origins*. Reading, MA: Addison-Wesley, 1997.

Guyer, Paul. *Kant on Freedom, Law and Happiness*. Cambridge: Cambridge University Press, 2000.

Hannam, James. *The Genesis of Science: How the Christian Middle Ages Launched the Scientific Revolution*. Washington, DC: Regnery Publishing, 2011.

Hare, J. *The Moral Gap*. Oxford: Clarendon Press, 1996.

Hasker, William. *The Emergent Self*. Cornell Studies in the Philosophy of Religion. London: Cornell University Press, 1999.

Hawking, Stephen. *A Brief History of Time*. New York: Bantam Books, 1988.

Hawking, Stephen, and Ellis, G. F. R. *The Large Scale Structure of Space-Time*. Cambridge: Cambridge University Press, 1973.

Hawking, Stephen, and Mlodinow, Leonard. *The Grand Design*. New York: Bantam Books, 2010.

Heller, M. *Creative Tension: Essays on Religion and Science*. Philadelphia: Templeton Foundation Press, 2003.

Holder, Rodney D. *God, the Multiverse, and Everything: Modern Cosmology and the Argument from Design*. Burlington, VT: Ashgate Pub. Ltd., 2004.

Bibliography

———. "The Realization of Infinitely Many Universes in Cosmology." *Religious Studies* 37.3 (Sept. 2001): 343-53.

Hou, Xian-guang, et al. *The Cambrian Fossils of Chengjiang, China.* Oxford: Blackwell, 2004.

Hoyle, Fred, et. al. "A State in C12 Predicted from Astrophysical Evidence." *Physical Review Letters* 92 (1953): 1095.

———. "The Universe: Past and Present Reflections." *Annual Review of Astronomy and Astrophysics* 20 (1982): 1-35.

Jacob, François. "Evolution and Tinkering." *Science* 196 (1977): 1161-1166.

Jaki, Stanley L. "The Biblical Basis of Western Science." *Crisis Magazine* (Oct. 1, 1997): 17-20. https://www.crisismagazine.com/1997/the-biblical-basis-of-western-science-2.

Jantzen, Benjamin. *An Introduction to Design Arguments.* Cambridge: Cambridge University Press, 2014.

Jaynes, Julian. *The Origin of Consciousness in the Breakdown of the Bicameral Mind.* Boston: Mariner Books, Houghton Mifflin, 2000.

Jastrow, Robert. *God and the Astronomers.* New York: W. W. Norton, 1978.

Johnson, Phillip E. *Defeating Darwinism by Opening Minds.* Downers Grove, IL: InterVarsity Press, 1997.

Jordan, Pascuel. *Die Herkunft der Sterne.* 2 Auflage. Stuttgart: Wissenschaftliche Verlagsgesellschaft, 1947.

Krauss, Lawrence M. "The End of the Age Problem and the Case for a Cosmological Constant Revisited." *Astrophysical Journal* 501 (1998): 461-466.

Kurtz, Paul. *Forbidden Fruit: The Ethics of Secularism.* Amherst, NY: Prometheus Books, 1988.

Larson, K. *Cosmology 101.* Westport, CT: Greenwood Press, 2007.

Lewis, C. S. *God in the Dock: Essays on Theology and Ethics.* Grand Rapids, MI: Wm. B. Eerdmans Publishing Co., 1970.

———. *Mere Christianity.* New York: The Macmillan Company, 1943.

GOD DOES EXIST!

———. *The Problem of Pain: How Human Suffering Raises Almost Intolerable Intellectual Problems*. New York: Macmillan Publishing Co., 1962.

Lincoln, Maya and Wasser, Avi. "Spontaneous Creation of the Universe *Ex Nihilo*." *Physics of the Dark Universe* 2.4 (Dec. 2013): 195-199. https://www.sciencedirect.com/science/article/pii/S221268641300037X.

Linville, M. "The Moral Argument," in *The Blackwell Companion to Natural Theology*, first edition, W. L. Craig and J. P. Mooreland, eds. West Sussex: Wiley-Blackwell, 2009.

McCulloch, Gregory. *The Mind and Its World*. The Problems of Philosophy. London: Routledge, 1995.

McGrath, Alister. *A Fine-Tuned Universe*. Louisville, KY: Westminster John Knox Press, 2009.

McMullin, Ernan. "How Should Cosmology Relate to Theology?," in *The Sciences and Theology in the Twentieth Century*. A. R. Peacocke, ed. Notre Dame, IN: University of Notre Dame Press, 17-57.

Meyer, Stephen C. *Signature in the Cell: DNA and the Evidence for Intelligent Design*. New York: HarperCollins Publishers, 2009.

———. "Evidence for Design in Physics and Biology: From the Origin of the Universe to the Origin of Life," in *Science and Evidence for Design in the Universe*, 53-111. The Proceedings of the Wethersfield Institute, Vol. 9. San Francisco: Ignatius Press, 2000.

———. "The Return of the God Hypothesis," *Journal of Interdisciplinary Studies* 11 (1999): 1-38.

———. *The Return of the God Hypothesis*. New York: HarperCollins Publishers, 2019.

Mithen, Stephen. *The Prehistory of the Mind: A Search for the Origins of Art, Religion and Science*. London: Thames and Hudson, 1996.

Moritz, Joshua. "Big Bang Cosmology and Christian Theology," in *Theology and Science: From Genesis to Astrobiology*. J. Seckbach and R. Gordon, eds. Singapore: World Scientific Publishing, 2018.

Moya, Andrés, et al. "The Evolution of RNA Viruses: A Population Genetics View." *Proceedings of the National Academy of Sciences* 97.13 (June 20, 2000): 6967-6973.

Bibliography

Muggeridge, Malcolm. *The End of Christendom*. Grand Rapids, MI: Eerdmans, 1980.

Muncaster, Ralph O. *Dismantling Evolution: Building the Case for Intelligent Design*. Eugene, OR: Harvest House Publishers, 2003.

Nagel, Thomas. *Mind and Cosmos: Why the Materialist Neo-Darwinian Conception of Nature Is Almost Certainly False*. New York: Oxford University Press, 2012.

Newman, John Henry. *An Essay in Aid of a Grammar of Assent*. London: Burns, Oates, and Co., 1870.

Penrose, Roger. *The Emperor's New Mind: Concerning Computers, Minds, and the Laws of Physics*. Oxford: Oxford University Press, 1989.

———. *Shadows of the Mind: A Search for the Missing Science of Consciousness*. Oxford: Oxford University Press, 1994.

———. *The Large, the Small, and the Human Mind*. Cambridge: Cambridge University Press, 1997.

Plantinga, Alvin. *God and Other Minds: A Study of the Rational Justification of Belief in God*. Ithica, NY: Cornell University Press, 1967.

Ramsey, Frank P. "Truth and Probability." *Readings in Formal Epistemology*. Horacio Arlo-Costa, et al., eds. Springer Graduate Texts in Philosophy, 1. Switzerland: Springer, Cham, 2016.

Rashdall, H. "The Moral Argument for Personal Immortality," in *King's College Lectures on Immortality*. London: University of London Press, 1920.

Ratzsch, Del. *The Battle of Beginnings: Why Neither Side Is Winning the Creation-Evolution Debate*. Downers Grove, IL: IVP, 1996.

Ritchie, A. *From Morality to Metaphysics: The Theistic Implications of Our Ethical Commitments*. Oxford: Oxford University Press, 2012.

Ross, Hugh. *The Creator and the Cosmos*. Colorado Springs, CO: NavPress, 2001.

———. *The Fingerprint of God*. 2nd edition. Orange, CA: Promise Publishing, 1991.

GOD DOES EXIST!

Ruse, Michael. "Evolutionary Theory and Christian Ethics," in *The Darwinian Paradigm*. London: Routledge, 1989.

Saward, Mark. "Fine-Tuning as Evidence for a Multiverse: Why White is Wrong." *International Journal for Philosophy of Religion* 73 (2013): 243-253.

Schaefer III, Henry F. "The Big Bang, Stephen Hawking, and God." 2004 New College Lecture Series. Center for Computational Quantum Chemistry. University of Georgia, Athens, GA. October 13, 2004. https://www.newcollege.unsw.edu.au/downloads/File/multimedia/pdfs/ 1c383cd30b7c298ab50293adfecb7b18.pdf.

Shroeder, G. L. *Genesis and the Big Bang*. New York: Bantam Books, 1992.

Sorley, W. R. *Moral Values and the Idea of God*. Cambridge: Cambridge University Press, 1918.

Spitzer, Robert J. *New Proofs for the Existence of God: Contributions of Contemporary Physics and Philosophy*. Grand Rapids, MI: Wm. B, Eerdmans, 2010.

Stark, Rodney. *How the West Won: The Neglected Story of the Triumph of Modernity*. Wilmington, DE: Intercollegiate Studies Institute, 2014.

Stoeger, W. "God, Physics and the Big Bang," in *The Cambridge Companion to Science and Religion*. P. Harrison, ed. Cambridge: Cambridge University Press, 2010.

Swinburne, Richard. "Argument from the Fine-Tuning of the Universe." *Modern Cosmology and Philosophy*. John Leslie, ed. New York: Prometheus Books, 1998.

———. *The Existence of God*. Revised edition. Oxford: Oxford University Press, 1991.

Taylor, A. *The Faith of a Moralist*. London: Macmillan, 1930.

———. *Does God Exist?* London: Macmillan, 1945.

Thaxton, Charles B., Bradley, Walter L., and Olsen, Roger L. *The Mystery of Life's Origin: Reassessing Current Theories*. New York: Philosophical Library, 1984.

Bibliography

Torrance, Thomas. *Divine and Contingent Order*. Oxford: Oxford University Press, 1981.

Trefil, James S. *The Moment of Creation: Big Bang Physics from Before the First Millisecond to the Present Universe*. New York: Scribners, 1983.

Vedral, Vlatko. *Decoding Reality: The Universe as Quantum Information*. Oxford Landmark Science. Oxford: Oxford University Press, 2012.

Webster, Bill. *Psyche* 2.18 (July 1995): 1-3.

Weisman, C. M., and Eddy, S. R. "Gene Evolution: Getting Something from Nothing." *Current Biology* 27.13 (July 10, 2017): R661-R663.

White, Roger. "Fine-Tuning and Multiple Universes." *Noûs* 34.2 (2000): 260-76.

Winograd, T. "Thinking Machines: Can There Be? Are We?," in T. Winograd & Fernando Flores. *Understanding Computers and Cognition: A New Foundation for Design*. Norwood, NJ: Ablex, 1986.

Whitehead, Alfred North. *Science and the Modern World*. New York: Macmillan Company, 1925, 1953.

Whiteside, R. L. *A New Commentary on Paul's Letter to the Saints in Rome*. Denton, TX: Whiteside, 1945.

Yavelberg, Ilan. "How Was the Universe Created Out of Nothing?" *Innovations Report* (March 13, 2014). https://www.innovations-report.com/html/reports/physics-astronomy/how-was-the-universe-created-out-of-nothing.html.

Author's Biography

Daniel H. King, Sr. was born in 1948 in Union City, TN. At age six his family moved to Warren, MI, and he grew up there and graduated from Lincoln High School in Warren. He was a wrestler in High School and for his first two years of college, until a serious shoulder injury permanently sidelined him from the sport.

He married his High School sweetheart, Donna Chapman, and has been happily married to her for 52 years. They have two children: Dan Jr. and Jennifer. Dan has preached for churches in Memphis, TN, Downers Grove, IL, and Lakeland, FL, but most of his local church work has been in Middle Tennessee. Presently he lives in Columbia, TN and is associated with the Locust Street church of Christ in nearby Mount Pleasant, where he serves as the local preacher.

Author's Biography

He has written extensively in many religious journals, both popular and professional. He has been a writer for *Truth Magazine* for over 40 years, and presently serves on the board of directors for Truth Publications, Inc., and as Vice-President and Publications Committee Chair of the organization.

Dan attended Wayne State University, David Lipscomb College (B.A.), Harding Graduate School of Religion (M.A.), and Vanderbilt University (PhD). His special area of competence is in Old Testament language and literature. He served as an adjunct professor at Tennessee State University in 1976 and at Florida College during 1984-88.

For 26 years he worked as an independent financial consultant to hundreds of clients. He specialized in investments and retirement planning. He retired from that business several years ago.

He has authored several tracts and numerous books: *Hebrew and Hellenistic Thought in the Book of Wisdom*, *We Have a Right* (with Mike Willis), *Responsibility and Authority in the Spiritual Realm* (with Leon Boyd), *At the Feet of the Master Teacher*, *Commentary on the Gospel of John*, *Commentary on the Epistles of John*, *Commentary on the Book of Hebrews*, *Commentary on the Book of Daniel*, *Commentary on James*, *The Days of Creation*, *Searching for Happiness?*, and *"I Saw the Heaven Opened": A Commentary on Revelation*, along with *Daniel*, *Ezekiel*, *Song of Solomon*, *Hebrews* and *Revelation* in the Bible Text Book adult workbook series. Currently he is engaged in writing a verse-by-verse commentary on the book of Proverbs for the Truth Commentary series.

www.ingramcontent.com/pod-product-compliance
Lightning Source LLC
Chambersburg PA
CBHW050850160426
43194CB00011B/2096